OLD HICKORY

OLD HICKORY

A LIFE OF ANDREW JACKSON

BURKE DAVIS

THE DIAL PRESS   NEW YORK

Published by
The Dial Press
1 Dag Hammarskjold Plaza
New York, New York 10017

Manufactured in the United States of America

Second Printing—1978

Library of Congress Cataloging in Publication Data

Davis, Burke.
Old Hickory.

Bibliography: p.
Includes index.
1. Jackson, Andrew, Pres. U. S., 1767–1845.
2. Presidents—United States—Biography. 3. United States—Politics and government—1829–1837.
I. Title.

E382.D3   973.5'6'0924 [B]   77-24425
ISBN 0–8037–6548–7

To Thomas Bancroft Schlesinger

Contents

OLD HICKORY

Prologue:
The Backwoods Boy

The pallbearers had been drinking.

The funeral party scuffed over a snowy woods track in a hissing of sleet and crept down to a frozen creek, where the pallbearers halted and drank from bottles of whiskey, a treasure hoarded for such an occasion.

The widow and two infant sons rode in a wagon, a reeling bundle of quilts, jolted over the trail and snatched across the fords in a clatter of ice. The husband's coffin followed on a farm sledge drawn by an ox. The procession paused twice before cabins in clearings, where the widow descended to greet relatives; she was a plump red-haired woman in her late twenties, noticeably pregnant even in her heavy clothing. At each stop the men had more to drink.

There had been a wake the night before in the cabin where the dead man lay. Whiskey was passed in gourds to those who had crowded into the hut in the forest, and inevitably in the home of a man from Northern Ireland who had been only two years in the Carolina backwoods, the immemorial customs of the old country wake had been followed —the clock stopped and its face covered, mirrors turned to the wall, dishes and kitchen utensils hidden, psalms chanted and Bible verses read. The corpse lay exposed in orange firelight; it was thought that a plate of salt placed on the chest would prevent swelling.

It had been a long day on the trail and it was late afternoon when the funeral party had gone the twelve miles to Waxhaw Presbyterian Church and the wagon lurched up the slope of the cemetery, where a red pit had been hacked into the dense clay. The woman and children huddled in their quilts, waiting. The pallbearers arrived with the sled —but the coffin had disappeared. A noisy party went back down the trail and found the wooden box caught in underbrush on a creek bank, where it had fallen at the last crossing.

There was a brief service on the hillside in the sleet storm, with solace for the widow intoned in the alien accents of the Reverend William Richardson, a young Scot who had been schooled at the University of Glasgow and had somehow strayed into the back country. Carmine clods fell on the pine planks, a muddy mound grew in the snow, and the party disappeared. Wind swept the soiled ice of the churchyard. It was early March 1767.

A few days later, in a cabin not far away, the widow bore her third son, a boy named for his dead father: Andrew Jackson. He was to become the seventh President of the United States and the first great storm center of American democracy.

The Jacksons had emerged from obscurity in the north of Ireland, a family of linen weavers among the band of proud impoverished Scots-Irish in the tiny port of Carrickfergus, near Belfast. Andrew Jackson, Sr.,'s wife was Elizabeth Hutchinson, a small, spirited woman who bore him two sons in rapid succession and, tending her family by day, continued the drudgery of weaving flax by night, hoarding coins against the time she might join the immigrant waves bound for America. She was bewitched by the tales of Andrew's brother Hugh, an old soldier who had survived Braddock's defeat in the wilderness and had fought Indians from Canada to the Carolinas. When the Treaty of Paris had ended the French and Indian War, and new American lands were opening, Hugh prepared to recross the Atlantic, leading a party of twenty families, Andrew and Betty Jackson among them.

Hugh's young Irish wife refused to embark, forbade the soldier's return to America, and dissuaded most of the party from the voyage, but the Jacksons persisted. And so amid a throng of hopeful refugees had come the Jacksons of Carrickfergus, to land in a crowded northern port, to bargain for wagons and teams, and straggle south across Pennsylvania and the waist of Maryland through the Virginia settlements to the Carolina frontier, where their road became a capricious trail, meandering in the ancient tracks of buffalo and Indian traders and cattle drovers, fording scores of streams, near the end passing rivers with strange names: Dan, Haw, Deep, Yadkin, Catawba.

They were seldom alone, even on the fringe of the wilderness. It was 1765, when wagons almost beyond counting rolled the Carolina foothills as immigrants sought the rich lands of the frontier. At least 1,000 wagons passed through the North Carolina village of Hillsboro that year—and there were more from other directions. Newcomers also streamed into the uplands from the port at Charleston; the new lands filled rapidly.

Near the end of their journey the Jacksons passed the village of Salisbury on the Yadkin River, and, three or four days beyond, on the southeasterly road toward Charleston, halted in the Waxhaw settlement in the valley of the Catawba, on the border between the Carolinas. They were at home; four of Betty Jackson's married sisters were already settled in this neighborhood—the first of them, Jane, the wife of James Crawford, was becoming rich after only five years in the new country, the mistress of a farm whose fields were tended by slaves. Andrew Jackson began more humbly.

Neighbors and relatives helped him to raise a crude cabin near the head of Liggett's Branch, a tributary of Twelve-Mile Creek on the watershed of the Catawba River. The isolated tract was four miles off the road and ten miles from the Crawfords, rather poor land watered by an overgrown stream that twisted through heavily timbered hills. But the other Hutchinson sisters were nearby: Margaret, who had married George McKemey; and Mary and Sarah, the wives of two brothers, John and Samuel Lesley.

Even this land had been spoken for, and Jackson was forced to pay or promise to pay, for a share of the claim of Thomas Ewing on this 200 acres of wilderness. The tract was not surveyed until the spring of 1766, when Jackson had begun the cruel labor of clearing fields, girdling giant trees, and felling them to make small clearings. He made his first crop among the charred stumps before he injured himself, straining at a log. Within a few hours he was dead.

Tales of the boyhood of young Andrew Jackson in the Waxhaw settlement were to be preserved in traditions that assumed the unadorned simplicity of folklore—otherwise, his formative years were lost to history. Even the state in which he was born on March 15, 1767, was to become a matter of dispute inspired by faulty surveys, shifting boundaries, and a welter of claims and counterclaims by those who had stakes in the border country that lay between the Carolinas.*

---

*Jackson believed that he was born in South Carolina. His first recorded comment on his birthplace was in 1816, in response to a resolution of appreciation from the South

As the most promising of Betty Jackson's sons, Andy was sent to a Presbyterian academy at Waxhaw Church. He was reading by the age of five and at eight wrote "a neat, legible hand."

Since many men and women of the Waxhaw settlement were illiterate, much news of the day was given to the community by "public readers," who read newspapers, documents, and important letters before small gatherings. By tradition, at least, young Andrew performed this chore. At the age of nine Andy was chosen as public reader "as often as any grown man," and parroted news from the outside world in his shrill voice with the aplomb of a veteran. Many years later he was to recall with pride his youthful ability to "read a paper clear through without getting hoarse . . . or stopping to spell out the words."

Among the communications Andy recited was the Declaration of Independence, read from a newspaper before a group of thirty or forty of his neighbors in mid-July 1776, an omen of approaching war with England not unwelcome in Waxhaw. Only a month earlier Andy's relative, Captain Robert Crawford, had marched off with his local militia company to help repel a British assault on Charleston.

Perhaps encouraged by his performance as a reader, his pious mother began to hope that Andrew would become a preacher; but the boy was set apart from his young contemporaries in ways that were to shape another destiny.

At thirteen, lean and graceful, with a thick shock of dark reddish hair and bright blue eyes set deeply in a freckled face, he was already notorious for the ferocity of his temper. He was invincible at running or jumping, and a reckless horseman, but was too light to excel at wrestling, a favorite local sport. In these years he suffered from an ailment that caused him to drool uncontrollably, a failing that provoked many a battle with boys who taunted him for "slobbering." He would fight at drop of a hat and, as a friend said, "he'd drop the hat himself."

George McWhorter, an older schoolmate who made frequent jokes about Andrew's drooling, was challenged fiercely each time, but Jackson refused to give up although he was invariably beaten. A classmate who threw him in three out of four wrestling matches remembered, "He would never stay throwed. He was dead game and would never give up."

Carolina Assembly for his victory at New Orleans. He then paid tribute to "that State which gave me birth," and repeated this positive belief in later years. North Carolina's claim to Jackson's nativity was not to be raised until fifteen years after his death.

The Waxhaw settlement drew its name from an Indian tribe that once lived in the region.

Some of his friends once handed Andy a musket loaded to the muzzle with powder and waited for him to fire it, but their joke was spoiled by Andy, who though he was knocked sprawling by the explosion, sprang up with blazing eyes and ready fists. "By God, if one of you laughs, I'll kill him."

Jackson was an infallible protector of younger boys of the neighborhood, yet his peers and elders found him arrogant, irascible, and overbearing; one Waxhaw boy remembered him as "the only bully he had ever known who was not also a coward."

Andy's interest in school waned quickly, and though he could read, write, and keep accounts, he never learned proper grammar or spelling. Outside the academy he was an apt student, famed for the fluency of his profanity in a community of accomplished veterans.

In 1778, at the age of eleven, Jackson joined a cattle drive to Charleston, and from his mother's share of the profits from the sale of the Waxhaw herd was sent to a "Classical School" a few miles from his home. No record of his scholarship there survives. In fact the earliest document preserved by Jackson revealed an interest in a nonacademic activity that was to be lifelong: "A Memorandum. How to feed a Cock before you him fight Take and give him some Pickle Beaf Cut fine. . . ."

War engulfed the backwoods settlement in the midst of Andy's boyhood. In 1779 his older brother Hugh died at the fierce little battle of Stono Ferry, in which a British invasion force was driven back into Georgia; and in the following May, after Charleston had fallen to a British siege, Lord Charles Cornwallis sent his relentless Irish cavalryman Colonel Banastre Tarleton raiding into the Carolina upcountry, setting off civil war between Whigs and Tories. Tarleton's troopers surprised a band of Whigs under Colonel Abraham Buford near Waxhaw, and killed more than 100 militiamen, many of whom were butchered after they had surrendered. Buford's wounded were carried to Waxhaw Church, where Betty Jackson and her sons helped to treat them, and Andrew heard survivors tell of helpless men hacked to death by British sabers as they cried for quarter.

After the massacre Betty Jackson and her family joined a refugee train into North Carolina, and when they returned a few weeks later under the protection of General Thomas Sumter and his little army, the Jackson boys could wait no longer. They enlisted with Colonel William R. Davie's backwoods cavalry. Andrew was thirteen years and four months old, and Robert sixteen. Andy, who knew the roads and was a veteran rider, served only as a mounted messenger, but performed so well that Davie gave the boy soldier a valuable pistol.

The full tide of war had now turned southward. To halt the invasion of Cornwallis, Congress sent General Horatio Gates, the hero of Saratoga; but his army was shattered in battle at Camden, South Carolina, in August, and redcoat raiders again swarmed the countryside. Betty Jackson and her sons once more fled to North Carolina, this time for three months. They returned to disaster.

In April 1781 Andy and Robert were captured by British and Troy raiders in a house near Waxhaw, where a dragoon officer "in a very imperious tone" ordered Andy to clean his boots. When the boy refused, protesting that he was a prisoner of war, the cavalryman slashed at his head with a saber, Andy threw up his arm to ward off the blow, and was cut severely on both head and hand. The officer then turned on Robert demanding that he clean his boots, and when he refused, opened a gash on his head.

The British and Tories took Andy's pistol and a fine Irish shotgun borrowed from his uncle James Crawford. They also plundered the house of valuables, smashed furniture, raped women of the farm family, and burned the house, before marching their captives to prison in Camden. Andy and Robert were fed once daily in their cell, scanty meals of bread and water. Their wounds were neglected, and a Tory took Andrew's coat and shoes. Smallpox spread through the stockade, and both Jackson boys came down with the disease. They were rescued by their mother, who rode to Camden, persuaded Lord Rawdon, the British commander, to release her sons and three other boys from Waxhaw, and took them home. The little band set out in a cold rain, with Robert so enfeebled that he was lifted onto a horse and held in the saddle by a companion. Mrs. Jackson rode the second horse, and Andrew walked the forty miles home barefoot, coatless, and hatless.

The Jackson boys were delirious when they tumbled into their beds at last. Robert died two days later, and Andrew was near death for several weeks. He had a wry memory of the ravages of smallpox. "When it left me I was a skeleton—not quite six feet long and a little over six inches thick! It took me all the rest of that year to recover my strength and get flesh enough to hide my bones." Andy's only solace was the recovery of his pistol and his uncle's shotgun, which were taken from a captured Tory by Colonel Davie's men, who then hanged the culprit.

Jackson retained a remorseless hatred of the British from these days, but later conceded that his companions bore much of the blame for atrocities that marked the struggle for the Upper Carolinas. "I am afraid," he said, "the Whigs did not lose many points in the game of hanging, shooting and flogging. They had great provocation, but . . . I feel bound to say that they took full advantage of it."

By the time Andrew had recovered from smallpox and his wounds, the Revolution was drawing to a close. Lord Cornwallis had moved to Virginia and dug in at Yorktown, where he was soon to be besieged in the last major action of the war. During the summer of 1781 Betty Jackson and two other women left for Charleston to nurse Waxhaw soldiers who were held on British prison ships in the harbor. Jackson was sobered by his mother's farewell. She wiped her eyes with her apron and gave him some advice: "Make friends by being honest and keep them by being steadfast." And more, "Andy . . . never tell a lie, nor take what is not your own, nor sue . . . for slander . . . *settle them cases yourself.*"

It was their final parting. Betty Jackson succumbed to "ship fever" and was buried in an unmarked grave outside Charleston. With the news of her death Andrew was given a pathetic reminder of his mother, a small bundle of her clothing. "I felt utterly alone," he said, "and tried to recall her last words to me." His mother's spirit was to exert a lasting influence on Jackson's life. In old age he would remember her as "gentle as a dove and brave as a lioness."

By the end of 1782 when the British evacuated Charleston, Andrew was fifteen; for the next three years he lived with friends and relations in Waxhaw.

He became a saddler's apprentice for six months or so, then returned to school, and by one report served for a time as a teacher. By a more persuasive tradition Andy devoted himself to pleasures he shared with young Charleston aristocrats who had come to Waxhaw as refugees. An early biographer noted that Jackson's abiding passion for fast horses was acquired during this time. "He ran races and rode races, gambled a little, drank a little, fought cocks occasionally . . . in the style usually affected by dissipated young fools of that day." It is likely that he also acquired from these young Charlestonians the courtly manners and dignified bearing that were to distinguish him in later life.

Amid these diversions came news from Ireland of the death of Andrew's grandfather, Hugh Jackson, a Carrickfergus merchant, who left the Waxhaw orphan a small fortune of 300 or 400 pounds sterling. Astride a fine horse that he had inexplicably acquired, Andy rode to Charleston, collected his legacy, and promptly lost it in a few days and nights of revelry with his Charleston friends and some brief encounters with swift Low Country thoroughbreds.

Penniless and in debt for his tavern bill, the sixteen-year-old Jackson wandered into a crowded barroom where a dice game was in progress and was challenged to a bet: $200 against his horse. Andy hesitated but briefly—if he lost, he would offer his landlord his saddle and bridle, promise to pay the balance of his bill, and walk home. He reached for the dice, rolled and won, and left the tavern at once. He paid his landlord and left Charleston, "with new spirits infused into me," though he carried in his purse only the meager remains of his inherited fortune. Jackson had gambled with dice for the last time.

Andrew departed Waxhaw forever a few weeks short of his eighteenth birthday, in December 1784. He gave no reason for his departure. Some of his neighbors surmised that Andy had wearied of recriminations over his wasted inheritance—but two generations later there was a persistent story of a blighted romance with Mary Crawford, the major's daughter. By Christmas, at any event, he was in the village of Salisbury, North Carolina, some seventy-five miles away, comfortably lodged at the Rowan House—4 shillings a day for man and beast.

Jackson had now reached the full height of manhood, cadaverously lean, though strong, wiry, and supple, with an air of almost compulsive eagerness in his bearing—"a lank, leaning-forward fellow," as one girl described him. His pale, pocked face was arresting if not handsome, and his forehead was marked with a scar that ran into his mop of auburn hair. He was not long in making himself known in his new home. Jackson was now seeking to enter the practice of law, which in the wake of the Revolution had become the most lucrative profession open to young men of the new states. Most of the Tory lawyers who had been dominant figures in many colonial towns were gone or had lost influence, and there was the framework of a new government to be raised in a country already expanding westward.

Salisbury, a cluster of fifty-odd houses along tree-shaded streets, was already old as southern frontier towns went, and its leading families lived well, in tall houses reminiscent of the mansions of the coastal settlements. In one of these houses lived Spruce Macay, a lawyer who had two young men reading law with him, aiding in the practice he conducted from a cramped one-room office in his front yard. Jackson joined Macay and began a long friendship with one of his student assistants, John McNairy.

Jackson also renewed an acquaintance with John Stokes, a brilliant, erratic lawyer who had lost a hand in the massacre of Buford's troops at Waxhaw, and now wore as a replacement a silver knob, which he delighted to bang on tables in taverns and courtrooms to attract attention or emphasize his arguments. Jackson became celebrated locally as a bon vivant and inspired tales of wild drinking parties, with mulatto mistresses and gambling for high stakes.

Years later, after Jackson had become famous, an old resident remembered him as "the most roaring, rollicking, game-cocking, card-playing, mischievous fellow that ever lived in Salisbury . . . the head of the rowdies hereabouts."

Andrew attracted several young women who met him at parties in Macay's house, and left a particularly vivid impression with Nancy Jarret, who never forgot her first encounters with him: ". . . full six feet tall and very slender, but . . . graceful. . . . His eyes *were* handsome . . . a kind of steel-blue . . . his ways and manners were most captivating. . . . We all knew that he was wild . . . that he gambled some and was by no means a Christian young man." Nancy noted that Jackson usually spoke slowly, "with good selected language," but that in excitement his speech became rapid and assumed a marked North Irish accent. Nancy was obviously taken with young Andrew: "Either calm or animated there was something about him I cannot describe except to say that it was a *presence.*" Jackson evidently practiced his wiles upon Miss Jarret, who remembered that though he talked with her frequently, he never once averted the glance of the steel-blue eyes from her face, not "for an instant."

John McNairy finished training under Macay and was admitted to the bar; but after a year in Salisbury Jackson's most memorable accomplishment was as manager of the Christmas ball, the leading social event of the year. Young men and women from the most prominent families of the region were halted during the dance by the arrival of the only local prostitutes, Molly Wood and her daughter Rachel. When these two appeared in the ballroom, the music and dancing stopped; while chaperones herded a bevy of giggling and embarrassed young ladies into a corner, Molly and Rachel showed their invitations—and Jackson confessed that he had sent the cards as a joke, confident that the two women would not appear. Though he apologized profusely, Jackson had not been fully forgiven many years later when his biographer, James Parton, heard the story from a witness who demanded that her name be withheld. This woman was thunderstruck when she heard that Jackson was running for President: "What! Jackson up for President? *Jackson? Andrew* Jackson? The Jackson that used to live in Salisbury? Why, when he was here he was such a rake that my husband would not bring him into the house! It is true he *might* have taken him out to the stable to weigh horses for a race and might drink a glass of whiskey with him *there.* Well, if Andrew Jackson can be President, anybody can!"

However devoted to dissipation he might have been, Jackson completed his legal training after two years with Macay and a final six months in the office of John Stokes, and was admitted to the bar on

September 26, 1787. Sartorially, at least, he was a new man. Nancy Jarret, who was drawn to the courthouse with several other girls to witness Jackson's ascension, saw him "in a new suit, with broad-cloth coat and ruffled shirt . . . his abundant suit of dark red hair combed carefully back . . . and, I suppose, made to lay down smooth with bear's oil."

The young lawyer had been subjected to the last formal training of his life. Not surprisingly he emerged virtually untutored from the haphazard reading of law and his brief days in backwoods schoolrooms. As a later historian observed, this was probably inevitable, since Jackson was unteachable, utterly self-reliant, and confident of his own judgment.

A judge who met Andrew on the backwoods circuit a few days after his licensing advised him to go "up west," into North Carolina's sparsely settled northwestern counties, and Jackson left for the straggling village of Martinsville, the seat of Guilford County, perhaps because John McNairy and Governor Martin of North Carolina lived nearby. Clients were scarce in this outpost, and Jackson may have clerked in a country store to augment his income. He did not go unnoticed. With his characteristic energy he organized the first celebration of the anniversary of the revolutionary Battle of Guilford Courthouse, an affair enlivened by speeches, horse races, and cockfights.

For a few weeks Jackson rode the circuit of backwoods country seats in upland North Carolina with other lawyers, judges, and court officials. He was admitted to practice in neighboring Surry County in November 1787, and stopped at a tavern operated by Jesse Lister, who later claimed that Jackson left a board bill unpaid. He was said to have defended a thief in this court, with the understanding that he would win an acquittal or collect no fee—and that when the case was lost, the defendant went to the whipping post and Jackson left town owing his board bill.* Young Andrew also gave a note for a gambling debt in this courthouse village to the lawyer William Cupples, who had not collected it eight years later.

Virtually no records of the twenty-year-old Jackson's scanty practice in these courts survive. He certainly knew little law, but he was an eager controversialist and a forceful, though not an eloquent speaker, who

---

*By tradition Lister canceled the debt a generation later with an entry in his account book: "Paid at the battle of New Orleans." Lister's daughter at any rate later presented the bill to President Jackson, who refused to honor it on the ground that he had always paid such debts, and that if it had been due, Lister would have presented it during his lifetime.

impressed his hearers as a young man of promise, bold and candid, with a notable sense of justice and the self-assured air of one born to leadership. Though it was not yet apparent to his contemporaries, he was also an incurable romantic, moved by a tendency to self-dramatization, and a gifted public performer, whose vivid career was to become one of the most memorable in the history of his country.

It was obvious to Jackson and McNairy that their prospects were not bright in the district around Martinsville, and one of them, probably the more aggressive Jackson, proposed that they move westward, into North Carolina's wilderness domain that stretched from the Appalachians to the Mississippi. Settlement of the western district of this frontier had only begun, in an outpost built by a few families on the banks of the Cumberland River, almost 200 miles beyond the scattered frontier villages in the mountains. A new government would rise in the wilderness territory, courts would be established, towns would grow, and industrious lawyers could build fortunes by acquiring land before the great migration of settlers had begun.

Before the end of 1787 the North Carolina legislature created a superior court in the Western District, and named John McNairy its first judge. McNairy, perhaps by prior agreement, was to appoint Jackson as prosecuting attorney as soon as they arrived on the Cumberland.

North Carolina had ceded the western region to the federal government as her share of the expenses of the Revolution, provided that Congress accepted the grant within two years; but mountain settlers, fearing that they were to be left without protection, seceded and created the state of Franklin. Under the leadership of the frontier hero John Sevier this upstart government had survived for three years in defiance of the Carolinians of the seaboard, whose own ties to the infant United States under the Articles of Confederation were tenuous indeed.

In the spring of 1788 Nolichucky Jack Sevier, captured and brought to trial for treason in the hill village of Morganton, North Carolina, was rescued by his followers and fled to live the life of an outlaw. The popular, handsome Indian fighter and hero of the revolutionary victory of King's Mountain was soon to be pardoned and become first governor of Tennessee. He was also to become Jackson's lifelong rival.

About the time of Sevier's flight Jackson, McNairy, and two or three other young lawyers passed through Morganton on their way across the mountains, and by May had reached the little hill town of Jonesboro.

1

"I have the good of the country at heart"

The arrival of the twenty-one-year-old Jackson in Jonesboro became part of a durable East Tennessee tradition, long embalmed in the memories of old men. The boy orphan from Waxhaw was apparently the only rider of the cavalcade who was to be remembered—a lean, erect figure riding one horse and leading another with bulging saddlebags, a brace of pistols before him and another in his belt, and a holstered long rifle behind, with a pack of foxhounds trotting by his side.

Years later when he was asked if Jackson had walked into Jonesboro, an old man who had observed his arrival roared: "Walk? Jackson walk? Good God. He never walked anywhere unless it was an absolute necessity. He came here riding a race horse and leading another first-rate horse."

Jackson recalled long afterward that his saddlebags had contained half a dozen books, all of them probably law books. He also carried salt, tea, tobacco, liquor, and surveyor's instruments. Other necessities that were likely included in his baggage went unrecorded—playing cards and some gamecocks from North Carolina's finest strains.

On May 12, 1788, the boy lawyer appeared in Jonesboro's log cabin courthouse, produced his license, and was admitted to practice in Washington County. He was not penniless when he arrived, in any event, for he soon bought a slave girl, one Nancy, who was about eighteen or twenty years old and valued at the handsome price of almost $300.

During the four months that Jackson and McNairy spent in Jonesboro, awaiting the passage of the first emigrant train over the Cumberland Trail, Andy came to public attention on the racetrack and in the courtroom. He boarded in the farmhouse of one Christopher Taylor, whose parlor served as his law office, but spent much of his time caring for his racehorse, which he claimed was the fastest in the region. Jackson soon found a challenger, a wealthy land speculator by the name of Colonel Love who lived in nearby Greasy Cove, the owner of a racer acknowledged as the champion of the settlements, already the conqueror of the fastest horses from the nearby Virginia Mountains.

Jackson arranged a race against Love's horse, an event that drew a large crowd to the half-mile track in Greasy Cove, in the valley of the Nolichucky River. The backwoods throng drank a good deal, staged a few fistfights, and wagered furs, cattle, horses, Negroes, crops, land, guns, iron, and a small amount of money.

Jackson's jockey, a black boy owned by Taylor, became ill shortly before the race so Jackson decided to ride himself. He appeared on his Carolina racer, threading his way through the crowd with "a haughty air of confidence and self-possession," and rode onto the circular track to meet Love's professional jockey astride the local champion.

The horses broke at the shout of "Go" from the judge, and raced neck and neck to within a few yards of the finish, when Love's horse spurted into the lead to pass under the string the winner. In the hubbub that followed, the chagrined Jackson cursed Love and his family as land pirates, and Love called Jackson "a damned long gangling sorrel-top soap stick." After a protracted argument Andy withdrew in defeat.

In one of his first law cases in Jonesboro Jackson found himself opposed by Waightstill Avery, a distinguished Princeton graduate who had been the first attorney general of North Carolina. Avery had befriended Jackson, but this did not deter the boy from twitting the older lawyer about his favorite authority, Matthew Bacon's *Abridgement of the Law,* a work that Avery invariably carried in his saddlebags, carefully swaddled in buckskin.

Avery retorted with stinging scorn, saying that Jackson knew nothing of this law case nor any other. Andy bellowed, "I may not know as much law as there is in *Bacon,* but I know enough not to take illegal fees!"

Avery turned on him furiously: "Do you mean to charge me with taking illegal fees?"

"I do, Sir."

Avery shook his finger under Jackson's nose and hissed into his face, "It's false as hell."

Jackson then ripped a blank page from a law book, scrawled a challenge to a duel, handed it to Avery, and stalked from the courtroom. To a friend who agreed to serve as his second, Jackson confided that he had no wish to kill Avery. He had meant to explain, he said, that Avery had innocently violated a recent law fixing a schedule of fees— but since he had been interrupted and insulted, he could not retract without appearing to be a coward. Avery sought to avoid trouble by ignoring Jackson in the courtroom the next day, which prompted the frustrated Andy to write a second challenge:

> Sir
>
> You recd a few lines from me yesterday and undoubtedly you understand me. My character you have injured; and further you have Insulted me in the presence of a court and a large audianc I therefore call upon you as a gentleman to give me satisfaction . . . & further . . . an answer immediately without Equivocation and I hope you can do without dinner untill the business is done . . . yr obt St
>
> Andw Jackson

Conciliators sought to prevent a duel, yet Avery felt that he had no alternative but to fight—or to make a show of doing so. At sunset the portly old man and the stern young Jackson met in a clearing at the edge of Jonesboro, raised their pistols, and fired into the air at a signal, fulfilling the demands of the Code of Honor. Duelists, seconds, and friends then shook hands amiably.

"Avery," Jackson said, "I knew if I hit you and didn't kill you immediately, your only comfort in your last moments would be your beloved Bacon. So I had my friend bring it to the ground."

Jackson's second unrolled a flat package to reveal a side of cured bacon and the group dispersed in laughter.

A brief entry in the courthouse records provided the only documentary evidence of this adventure:

> Watsel Avery having for want of Acts of Assembly Crept into an Era in Taking Two pounds instead of one pound six shillings and eight pence was by the Court freely pardoned at his own request.

The people of Jonesboro were said to have sympathized with Jackson in the affair, though some thought him "a little too fractious." The hot-tempered young lawyer was already winning a reputation for combativeness, but as a friend said of him, "No man knew better than Andrew Jackson when to get into a passion and when not."

Jackson and John McNairy left for the Cumberland settlements on September 25, 1788, with an immigrant train of sixty families, under escort of sixteen guards provided by the state. The party carried westward news of the final ratification of the Constitution of the United States, a prelude to the establishment of a permanent government, under General Washington as first President.

The 183-mile trail from Jonesboro to Nashville crossed the Cumberland Mountains, regarded as the most dangerous strip of wilderness in the region, a route fiercely defended by the Cherokees. In hopes of reaching safety the caravan was herded swiftly for two days and a night with infrequent halts of less than an hour, until it reached a campground chosen by the guards. The party fell asleep soon after nightfall, except for a few sentinels and Jackson, who was alarmed by the hooting of owls in the forest. He aroused a friend, "The owls—listen—there. Isn't that a little *too* natural?" Jackson insisted that Indians were approaching the camp, preparing to attack before dawn.

When experienced woodsmen confirmed Jackson's fears, the party broke camp and filed away in darkness. A few hours later five hunters who reached the campsite were attacked by Indians and four of them were killed as they slept.

Some nights later when four panthers attacked the Cumberland caravan's horses and tried to kill a colt, Jackson aided in the defense by shooting an adult and tomahawking a cub.

In the last week of October Jackson rode to the crest of a bluff above the Cumberland River and saw the city of Nashville for the first time: a cluster of cabins, bark tents, and wagons, two taverns, two stores, a distillery, and a courthouse, all surrounded by a rail fence that kept grazing herds of buffalo at bay. The lands that rolled down to the Cumberland had been prized Indian hunting grounds for centuries. A French settlement of 1714 on the site of a deserted Shawnee fort had flourished here for many years; Daniel Boone had passed this way long before the Revolution, when the place was known as Big Salt Lick. The nondescript village of Nashville, founded by James Robertson and John Donelson, was only nine years old.

The log courthouse, 18 feet square, was filthy and rundown. Horses were hitched to the whipping post and stocks. The one licensed lawyer was the spokesman for the debtors of the settlement, who had virtually halted business in the village by their defiance.

The twenty-six-year-old Judge McNairy took office on November 3, and with the aid of his boy prosecutor gave the settlement a taste of law and order. In a single day Jackson issued seventy writs to delinquent debtors on behalf of merchants and other property owners, with the result that local trade began to flourish—and Jackson found himself with more clients than he could handle. Overnight his private law practice marked him as a leader of the community. By the spring of 1790, little more than a year after his arrival, Jackson had served as counsel in 42 of the 192 cases on the Nashville docket, and was soon appearing in about half the cases tried there—usually for the defense —in such matters as fistfights, land squabbles, and thefts of livestock. Within a few weeks Jackson was riding the circuit of nearby county courts, and soon took the first of his long return journeys to court in Jonesboro, a trek he was to make twenty-two times in the next seven years.

From the start Jackson was paid for his services in farm produce, chickens, cattle, horses, and most importantly in land, which was cheap and plentiful, though most of it still legally belonged to the Cherokees. The solicitor had become a capitalist almost immediately after his arrival. He once told a friend that his first eight years of practice earned him in fees "land enough to make a county," and horses and cattle to stock a farm.

The year 1790 also brought new professional standing to Jackson, when Congress created the Southwest Territory in the country below the Ohio, and the twenty-two-year-old state solicitor became U.S. attorney general for the territory.

The young prosecutor did not settle in the village itself. For some reason he avoided the convenient, convivial, and notorious Red Heifer Tavern near the courthouse to become a boarder at the remote block-house of Colonel John Donelson's widow, some ten miles distant on the opposite side of the Cumberland, in an exposed location vulnerable to Indian attacks. The attraction may have been the widow's twenty-one-year-old daughter Rachel, who had recently returned home from Kentucky after a separation from her husband Lewis Robards.

When Jackson first saw her, Rachel Robards was not only beautiful but vivacious and winning, "the best story-teller, the best dancer, the sprightliest companion, the most dashing horsewoman in the western country." She was also alluring, celebrated for her "lustrous dark eyes," and, as one of her kinswomen said, "irresistible to men . . . beautifully moulded form, full red lips," her oval face "rippling with smiles and dimples." Her charms for Jackson evidently were not diminished by the fact that she smoked a pipe, like many women of the frontier.

Rachel was one of the eleven children of John and Rachel Stockley Donelson, who had arrived on the Cumberland in 1780 after an epic voyage by flatboat. John Donelson, the son of a Maryland shipowner, had migrated to Virginia, married the daughter of a prominent Eastern Shore family, and become a prosperous farmer, iron founder, and surveyor in Pittsylvania County. As militia commander and a member of the House of Burgesses he had become a friend of George Washington, and had helped to clear western lands for settlement by making treaties with the Cherokees.

After his friend James Robertson had led an advance party to the Cumberland, Colonel Donelson had followed with the main party of 160 men, women, and children, most of whom survived the 1,000-mile river journey despite frequent Indian attacks, disease, floods, freezing weather, and famine. He and Robertson became founders of Nashboro, the village on the site of Big Salt Lick that was to become known as Nashville.

At seventeen Rachel Donelson had married into the Robards family and had spent four years in her mother-in-law's imposing stone mansion near Harrodsburg, Kentucky, apparently happily, until her jealous husband drove her from home. Peyton Short, a young lawyer who boarded at the Robards house, had shown Rachel "perhaps a little more than ordinary politeness," and Lewis Robards, when he discovered Short and his wife in an animated conversation, assumed that the two were having an affair. Though the elder Mrs. Robards sided with Rachel against her son and Short vowed that they were innocent, Robards ordered Rachel "never to show her face in his house again." John Donelson had been killed on a surveying trip by unknown marauders, and his widow sent one of her sons to bring Rachel home.

The despondent Rachel returned to her mother's blockhouse to live as a recluse for weeks, refusing to attend parties and dances, or to appear in public even briefly. It was soon afterward that Jackson joined the household. He seemed to be smitten at once. George Davidson, a chore boy at the blockhouse, noted that the unfailingly polite Jackson was "particularly so to the beautiful Mrs. Robards." Trouble was not far away.

Jackson shared a bed in a cabin near the main house of the stockade with John Overton, another newly arrived lawyer who had come down from Kentucky. Overton had brought Rachel a message from her husband, who now begged to be forgiven, and she apparently relented, for Lewis Robards appeared. He was soon accusing his wife of being in love with Jackson.

Despite Rachel's protestations of innocence and Overton's efforts to convince him that his suspicions were groundless, Robards berated his wife so fiercely that she and her mother were frequently in tears.

The impending crisis in the Donelson stockade was postponed by Jackson's absence on a circuit of Judge McNairy's district, which ranged along the Cumberland from Gallatin to Ashland. In Gallatin the prosecutor discovered that his reputation as the scourge of debtors had spread across the frontier and made him numerous enemies. Jackson was talking with bystanders in the courtyard when a local bully shoved past and stepped on his foot. Jackson apologized and continued talking, but when the bully trod on his foot once more he snatched up a piece of wood and knocked the man down. It was Gallatin's last attempt to intimidate the new prosecutor.

When he returned to the Donelson stockade, Jackson denied to Robards that he was wooing Rachel and charged the Kentuckian with injustice to his wife. Robards became angry and threatened to kill Jackson, who reiterated his innocence, saying he was too weak to fight him physically but offering to meet him in a duel. The Kentuckian declined the challenge with a burst of profanity.

At John Overton's suggestion Jackson moved to another blockhouse nearby and Robards left for Kentucky, where Rachel returned to him briefly. But within a few weeks she found life with her husband unbearable, and fled after a quarrel. At the request of the Donelson family Jackson went to bring her back, a rescue soon to be given a sinister meaning by Robards in a court complaint: "Rachel Robards, did on the _____ day of July, 1790 elope from her husband, said Lewis . . . with another man." The other man, of course, was Andrew Jackson; but it was to be almost a year before he learned of the charge.

Jackson took Rachel to the home of her sister, Jane Hays, where she lived for a time. Robards again followed her, to make a final, futile plea for reconciliation. When he told friends that Jackson was too intimate with Rachel, Jackson sought him out: "If you ever again associate my name with your wife's I'll cut off your ears—I'm tempted to do it anyhow."

Robards served Jackson with a peace warrant, and had him marched before a magistrate by a constable and several guards, a procession that moved to an unexpected end. Jackson borrowed a hunting knife from a guard and made an elaborate examination of the sharp blade, glancing at Robards as he ran his thumb along its edges until his nervous accuser fled into a canebrake. Jackson appeared before the magistrate, who dismissed the case.

Somewhere in his travels of the district Jackson met a fascinating stranger, Captain André Fagot, a Frenchman who was serving as a Spanish agent in America, assigned to bring the new settlements under control of Spain. The urbane Frenchman evidently left a dazzling glimpse of the future of the Mississippi Valley with young Jackson, who wrote at once to enlist the aid of the district militia commander, Brigadier General Daniel Smith. Jackson urged Smith to write Esteban Miró, the governor of the Spanish Territory of Louisiana, requesting a commercial treaty that would lead to peace with the Indians and prosperity for the Cumberland. He also asked Smith to talk with Fagot before the Frenchman left for New Orleans. "I hope you will consider it well," the twenty-two-year-old wrote the veteran frontiersman, "as I have the good of the country at heart."

It is unlikely that Jackson influenced the Cumberland's older leaders in these negotiations, for it was obvious that the Spaniards were the only potential allies and protectors near at hand, and the western settlements had already been named Mero, in the governor's honor. But Smith did recommend Fagot to Governor Miró and sent a verbal message that might have changed the destiny of the United States. Miró reported this encouraging news to Madrid at once: "The inhabitants of the Cumberland . . . would in September send delegates to North Carolina . . . to solicit from the legislature . . . an act of separation," a move that would place "the Territory under the dominion of his Majesty."

General James Robertson, the influential founder of the Cumberland settlement, speaking for "every thinking person in this country," also sent a friendly letter to Miró, saying that "Nature seems to have designed the whole Western Country to be one people."

However dimly he foresaw the final struggle for control of the vast American west, young Jackson understood that the Cumberland settlements could not prosper without free passage of the Mississippi, and might not survive without allies in the endless Indian wars. His older contemporaries took note of his concern for the future, and his unstudied assumption of a role of leadership.

Jackson shared the fears of Smith and Robertson that the United States might expire and leave westerners to their fate. Though the U.S. Constitution had become effective, North Carolina had rejected it, and the men of the Cumberland felt more keenly their isolation behind the

Appalachian barrier. Almost unanimously leaders of the Southwest Territory sought an ally nearer and more powerful than the Americans of the Atlantic seaboard. The unspoken fear of the Cumberland settlers was that the British would return to wrest from the puny, divided republic the continent they had lost in the American Revolution. To no one in the west did that threat seem more ominous than to Andrew Jackson.

2

"A restless and enterprising man"

In October 1790, in response to a proclamation by Governor Miró offering free land to American emigrants, Jackson made the long, perilous journey to Mississippi, where he acquired a valuable tract of riverfront land thirty miles above Natchez at Bayou Pierre. He built a log house with the aid of slave labor and planned an elaborate plantation, complete with racetrack. Jackson became friendly with several prosperous Americans in Mississippi, among them Abner and Thomas Marston Green, Jr., who had migrated from Virginia. One of the Green family saw a boundless ambition in young Jackson, "a restless and enterprising man, embarking in many schemes for the accumulation of fortune, not usually resorted to by professional men."

Within six months Jackson was back in Nashville, increasingly busy in the courtroom. He also became more deeply involved with Rachel Robards, whose husband, still in Kentucky, threatened to return and carry his wife away by force. The thoroughly frightened Rachel made plans to flee to Natchez. She was offered passage with a flatboat flotilla commanded by Colonel John Stark, an old friend of the Donelsons, who was carrying traders on a 2,000-mile journey through the wilderness down the Cumberland, the Ohio, and the Mississippi. Jackson tried to dissuade Rachel from taking the dangerous trip. When she insisted, he confessed to Overton that he loved her and regretted that he had "innocently and unintentionally" caused her unhappiness. Colonel Stark, anxious for added protection for Rachel and his own family on the passage through Indian country, urged Jackson to join the flotilla, and after some hesitation, Jackson agreed. He turned over his law practice to Overton, and left with Stark and Rachel in the late winter or early spring of 1791.

Overton, at least, was convinced that Jackson's sole concern in joining the expedition was Rachel's safety, since he had observed during their tours of backwoods courts that Jackson never joined other young men who "were indulging in familiarities with young females of relaxed morals." When he reflected on Jackson's "singularly delicate sense of honor and . . . chivalrous conceptions of the female sex," Overton concluded that the premarital relations of Jackson and Rachel were undoubtedly "honorable and virtuous."

Jackson returned from Natchez in May 1791 to resume his practice and career as U.S. attorney, leaving Rachel on the plantation of his friends, Mr. and Mrs. Abner Green. He found Mrs. Donelson near hysteria over the most recent news from Kentucky: Robards had petitioned for a divorce on grounds that Rachel had deserted him the previous summer to live in adultery with Jackson.

For once the hotheaded Jackson suppressed his impulse to take revenge, "to pursue Robards and at the pistol's point make him retract," as a family historian put it. Jackson was in love, and instead of stalking Robards, he asked Mrs. Donelson's permission to marry Rachel. The widow was overcome. "Mr. Jackson, would you sacrifice your life to save my poor child's good name?" Jackson's reply, by the only surviving account, was gallantry itself, "Ten thousand lives, Madam, if I had them." He left immediately for Natchez to be married.

Inexplicably Jackson accepted the unofficial report of Rachel's divorce as authentic. Despite the limitations of his legal experience he was aware that divorces were rare and not easily obtained; yet in his haste he made no effort to investigate, even to read the Virginia statute, and thus knew little or nothing of the steps Robards had taken.

Since Kentucky was still a part of Virginia, Robards had appealed to his brother-in-law, Representative Jack Jouett, to introduce a bill in the Virginia legislature—the usual procedure for obtaining a divorce at the time. The popular Jouett, a hero of the Revolution, was aware of Robards's jealous nature and felt that he had wronged Rachel in the affair of Peyton Short, but was now persuaded to help him win a divorce. The General Assembly, however, did not grant an outright divorce, but merely passed a bill enabling Robards to take his case into court. The act specified that Robards must publish a notice of his suit for eight consecutive weeks in the *Kentucky Gazette* so that Rachel might appear to plead her case. Finally the act provided for a jury trial:

... To inquire into the allegations contained in the declaration ... and if the jury ... shall find in substance that the defendant hath deserted the plaintiff that she hath lived in adultery with another man since such desertion ... thereupon the marriage ... shall be totally dissolved.

Rachel and Andrew were married near Natchez in August 1791, in the home of Thomas Marston Green, Jr., and spent a month's honeymoon in Jackson's cabin at nearby Bayou Pierre. They were back on the Cumberland by October. Within a few weeks Jackson bought Poplar Grove, a 330-acre riverfront farm, from Rachel's brother John, and the twenty-four-year-old bride and groom settled happily into the life of the Middle Tennessee frontier.

Jackson was appointed judge advocate of the county militia, his first military post, and elected a trustee of a new local school, the Davidson Academy. As attorney general he was paid £40 for each case, and since he was intimately involved in most public transactions, opportunities for profit inevitably came to his attention. His private practice was still flourishing; he tried 206 of the 435 cases on the Nashville docket in 1793, and almost 300 of 400 the following year. Since his fees were still usually paid in land at the rate of about 10 cents an acre, his holdings literally accumulated more rapidly than he could accurately determine their extent. In terms of land ownership Jackson was one of the wealthiest men in Tennessee. He was also acquiring more slaves and probably had a dozen or so on his farm on the Cumberland.

The outbreak of a new Indian war threatened the settlements in 1792 and 1793. The Cherokees, enraged at the constant violation of treaties by white settlers and speculators, invaded the Cumberland in force. The Poplar Grove plantation was cut off from Nashville and the blockhouse of Robert Hays, Jackson's brother-in-law, was besieged and two men killed. Jackson almost lost his life when Cherokees attacked the territorial capital of Knoxville in August 1793. He and an officer left a fortified outpost to scout the enemy and walked into an ambush; the officer was killed, but Jackson escaped to spread the alarm.

John Sevier asked federal approval of a raid into Cherokee country. When there was no response, he mustered his brigade of East Tennessee militia and plunged into the mountains, guided by an escaped captive of the tribe. This raid, known as the Nickajack expedition, left Cherokee towns in ashes, destroyed crops, and inflicted such heavy casualties among warriors, women, and children that the power of the tribe was broken. In the peace that followed, white emigrants swarmed into Tennessee by the thousands.

In December 1793 when Jackson and John Overton were attending court in Jonesboro, Overton happened upon a copy of a recent court record from Harrodsburg, Kentucky. Only a few weeks before, on September 27, a jury had granted Lewis Robards a divorce on the finding that

> . . . the defendant, Rachel Robards, hath deserted the plaintiff, Lewis Robards, and hath, and doth, still live in adultery with another man. It is therefore considered by the court that the marriage between the plaintiff and the defendant be dissolved.

Jackson was staggered by the news. Since he and Rachel had married on the assumption that the legislative act of 1791 was final, they were technically guilty of adultery—and Rachel of bigamy. Not only had Lewis Robards delayed two years before obtaining his divorce; he had failed to publish notice for eight weeks in the widely circulated *Kentucky Gazette,* as if to cloak his plans in secrecy.

Overton suggested a second wedding, but Jackson refused indignantly. "Every person in the country," he said, understood that he and Rachel had been properly married in Natchez, and were legally man and wife, whatever the maneuvers of Robards. Only after hours of pleading was Overton able to persuade the stubborn Jackson that his responsibility to Rachel outweighed all other considerations. They were remarried in a brief, subdued ceremony on January 17, 1794. Over the minister's voice as he read the stately phrases of the ceremony there almost certainly rang in Jackson's memory Rachel's stricken cry when he first told her of Lewis Robards's charges: "I expected him to kill me, but this is worse."

Despite its troubled beginnings the marriage was to endure in apparent happiness until Rachel's death, marked throughout by mutual warmth and affection. Jackson could not have been unaware of the advantages of this link with one of the most prominent, and numerous, Tennessee families, and he had obviously weighed Rachel's other qualifications for matrimony. He once advised his ward, Andrew Jackson Hutchings, that he should choose a wife with care, "one who will aid you in your exertions in making a competency and will take care of it when made. . . . Look at the economy of the mother and if you find it in her you will find it in the daughter." He praised Rachel as a model:

"Recollect the industry of your dear aunt, and with what economy she watched over what I made, and how we waded thro the vast expence of the mass of company we had. Nothing but her care and industry, with good economy could have saved me from ruin. If she had been extravagant the property would have vanished and poverty and want would have been our doom. Think of this before you attempt to select a wife."

Jackson now turned to a bold scheme to capitalize on the growing value of his lands, confident that he could make a fortune by converting them to goods and establishing a trading post. In the early spring of 1795 he set out for Philadelphia, prepared to sell more than 30,000 acres of his own, 50,000 he owned jointly with John Overton, and 18,000 acres for a friend. He discovered that trading in the Quaker city was an art quite unlike the easy ways of bartering on the frontier. He spent three weeks haggling and fuming over delays, complaining of "difficulties such as I never experienced before. . . . The Dam'st situation ever man was in."

At last Jackson sold about 29,000 acres of the land he shared with Overton, for a price of $10,000. The buyer was David Allison, a speculator and merchant who gave in payment a series of notes to mature at intervals over the next four years. With these notes, which he endorsed, Jackson bought some $6,500 worth of merchandise—cloth, buttons, thread, cigars, ivory combs, hats, shoes, china, tools, knives, salt, sugar, coffee, wine, gunpowder, grindstones, nails, cowbells.

He shipped the heavy goods to Pittsburgh by wagon, arranging for the purchase of a boat to carry them down the Ohio River to Kentucky, from where they were to be taken by wagons to Nashville. He reached home belatedly in June, "fatigued even almost to death."

While his merchandise was moving laboriously through the country, Jackson bought a new home, a tract of fine farmland known as Hunter's Hill, where he began the building of a large frame house overlooking rolling meadows and his private ferry on the bank of the Cumberland. He also hired an estate manager, as if he foresaw that he was to become an absentee planter for most of his life. By now he had become an active horse trader, resolved to build the finest stable of racing stock on the frontier. Among his numerous correspondents was Wade Hampton of South Carolina, from whom he acquired a few thoroughbreds. Within a few months Jackson was caught up in a new phase of his political career, as a founding father of the state of Tennessee.

In 1796 after a census revealed a population of 76,000 in the Southwest Territory, a convention met in Knoxville to prepare for statehood. Jackson was one of the fifty-five delegates, and the second man chosen for a committee assigned to write the constitution. Jackson first appeared as a champion of the masses during debate on the constitution, opposing the exclusion of clergymen from public office on the ground that it was undemocratic, and favoring a two-house legislature as more responsive to the will of the people than the unicameral plan at first proposed. Jackson also approved the liberal provisions for voting and officeholding: any man could vote after six months' residence and any freeholder after one day; owners of 200 acres could serve in the legislature, and owners of 500 acres could become governor.

Delegates noted that Jackson did not introduce resolutions he favored, but deferred to his seniors and strongly supported them once they had spoken. He was not a roaring orator of conventional frontier style, but was "fluent, forceful and convincing," speaking slowly unless excited, in rather inelegant but always lucid style. A friend remembered: "No one ever listened to a speech from Andrew Jackson who . . . had the least doubt as to what he was driving at. . . . He talked to them. He did not orate." Jackson's gestures were somewhat awkward but forceful, and his hearers remembered longest the frequent stabbing of his gaunt forefinger, aimed like a pistol to emphasize his points.

Though it was not officially recorded, an enduring tradition credits Jackson with the naming of the new state over the opposition of Sevier, Robertson, and McNairy, who favored "Franklin" or "Washington." Jackson, it was said, rejected the names of individuals, reminding delegates that most eastern states had been named for kings and queens, English noblemen or English counties. He argued that independent Americans should not mimic the British and urged delegates to name their state for the Tennessee, "the Great Crooked River" that rose in the mountains to the east and flowed through the most fertile valleys of the territory. The musical Cherokee word "Tennessee" was irresistible, he said. "It has a flavor on the tongue as sweet as hot corn-cakes and honey." The delegates adopted the name by a majority of about two-thirds, and the sixteenth state entered the American Union as Tennessee.

The convention completed its work in twenty-seven days, after producing a constitution praised by Jefferson as the most democratic yet adopted by a state; but Tennessee's admission to the Union was delayed by the conservative Federalists, who foresaw a parade of new western states as a threat to their continued rule. Largely due to the leadership of Jefferson's disciple Aaron Burr in a pioneer congressional struggle along party lines, Tennessee was admitted to the Union June 4, 1796.

John Sevier became governor, and the legislature named William Blount and William Cocke to the Senate and Jackson to the House of Representatives.

Though its constitution was proletarian by contemporary standards,

Tennessee began statehood under the leadership of an embryonic frontier aristocracy, a ready-made Establishment representing the propertied class. All officers were chosen in advance, without recorded opposition. This paradox was baffling to politicians of the eastern states (and to many twentieth-century historians), who failed to perceive that the adventurers of the frontier were virtually without class-consciousness. Except for the presence of its 11,000 slaves, the infant state of Tennessee was a highly fluid democratic society and its founders cherished ideals of equal opportunity for all. The specter of class exploitation and the menace of unbridled speculation had not risen. In this time the twenty-nine-year-old Jackson, already a respected leader, began to imbibe the rather vaguely defined political views that were to preoccupy his countrymen for many years—views perhaps naïve and superficial, arrived at intuitively rather than intellectually, but views passionately held and defended.

Though he was a capitalist, speculator, and frontier aristocrat, Jackson thought of himself as an egalitarian, a champion of the people and a defender of right of the common man to rise in the world to the limit of his abilities.

Jackson's political education was augmented by painful lessons in the economics of speculation. David Allison was bankrupt and the Philadelphia merchants called on Jackson to retire Allison's notes as they came due—in cash rather than land or produce of the frontier, where cash was seldom seen. When the first of Allison's notes was due and he was unable to pay, Jackson traded his new store for 33,000 acres of fine land, which he sold in turn to James Stuart of Knoxville for 25 cents an acre. In partial payment—more than half the total—Jackson accepted a draft for about $4,500 on Senator Blount, who was indebted to Stuart. By now more than 60,000 acres accumulated by Jackson and John Overton had been lost, or were in danger.

The congressman-elect packed Blount's draft in his saddlebags, leaving for the 800-mile ride to Philadelphia in late October 1796. He was forty-two days on the route, trading horses occasionally, and reached the capital on a young black stallion he said was worth three times as much as the horse he had ridden from home. He was to keep the stallion in his stud for years.

3

"Great God!
Do you mention *her*
sacred name?"

Jackson took his seat in the House of Representatives December 5, 1796, clad in the unaccustomed grandeur of a new black suit from a Philadelphia tailor shop; but one sophisticated observer penetrated his disguise at a glance. The Swiss-born Albert Gallatin of Pennsylvania saw him as "a tall, lank, uncouth-looking personage, with long locks of hair hanging over his face, and a queue down his back tied in an eel skin; his dress singular, his manners and deportment those of a rough backwoodsman."

Two days after the arrival of Jackson, President Washington appeared in the chamber to deliver his farewell address to Congress, a grave, reserved figure who spoke in a high, thin voice but with the authority of a founder of the republic, as he reviewed the accomplishments of his administration. Most members of the House were moved by the scene and thoughts of Washington's retiring to private life, and some of them crossed party lines to approve a respectful response to his "mildly partisan" address.

A committee prepared a resolution acceptable to Washington's Federalist party, but House Republicans refused to give it unanimous support, and for two days subjected the reply to a painstaking review, challenging the implications of virtually every line, determined to withhold blanket approval of the Washington administration, which they considered dangerously aristocratic. When the President's critics failed to amend the document and the matter came to a vote, only twelve extreme Republicans held out to the last, refusing to endorse the resolution. One of these was Jackson. Another was the young New York aristocrat Edward Livingston, "a republican by theory," in contrast to Jackson, whose views had been formed "by environment and by every instinct of his nature."

Jackson's resentment was undoubtedly aroused by the popular attitude that the father of his country was a sacred figure, and that his opinions were unassailable. Jackson later defended his challenge to the reply of the House to Washington: "I didn't vote against anything in the document but against 'the King's Speech,' a servile mutation of the old English practice of addressing the head of state. It may be well enough in countries that have a king, but I thought it absurd in a country where none existed or could exist."

From this beginning Jackson won friends among Republican leaders, including Livingston, Nathaniel Macon of North Carolina, Aaron Burr, and the Virginians Stevens Mason, Henry Tazewell, and John Randolph of Roanoke, all of whom detected in the rough and inexperienced Jackson the indomitable spirit of a future leader. He was to correspond with these men for years.

With these allies and the support of Albert Gallatin and James Madison, Jackson worked a minor miracle for his constituents. An officer who had marched with John Sevier's unauthorized raid against the Cherokee towns asked Congress to pay him for his service, and was brusquely refused when the Secretary of War assailed the punitive expedition as inhumane and unlawful.

Jackson was so aroused that he introduced a resolution to have all expenses of the expedition paid, some $23,000, arguing that the Cherokee raid was launched in self-defense, that the capital had been under siege and Sevier's 1,200 troops attacked in their camp. "The knife and the tomahawk were held over the heads of women and children. . . . It was time to make some resistance. Some of the assertions of the Secretary of War are not founded in fact."

When his measure was shunted aside to the Committee on Claims and apparently certain death, Jackson protested: "I own that I am not very well acquainted with the rules of the House, but . . . [why] this very circuitous mode of doing business?" The next day Jackson reintroduced his bill with a brief, forceful speech. If the House refused its support, Jackson said, militia discipline would be undermined; volunteers should not be denied pay for their services. He was on his feet four times during the debate. Madison and Gallatin were so impressed by the forthright challenge that they joined the fight and had the bill sent to a special committee of which Jackson was chairman. The House then approved reimbursement for Tennessee's Indian fighters.

Otherwise Representative Jackson merely cast his votes, deserting his party only once to vote for expanding the navy by building three frigates, a move his fellow Republicans feared would strengthen the hand of John Adams, the President-elect. Jackson voted against paying tribute to Algiers, whose ships were preying on American commerce —and also opposed an appropriation of $14,000 for the purchase of furniture for the presidential mansion in the raw new capital city of Washington.

Jackson left for Tennessee in early March 1797, soon after the adjournment of Congress. He was homesick, and worried about his wife. He had written Robert Hays, his brother-in-law: "Attend . . . my Dear little Rachael [sic] and sooth her in my absence. If she should want anything get it for her." Jackson wrote Rachel of his yearning to "be restored to your arms . . . Dear Companion of my life." His only wish was that they would never be separated again. "I mean to retire from . . . publick life. . . . Could I only know you . . . enjoyed Peace of Mind, it would relieve my anxious breast and shorten the way . . . until . . . I am restored to your sweet embrace."

Jackson also returned home in financial distress. Senator Blount, caught up in Allison's failure, could not pay his draft and Jackson was forced to sell it for a fraction of its face value. He had lost the 33,000 acres of land as well as his store.

Jackson recovered quickly from political fatigue. He resigned his House seat promptly enough, leaving it to William C. C. Claiborne, a wandering politician who had made his way west by way of New York and Pennsylvania—but within six months Jackson was on his way back to the capital once more, this time as a senator from Tennessee. He agreed to take the seat vacated when his friend Blount was expelled from the Senate for the "high misdemeanor" of conspiring with British agents to wrest the territory of West Florida from Spain. This bold scheme of aggression, though it sent shock waves through the national capital, was applauded by Tennesseans, who were determined to open the Mississippi to their trade at any cost. Blount was immediately elected to the state Senate.

Jackson left reluctantly for Philadelphia, pausing once on the long ride to write Robert Hays: "Try to amuse Mrs. Jackson. I left her *Bathed in tears*"—a sight which had given him "more pain than any event in my life."

The new senator, in any case, managed to mask his remorse as he took his seat in November 1797 resplendent in a fashionable black coat with velvet collar and "florintine breeches." He settled into a dull session in which he failed to cast a single recorded vote, though his colleague, Senator William Cocke, voted on every roll call. Jackson's legislative duties seem to have been limited to negotiations for the new boundaries of Cherokee lands in Tennessee; but his chief concern was the threatened war with France, which hung over the country through months of unpromising negotiations. French warships seized American vessels, and a delegation led by John Marshall arrived in Paris only to be refused recognition by the Directorate. Though Jackson fumed because the patient, cautious John Adams did not declare war, his true sympathies were with the French. Napoleon was his ideal, and in January 1798 when the emperor turned his back on conquered Europe and gathered an army on the Channel for an invasion of England, the junior senator from Tennessee was elated. "Should Bonaparte make a landing on the English shore, tyranny will be humbled, and a republic will spring from the wreck, and millions of distressed people will be restored to the rights of man."

Jackson renewed his friendships with Edward Livingston and Aaron Burr during the session. He was especially stimulated by Livingston. "I felt myself suddenly attracted toward him," Jackson wrote, "by the gentleness of his manners; the charm of his conversation . . . by the profound acquaintance he already possessed of the theories of society . . . by his unlimited confidence in the sagacity of the people, and of their capability of self-government. . . ."

Jackson was also drawn to Burr, who had first won his heart by fighting for the admission of Tennessee to the Union. He admired Burr's courtly manner, which he apparently took as a model; he dined at least once in the Burr home, a sumptuous meal whose fine wines were to linger in Jackson's memory for life.

But the senator's exposure to Philadelphia society was brief. A worldwide depression set off by England's suspension of specie payments during the Napoleonic wars had now swept the United States. David Allison had been imprisoned for debt, and Jackson's losses on his mercantile venture were total. In April 1798 he resigned his Senate seat and hurried home to cope with his financial affairs.

To his relief Jackson found that the Hunter's Hill plantation had been thriving under the watchful eye of Rachel. He confessed that her handling of the black farm laborers was more effective than his own indulgent methods. "They take advantage of me in all kinds of ways," he said, "but they don't try any monkeyshines with her." In hope of increasing profits he bought one of the earliest cotton gins, which had been introduced only four years before, and Hunter's Hill was soon processing its money crop with the first gin in the Cumberland Valley. Jackson also built a distillery, and sold his whiskey for 75 cents a gallon in the new store he opened with a partner, Thomas Watson. Both Andrew and Rachel waited on the trade, which was apparently brisk from the start.

General Robertson's son Felix retained a vivid memory of Jackson as a merchant: "A cool, shrewd man of business . . . prompt and decided. No chaffering, no bargaining. . . . A man of soundest judgment, utterly honest, *naturally* honest; would beggar himself to pay a debt, and did so; could not be comfortable if he thought he had wronged anyone. He was swift to make up his mind, yet was rarely wrong, but whether wrong or right, hard to be shaken. . . ."

Robertson also observed that Jackson harbored the proverbial countryman's distrust of banks and cheap currency: "He was a bank hater from an early day. Paper money was an abomination to him, because he regarded it in the light of a promise to pay that was almost certain, sooner or later, to be broken. For his own part, law or no law, he would pay what he owed; he would do what he said he would."

But public service took Rachel's ambitious husband from her once more. Jackson's new mercantile career was hardly six months old before he was appointed to the Superior Court, a bench that served as the state's Supreme Court when its three judges sat together. Jackson's salary was $600 a year, second only to the governor's handsome income of $750. He had begun a six-year career on the bench that was to make him a popular figure throughout Tennessee.

The new judge traveled almost constantly between Nashville, Knoxville, and Jonesboro, acquiring an extensive personal acquaintance with the state's people wherever he held court, and in the cabins where he spent so many nights as a guest. His open, friendly manner won many friends and the tales he told before the hearth fires of his hosts were so frequently repeated as to become part of Tennessee folklore.

Few of Jackson's recorded decisions were to survive, but Tennessee tradition in the years after his death held that his decisions were, in the words of an early biographer, "short, untechnical, unlearned, sometimes ungrammatical, and generally right." This assessment would have pleased Jackson, who compensated for his deficiencies in legal knowledge with a strong sense of justice and impartiality, expressed with courage and almost unfailing common sense. He once held forth his ideal to a jury as if proposing a conspiracy of laymen to circumvent the baffling complexities of legal tradition: "Do what is *right* between these parties. That is what the law always *means.*" Jackson's success on the bench was made possible by the simplicity of most cases, which could be decided equitably by an impartial layman of sound judgment.

He seldom deliberated long over decisions—once deciding fifty cases in fifteen days—and some lawyers felt that he was inclined to make snap judgments. His critics also claimed that he was prone to side with the defense in criminal cases and that the leniency he revealed in charges to juries resulted in too many acquittals.

Judge Jackson occasionally revealed a disregard for precedent that delighted his supporters and perplexed lawyers who practiced in his court. In 1803 he heard a complex land case in Nashville involving titles that had been clouded years earlier in a decision by Judge McNairy—with the assistance of District Attorney Jackson. Jackson reversed McNairy's decision. An appeal was filed that cited one of Jackson's own arguments, but he denied the plea on the grounds that the federal court had no appellate jurisdiction—and because McNairy's decision had been contrary to the law and the facts. When a complaining attorney pointed out that the decision was based on the arguments of District Attorney Jackson, Judge Jackson replied that his oath as district attorney had bound him to protect the interest of the government, but that his oath as judge bound him to rule impartially between private citizens. Jackson added that there was nothing to prevent him from changing his opinion in the light of experience, study, "and graver responsibility." The decision stood.

There were times when Judge Jackson appeared to be hypersensitive to public opinion. Near the end of his service on the bench he was to hear a case involving one of his bitter enemies. Jackson sought out the man's attorney, George Rutledge: "You know that the personal relations between your client and me are not friendly."

Rutledge said he was aware of the hostility.

"This is the last court I'll ever hold here. I'm going to retire from the bench. If this case goes against your client, people will say it was because the judge was against him personally. God knows, George, that I would be as fair to him as to the best friend I have in the world; but there are people who would never believe it. On the other hand, if it should go in his favor, there are people who would say that . . . knowing that everybody knew the plaintiff and he were at outs, the judge would stand up so straight as to fall over backward. Don't you see?"

Rutledge asked, and was granted, a postponement until the next term of court.

Judge Jackson achieved the stature of legendary hero of the frontier in March 1803 after a memorable encounter with Russell Bean, an eccentric gunsmith.

Bean, who had left his wife and children to spend a year in New Orleans, returned to Jonesboro to find his wife nursing an infant—a child sired by one Allen, a local merchant. Bean promptly cut off the child's ears close to the head. "There," he said, "I reckon I've marked it so it'll not get mixed up with my chaps."

Bean was arrested, convicted, branded in the hand, and imprisoned, but escaped and went into hiding for several weeks while he stalked his wife's seducer. The gunsmith emerged one night during one of Jackson's terms of court in Jonesboro to find the town in an uproar, its streets thronged with people who had turned out to fight a fire at the stables of a tavern. Amid the spreading blaze and trumpetings of terrified horses Judge Jackson had taken command, organized a bucket brigade, and sent men to cover the roofs of nearby houses with wet blankets.

Bean burst into the mêlée, tore stable doors from their hinges to free the horses, clambered to a rooftop to help spread blankets and, as a witness said, "did more than any two men, except General Jackson, in saving the town." When the fire was out, Bean defied the sheriff and went off in search of Allen once more.

The next morning Jackson assembled a posse to capture the gunsmith and ordered him brought into court by the sheriff, who reported that no one could arrest Bean. The fugitive was encouraged by townspeople, who felt that he was being persecuted, while the merchant Allen had escaped scot-free. Jackson lectured the sheriff on his duty before a crowded courtroom and adjourned the session for the noon meal, but had no sooner appeared on the street than the exasperated sheriff deputized him and two other judges to capture Bean. Jackson's companions protested that as judges they could not be deputized, but Jackson merely called for a pistol. Then, followed at a respectful distance by a crowd, he approached Bean with his weapon ready. Bean gave up his arms, followed Jackson into the courtroom, and stood patiently while he was pronounced guilty and ordered to pay a fine.

Shortly before leaving the bench, Jackson came into conflict with John Sevier—by now the three-term governor of the state, idol of East Tennessee, and in terms of the mythology of campaign oratory the champion of the common people and sworn enemy of the "neebobs" of the west, plantation owners like Judge Jackson and his friends.

Rivalry between these two forceful men had begun during Jackson's term in the House of Representatives, when he discovered that Sevier and his friends had acquired about one-fifth of the state of Tennessee by the use of forged warrants and other frauds. Jackson informed Governor Ashe of North Carolina, who launched an investigation that uncovered 165 bogus warrants in Sevier's hands—a fraud that could not be proven because the entry books had been destroyed.

The old veteran next clashed with Jackson over military office. In 1801 when Governor Sevier had served the three consecutive terms allowed by the constitution, he was succeeded by Jackson's friend, Archibald Roane, under whose administration the Tennessee militia held an election to choose a major general. The field officers cast an equal number of votes for Jackson and Sevier, and Governor Roane then cast the deciding vote for Jackson. Sevier was outraged; he was the hero of King's Mountain and the veteran of some thirty-five battles against Indians—and Jackson had no military experience. Sevier had a dream which he noted in his diary: his father appeared to him and denounced Jackson as "a very wicked, base man, and a very improper person for a Judge."

When Roane ran for reelection, John Sevier campaigned vigorously to regain the office he regarded as his private fief. In an effort to aid Roane, Jackson published the facts of the vast land frauds perpetrated by Sevier and his friends; but though the story created a sensation, Sevier convinced voters that he was being persecuted, and won the governorship once more after a bold campaign of subterfuge and evasion.

The old warrior had resumed office in Knoxville when Jackson arrived to hold court. The rivals met on the steps of the courthouse on October 1, 1803.

Jackson emerged from his courtroom to find Sevier delivering a speech before a crowd of legislators and hangers-on, apparently in hopes that Jackson would appear. Nolichucky Jack, as usual, recounted his services to Tennessee and rattled his old cavalry saber in its scabbard as he trumpeted the roll of his victories against the Indians. When he caught sight of Jackson, Sevier nodded and made an insulting reference to the judge.

"I've performed some public services myself," Jackson said, "which I believe have met with approval."

"Services!" Sevier bellowed. "I know of no great service you have rendered the country except taking a trip to Natchez with another man's wife!" He drew his saber.

Jackson's eyes blazed with wrath. "Great God! Do you mention *her* sacred name?" He swung his walking stick at Sevier's head.

The crowd pressed in upon them. Several pistol shots were fired and a bystander grazed by a bullet before friends separated Jackson and Sevier and led them away.

Jackson sent a challenge to the governor's mansion. Sevier protested

to friends that his courage was so well known that he could decline
without criticism, that he was too old to fight, and that his death would
leave his family impoverished, but finally replied that he would
meet Jackson, though not in Tennessee, where dueling had been out-
lawed.

Jackson scorned Sevier's subterfuge, and offered to fight in Virginia, North Carolina, Georgia, or Indian Territory, "if it will obvi-
ate your squeamish fears. . . . You must meet me tween this and
four o'clock this afternoon . . . or I will publish you as a coward."
Jackson's friends sought to dissuade him but the infuriated judge
persisted. He would resign from the bench if need be, but he
would defend his wife's honor. He sent Sevier a final challenge:

> In the publick streets of Knoxville you appeared to pant for combat.
> You ransacked the vocabulary of vulgarity . . . you . . . took the sacred
> name of a lady in your polluted lips, and dared me publickly to chal-
> lenge. . . . I have spoken for a place in the paper for the following
> advertisement:
>
> ". . . Know ye that I Andrew Jackson, do pronounce, publish, and
> declare to the world, that his excellency John Sevier . . . is a base coward
> and poltroon. He will basely insult, but has not the courage to repair.
> ANDREW JACKSON."
>
> You may prevent the insertion of the above by meeting me in two hours
> after receipt of this.

Sevier delayed for twenty-four hours, then made an evasive answer.
Jackson published his notice in the *Gazette* and, in the belief that Sevier
would follow, set out with Thomas J. Van Dyke, an army doctor, for
the Cherokee reservation, where he waited five days before Sevier
arrived with a party of armed men.

Jackson drew his pistols and strode toward Sevier, who dismounted
and approached with two pistols ready. The two halted about twenty
paces apart, cursing each other steadily.

"Damn you, Jackson," Sevier cried, "fire away." The antagonists
continued to shout for a few moments, then put away their weapons,
but Jackson rushed forward abruptly with his stick raised, shouting that
he would cane Sevier. The governor drew his saber, which so frightened his horse that he ran away carrying Sevier's pistols. Jackson drew
a pistol once more, and Sevier dashed behind a tree. "Damn you,
Jackson, will you fire on a naked man?"

The governor's seventeen-year-old son, George Washington Sevier, drew a pistol on Jackson, and Dr. Van Dyke, in turn, drew on the boy. At that moment others of the Sevier party approached, persuaded the men to put away their arms, and led Jackson and Sevier from the field, the antagonists bellowing curses at each other until they could no longer be heard.

4

"I'd have hit him if he'd shot me through the brain!"

As a loyal Republican Jackson had supported Thomas Jefferson in his presidential races against John Adams in 1796 and again in 1800, when the Virginian was elected after a bitter campaign. Jackson remained faithful despite charges that Jefferson was an atheist, an unpatriotic coward, an immoral embezzler, and "the great arch priest of Jacobinism and infidelity."

The judge did not record his sympathies during the spectacular final phase of Jefferson's election, which took place in the House of Representatives after a tie in the electoral vote between Jefferson and Aaron Burr. The House was deadlocked through thirty-six ballots over a hectic period of six days, during which there were rumors of an armed uprising to defend the Constitution. It was said that 70,000 men were under arms in Massachusetts. Though Burr had nominally run as a candidate for Vice President, he eagerly accepted the opportunity to defeat Jefferson in the House, and the new régime opened with a distinct coolness between the leaders of the party.

Jackson was electrified by the first great event of Jefferson's administration, the Louisiana Purchase. He wrote the President of this "golden moment . . . when all the Western Hemisphere rejoices," and began a campaign to win for himself the governorship of the new territory. Like most Americans Jackson disregarded the fact that the boundless western lands had been bought by a President with dubious authority to purchase, from an emperor who had no right to sell, and that the Spanish flag still flew over New Orleans. The eager Americans of the west were the chief beneficiaries of Napoleon's move to frustrate the ambitions of Great Britain by betrayal of the Spanish, and they were not to be denied. General James Wilkinson and a small force of U.S. regulars soon floated down the Mississippi to occupy New Orleans without incident, and without demonstrations of welcome from native Creoles.

Jackson put forth his name as a candidate for governor of Louisiana indirectly through his friends in Tennessee, and despite his embarrassed financial condition, prepared to plunge into new trading ventures and speculations. The judge was so short of cash that he was forced to pledge his salary in advance to pay a $375 freight bill for iron shipped from East Tennessee. He shipped some 56,000 pounds of cotton and a large lot of hides and furs to New Orleans under instructions to sell them at any price, "to save ourselves." He sent his neighbor John Coffee into the Illinois Territory to offer as much as $35,000 for property surrounding some salt springs before new settlers swarmed into the region. Coffee was a friend and silent partner in these enterprises, a huge, taciturn, self-educated man who was soon to marry one of Rachel's numerous nieces, and was to remain Jackson's loyal ally for life. Jackson also acquired a new partner to succeed Thomas Watson—John Hutchings, a rather ineffectual young man whose chief asset seems to have been that he was Rachel's nephew.

In the spring of 1804 Jackson left for Philadelphia to arrange a new line of credit and buy more merchandise, but the chief purpose of his trip was almost certainly to seek the governorship of Louisiana. He stopped in Washington in hope of seeing Jefferson. When he discovered that the President had gone to Monticello, however, Jackson did not follow him, since "it would have been perhaps construed as the call of a courteor"—and despite his eagerness for the post which would have ended his financial worries, Jackson declared, "of all characters on earth I . . . despise a man capable of cringing to power for a benefit or office . . . before I would violate my own ideas of propriety, I would yeald up any office in the government. . . ."

His chief rival for the office was William C. C. Claiborne, whose appeal to the President was obvious to Jackson: "He has the advantage of birth in Virginia; a great thing in the eyes of T.J." The judge's fears were confirmed. By the time he reached Philadelphia, Jackson learned that Jefferson had named Claiborne as governor of Louisiana.

The President's rejection of Jackson was undoubtedly based on the unfavorable impression the impulsive Tennessean had left with him during the Senate session of 1797–98. "His passions are terrible," Jefferson remembered later. "He could never speak on account of the rashness of his feelings. I have seen him attempt it frequently, and as often choke with rage." Since Jefferson had no opportunity to judge Jackson's obvious qualities of leadership outside the formal forum of the Senate, where the frontiersman was out of his element, the more amenable but superficial Claiborne presented the safer choice.

Jackson's pride was wounded by his failure, and he never publicly revealed his effort to win the post. He managed, in fact, to convince himself that he had not sought to become governor. He wrote Edward Livingston, who had now migrated to New Orleans, protesting that he could not be tempted by the governorship unless it had come unsolicited. "I have not applied for it. As you know, I have not the courteor's arts. I would not dance before the throne of power for the throne itself."

After establishing credit with the Bank of North America in Philadelphia and buying $12,000 worth of merchandise and some elegant chairs and a sofa for Rachel, Jackson returned to Tennessee. He stopped in Virginia to purchase three brood mares from the Berkeley estate, all from the bloodlines of the legendary early American sire, the Godolphin Arabian.

Jackson found himself on the brink of ruin when he reached home. The freight bill of more than $1,600 for shipment of his merchandise took all of his cash, and John Hutchings returned from New Orleans to report that his cotton and furs had brought so little as to barely cover the costs of the journey. Once more Jackson moved resolutely to save himself. He resigned from the bench to devote full time to his personal affairs, becoming a private citizen for the first time in sixteen years. He also sold 25,000 acres of unimproved land in other parts of the state, and his beloved home at Hunter's Hill. He moved to a new farm known as the Hermitage, a 640-acre tract 2 miles away where he settled Rachel and her new furniture into a log house, built a connecting cabin for guests, and began life anew. The main building was a two-story blockhouse with one large room on the first floor, with a lean-to shed in the rear. Meals were cooked in the large fireplace, and the big room served as parlor, living room, dining room, and kitchen. The Jacksons were to live in this building for fifteen years.

He opened a new store at Clover Bottom on Stone's River, some three miles from the Hermitage, with branches in the towns of Lebanon and Gallatin. Jackson advised his Philadelphia creditors that he expected to pay his debts the next spring, but it was not to be. He was irresistibly tempted by the building of a racetrack near his store, and when its owners had financial difficulties, the Jackson and Hutchings firm assumed control. In a flush of optimism Jackson expanded his Clover Bottom operations by building a tavern and boatyard.

By spring of 1805 the Philadelphia creditors had become insistent: "Sorry we are to say you have betrayed that Confidence we had placed in you." And, "we certainly have expected and ought . . . to have our money . . . and we cannot help thinking from the Character and knowledge we have of General Jackson but what . . . it must have been sent. If not, we must beg . . ."

Jackson's neighbor Edward Ward, who had bought Hunter's Hill, was now some $1,450 in arrears with his payments. Jackson insisted upon payment, reminding Ward: "When you recollect that I turned myself out of house and home by the sale of my possessions to you, purely to meet my engagements, you must know . . . the sacrifice of ease and comfort that I made. . . . My creditors are growing clamorous and I must have money. . . ."

In these straits merchant Jackson turned to horse racing in hope of restoring his fortunes. He made an unpromising beginning in the spring races, when his Indian Queen was defeated by the local champion, the gelding Greyhound. In an effort to recoup his loss Jackson bought another of Greyhound's victims, the bay stallion Truxton, whose owner, Major John Verell, had been brought to bankruptcy by the loss of the race. Jackson fell in love with the powerful horse at first sight. He felt that with proper conditioning Truxton would become a champion. Despite his formidable debts Jackson paid $1,500 for the big bay, assuming some $1,100 of Verell's debts and paying the balance with three geldings, with the promise of two more geldings if Truxton won a purse during the year. Then, with a sublime confidence in his eye for horseflesh, he arranged a return match with Greyhound for $5,000, put Truxton through four or five months of rigorous training, and in the fall defeated Greyhound with ease. The race had hardly ended when he also bought Greyhound, and with him won another $5,000 race at the next meet against Captain Joseph Erwin's horse Tanner. The victories established Jackson as the leading horseman of the region and temporarily relieved his financial distress.

Captain Erwin then challenged Jackson to another race, matching his well-known stallion Ploughboy against Truxton for $2,000, with $800 to be paid in case of a forfeit. Jackson had three partners in the stake—his neighbor William P. Anderson, Major Verell, and Captain Samuel Pryor, who was Truxton's trainer. Erwin's partner was his son-in-law Charles Dickinson, a young lawyer who had recently migrated from Maryland.

The twenty-seven-year-old Dickinson, a successful lawyer who had been trained under John Marshall, was known for his urbane manner, dissipated habits, and extraordinary skill as a marksman. He was already a man of means, a speculator in farm produce, land, horses, and slaves. His relations with Jackson had been strained for some time, since he had made insulting remarks about Rachel in public. Jackson had confronted the young man, who apologized lamely, saying that if he had made offensive statements, he had done so while he was drunk. Jackson accepted this, but soon afterward when he heard that Dickinson had repeated his insults in a Nashville tavern, he asked Erwin to restrain his son-in-law, charging that he was being used by John Sevier's friends, who hoped to provoke a duel.

Erwin's horse Ploughboy went lame during training for the race and was withdrawn by Erwin and Dickinson, who paid the forfeit. The postponed race involved Jackson in a tragic quarrel with Dickinson. One Saturday when a crowd gathered at the Clover Bottom store, William Anderson's brother Patton repeated his version of the forfeiture of the race, and Jackson interrupted to correct him. In fact, he said, Erwin and his friends had attempted no subterfuge. Erwin had offered $800 in notes not yet due, and Jackson insisted that at least half the payment must be in due notes, since his partners Verell and Pryor needed cash at once. Dickinson then produced due notes for $400. Jackson made the transaction clear to his listeners, but this was not enough. Thomas Swann, one of Dickinson's young friends, intruded into the conversation and later took Dickinson a distorted view of Jackson's explanation. To Dickinson's demand for satisfaction Jackson responded that someone had told "a damned lye."

This brought a heated exchange between Swann and Jackson in which Jackson told the boy he was being used as a dupe, and added, "The base poltroon and cowardly talebearer will always act in the background. You can apply the latter to Mr. Dickinson . . . I write it for his eye."

In reply Dickinson wrote Jackson, branding him as a liar and a coward and daring him to issue a challenge. Young Swann also wrote, "Think not I am to be intimidated by your threats. No power terrestial shall prevent the settled purpose of my soul. . . . My friend the bearer of this is authorized to make complete arrangements in the field of honor."

When Jackson learned that Dickinson had left for New Orleans before sending his challenging note, he made no reply, but sent Swann word that though he would not fight him, he intended to cane him upon sight.

A few days later Jackson met Swann in a crowded Nashville tavern, caned him, and was on the point of shooting it out with the young man when Swann apologized.

The affair was prolonged by Swann's friend Nathaniel McNairy, a younger brother of Judge John McNairy, who called on Jackson to demand satisfaction for the caning. Jackson refused to "degrade himself" in a formal duel but agreed to meet Swann in some isolated spot if it were acknowledged that this was not to be a fight between gentlemen.

Swann and Jackson then published statements in Thomas Eastin's Nashville paper, the *Impartial Review and Cumberland Repository*, Jackson dismissing McNairy as a meddler and Swann as "the puppet and lying valet for a worthless, drunken, blackguard scoundrel . . . Charles Dickinson."

Jackson was obviously saving himself for Charles Dickinson, who sent word that he was taking target practice from his boat on the voyage to New Orleans. The aged General James Robertson, founder of Nashville, urged Jackson to avoid a fight, since his courage needed no vindication. The old man warned that the slaying of Dickinson would make Jackson miserable for as long as he lived, and cited Burr's duel with Alexander Hamilton: "I suppose if dueling Could be Jestifiable it must have bin in his case and it is beleaved he has not had ease of mind since the fatal hour. . . . Once for all let me tell you . . . avoid . . . a duel."

It was too late. The race between Truxton and Ploughboy, the ostensible source of the feud, was now rescheduled. An announcement in the *Impartial Review* reflected Tennessee's growing excitement over the involved affair:

> On Thursday the 3d of April next will be run the greatest and most interesting race ever run in the Western country between *Gen. Jackson's* horse
>
> TRUXTON
> 6 years old carrying 124 pounds and *Capt. Joseph Erwin's* horse
>
> PLOUGHBOY
> 8 years old carrying 130 lbs. . . . For the sum of 3,000 dollars.
>
> No stud horses can be admitted within the gates, but such as contend on the TURF—and all persons are requested not to bring their dogs to the field, as they will be shot without respect to the owners.

Though race day dawned cold and gray, with a threat of rain, the throng that swarmed into Clover Bottom was the largest civilian crowd

Jackson had ever seen. His friends feared that the audience was to be disappointed, for Truxton had gone lame two days earlier under Jackson's strenuous training regimen. Men who gathered at the paddock saw the bay's injury at a glance—a swollen thigh that made it obvious Truxton would not be at his best today. Jackson's manner was grave but he insisted stubbornly that the race must go on.

Jackson's trainer, Sam Pryor, and other friends urged him to pay the forfeit and race another day, arguing that Truxton's injury was serious, and he faced almost certain defeat. Jackson hesitated only briefly, going over the horse one last time, stroking his head, speaking in a low voice, and looking into his eyes. He straightened and said, "It's all right, gentlemen. Truxton will run."

Truxton's supporters had come early, many of them bringing their most valuable property to throw into the betting—herds of horses and droves of slaves, both of which were turned into pens to await the end of the race. Erwin's exultant backers hurried through the crowd, seeking wagers. Major William B. Lewis offered to bet an unlimited amount, but found takers for only $2,000. The Truxton men slowly, rather reluctantly, made their bets, a total of about $10,000 by race time, approximately half the amount Jackson had expected.

Under dark, low-hanging clouds the horses moved out for the first of the two-mile heats and were off at the tap of a drum. The crowd roared as the injured Truxton took the lead, held on through the first mile, and drew ahead steadily through the grueling finish to win going away.

The cheers of Jackson's supporters ceased as his jockey slowed the winner. Truxton limped visibly—he was now also lame in a front leg. When Jackson reached him, he saw that on one of the animal's sound legs "the plate had sprung and lay across the foot." The bay seemed to be out of it, but Jackson refused to halt the race.

The two horses went back to the post in a driving rain. The huddled crowd peered through the storm in astonishment as the raw-boned bay pulled away from Ploughboy with ease, giving no sign of his injuries. Once more he ran away from his rival, and though his rider used neither whip nor spur, Truxton won by 60 yards. It seemed to Jackson's neighbors that Truxton had imbibed the indomitable spirit of his master.

Jackson sent an enthusiastic account of the race to John Hutchings in New Orleans, who replied ruefully that Dickinson had left the city before the news of Truxton's triumph arrived and that he had missed the pleasure of observing the young man's "aggoney."

At this point Aaron Burr appeared in Tennessee on a mission that was to link Jackson's name with a dramatic and mysterious plot against the United States. Burr, who had been indicted for murder in New Jersey after killing Alexander Hamilton, went into hiding on an island off the Georgia coast for a time, but boldly reappeared in Washington when Congress convened in December 1804, and presided over the Senate until the end of the session. He left after a dignified speech of farewell that moved even his enemies to tears, and traveled through the west, where he was given a hero's welcome. Burr's role in gaining the admission of Tennessee to the Union had not been forgotten.

Burr had been secretly conferring with British and Spanish ministers in Washington, hatching a vague plot to create a new nation in the Lower Mississippi Valley. He had also been in touch with the American military commander in New Orleans, General James Wilkinson, whom he had known since the days of the Revolution. Wilkinson, who had been in Spanish pay for several years, remained a Spanish spy while commanding U.S. forces in Louisiana. Burr was lionized in Cincinnati and Louisville and in Frankfort, Kentucky, where he talked with men who had taken part in an earlier Spanish plot to annex Kentucky. Though he said publicly that he was recruiting colonists to settle on the Ouichata River in Louisiana, it was understood that Burr's goal was an invasion of Texas, which most westerners approved.

He told conflicting stories of the pledged support of both the English and the Spanish, and said he planned to seize Florida, or Texas, or Mexico—each audience was left with a different conception of his scheme. In these weeks Burr left behind such a confusing trail that his actual purpose was never to be precisely known.

Burr undertook a long side journey to visit Jackson, apparently to renew their acquaintance formed in the Senate seven years before. In May 1805 the ex-Vice President arrived at Nashville, where he was honored with a banquet and ball, and was then carried off to the Hermitage for a stay of almost a week.

Burr evidently told Jackson only of his projected settlement in Louisiana, but hinted that he would march into Texas only in case of war with Spain, a move Jackson approved but regarded as hazardous, even though Burr insisted that he had the secret support of the Secretary of War, Henry Dearborn.

Jackson gave Burr a boat to carry him down the Cumberland and the restless empire-builder moved on to New Orleans, where he found great enthusiasm for his project. In August, as he had promised, Burr returned to the Hermitage for a week's visit, a most pleasant one, he wrote a friend; he praised his host as "one of those prompt, frank, ardent souls whom I love to meet."

Jackson was impressed by Burr's energy but dubious of his chances of success in the southwest. He felt that the ex-Vice President relied too heavily on the promises of strangers. As Jackson told John Overton later, "Burr is as far from a fool as I ever saw, and yet he is as easily fooled as any man I ever knew."

Burr soon left for the east, from where he corresponded occasionally with Jackson, discussing the threatened war with Spain, for which westerners had agitated throughout years of quarreling with Spanish officials in Florida and the Mississippi Valley. There would be no war with Spain, Burr reported. As Jefferson's kinsman John Randolph had charged on the floor of the House, the President refused to take a strong stand in the Spanish disputes, trusting to dollar diplomacy to settle the conflict. Burr reported that Jefferson was attempting to buy Florida for $2 million. "This secret is a secret to those only who are best entitled to know it—our own citizens." Burr also warned Jackson of another threat of war. General Francisco Miranda, a South American adventurer, was fitting out an expedition in New York with plans to invade Venezuela. France and Spain were likely to retaliate by seizing New Orleans, Burr warned—and in that case only a western army could protect U.S. interests in the southwest. "Your country is full of fine materials for an army . . . a brigade could be raised in West Tennessee which would drive double their number of Frenchmen off the earth." Burr then asked for a list of Tennessee officers, which he said he would "recommend to the Secretary of War" in case troops were called out. After consultation with General Robertson and others, Jackson sent Burr a roster of officers for his two imaginary regiments.

Charles Dickinson was also back in Nashville in May 1805, where he placed an insulting notice about Jackson in the *Review* for publication on the twenty-fourth. John Overton's brother Tom, a militia general, carried the news to Jackson, who asked him to return to Nashville and read the article before publication. Overton reported that the notice was scurrilous. "General, you must challenge him."

Dickinson had written of Jackson, "I declare him, notwithstanding he is a Major General of the militia of Mero district, to be a worthless scoundrel; A poltroon and a coward!—A man who, by frivolous and evasive pretexts, avoided giving the satisfaction which was due to a gentleman whom he had injured."

Within an hour Tom Overton delivered Jackson's challenge to Dickinson, who accepted. Arrangements were made at once. The duel was to be fought in Kentucky, just across the state line, and despite Jackson's protests over the delay, was set for May 30. The seconds agreed that the duelists should stand 24 feet apart, with pistols held downward at their sides, ready to shoot on command. Both the choice of position and the right to give the firing command were to be determined by lot.

Jackson rose before dawn of May 29, telling Rachel that he must settle some trouble with Dickinson and would be gone for two days. She asked no questions. By 6:30 A.M. the general was in Nashville, where he met Overton, a surgeon, and two other men, and left for Kentucky.

Dickinson had kissed his pregnant young wife goodbye and told her only that he was leaving, but would be home the next evening without fail.

Tales of the day-long rides of the duelists to the meeting place, though probably apocryphal, lingered in Tennessee tradition for many years afterward. Dickinson, it was said, entertained his young companions with exhibitions of his marksmanship along the way, once firing four shots from a distance of 24 feet into a space the size of a silver dollar. He was also said to have severed a string with a bullet from the same distance, leaving it hanging by a tavern door and calling to the landlord, "If General Jackson comes along this road, show him *that!*" In any event Dickinson's party moved noisily on its way, shouting and laughing and occasionally racing the horses to plunge across streams.

Jackson mentioned the duel only twice during the long ride, once to say he hoped Dickinson would be prompt, and then, speaking of his skill: "He's a quicker shot than I am, probably a better one. He's sure to fire first. The chances are nine out of ten he'll hit me—but that won't matter. I'll take my time, aim deliberately, and kill him if it's the last thing I do."

The general also talked of British seizures of American ships and sailors, the growing threat of war, and his fears that Jefferson would be too weak to cope with the British. Perhaps the next President would be less timid. "We must fight England again before long. I wasn't old enough to be of any account the last time. I only hope we'll go to war before I'm too old to fight."

Overton smiled. "What age do you think that might be?"

"About a hundred years, if England's the enemy!"

Jackson also talked at length of Burr, saying his scheme of western settlement was doomed to failure. "The Federalists will jump Burr, tooth and toenail, and when they do Jefferson will run like a cottontail rabbit. He's the best Republican in theory and the worst in practice I've ever seen."

He spoke of Burr's duel with Hamilton, and added that, though he'd liked Hamilton personally, "his political views were all English; not in the least American." Jackson's manner was calm and assured, but Overton noted that he failed to take his customary small drinks of whiskey at intervals during the day, and drank only a mint julep when the party halted at noon.

Late in the day when his group stopped at a tavern, Jackson learned that Dickinson's party had already passed, to spend the night two miles down the road. "That's good news," he said. "They won't keep us biting our thumbs any longer."

The general ate a large supper—waffles, fried chicken, and sweet potatoes—then sat on the tavern porch until ten o'clock, smoking his pipe and talking with the other guests. He slept so soundly that Overton roused him with difficulty the next morning.

Jackson led the party to the Red River and rode across the shallow stream to the Kentucky shore. One of his friends asked, "How do you feel about it now, General?"

"Oh, all right. I'll wing him, never fear." Two of the men halted near the river; Jackson walked forward into the woods with Overton and his surgeon. It was about 7:00 A.M.

Dickinson and his party were waiting in a clearing in a poplar forest. Dr. Catlett won the choice of position by lot, but since the rising sun had not reached the clearing, this gave Dickinson no advantage. Overton won the right to give the command to fire.

Overton produced Jackson's pistols, handsome weapons with 9-inch barrels which fired 1-ounce balls of seventy caliber. Dickinson chose one of them and the duelists took their places at pegs 24 feet apart. Dickinson wore a short blue coat and gray trousers, and Jackson a long frock coat buttoned carelessly over the chest, its loose folds concealing his spare figure. Young Dickinson exuded confidence. Jackson stood stiffly erect, with an air of intense concentration.

Overton called, "Gentlemen, are you ready?" Both men responded immediately.

"Fire!"

Dickinson's pistol blazed instantly. Dust rose from Jackson's loose-fitting coat and his left hand flew to his chest. The long face grimaced with pain but the erect form was motionless. He raised his pistol.

Dickinson stepped backward. "My God! Have I missed him?"

Overton raised his pistol and ordered him back to the mark.

Dickinson stepped forward, folded his arms, and waited, staring at the ground. Jackson stiffened and took aim. The hammer halted at half-cock. Jackson deliberately recocked it and fired. Dickinson reeled and fell to the ground. His seconds propped the wounded man against a bush and Dr. Catlett loosened his clothing to find that the heavy ball had passed through his body just below the ribs, lacerating the intestines.

Overton walked to the spot and returned to Jackson.

"He won't want anything more of you, General."

Jackson and his party turned away immediately. When they were out of sight, Overton saw that Jackson's shoe was full of blood.

"My God, General, are you hit?"

"Oh, I believe he pinked me."

Jackson unbuttoned his coat to reveal a stain of blood across his shirt and waistcoat. "I don't want those people to know," he said. "Let's move on."

When the wound was examined soon afterward it was found that Dickinson's bullet, deflected by the breastbone, had torn a deep furrow through the chest muscles, broken one or two ribs, and lodged in the chest cavity.

"He misjudged his aim because of your loose coat," Overton said. "He missed your heart only an inch or so."

"I'd have hit him," Jackson said firmly, "if he'd shot me through the brain! . . . Did you notice Dickinson's mistake? . . . When he came back to the mark he folded his arms across his chest. If he had let his right arm hang down to cover his side, it would probably have turned my bullet."

Jackson sent a bottle of wine to Dr. Catlett for Dickinson's use, and offered the aid of his own surgeon. Catlett replied that the wounded man was beyond the need of surgery.

Dickinson lingered through the night, conscious to the end, "cursing his ill luck almost with his last breath." Someone told him that Jackson had been severely wounded after all, and was dying. Dickinson seemed content. He spoke suddenly to his doctor, "Why did you put out the candles?"

A moment later he was dead.

Rachel, who heard the news within a few hours and understood completely, cried impulsively, "Oh, God have pity on the poor wife . . . the babe in her womb!"

Soon after the funeral Jackson learned that Dickinson's friends and relatives had asked editor Eastin to publish the next issue of the *Impartial Review* with black borders, in mourning. Jackson, who saw this emotional appeal as an attempt by his enemies to destroy him, dictated a letter to Eastin:

> Though I know your personal attitude, I yet believe you to be a fair man. . . .
>
> Presuming that the whole public is not in mourning for this event, in

justice to that whole public it is only fair and right to set forth ALL THE NAMES of those citizens who have made the request . . . in order that the real public might judge whether the true motives of the signers were "a tribute of respect for the deceased," or something else. . . .

When Eastin showed this letter to Dickinson's friends, almost half of the seventy-odd petitioners withdrew their signatures. Jackson looked over the forty-seven published names with satisfaction. Now, he told his friends, he had a guide to men in Nashville who would bear watching. He seemed to feel no remorse. In his eyes Dickinson was merely a sworn enemy who had long plotted to murder him and had died in the attempt, a sacrifice to partisan politics.

Jackson's phenomenal popularity in Tennessee waned after the Dickinson duel. Gossips repeated his casual remark that he had merely been "pinked," and revived tales of his quarrel with Sevier. Except for friends and neighbors, few people were aware that Jackson's wound was serious, and almost no one realized that Dickinson's insults to Rachel had precipitated the duel. Even John Overton was led by Jackson to believe that the duel had grown out of the racing squabble.

Joseph Erwin published an account of the duel, charging that Jackson had shot Dickinson in cold blood after his pistol failed to fire at half-cock. Erwin maintained that the agreement gave Jackson no right to fire under such circumstances, and that he had taken "unguarded, illiberal and unjust advantage" of Dickinson. The seconds of both men, however, issued a statement insisting the duel had been conducted fairly, according to the agreement.

Jackson recovered slowly from his wound. Dickinson's bullet had lodged so near his heart that removal would be dangerous; it was to remain there for the rest of the general's life.

5

"I would cut his throat with as much pleasure as I would cut yours"

In September 1806 Aaron Burr returned to the Hermitage, where Jackson welcomed him as "still a true and trusty friend to Tennessee," and invited Overton, General Robertson, and others to greet him. At Jackson's suggestion Burr was honored with a public ball, where an admiring crowd watched the general pass among the guests, introducing Burr as his friend and Tennessee's godfather. Burr was also entertained by several of Nashville's leading citizens, including General Robertson. Burr was full of dazzling but formless dreams of empire. He had now left the east forever, he said. His daughter Theodosia had come west with him, and was waiting on Blennerhasset Island in the Ohio River, ready to accompany his expedition down the Mississippi. His account of his ambitious scheme aroused the suspicions of the astute old General Robertson, who pressed Burr for details and questioned him pointedly about Jefferson's attitude toward his plans; but, the old man said, "he was so guarded, I gained but little satisfaction."

Burr disappeared within a few days, but in early November sent Jackson an order for five large riverboats and provisions, for which he paid in cash—$3,500 in Kentucky banknotes. Jackson and Coffee accepted the contract for the boats and ordered provisions. The work began at Clover Bottom under Coffee's direction. Jackson's friend Patton Anderson also raised a company of seventy-five men to accompany Burr's expedition.

Carpenters were still hammering away at Burr's boats in Clover Bottom when a young stranger appeared at the Hermitage with a letter of introduction to Jackson. The visitor was a Captain Fort, who said he was on his way to join Burr. It was this young man (whose identity was never to be established) who first alarmed Jackson and opened his eyes to the menace of Burr's scheme. Fort spoke of Burr's plans with the knowing air of a conspirator. The purpose of the project, he said casually, was to "divide the Union." When the startled Jackson asked how that was to be done, Fort said, "By seizing New Orleans, closing the port, taking Mexico and uniting with the western part of the country."

"How can he do that?"

"With Federal troops, led by General Wilkinson."

Fort conceded that Wilkinson had told him nothing of the plot, and could not say positively that Burr was involved. "I hardly know Colonel Burr," he said.

Under Jackson's persistent questioning Fort said his information came from Samuel Swartwout in New York, one of Burr's lieutenants. When he saw that he had gone too far, Fort tried to allay Jackson's fears by changing his story. It was too late. Jackson turned at once to spread the alarm.

He wrote to Daniel Smith, his successor in the Senate, warning that "there is a plan on foot . . . in concert with Spain to seize Neworleans and Louisiana, and divide the union." He confessed that he could not name names, but outlined a plot of "a designing man": Spain was to send troops into Louisiana, Wilkinson would lead an expedition into Mexico, while a band of American frontiersmen floated from the Ohio to capture New Orleans with the connivance of Governor Claiborne. "I hope I may be mistaken but I as much believe that such a plan is in operation as I believe there is a god. . . ." Jackson urged Smith to warn Jefferson at once: "The government must watch over their general . . . and give orders for the defense of Neworleans."

Jackson also wrote to Jefferson, offering to march with his Tennessee troops "in the event of . . . aggression . . . FROM ANY QUARTER."

He then sent a warning to Governor Claiborne, as if he had no doubt of his loyalty. Jackson recalled their earlier friendship in Tennessee, and added:

> I fear *treachery* has become an order of the day . . . put your town in a state of defense . . . and defend your city as well against internal enemies as external. . . . *I fear you will meet with an attack from quarters you do not at present expect.* Be upon the alert; keep a watchful eye upon our General

[Wilkinson] and beware of an attack as well from our own country as
Spain. . . . I love my country and government. I hate the Dons; I would
delight to see Mexico reduced; but I will die in the last ditch before I
would yield a foot to the Dons, or see the Union disunited.

Jackson also wrote Burr, demanding an explanation. Until his suspicions were cleared, he wrote, "no further intimacy was to exist between
us."

Jackson and Coffee agreed that the firm would do no further business with Burr, though the boats contracted for must be completed.

Burr replied promptly to Jackson, protesting his innocence and offering "the most sacred pledges" that he was not involved in a plot
against the United States. Within a day or two Jackson had news of a
farcical court hearing in Frankfort, Kentucky, where U.S. District Attorney Joseph Daviess had demanded Burr's arrest for treason. Federal Judge Harry Innes, who had aided James Wilkinson in the Spanish
plot to annex Kentucky, called a grand jury to hear evidence. Burr
appeared in a packed courtroom with his young attorney Henry Clay
—but the jury was dismissed at the request of Daviess, whose most
important witness had fled the state. Court adjourned amid cheers of
the crowd.

But time was running out for Aaron Burr. Wilkinson, who sensed
disaster, sought to conceal his own involvement by betraying Burr
in an insinuating letter to Jefferson—at the same time demanding
$110,000 from the Mexican government for this service. At the end of
November Jefferson issued a proclamation exposing a conspiracy
against Spain by "sundry persons" and ordering the arrest of the
plotters. Ohio officials seized Burr's small fleet at Marietta, and except
for thirty men who escaped down the river, the ex-Vice President's
supporters deserted him. Before this news reached Tennessee, Burr
reappeared at the Hermitage; on finding that Jackson was away, he
took a room in the nearby tavern at Clover Bottom.

When Jackson and Coffee appeared, Burr begged them to continue
their aid, swearing "upon his honor" that Jefferson approved all that
he was doing. He showed them a blank commission signed by the
President. "There, gentlemen, I suppose this will satisfy you."

Jackson was convinced. He delivered the two boats Burr requested,
and also sent with him Rachel's seventeen-year-old nephew, Stockley
Hays, who was on his way to school in New Orleans—though he did
not send Patton Anderson's troops. Burr's party shoved off downriver
on December 22, less than a week before news of Jefferson's proclamation reached Nashville.

Burr was burned in effigy in Nashville on December 31, 1806, before an excited crowd that was harangued by Thomas Swann and Joseph Erwin, who hinted broadly that Andrew Jackson was implicated in the plot of his crony Aaron Burr.

At the Hermitage Jackson was already caught up in the defense of the Union against the proclaimed menace by Burr, and in a furious protest at insinuations of his own disloyalty from another quarter.

On January 1, 1807, Jackson received from Secretary of War Henry Dearborn a message—he refused to dignify it as an order: "A milk and water thing . . . the merest old woman letter you ever saw."

Dearborn's letter was as insubstantial as tales of the plot itself, except in its inference that Jackson himself might be implicated:

> . . . *It appears that you have some reason for suspecting that some unlawful enterprise is in contemplation on the western waters. . . .*
>
> *It is presumed that the Proclamation of the President . . . will have produced every exertion . . . and . . . that you will have been among the most jealous opposers of any such unlawful expedition, as appears to be initiated, by a set of disappointed, unprincipled, ambitious or misguided individuals, and that you will continue to make every exertion in your power, as a General of the Militia, to counteract and render abhortive, any such expedition. . . . About Pittsburg it is industriously reported among the adventurers, that they are to be joined, at the mouth of the Cumberland, by two Regiments under the Command of General Jackson—such a story might afford you an opportunity of giving an effectual check to the enterprise if not too late I am etc.*
>
> *Henry Dearborn*

Blazing with rage at the insinuation that he was involved in Burr's plot, Jackson responded briefly to Dearborn: "The first duty of a soldier is to attend to the safety . . . of his country. The next is to attend to his own feelings when they have been . . . wantonly assailed."

Though he complained that Dearborn had made his meaning deliberately obscure, and that no one could say whether the Secretary wished to arrest Burr, Jackson prepared for action. He called up volunteers, put two brigades under arms, and sent word to Captain Bissell, commander of an army post at Fort Massac on the Ohio, to intercept any armed vessels. Bissell was to call on Jackson for reinforcements in case of need.

Jackson then turned to his unfinished business with Secretary Dearborn in such a state that he made several false starts at writing a letter. He began one apoplectic condemnation, tore it up, and began afresh:

Henry Dearborn, Sir. . . . Colo. B. received at my house all that hospitality that a banished patriot . . . was entitled to. . . . But sir when proof shews him to be a treator I would cut his throat with as much pleasure as I would cut yours on equal testimony.

Jackson put that aside and wrote a final, hardly less scathing challenge to the Secretary:

You stand convicted of the most notorious and criminal acts of dishonor, dishonesty, want of candour and justice. . . . You say Sir that it is industriously reported amongst adventurers that they are to be joined at the mouth of Cumberland by two regiments under the command of Gnl Jackson. Such a Story might afford him an opportunity of giving an effectual check to the enterprise, if not too late. After I have given the most deliber[ate] consideration to your expressions . . . I cannot draw from them any other conclusion but this: that you believed me concerned in the conspiracy [and] that I was a fit subject to act the traitor of traitors, as others have done . . . and that the . . . Secretary of War . . . [could] buy me up without honour.

Jackson branded Dearborn's letter as "unworthy of a man of honor." As to the Secretary's resentment of these charges: "I care not where, when, or how he shall." Whatever defense Dearborn could make, Jackson said finally, "cannot be . . . either tenable or true."

Dearborn made no reply to this outrageously insubordinate letter, reinforcing Jackson's suspicions that the Secretary and other Washington officials had been involved in the plot. He now believed that James Wilkinson had been the actual traitor, and he was not persuaded by Senator Smith's report from Washington that "the President confides in his fidelity."

Captain Bissell's reply to Jackson's warning ridiculed the threat of danger to the country. Colonel Burr had passed Fort Massac and gone down the river with sixty men in ten boats. The vessels were unarmed. Burr floated downstream for several days before he realized that the hunt was on, and that Wilkinson was waiting to trap him in New Orleans. The adventurer then deserted his boats to flee into the wilderness. He was captured in disguise soon afterward a few miles from the border of Florida, where he would have been safe under Spanish protection.

Even now Jackson refused to believe that the adventurer was a traitor. "If Burr has any treasonable intentions in view he is the basest of all human beings," he wrote. Jackson told the Tennessee congressman George Campbell that Burr had talked at length of settling on the Washita, and that in case of a war with Spain, he was certain of a regular army commission that would enable him to invade Mexico. This, Jackson was convinced, was the extent of Burr's plan.

Jackson denounced the capture as an outrage: "The mode of Burr's seizure in Alabama corroborated the farce of the Jo Daviess persecution in Kentucky. It looked to me as if Jefferson had brought over here some of those *lettres de cachet* they used in the French Revolution when they wanted to cut a man's head off because he didn't agree with them."

But Thomas Jefferson, though he regarded the explosive master of the Hermitage warily, was never in doubt as to his loyalty to the country. The President told George Campbell that he was "perfectly satisfied with the attitude of General Jackson . . . he had followed a straightforward, manly and patriotic course."

When Burr was tried for treason in Richmond, Virginia, in May and June 1807, Jackson was subpoenaed as a witness. Chief Justice John Marshall presided over the trial before a tense crowd in the hall of the House of Delegates, a hearing that degenerated into a charade. Burr appeared with an honor guard of 200 well-dressed civilian supporters who escorted him from the nearby penitentiary. Upon Burr's protest that a U.S. senator and an ex-senator, both Jefferson's friends, had been illegally drawn for the grand jury panel, they were dismissed by Marshall. Jefferson's cousin and sworn enemy John Randolph of Roanoke, the brilliant and eccentric gadfly of the House of Representatives, was named chairman of the jury. Burr's lawyers then demanded that Jefferson be called, and after four days of heated arguments, Marshall issued a subpoena, which the President defied. Jefferson refused to appear.

District Attorney George Hay asked postponements day after day, awaiting the appearance of General James Wilkinson, whose testimony, it was said, would prove that Burr had plotted treason. Wilkinson was twenty days late in arriving.

The prosecution's tactics of delay reinforced Jackson's belief in Burr's innocence and roused his wrath against the Jefferson administration. He felt this was a personal attack on Burr by Jefferson to destroy him. He wrote a friend in Tennessee, "I am still detained here . . . I am more convinced than ever that treason never was intended by Burr; but if it ever was, you know my wishes—that he may be hung. I am sorry to say that this thing has assumed the shape of a political persecution. . . ." Jackson made no secret of his feelings. He attacked

Wilkinson and Jefferson in public, the general as a "double traitor" and Jefferson as a coward who placed himself above the law. His suspicions of Wilkinson were shared by members of the grand jury, which failed by a margin of two votes to place the general himself in the dock with Burr—and events soon reinforced Jackson's prejudice against Jefferson.

In late June news reached Richmond that the British warship *Leopard* had attacked the smaller U.S. frigate *Chesapeake,* killing or wounding twenty-one men to seize four alleged deserters. A few days later when he learned that Jefferson had made a mild diplomatic protest, rather than a declaration of war, Jackson announced in a newspaper that he would address the public from the steps of the State House the next day.

He spoke extemporaneously for about an hour, an impetuous attack upon Jefferson and the "base and treacherous" James Wilkinson:

> . . . Mr. Jefferson has plenty of courage to seize peaceable Americans by military force and persecute them for political purposes. But he is too cowardly to resent foreign outrage upon the Republic. Here an English man-of-war fires upon an American ship of inferior force, so near his Capital that he can almost hear the guns, and what does he do? Nothing more than . . . recommend to Congress a bill laying an embargo and shutting our commerce off from the seas. If a man kicks you downstairs you get revenge by standing out in the middle of the street and making faces at him! . . .

As to Burr's trial, Jackson said,

> This persecution was hatched in Kentucky. The chicken died and they are trying to bring it to life here. . . . Mr. Jefferson can torture Aaron Burr while England tortures our sailors.
>
> This grand state is full of good Republicans [Democrats] and many of them may not like to hear such sentiments about their own great man. Whatever he does or fails to do is right in their eyes, no matter how cruel to Americans or how dastardly toward the English. But the East is different from the West. Out there the political air is pure. . . .
>
> A year ago or more I gave at a dinner to Aaron Burr in Nashville the toast, "Millions for defence; not a cent for tribute." They change that tune on this side of the mountains. Here it seems to be—"Millions to persecute an American; not a cent to resist England!" Shame on such a leader! Contempt for a public opinion rotten enough to follow him!

"He can talk as well as shoot," one listener said.

"Yes, and talks as if he's ready to shoot it now."

The Richmond editor Thomas Ritchie foresaw that the speech would make Jackson a national democratic leader: "He spared none. His style of speaking was rude but strong. It was not the polished oratory Eastern audiences were accustomed to hear." The force of Jackson's speech reminded Ritchie of the blows of an ax, felling a giant tree.

When the trial continued to drag on, Jackson demanded that Hay take his testimony or release him, so that he could return home. "I don't believe there is a particle of sincerity or honesty in the case against Burr and it's an outrage to keep honest men dancing fools' attendance on such a miserable farce."

Jackson was dismissed and left for home, but in his wake the government salvaged the farce with a temporary victory when Burr was ordered held for trial. The grand jury rejected all evidence against Burr except a coded message he had sent to Wilkinson, claiming that British support for their scheme was assured, that he could muster as many as 1,500 troops, and ending with flourish: "The gods invite us to glory and fortune; it remains to be seen whether we deserve the boon."

The case against Burr finally collapsed when a regular jury found him not guilty. And when Jefferson sought to try him on a lesser charge of "high misdemeanor," Burr fled to Europe, where he was to wander for almost four years, friendless and impoverished, involving himself in other fantastic schemes.

Jackson returned home to oppose James Madison's election in 1808 but succeeded only in causing a split in the Democratic party in Tennessee, since he was opposed by Federalists and Jeffersonian Democrats.* Jackson proposed moving the state capital from Knoxville to Nashville, which alienated East Tennesseans. He also favored a land court to settle title controversies, which was resisted by all who held dubious title to land granted under forged warrants. Thus Jackson, when urged to run for governor, wisely resisted the temptation and stepped aside in favor of his friend Willie Blount. Blount's election unified the party.

In Jackson's eyes the election of James Madison was a disaster, prolonging the policy of appeasing British aggressors. And the failure of a movement to remove James Wilkinson from command outraged

---

*For the sake of clarity Jackson's party is referred to hereinafter as Democrat, though they were to call themselves Republicans and Democrat Republicans for some years.

him. "On the eve of war," he fumed, "and a Treator at the head of the army!" War was very much on Jackson's mind. He remained convinced that the British would invade the country once more, and continued to prepare himself and his militia for action. A friend noted that his library now consisted of a few well-worn volumes—a book on horse breeding and handling, French and English army regulations and tactics, a history of Marlborough's campaigns, and some pamphlets on the battles of the Revolution. His leisure time was spent in studying military problems, and he alerted his militiamen at every threat of a possible war with England. The commander who had never fought a battle thought of himself as a general whose civilian troops could overcome all odds. "My only pride is that my soldiers has confidence in me, and on the event of war I will lead them to victory. Should we be blest with peace I will resign my military office and spend my days in the sweet calm of rural retirement." Though he was spoiling for a fight, he feared that the timid Congress would appease the British, whatever the provocation. "I am well aware that no act of insult, degradation or contumely offered to our government will arouse them from their present lethargy. . . ."

Jackson finally concluded that he was not destined to become a merchant prince, unlike so many of his contemporaries who accumulated fortunes in the early years of the Mississippi trade. Jackson and Hutchings went out of business in 1808, with their debts only slightly smaller than assets—most of the latter in the form of accounts receivable which many customers were unable to pay. The silent partner John Coffee gave Jackson notes for his share of the debts, and returned to his career as a surveyor. But soon afterward when Coffee married one of Rachel's nieces, Jackson presented the notes to the bride as a wedding gift.

Jackson now turned to the pleasures, and profits, of the Hermitage and its growing stable. He sold his racetrack to the Nashville Jockey Club and concentrated on the development of his own stock. For five years his stable had made money for him; Truxton alone had won more than $20,000.

The big bay stallion, in fact, made more money for Jackson than any other single piece of property he ever owned. During his prime Truxton was undefeated in a two-mile heat and sired more than 400 colts who were winners on the tracks. Horses of his blood were dominant in the southwest until the advent of the great thoroughbred racer and stud Lexington in Kentucky.

Truxton remained Jackson's favorite: "His performances on the turf have surpassed those of any horse of his age that has ever been run in the Western country. . . . Truxton by old sportsmen and judges is admitted to be amongst the best distance horses they ever run or ever had to train. . . . His speed is certainly known to all of those who have run against him."

Just before retiring at night Jackson invariably went to the bay's stable, where he inspected the horse and his stall with care. The stallion seemed to respond to Jackson: in his old age, when he became unruly and bad-tempered, Truxton could be managed only by the general.

During these years Jackson kept fifty to sixty horses at the Hermitage and sold brood mares and young stallions in almost every season. Before 1812 the progeny of Truxton and the Berkeley brood mares Jackson had brought from Virginia were beginning to reach marketable age. The Hermitage colts were usually sold before foaling. As one of his biographers said, "General Jackson was, beyond question, the most capable horse breeder and horse handler of his time."

Cockfighting was another of the passions of Jackson's new life at the Hermitage, and his sponsorship increased the popularity of the sport in western Tennessee. He challenged his friend and neighbor Patton Anderson to a main on July 4, 1809, an event that became a festival for amateur cockfighters of the region. For a day or so in advance the roads to Nashville were crowded with wagons and ox carts loaded with crates of fighting cocks.

Jackson's cocks won the contest against Anderson's in four days of bloody dueling, during which Jackson remained at the pit to the end, drinking mint juleps, encouraging his handlers and their birds, obviously relishing the excitement. On the third day, when one of his severely wounded cocks was revived, and killed its opponent with a lucky stroke of its spurs, Jackson called to a friend, "There's the greatest emblem of bravery on earth. Bonaparte is not braver!"

The size of the Jackson-Anderson wager was not reported, but Colonel Isaac Avery saw "large sums of money and several horses change hands." Avery was puzzled by Jackson's addiction to the cruel sport: "I suppose it was ennui, or want of excitement, that made him do it."

Jackson never lost his enthusiasm for cockfighting. One of his contemporaries retained as his most vivid memory of the general a scene at a cockpit in the heart of Nashville when Jackson, transported by excitement, shouted like a boy, urging his birds to victory or death:

"Hurrah, my Dominica! Ten dollars on my Dominica! . . . Hurrah, my Bernadotte! Twenty dollars on my Bernadotte! Who'll take me up? . . . Well done, Bernadotte!"

The Hermitage was now constantly thronged by guests, Jackson's friends from all parts of Tennessee and beyond, in addition to the usual swarm of Rachel's almost numberless tribe of relatives. There were also strangers by the score, welcomed in the open hospitality of the time. Jackson was an almost aggressively generous host. When Daniel Boone's son visited Nashville for several weeks on business for his father, and put up in a cheap hotel on the outskirts of Nashville, Jackson sought him out and took him to the Hermitage. "Your father's dog should not stay in a tavern where I have a house," he said. James Parton, gathering material for his biography from Jackson's Tennessee neighbors, was told by one of them, "Put down in your book that the General was the prince of hospitality; not only because he entertained a great many people but because the poor, belated peddler was as welcome at the Hermitage as the President of the United States and made so much at his ease that he felt as though he had got home."

Jackson also devoted much of his time to making a model farm of the Hermitage, which was now worked by twenty slaves. He insisted upon the most advanced farming methods and equipment, bought newly developed seeds for his crops, and frequently worked in the fields, driving himself grimly to keep pace with his black laborers despite his increasingly frail health. He had suffered periodically from fevers since his boyhood bout with smallpox; dysentery weakened him and robbed him of his appetite, and Dickinson's bullet caused discomfort and congestion in his chest.

His presence alone brought new happiness to Rachel, who mothered him as she did virtually all others on the farm, black and white. The misery she had known during his twelve years of almost constant absence had ended, forever she hoped. At forty-three she retained some of her youthful beauty despite her short, thickening figure; her hair was still jet-black, she seemed as lively and vivacious as ever, and her sweet, kindly face was usually wreathed in smiles. Except for the fine lines caused by long exposure to the sun, her dark, round face was unwrinkled. She still wore the plain dress of the mistress of a working farm and her unaffected manners and speech were those of the frontier. Even visitors who were prone to criticize her lack of education took note of her intelligence and her warmth and friendliness. She had taken solace in religion during the years of Jackson's absence and was endlessly busy helping others, the slave families, neighbors, and passing strangers. To the people of a wide neighborhood she was known universally as Aunt Rachel. The chief sorrow of her life was that she had no children of her own; several miscarriages and infant deaths had ended her hopes of raising a family at the Hermitage.

The Jacksons had taken in John and Andrew Donelson, the sons of her dead brother Samuel, and later welcomed William Smith, a "pathetic child" born unexpectedly to elderly neighbors. Jackson was also guardian to the four children of his late friend Edward Butler, and was unofficial guardian to the two sons of Butler's brother Thomas. Rachel continued to grieve. Once when Jackson was tumbling on the floor at play with the Donelson boys she burst forth, "Oh, husband! How I wish we had a child!"

Jackson put his arms about her to halt her tears. "Darling, God knows what to give and what to withhold."

In January 1810 Rachel brought still another child to the Hermitage, one of twin sons borne by the wife of her brother, Severn Donelson. Since the mother had come near death in childbirth, and could not suckle two infants, Rachel had begged for the boy, who was adopted by the Jacksons and christened Andrew Jackson, Jr.

Revived gossip about Rachel and their marriage now tormented Jackson. He heard that a woman in a nearby county had repeated the old tales of Rachel's adultery and impulsively sent a friend to investigate, insisting upon "a strict inquiry." It was a hopeless quest after a will-o'-the-wisp, his investigator reported: "I cannot learn that Betsy has said anything injurious of Mrs. Jackson." The frustrated general went so far as to ask a woman of his neighborhood for information, and drew the same response, "I pledge you that Mrs. Bell did not either directly or indirectly say anything to injure the reputation of Mrs. Jackson."

Jackson's reputation as a fearless, and occasionally violent, frontier hero still flourished in tales savored by admiring Tennesseans.

It was said that the general was riding in his carriage on a lonely road when he was halted by two drunken wagoners, who ordered him to get out and dance for them.

"I can't dance without my slippers," Jackson said, "and they're in my trunk."

"Get 'em!"

Jackson opened his trunk, snatched a pair of pistols, and advanced on the bullies "with that awful glare in his eyes before which few men could stand."

"All right, you infernal scoundrels, you shall dance for me. Dance! DANCE!"

When the wagoners had jigged about for a few moments, Jackson lectured them and sent them on their way.

There was also a story of Jackson's enforcing law and order at pistol point during a brawl at Clover Bottom, when he stood at the starting post, glaring defiance over his ready weapons, to prevent jockeys from running a race he believed had been fixed.

It was a Clover Bottom racing meet too that prompted Old Hickory to a defense of his hotheaded friend and neighbor Patton Anderson, an incident that was to become a popular theme in the Jackson legend. One evening when a crowd of excited men pursued Anderson toward the stable, Jackson halted them at his fence. He recognized some of them as Anderson's enemies, and sought to detain them until his friend could reach shelter. He protested the cowardly attack on a lone man and promised to have Anderson meet any one of them in a duel at dawn.

When he saw that the men were determined, Jackson, who was unarmed, reached into his pocket, drew out a tobacco box, and raised his arm. "I'll shoot the first man who tries to cross that fence," he said. The crowd could not see the tobacco box in the darkness, and when Jackson snapped it shut with a click like the cocking of a pistol, they fled. Jackson enjoyed telling the story for years: "They scampered like a flock of deer. I knew there were men in that crowd who were not afraid to meet me or any other man—but no man is willing to take the chance of being killed by an accidental shot in the dark."

Anderson's salvation was temporary indeed, for Jackson's belligerent friend was soon murdered in the courthouse yard at Franklin, Tennessee, in the eruption of an old feud. Jackson plunged furiously into the subsequent trial, insisting that David Magness, the killer, should hang. The general descended upon Franklin with a number of his friends, delivered a fiery speech on the case to a tavern crowd while he was half-drunk, and when he was called as a character witness, made a valiant but futile effort to aid the prosecution.

The celebrated trial lawyer Felix Grundy, who was to become a U.S. Attorney General, grilled Jackson as to the reputation of the combative Anderson, seeking an admission that the slain man had made numerous enemies. Jackson burst forth, "Sir, my friend was the natural enemy of scoundrels!"

When Magness escaped with a light sentence for manslaughter—he was merely branded on the hand—the infuriated ex-judge, senator, and congressman Jackson shook his fist under the nose of Newton Cannon, one of the jurors, and warned him that he was "a marked man."

In 1811 Jackson was unexpectedly faced with financial disaster once more. His friend Judge George Campbell, who had left Congress for the bench of the State Supreme Court of Errors and Appeals, discovered that a case involving the David Allison bankruptcy had been improperly decided. Allison had died in debtor's prison after mortgaging 85,000 acres on Duck River in an effort to free himself. Norton

Prior, who held the mortgage, had asked Jackson to join a foreclosure action against Allison's heirs; but since he was on the bench at the time, Jackson turned over the case to John Overton, who won a verdict in federal court. As a result Jackson acquired 5,000 acres, which he sold to several buyers, guaranteeing the titles for the value of the land at the time defects of title might appear, rather than the value of the raw, undeveloped wilderness acres. Since the Duck River region was now prosperous farm country, the land was worth a fortune. Campbell reported that Jackson was legally responsible, since the titles were faulty—the federal court which awarded Overton's verdict had lacked jurisdiction.

Jackson was so alarmed that he took his case to Senator Jenkyn Whiteside, said to be the shrewdest lawyer in Tennessee. Whiteside advised him to do nothing, since the Allison heirs could not know the titles were faulty, and would therefore make no trouble. If he approached the heirs and they refused to cooperate, Jackson would be ruined. But Jackson would have none of this. He was determined to preserve his personal honor and make good his obligation to "those honest men" on Duck River at the risk of losing everything. "I told Mr. Whitesides that I had never sold any land but what I thought the title was good," he wrote, and was off on the long ride to Georgia, where he found Allison's impoverished heirs. Jackson explained that he had a claim against David Allison's estate for $20,000, and that he would exchange it for a release on the 85,000 acres in question. The Allisons agreed, and Jackson returned to the Hermitage with his estate and his honor intact, but with a growing sense of frustration. For all its pleasures "the sweet calm of rural retirement" had begun to pall, and the frontier on which he had spent the exciting days of his youth had rolled westward. Jackson was painfully aware that his behavior as a violent partisan of racetrack and tavern brawls reflected no credit on the state's founder, congressman, senator, and judge.

In the grip of one of the rare periods of depression in his life, Jackson considered leaving Tennessee and following the beckoning frontier into Mississippi Territory. In the wake of the Dickinson duel, the Burr episode, his financial reverses, and a revival of the gossip about Rachel, Jackson confessed to a friend that he could not shake off his mood of growing despair. He felt a compulsion for "some new pursuit to employ my mind and thoughts . . . to divest myself of those habits of gloomy and peevish reflections. . . ." He was also restless because he saw no warfare in his future. He feared that "as a military man I shall have no amusement or business, and indolence and inaction would shortly destroy me."

His contemplated move to the west was not merely a passing thought. He sent one of Rachel's nephews on a scouting trip to Mississippi and wrote to Louisiana for a report on the climate and growing conditions. He also asked Senator Whiteside to obtain for him the judgeship of Mississippi, and went so far as to offer the Hermitage for sale to a number of wealthy men, among them Colonel Wade Hampton of South Carolina, who rode out to Tennessee to inspect the property but did not buy it, though he praised it as an "elegant seat and fine tract of land."

Rachel's nephew Donelson Caffrey, reporting from Natchez, advised Jackson to remain at the Hermitage: "You have nearly got through all your embarrassments. You have a delightful farm, from the products of which you will at least be able to live comfortably; by the respectable and well-informed part of the country you are highly esteemed. . . ." Caffrey added a warning that Jackson would not escape critics and enemies in the southwest, since he would discover a good deal of "human baseness" among the strangers he would encounter in Mississippi.

6

"We are the free born sons of . . . the only republick . . . in the world!"

War with England threatened the country throughout the early months of 1812. The long-smoldering quarrel had become so ominous by February that Congress authorized President Madison to raise 50,000 volunteers, to be called up in an emergency.

This news was carried to Jackson by Thomas Hart Benton, a young lawyer from Franklin, Tennessee, who rode thirty miles through a sleet storm to the Hermitage, and found the general seated before a log fire in the great room of the blockhouse. Jackson held two-year-old Andrew on his lap, and at his feet was a lamb brought in from the storm at the boy's insistence.

Benton proposed a plan for raising troops by expanding the militia and organizing units from three sections of Tennessee. Jackson accepted, named Benton as his aide, and with his assistance prepared a ringing call to the troops:

> VOLUNTEERS TO ARMS!
> Citizens! Your government has yielded to the impulse of the nation.
> . . . War is on the point of breaking out between the United States and
> . . . great Britain! And the martial hosts . . . are summoned to the Tented
> Fields! . . .
> . . . Shall we, who have clamored for war, now skulk into a corner?
> . . . Are we the titled Slaves of George the third? the military conscripts

of Napolon? or the frozen peasants of the Rusian Czar? No—we are the free born sons of . . . the only republick now existing in the world . . .!
. . . We are going to fight for the reestablishment of our national charactor . . . for the protection of our maratime citizens . . . to vindicate our right to free trade. . . .

Benton was a handsome, sturdy young migrant from North Carolina, whose family Jackson had known during his early law career. Fifteen years Jackson's junior, this self-trained lawyer was already known as a flamboyant courtroom orator and a leader of the state's younger Jeffersonian Democrats. Benton returned to Franklin and turned energetically to recruiting. His patriotic appeals made in speeches throughout his district raised a regiment of some 700 troops, which he commanded as colonel.

Jackson's troops were organized and drilled for weeks, while a divided Congress wrangled over the issue of war or peace. The war was strongly opposed in the east, with Connecticut, Rhode Island, and Delaware voting unanimously for peace, New York nearly so, and Massachusetts favoring it by a narrow margin. But on June 18 the nation was pushed into the conflict by the young "War Hawks" of the west and south, led by Speaker Henry Clay of Kentucky, Felix Grundy of Tennessee, and John C. Calhoun and Langdon Cheves of South Carolina.

The nation was hopelessly unprepared for war. The 6,000 regular infantrymen were scattered in posts from Canada to New Orleans; there were a handful of others—500 artillerymen with a few light guns, and 500 dragoons, also widely scattered. The available officers were aging generals of the Revolution—except for the veteran William Henry Harrison of the Indiana Territory, and the inexperienced but aggressive Jackson, whose talents were unsuspected outside Tennessee.

The U.S. navy consisted of six frigates and seven sloops and brigs, to oppose the world's leading naval power. Once she had overcome the French, Great Britain could blockade the coast with 1,000 ships, and transport an army of 100,000 to reconquer her North American colonies.

James Madison had anticipated the call to war. Six days before the formal declaration the President's express riders had dashed out from Washington to alarm the country. The news was carried to the southwest by one of Jackson's former jockeys, Billy Phillips, who had once ridden Truxton to victory. An aging veteran of the Revolution saw the express rider gallop through the village of Lexington, North Carolina, on his way: "Bill Phillips has tore through this little place without stopping. He come and went in a cloud of dust, his horse's tail and his own long hair streaming alike in the wind. . . . But as he passed the tavern . . . he swung his leather wallet . . . above his head and shouted —'Here's the Stuff! Wake Up! War! WAR WITH ENGLAND! WAR!!!'

"Then he disappeared down the Salisbury road like a streak of Greased Lightnin!' "

Phillips raced into Nashville in the dusk of June 21, after galloping 860 miles in 9 days. He was soon to resign as a courier and join Jackson's troops.

Jackson offered Governor Blount the services of 4,000 men within 10 days, and promised that he could march them to Quebec within 3 months. He was willing to serve anywhere, he said. "In behalf of the indomitable men I have the proud honor to command, I beg to assure the President that wherever it may please him to find a place of duty for them, he can depend upon them to stay there till they or the last armed foe expires."

Blount passed this message to the War Department with a recommendation of Jackson:

> He loves his country and his countrymen have full confidence in him. He delights in peace; but does not fear war . . . he feels a holy zeal for the welfare of the United States, and at no period of his life has he been known to feel otherwise. His understanding and integrity may be confided in. He is independent and liberal in mind. . . . He ought to command his volunteers.

The War Department made a perfunctory acceptance of Jackson's troops, but sent no orders. General Henry Dearborn was ordered to move against Quebec—and was to delay for nine months before going on a futile campaign that ended in defeat.

The war opened with a series of American disasters. The British won an easy victory on the Great Lakes when General William Hull surrendered Detroit without firing a shot. Jackson urged the War Department to send him to recapture Detroit, "so basely yielded to the enemy." He wrote Senator George Campbell, "the news of Hull's surrender almost killed me . . . I could not understand it, could hardly believe it . . . maybe after a while someone will whip the English . . . God knows I would like the chance to try it! My Division is ready any minute!" But though two Tennessee regiments were ordered to join General William Henry Harrison in the northwest, Jackson was not called. He appeared to have been forgotten in Washington.

To Aaron Burr, returning to New York penniless after his European exile, the administration's bias against Jackson was no mystery. Burr told his friend Martin Van Buren, "I'll tell you why they don't employ Jackson. It's because he's a friend of mine." And to the New York congressman John Sage, Burr said urgently, "I know my word's not worth much with Madison, but tell him for me there's an unknown man in the West, named Andrew Jackson, that will do credit to an army commission."

At last, in November, Governor William Blount was ordered to send 1,500 Tennessee troops to serve under James Wilkinson at New Orleans, but even then there was no mention of Jackson. Only when Blount took the initiative and commissioned Jackson as major general of United States volunteers did the impatient amateur soldier enter the war at last, without a blessing from Washington.

Despite his resentment that the War Department had not "daigned to name me," Jackson assured Blount that he asked nothing more than a chance to fight. He would gladly have served at a sergeant's pay, he said. As to serving under James Wilkinson, "It is a bitter pill . . . but I go in the true spirit of a soldier. . . . Should he get troublesome a way may be found, I think, to deal with him . . . I want no trouble, but will be prepared should any come." He packed his dueling pistols.

More than 2,500 men assembled in Nashville the first week in December in response to Governor Blount's call for 1,500. They arrived in bitter weather when the Cumberland River was frozen from bank to bank, for the first time in memory. Jackson's quartermaster, Major William B. Lewis, had provided 1,000 cords of wood, preparing for weeks of encampment, but the troops burned the entire supply the first night. Jackson and Lewis spent the night prowling through the camp to help care for men and animals. At six o'clock the next morning Jackson entered a tavern, where a civilian who had just risen from a warm bed complained that the troops were being mistreated. "It's a shame," he said, "that the men should have to stay out on such a night, while the officers have the best accommodations in town."

Jackson roared, "You damned infernal scoundrel, sowing dissatisfaction among the troops! Why, the quartermaster and I have been up all night, making the men comfortable. More of that talk and I'm damned if I don't ram that red-hot andiron down your throat."

Jackson's little division was made up of 2 infantry regiments of some 900 men each, led by Benton and Colonel William Hall, a veteran of John Sevier's Indian campaigns, and a mounted regiment of 700 men led by John Coffee. Among Jackson's other officers were William Carroll, his inspector general, a tall, stylishly dressed Nashville merchant who had migrated from Pittsburgh, Pennsylvania; and the general's handsome secretary, John Reid, an accomplished writer who was to become Jackson's first biographer. All of the troops were riflemen, for Jackson accepted only those who carried the long-barreled weapons. "Smooth-bore muskets don't carry straight," he said. "They may be good enough for Regular Soldiers, but not the Citizen Volunteers of Tennessee."

Jackson had seen to it that these men were not only drilled regularly, but also well armed and equipped for action. The general had spent as much of his own money on his division as the state had appropriated, and each year, during their annual muster, he had promised the troops action: "War with England must come soon. They will invade Louisiana and send the Indians out to massacre. When that day comes, the rifles of Tennessee must save the country!"

Thanks to a law written by Jackson when he took office as major general, the Tennessee militia was unencumbered by the restriction, in effect in all other states, that it could not cross its borders. Jackson's volunteers could march wherever danger threatened.

At last, on January 7, 1813, the infantry shoved off in a fleet of flatboats and keelboats amid the ice floes of the Cumberland, and Coffee led his cavalrymen on the overland route down the Natchez trace. Jackson wrote Rachel as the boats struggled down the Ohio, thanking her for the gift of a miniature portrait, which he said he intended to wear "near my bosom." He was distressed by their separation, he said, and by her grief caused by the tales of gossips:

> I thank you for your prayers. I thank you for your determined resolution to bear our separation with fortitude. We part but for a few fleeting weeks when . . . Providence . . . will restore us to each other's arms.
> . . .
>
> It is now 1 O'clock in the morning—the candle nearly out. . . . May the angelic hosts that reward and protect virtue and innocence and preserve the good be with you until I return. . . .

Jackson's infantry reached Natchez on February 15 after floating 2,000 miles in 39 days, having survived grinding ice floes and an earthquake that shook the Lower Mississippi Valley. Coffee's cavalry was waiting nearby. There was also an anguished reply from Rachel:

> *Your letter . . . was everything to me . . . my thoughts, my fears, my doubts distress me. . . . Do not my beloved husband let love of country, fame and honor make you forget. . . . You will say this is not the language of a patriot, but it is the language of a faithful wife. . . .*

Our little Andrew often does he ask me in bed not to cry, papa will come again and I feel my cheeks to know if I am shedding tears. . . .

Your dearest friend on earth,

RACHEL JACKSON

Jackson also received an unwelcome order from Wilkinson: he was to remain in Natchez, where the health of the troops would be better, and where they would be in position to strike at Pensacola, Mobile, or New Orleans in case of a British invasion. Jackson accepted this, but became restless after two weeks of idling in camp. When he learned of a fresh American defeat in Canada he again offered to lead his men northward, and word of this somehow reached Rachel at the Hermitage. She wrote the general accusingly: "Oh how hard . . . Love of Country the thirst for Honour . . . is your [ruling] motive."

Near the end of March, after keeping his men waiting in idleness for six weeks at Natchez, Jackson received a terse order from John Armstrong, the new Secretary of War:

> The causes of embodying and marching to New Orleans the corps under your command having ceased to exist, you will on receit of this consider it dismissed from public service and . . . have delivered over to Major General Wilkinson all articles of public property.
>
> You will accept for yourself and the corps the thanks of the President of the United States.

Armstrong, who had been in office two days, probably did not realize the hardships his order entailed, but the stranded general of Tennessee volunteers was in no mood for philosophical contemplation.

Jackson seethed with anger over "the wicked machinations" of Wilkinson and Armstrong in disbanding his division 800 miles from home, the men unpaid, their shoes and clothing worn out, and short of provisions or transportation. He sent Armstrong and Wilkinson "very severe" but respectful replies, refusing to demobilize his troops in Natchez. To Wilkinson he wrote that if he were not furnished food and enough wagons to carry his sick men,

> I shall dismount the cavalry, carry them on, and provide the means for their support out of my private funds. If that should fail I thank God we have plenty of horses to feed my troops to the Tennessee, where I know my country will meet me with ample supplies. These brave men, at the call of their country, voluntarily rallied. . . . They followed me to the field; I shall carefully march them back to their homes. It is for the agents of

the government to account to the State of Tennessee and the whole world for their singular and unusual conduct to this detachment.

Jackson also wrote Governor Blount, urging him to have food for the troops waiting at the Tennessee line, and threatening to raid the countryside if necessary, an alternative which "altho it might alarm those who are enjoying plenty and comfort at home, yet it will be resorted to by soldiers who think that their country is not grateful, and who are pinching under lean gripe of hunger. Provissions I must have and hope you will save me from the unpleasant necessity of procuring them *vie et armis.*" To his men he announced that he would move them home "on my own means and responsibility," if they had to eat their horses on the way.

Since he suspected that Wilkinson would try to recruit his stranded men for duty, he ordered his sentries to keep watch for regular army recruiting officers and to drum them out of camp if they appeared. He hired eleven wagons to carry his sick men, obligating himself to pay the costs of $10 per day for each wagon to and from Tennessee. He insisted that Wilkinson's quartermaster give him twenty days' rations and persuaded Natchez merchants to sell his men clothing on credit. All told, he drew drafts for $12,000 on the quartermaster of the Department of the South, for which he had no authority, and then began the march home. He turned over his three horses to sick men and walked all the way to Tennessee, moving constantly along the column to attend to the sick men, the distribution of food, and the widening of roads and building of bridges.

Somewhere along the route one of his soldiers gave him the nickname he was to bear for life. "He's tough," one of them said, "tough as Old Hickory."

Despite their failure to see action during the abortive expedition, the troops were welcomed home in a public ceremony at Nashville, where they were presented with handsome new flags made by Tennessee women. Otherwise the state's prompt response to the emergency call drew little attention.

Government auditors refused to honor Jackson's drafts for the transportation of his troops, and the general was threatened with suits by contractors. He was personally liable for debts of $12,000 or more.

Thomas Benton, who was going to Washington to seek a regular army commission, offered to intercede, hoping to force the War Department to pay the bills. Armed with letters of introduction from Jackson to influential men in the capital, Benton soon won a commission as lieutenant colonel, but his negotiations in Jackson's behalf were frustrating. Tennessee's congressional delegation was unable to help, and Secretary of War Armstrong said he could do nothing. After several weeks Benton became desperate: "Ruin seemed to be hanging over the head of Jackson and I felt the necessity of some decisive movement." He gave up attempts at persuasion and threatened Secretary Armstrong with political retaliation. Since Jackson's troops had been drawn from virtually "every substantial household" in Tennessee, Benton said, the state was united in its concern for the welfare of the division, and Washington's failure to meet its obligations would be remembered at the next election. Two days later Armstrong ordered that Jackson's drafts be honored.

During Benton's absence Jackson became involved in yet another brawl, this time quite against his will. Inspector General William Carroll, who had made enemies during the expedition by his efforts to improve efficiency, was challenged to a duel by one of Jackson's lieutenants. Carroll refused on the ground that the young man was not a gentleman, but the quarrel continued and at last Thomas Benton's younger brother Jesse issued a challenge to Carroll. Jesse was eccentric and excitable, and though he had a reputation as a coward, he was frequently involved in squabbles. But since he qualified as a gentleman he could not be ignored. Carroll accepted the challenge and asked Jackson to be his second.

Jackson protested that he was too old, but Carroll insisted. Several young men, he said, were conspiring to chase him out of the state so that one of them could win his commission. Jackson advised Carroll to settle the quarrel, and rode into Nashville himself and persuaded Jesse Benton to accept an amicable settlement. But within a few days the feud was revived by some of Jackson's enemies, among them Thomas Swann and Joseph Erwin. Jackson was infuriated by the revival of the Dickinson affair and implications involving Rachel. He agreed to serve as Carroll's second and the duel was arranged. It was to become a memorable meeting.

Jesse Benton fired first and missed, then turned, panic-stricken, and squatted before Carroll, who deliberately shot him in the buttocks. The wound incapacitated Jesse for only a few days, but was to provoke laughter in Tennessee for the rest of his life.

Thomas Benton learned of the duel before he left Washington, and was outraged by Jackson's role when he read a distorted account of the affair from Jesse, who charged that the general had precipitated the fight. Thomas grew more indignant after his return to Tennessee, where gossips took him more tales of Jackson's hostility. Benton threatened revenge, and Jackson wrote to ask if he had talked of challenging him. Thomas denied that he had done so, but said he considered it "very poor business of a man your age and standing to be conducting a duel about nothing between two young men who had no harm against each other." Thomas also accused Jackson of conducting the duel in "a savage, unequal, unfair and base manner." He stopped short of issuing a challenge, but said defiantly, "The terror of your pistols is not to seal my lips."

Jackson made a mild response, saying that men of honor did not "quarrel and brawl like fish women," and it appeared that the trouble would blow over, until gossips told Jackson of Benton's continued insults. The general lost his temper and swore that he would horsewhip Thomas on sight. Their next meeting, six months later, made it apparent that both men were spoiling for a fight.

On September 4 Thomas and Jesse Benton, both armed, arrived in Nashville and stopped at the City Hotel, just across Court House Square from their customary hotel, the Nashville Inn. Jackson arrived a few moments later, carrying a riding whip and wearing pistols and a small dress sword. He was accompanied by John Coffee and Stockley Hays, who were also armed. News of an impending duel spread through the town.

At about nine o'clock the next morning Jackson and Coffee crossed the square to the post office, passing near the City Hotel, where Thomas Benton stood in the doorway, glaring down at them.

"Do you see him?" Coffee said.

"Oh, yes, I've got my eye on him," Jackson said. He led the way to the post office.

On their return Jackson and Coffee passed along the walk in front of the City Hotel, where Thomas and Jesse Benton were waiting. Jackson wheeled on Thomas with his whip raised. "Now, you damned rascal," he said, "defend yourself!"

Benton reached for a pistol, but Jackson snatched his own pistol from a pocket and held it at Benton's breast. Thomas walked backward slowly, followed by Jackson until the two reached the rear door of the hotel. As Jackson entered the building, Jesse Benton hurried in behind him and fired. Jackson lunged forward, shooting as he fell. Blood gushed from his shoulder.

Thomas fired twice and Jesse aimed at Jackson once more, but a bystander threw himself over the prostrate general.

Coffee charged into the smoky corridor, firing wildly, then clubbed his pistol and moved toward Thomas Benton, who fell backward down a flight of stairs.

Stockley Hays then thrust at Jesse with a sword cane, and when his blade snapped on a button, drew a long-bladed knife, forced Jesse to the floor, and stabbed him several times before Jesse thrust the muzzle of his remaining pistol into Hays's body. The weapon failed to fire.

Other men rushed in to aid the brawlers. Jackson was carried to the Nashville Inn, where his welling wounds soaked two mattresses with blood before the flow was stanched. The left shoulder had been shattered by Jesse Benton's heavily loaded pistol; a slug had torn through the muscle and a ball was embedded in bone.

As several doctors worked over Jackson, the Bentons stood before the inn, shouting insults and daring him to come out. Thomas snapped the small sword that Jackson had dropped during the fight, denounced him as an assassin, and went off with Jesse, still calling threats.

Jackson's doctors, with one exception, urged amputation of the shattered arm, but the dazed general shook his head. "I'll keep my arm," he said firmly. No attempt was made to remove the ball. The badly lacerated shoulder was bound with a slippery elm poultice and Jackson was taken to the Hermitage, where he was unable to leave his bed for three weeks.

Thomas Benton returned to his home in Franklin, hounded, he said, by Jackson's "puppies," who sought revenge. "I am literally in hell here," he wrote a friend, "all the puppies of Jackson are at work on me. . . . I see no alternative but to kill or be killed, for I will not crouch to Jackson; and the fact that I and my brother defeated him and his tribe . . . will for ever rankle in his bosom. . . . My life is in danger." Soon after Benton moved to Missouri. He was not to see Jackson again for ten years.

7

"Other chastisements remain to be inflicted"

he Indian chief Tecumseh, a gifted and courageous soldier and administrator, had spent four years in the attempt to unify the tribes of the Mississippi Valley, traveling tirelessly from the Great Lakes to the Gulf of Mexico urging a joint defense. Soon after Jefferson became President and whites bought hunting grounds on the Wabash River, Tecumseh began his campaign of resistance. He was a formidable foe, as William Henry Harrison said, "one of those uncommon geniuses which spring up occasionally to produce revolutions." Tecumseh insisted that the North American continent was owned by all Indians in common and that no single tribe or ruler had the right to barter away the land:

> The Great Spirit gave this land to his red children; he placed the whites on the other side of the water; they were not contented with their own, but came to take ours from us. They have driven us from the sea to the lakes; we can go no further . . . the Great Spirit ordered us to come here, and here we will stay.

When Harrison said he could do no more than report to the President, Tecumseh replied, "Well, as the great chief is to determine the matter, I hope the Great Spirit will put sense enough into his head to induce him to give up this land; it is true, he is so far off he will not be injured by the war; he may sit still in his town and drink his wine, whilst you and I will have to fight it out."

Tecumseh's influence was nowhere greater than among the Creeks, whose domain covered almost 50 million acres in the Lower Mississippi Valley. In a war council at an ancient town on the Tallapoosa River, he made an eloquent plea for unity by standing like a statue amid scores of silent watchful tribal chiefs. Tecumseh held a war club high over his head, then dramatically loosened one finger after another until the club fell to the ground. Young warriors in the council house were deeply impressed. In the autumn of 1811, while Tecumseh was urging the Creeks, Cherokees, and Seminoles to prepare for war, his plans were jeopardized when his brother, the Prophet, at the head of 900 warriors, attacked Harrison in the Battle of Tippecanoe and suffered a disastrous defeat. The well-trained nucleus of Tecumseh's army was destroyed.

As a British general Tecumseh led the first attacks on American settlements at the outbreak of the War of 1812, and in the fall of that year he returned to press the Creeks to join him, citing British victories at Detroit and in Canada, and promising aid from the English and Spanish.

One of Tecumseh's converts was the half-breed William Weatherford, Chief Red Eagle, the son of a Scots trader. Weatherford was the nephew of Alexander McGillivray, a legendary chief of the Creek nation, who had died as a brigadier general of the United States, leaving a fortune to his heirs. McGillivray—who was of French, Spanish, Scottish, and Creek ancestry—had ruled the Creeks for more than twenty years, the acknowledged emperor of the southern border. William Weatherford was his worthy successor, intelligent and fearless, and an implacable foe of the Americans who were encroaching upon Creek lands. He became the leader of the tribe's war party, the Red Sticks.

For six months after Tecumseh's visit Weatherford prepared the Creeks for war, raising 7,000 warriors in such secrecy that the whites of the southwest took no alarm.

The Red Sticks struck at noon on August 30, 1813, at Fort Mims in southern Alabama, a stockade crowded with refugee families. Warriors poured through the fort's open gate and killed, scalped, and mutilated 400 whites, including all the women and children. The only survivors were about a dozen white men who escaped into the swamps, and a number of Negroes who were taken into slavery by the Creeks.

When news of the massacre reached Nashville on September 18, there was a spontaneous demand for punishment of the Creeks. A town meeting was called and a committee was named to confer with Jackson and Governor Blount.

Enoch Parsons of the Tennessee legislature, who took Jackson word that the militia had been called out, found Old Hickory swathed in bandages and racked by pain as a result of his brawl with the Bentons. But when he expressed his regret that Jackson was unable to march with the troops, the commander snapped, "The devil in hell I'm not. . . . These people must be saved. . . ." The defiant voice died away in a groan.

Parsons left the room convinced that the general could not accompany the troops; but two hours later he received fifty copies of the marching orders, which ended firmly, "The health of your general is restored. He will command in person."

War news from the north was now more encouraging. Commodore Perry had defeated a British flotilla on Lake Erie, and General Harrison had crushed Tecumseh's band on the Thames River, a battle in which Tecumseh had been killed. While these victories were celebrated in the north, southern states were left to deal with their own crisis.

Despite his wounds Jackson assumed command from his bedroom. He sent scouts into the Creek country to report on the strength and location of the enemy, and to persuade some of the Creeks and Choctaws to become his allies. He called on the state for provisions and made a plan of campaign: he intended to burn Creek towns, defeat isolated warrior bands, and push all the way to Mobile, opening a road from Tennessee to the Gulf—and then, though he said nothing of it, he planned to seize West Florida and Pensacola, so that the Spanish could no longer incite the Creeks to war.

He threatened grim warfare. In a letter to a friend he declared, "The late fracture of my left arm will render me for a while less active than formerly. Still I march and before we return, if the general government will only hands off—we will give peace in Israel."

Jackson ordered his division to meet at Fayetteville, Tennessee, near the Alabama border, and sent Coffee in advance to Huntsville, Alabama, where he arrived on October 4 with almost 1,300 men.

It was now nearly a month since the Benton duel, but though Jackson was unable to wear a coat sleeve because of the pain in his shoulder, he began the march southward, his left arm in a sling, forced to mount with the aid of two men. He was late in reaching the rendezvous at Fayetteville but had sent John Reid ahead with an address to the troops, a document written by Reid from ideas that were unmistakably Jackson's own:

"We are about to furnish these savages a lesson of admonition . . . we have borne with their insults, and submitted to their outrages. . . . But the blood of our women and children recently spilt at Fort Mims, calls for our vengeance. . . . Our borders must no longer be disturbed by the war-whoop. . . . The torch that has been lighted must be made to blaze in the heart of their own country."

Jackson found fewer than half the expected 2,000 men were waiting in Fayetteville, but he was pleased to learn that the Creeks were marching in his direction, rather than southward to attack Mobile as he had feared. He also found morale high. As the volunteer Davy Crockett said, the men were "all determined to fight, judging from myself, for I felt wolfish all over."

On October 11, when he received a report that Coffee's force was endangered by the approach of the Creeks, Jackson hurried his troops to the rescue, driving them the thirty-two miles to Huntsville in five hours, only to discover that the report was false. Jackson then made a leisurely march to the Tennessee, joined Coffee's mounted men, and halted for a few days to cure the blistered feet of his men, determined to strike into the heart of the Creek country whether or not he was supported by forces ordered out from other states: "I had expected reinforcements from East Tennessee, and a cooperation from Georgia; but I begin to be apprehensive that their movements will be too slow for mine. I cannot bear to be idle, eating the public beef to no purpose." The public beef supply was to become virtually invisible, a threat already foreseen by Jackson: "There is an enemy I dread much more than I do the hostile Creek . . . that meagre-monster 'Famine.' "

The army of 2,500 men and 1,300 horses was now on the verge of the Creek country, a land of pathless woods and swamps seldom penetrated by white men. The task of supplying the column in the wilderness was formidable—10 wagonloads of provisions daily; 1,000 bushels of grain, 20 tons of meat, and 1,000 gallons of whiskey each week.

Civilian contractors had shipped supplies down the Tennessee River but were delayed by low water, and Jackson was already short of food for the troops. He dismissed one group of contractors, hired another, and raged at their failures, but it was in vain. He sent Major Lewis back to Nashville to expedite delivery, ordered Coffee's cavalry to scour the nearby country for food, and moved toward the Ten Islands of the Coosa River, where he was told that a Creek war party threatened a fort held by friendly Indians.

After three days of cutting roads over the supposedly impassable ridges of the Raccoon Mountains, Jackson reached Thompson's Creek on the Tennessee to find no provisions. He put his men to building a stockade, which he called Fort Deposit, and spent three days writing pleas for supplies. But though, as he said, he dreaded famine worse than the enemy, "I shall leave this encampment in the morning direct for the Ten Islands."

While he was on this march, with his column dogged by Creek scouts, Jackson received a message from the friendly Cherokee chief Pathkiller, word that William Weatherford had threatened to destroy tribes that refused to join his cause. Jackson dictated a reply to Reid: "Brother, the hostile Creeks will not attack you until they have had a brush with me; & that I think will put them out of the notion." Within a week the Tennesseans reached the Coosa near the Ten Islands, and here Jackson began a second outpost, called Fort Strother. Thirteen miles away, at the Creek town of Tallushatchee, a band of warriors had gathered. On November 2 Jackson sent Coffee and 1,000 horsemen to destroy this town. It was the horseman's first battle, but he planned and fought it like a veteran.

Coffee encircled the village, sending an advance party to draw the fire of the enemy and then fall back to the main body in feigned panic. The Creeks charged recklessly, only to be checked by a heavy volley and driven back into the village where they fought desperately to the last man, the whites rushing in to fire through the doors of the huts until the warriors were wiped out. "We shot them like dogs," Davy Crockett said.

About fifty warriors ran into one hut, guarded by a squaw who sat in the doorway, drawing a heavy bow with her feet and hands. She killed a young lieutenant, which so infuriated the riflemen that they shot her twenty times, set fire to the hut, and burned the fifty warriors.

Coffee rode through the mêlée, roaring encouragement to his men. His dapple gray stallion was shot four times and seven bullets tore the colonel's uniform, but horse and rider survived. Other squaws and children also died in the massacre, which claimed almost 200 Creek lives. Five of Coffee's men were killed and forty-one wounded.

Among the eighty-four prisoners herded back to camp was a three-year-old boy whose mother had been killed. Jackson told the Indian women to feed him, but they refused. "No, all his family are dead. Kill him, too." The general took the boy to his tent and fed him on brown sugar and water until he could be sent to Huntsville, to await Jackson's return. Old Hickory gave the boy the name Lincoyer.

Hungry soldiers returned to the ruins of Tallushatchee the next day and grubbed for food among the charred bodies. A potato cellar was found beneath a hut in which many Creeks had been roasted and was quickly emptied, though the fat of the incinerated bodies had covered the potatoes until "they looked like they had been stewed with fat meat," Crockett said. The young woodsman did not enjoy his meal. "I had a little rather not eat them, if I could have helped it."

Though Jackson reported that he had retaliated for the massacre of Fort Mims, he realized that his campaign had only begun—the Creeks would remain a menace until they were virtually destroyed.

Some thirty miles from Jackson's fort was a stockade at the Indian town of Talladega, where about 150 friendly Creeks had taken refuge, besieged by more than 1,000 hostile warriors. Just as the defenders were running out of food and water and surrender seemed inevitable, a chief dressed in a hog skin crept out of the fort and through the enemy camp, grunting and rooting, and escaped to Fort Strother where he burst into camp, yelling for "Captain Jackson." The chief disappeared into Jackson's tent and within a few moments the army was ordered to prepare for marching.

By now General Cocke and his East Tennessee troops were nearby, and a vanguard led by General White was expected the next day. Jackson moved to the relief of the besieged fort, sending word to White to protect the camp during his absence. Jackson marched at 1:00 A.M. November 8 with 800 horsemen and 1,200 infantry, crossed the Coosa by mounting an infantryman behind each cavalryman, and plunged into the overgrown country. By the end of the day he halted within six miles of Talladega.

In misery from dysentery, Jackson sat against a tree all night as his scouts came and went, reporting on the enemy. At midnight he received a message from General White saying he could not protect Jackson's base, since he had been ordered to rejoin General Cocke. Jackson had the choice of exposing his 200 sick and wounded at Fort Deposit or allowing the friendly Creeks to be massacred—a disaster that would spread terror across the frontier. Old Hickory did not hesitate.

At 4:00 A.M., without having slept, he moved to attack, and by sunrise was near the fort in line of battle. He formed his troops in three lines, militia on the left and volunteers on the right, with Coffee's mounted troops on the wings, advancing in crescents to encircle the enemy. Under Jackson's orders the vanguard met the hostile Creeks, fired four or five rounds, then retreated to the main army to lure the enemy within range of the massed rifles. The Creeks burst from hiding "like a cloud of Egyptian locusts, and screaming like devils," their bodies painted scarlet and "as naked as they were born." The Indians struck with such fury that a few confused militia companies fled. Jackson dismounted a reserve cavalry unit to fill the gap, the militia rallied, and a heavy fire swept the tribesmen, many of whom were armed only with tomahawks and bows and arrows. The tribesmen rushed one flank and when many of them fell, "they then broke like a gang of steers" for the opposite line, and ran back and forth, shot down by the hundreds. After a brief, wild fight at close quarters the Creeks broke through Coffee's lines and escaped, pursued for three miles by riflemen.

Almost 300 Indian bodies were found on the field, and it was obvious that many had been wounded. Jackson's losses were seventeen dead and eighty-three wounded.

Jackson fed his men and horses a sparse meal of ground corn, buried his dead in a common grave, put the wounded on litters made from the skins of dead horses, and moved the next day toward Fort Strother, where he found the sick and wounded suffering from hunger. The general had brought his own food on the expedition, but had left most of it at Strother, telling his surgeons to use it in case of need. When he found that only a few pounds of biscuit remained of his stores, Jackson had it distributed among the wounded. As an example to his men, he went to the spot where his cattle had been slaughtered and pawed among the scraps and entrails to find a few mouthfuls to eat. Tripe, he told his troops, would keep them alive. By now his dysentery was almost unbearable. He sought relief by hanging himself from a bent sapling, dangling by his sound arm for hours, racked with pain, his long face grim and impassive, wrinkled, yellow; he seemed to be "half dead, except for the fire in his dark blue eyes." The general's only medicine was weak gin and water, which he sipped occasionally.

For several days, while the troops lived on the last of the lean cattle, Jackson and his staff took only the tripe, which they boiled and ate without bread or seasoning, even that a ration that was soon to be reduced. The army's horses had grown feeble and the men were becoming desperate. "We commenced eating beef hides," Crockett said, "and continued to eat every scrap we could lay our hands on." One day as the general sat under a tree eating, a half-starved soldier begged him for food. Jackson drew a few acorns from his pocket. "This is the best and only fare I have," he said. The tale was repeated throughout the camp by admiring troops, but it did little to halt the growing complaints of hungry men.

The general refused to consider abandoning his winter campaign despite the failure of his supply system and the disappearance of the East Tennessee troops. Messengers left daily on the homeward route, bearing Jackson's demands for aid, one of them an angry denunciation of James White: "General White, instead of forming a junction with me, as he assured me he would, has taken the retrograde motion, after having amused himself with consuming provisions for three weeks in the Cherokee nation, and left me to rely on my own strength."

The general's humor was not improved by news that the East Tennessee troops had attacked the village of a peaceful tribe and prolonged the campaign. Jackson's two quick victories against the Creeks had so stunned the Indians of the region that the small tribe of Hillabees sent a messenger to Fort Strother to sue for peace. Jackson replied that he would not make war on friendly tribes, but before the message could be delivered, General White, unaware of the offer of peace, destroyed a Hillabee town, killed 60 warriors, captured 250 women and children, and returned to Cocke's camp. The Hillabees rejoined the war, resolved to fight to the last man and take revenge for the betrayal, for which they blamed Jackson.

Some of Old Hickory's troops, after ten days of being virtually without food, took matters into their own hands. The militia brigade secretly planned to march home; but Jackson got wind of the plan, rose early in the morning, and blocked their path with the volunteers. The militiamen returned to camp, but the volunteers themselves grumbled all night and began the march homeward the next morning—only to find the stern Jackson in their path with the militiamen at his back, their rifles at the ready. Though the volunteers went back to camp, Jackson realized that he would soon lose control. He urged his men to stay with a promise that supplies would soon be delivered, but when one regiment of volunteers voted to go home, and said they would remain only three or four days longer, Jackson yielded.

He left about 200 volunteers to guard the sick and wounded and marched the others toward Fort Deposit, with an agreement that they would return when they met a provision train. When they met a herd of 150 cattle and 9 wagons of flour a few miles from the fort, the hungry men butchered and cooked several cattle; but after they had eaten, and Jackson ordered a return to the fort, one company moved defiantly into the road toward Tennessee.

Jackson spurred his horse past the mutineers and faced them with only a few of Coffee's cavalrymen at his back. He ordered the troopers to fire on command, and the leading files of the company turned back after one glance at the general's stern face. Jackson rejoined the main body. When he found the volunteer brigade also forming to march home, he snatched a musket from a soldier, rested its barrel on his horse's neck, held it with his one good arm, and swore that he would shoot the first man who moved.

Coffee and John Reid moved to the general's side. The three motionless figures waited until men in the front ranks averted their eyes and led the sullen troops back to camp. Jackson returned the borrowed musket. "Hell, General," the soldier said, "that thing won't fire. It's been busted for weeks."

Major Lewis arrived with a supply train a few days later—and with news that the United States had assumed support of the army for the campaign. Jackson made plans to march against the Creeks once more, but was defied by the volunteers, who insisted that their time was up on December 10. Jackson argued that these men had spent 6 months of the year at home before leaving, and that they were liable for 365 days of service. Several of the general's friends urged him to compromise, but he remained furiously adamant.

On December 9 an officer burst into Jackson's tent to report that the brigade of volunteers was in mutiny and planned to slip away in the night. Jackson placed his two small cannon on a nearby hillside, formed the mutinous brigade outside the fort, rode before the sullen volunteers, and "disgorged his rage" in an emotional address, warning the men that disgrace awaited them if they marched home. "If you go, you will go over my dead body. I'll do my duty at all costs . . . I have done with entreaty. If you persist, this matter will soon be decided."

He gazed briefly at the soldiers he had "once loved as his father loves his children," and after a moment of silence he ordered the artillerymen to light their matches. He spoke quietly to the mutineers. "Will you obey or not? I demand an explicit answer." There was no reply, but Jackson did not stir, though his horse stood in the field of fire between the cannon and the mutineers. Whispers began in the ranks, then an officer stepped out and told Jackson the men would remain until reinforcements arrived. But though the brigade went back into the fort, the troops continued to demand a release so insistently that Jackson realized they would be useless in battle. Three days later, when General Cocke reached the fort with 1,450 fresh men, Jackson sent Hall's veteran brigade to Tennessee. The men had hardly disappeared before Cocke told Jackson that the reinforcements themselves expected to go home ten days later, when their enlistments expired.

The general sent almost half of the newcomers home the next day, raging impotently and hurling insults after them, wishing, he said, that each of the deserters had a "smock-tail in his teeth, with a petticoat as a coat of mail to hand down to posterity." In the midst of all this, while Jackson was holding Fort Strother with a handful of men, he discovered that Governor Blount, too, had deserted him. Discouraged by tales of officers who had led the deserters home and irritated by Jackson's continued demands, Blount rejected Jackson's pleas for more men, saying that he had already called out all the troops approved by the legislature and Congress. He advised that Jackson abandon Fort Strother and fall back to the Tennessee River to await reinforcements before completing his campaign.

Jackson fumed about Blount's "damd milk and water observations," and wrote him "a gulger that will make him look and see his own situation."

The "gulger" was a defiant rejection of Blount's suggestion. Jackson reminded the governor that the Tennessee legislature had pledged its word to keep troops in the field so long as the border was menaced. He urged Blount to stand firm:

> And are you my Dear friend sitting with yr. arms folded . . . recom-
> mending me to retrograde to please the whims of the populace. . . . Let
> me tell you it imperiously lies upon both you and me to do our duty
> regardless of consequences of the opinion of these fireside patriots, those
> fawning sycophants, or cowardly poltroons. . . .

He warned of the dangers to the frontier if 5,000 now hesitant Choctaws, Cherokees, and friendly Creeks joined Weatherford's marauding bands, and begged Blount to meet the challenge at all costs:

> Arouse from yr. lethargy—despite fawning smiles or snarling frowns—
> with energy exercise yr. functions—the campaign must rapidly progress
> or . . . yr. country ruined. Call out the full quota—execute the orders of
> the Secy. of War, arrest the officer who omits his duty . . . save yr. frontier
> from being drenched in blood. . . . What retrograde under these circum-
> stances? I will perish first. No, I will do my duty.

Blount responded generously and sensibly to this stinging letter. He ordered 2,500 more West Tennesseans to Jackson, with another division from East Tennessee to follow. Jackson did not wait for them.

On January 16 he left Fort Strother with 900 men, horsemen led by Colonel William Carroll and infantrymen under Brigadier General Isaac Roberts, marching southward in search of William Weatherford who was gathering a strong force of Creeks. Joined by about 300 friendly Creeks at the Talladega Fort, Jackson's little army pressed on toward Weatherford's fortified post at the Horseshoe Bend of the Tallapoosa River. Jackson reached Emuckfaw Creek, within three miles of the Bend, and went into camp when scouts brought word that a Creek war party was nearby. He had piles of brush built a few yards away, ready to be fired at a signal, formed his men in a hollow square, and ordered them to sleep on their arms.

Weatherford attacked in the darkness before dawn, but the raw troops were ready. The Creeks were exposed in the light of the burning brush piles and held off for half an hour until daylight, when Coffee led a charge that drove them out of sight. They returned to the attack a few hours later. Jackson's troops fired steadily at the advancing Creeks, then made a second charge that drove them back to their fort. A few of Jackson's men were killed, among them Rachel's nephew, Alexander Donelson. One of the wounded was John Coffee. Jackson's men slept on the battlefield but began a retreat through the forest the next day, shadowed by Creek scouts on either side.

Weatherford attacked once more at dawn of January 24, as the army was crossing Enotachopco Creek, with troops spread out on both sides of the stream. Jackson had given detailed orders for defense at the crossing: the rearguard was to hold its line until the leading files recrossed the creek to the right and left to surround the attackers. Jackson watched from the bank of the stream, expecting to see the enemy cut off and destroyed. "But to my astonishment and mortification . . . I beheld the right and left columns of the rear guard precipitately give way." Two of Jackson's colonels fled across the creek toward safety.

Only Carroll and twenty-five men stood to fight off the Creek attack, as panic-stricken Tennesseans tumbled down the stream bank. Davy Crockett felt that the new colonel saved the army from massacre; "if it hadn't been for Carroll, we should all have been licked, for we were in a devil of a fix . . . and the Indians pouring it on us, hot as mustard. . . . I will not say exactly that the old general was whipped . . . but I know I was mighty glad when it was over."

Jackson was in the midst of the retreat, swearing at the fleeing men, some of whom turned back to face the Creeks "when they heard his voice and beheld his manner." The general moved so recklessly amid the fire that "cowards forgot their panic . . . and the brave would have formed round his body a rampart with their own." The wounded Coffee left his litter, mounted, and plunged across the stream, leading a company to aid Carroll. The artillerymen fired several rounds of grapeshot at the enemy, but could not reach the most deadly Creek sharpshooters, who were concealed in a huge hollow log.

Six or eight young artillerymen were killed and Lieutenant Robert Armstrong was wounded; but the Creeks finally gave way before the volleys of grapeshot and were chased by Carroll's men, who counted twenty-five Indian bodies in the woods. The Tennesseans resumed their march.

In these two skirmishes Jackson had lost 24 killed and 71 wounded; Indian losses could not be determined, beyond 189 bodies found on the fields. This was to be Jackson's only move against the Creeks which ended indecisively, but he felt that he had hastened the end of the campaign by inflicting heavy casualties and undermining Creek morale. These little victories in wilderness skirmishes, which lost nothing in the retelling, were rarities of the war, hailed exultantly in the southern press and mentioned frequently even in the north, where the administration's war was unpopular. Cheered by news of one general who won battles and made no excuses, people began to ask: "Who is this General Jackson?" From his distant headquarters in Charleston, South Carolina, General Thomas Pinckney, commander of the Southern District, wrote the War Department: "I take the liberty of drawing your attention to the . . . communications of General Jackson. Without the personal firmness, popularity, and exertions of that officer, the Indian War, on the part of Tennessee, would have been abandoned." The Secretary of War sent Jackson congratulations and passed on a commendation from the President.

But news of Jackson's victories brought only anguish to Rachel, who wrote in despair:

MY DEAREST LIFE:

I received your letter by Express. Never shall I forgit it I have not slept one night since. What a dreadfull scene it was—how did I feel. I never can disscribe it. . . . My dear pray let me conjur you by every Tie of Love of friendship to let me see you before you go againe I have borne it until now it has thrown me into feavours I am very unwell . . . I cannot sleepe all can come home but you I never wanted to see you so mutch in my life . . . I must see you pray my Darling never make me so unhappy for aney Country. . . . You have now don more than any other man ever did before you have served your country long enough . . . oh Lorde of Heaven how can I beare it . . . my prayers my tears is for your safety Day and night farewell . . . —health and happy Days untill we meete—Let it not be long from your Dearest friend and faithfull wife until Death

Jackson was soon almost overwhelmed with troops at Fort Strother —5,000 Tennessee volunteers and 600 regulars of the 39th U.S. Infantry, in whose ranks was the boy ensign Sam Houston. The general sent home the remnant of his old army and welcomed back most of Coffee's veteran cavalry brigade, as well as a number of Choctaws who sensed that the tide of war had turned and came in as volunteers.

Jackson began to enforce an even sterner discipline, as if determined to hold together the new army at all costs. He announced that the next man convicted of mutiny would be shot. General Cocke, who was

bringing reinforcements from East Tennessee, was delayed by food
shortages and mutinous troops. When Jackson was told that the march
had been slowed because of Cocke's jealousy, he sent a hasty and
imperious dispatch to one of Cocke's brigadiers, ordering the arrest
of any officer of any rank who incited the men to mutiny. Cocke resigned in protest and went home to face a court-martial, which acquitted him. Jackson also placed General Isaac Roberts under arrest after
a squabble. Four captains were tried by a court-martial and found
guilty of mutiny and desertion.

Despite his weakness from dysentery and the strain of a slow recovery from his shoulder wound, Jackson insisted upon attending to the
details of the reorganization, corresponding extensively, and supervising completion of the fort, building of the road, arrival of troops, and
deliveries by contractors. He was said to be the last to retire and the
first to rise. "We have not slept three hours in four nights," he wrote.
"Reid and myself are worn out." Eager to return to the Horseshoe
Bend, Jackson ordered powder, lead, and supplies for 20 days brought
to Fort Strother, and put 500 men to work on the road from Fort
Deposit and others to building boats to float down the Coosa.

Twice during these hectic days Jackson had turned aside to deal with
his creditors back home. He had renewed old notes for some $1,750
and drawn up a statement of all his personal debts in case of his death.
He wrote Rachel: "On the subject of my private and Domestic concerns, you and Col. Hays and Mr. John Hutchings must regulate it. I
have not time to spend many thoughts upon worldly pelf or gear. My
station is arduous and my duty severe."

When all was ready, after six weeks of labor, Jackson began to think
of himself as a public figure of national stature. He reported to Major
Lewis that he expected to crush the remaining Creeks within a few days
—and added that it might be well to publish the congratulatory letters
from Pinckney and the Secretary of War, prefaced by "some modest
remarks as coming from myself." The threat of mutiny distracted him
once more.

In General Roberts's 29th Regiment was a company led by a Captain
Harris, whose men had enlisted for three months. The troops were
marched to within a few miles of Jackson's camp, where Roberts halted
them and rode forward to get Jackson's assurance that he would accept
the men for ninety days. Jackson refused; they must serve at least six
months. When the brigade marched for home, Jackson denounced the
men as deserters and ordered Roberts to bring them to camp or put
them in county jails—but said he would accept all those who returned
willingly to duty, for a three-month term.

Captain Harris's company returned home and then to camp, this time bringing Private John Woods, a seventeen-year-old farm boy who had volunteered as a substitute for an older brother who remained at home.

On a rainy February morning when the hungry, shivering John Woods had left his guard duty with the permission of the officer of the guard, and was eating breakfast at his tent, the officer of the day approached and ordered the men nearby to pick up the bones and refuse about the tents. Woods explained that he had left his post with permission and was about to return. The officer angrily ordered the arrest of Woods, who snatched his gun and threatened to shoot the first man who approached him. Jackson overheard someone say that a man was in mutiny and rushed from his tent. "Where's the damned rascal? Shoot him! Shoot him!"

Woods was put in irons, tried by a court of five officers, found guilty, and sentenced to death; but though the boy was bitterly defiant, he was confident, like the rest of the army, that Jackson would never shoot a militiaman. Under the impression that the boy had been in camp previously and marched home with mutineers, Jackson declared that Woods was "twice guilty," and ordered his execution to proceed. The general concealed his distress over the incident. He spent two sleepless nights weighing the prisoner's life against the safety of the army. He considered commuting the sentence to flogging, or to branding Woods as a deserter with the letter D and drumming him out of camp, but concluded that he must disabuse the militiamen of their conviction that military law forbade capital punishment.

When Woods faced the firing squad, Jackson paraded the troops so that every man witnessed the execution—except for the general himself. Jackson rode out of camp beyond hearing of the fatal volley, and when it was over wrote Governor Blount, "It certainly was for the best. But it was a fearful ordeal for me. I hope it may never be repeated."

At noon on March 16, a few hours after Woods had been shot, Jackson loaded his somber troops into boats and moved downstream on the Coosa's spring floodtide, leaving behind about 500 men to hold Fort Strother and 400 others on the route to guard his line of communications.

Scouts brought word that Weatherford, with the remnants of the Creeks, about 1,000 men, was camped at Horseshoe Bend some 50 miles away. Jackson moved at once, with Coffee's mounted riflemen leading the way, and camped within five miles of the Bend at nightfall of March 26. Coffee reported the Indian position as impregnable, except to artillery: a peninsula of about 100 acres of rough and heavily timbered ground that rose slightly from the water. Across the neck the Creeks had built a zigzag breastwork of logs 450 yards long and from 4 to 8 feet tall, pierced by a double row of portholes. The zigzag construction of the works would expose Jackson's attacking troops to both direct and raking fire, and behind the breastwork lay a jumble of logs and cut underbrush, affording cover for the defenders. To the rear, at the tip of the peninsula, were a few riverside huts, with hundreds of canoes beached nearby available for a retreat. The stronghold lay in the heart of the Creek country, surrounded by 100 miles of unbroken wilderness of forest, swamps, and canebrakes.

More than 900 warriors and 500 women and children had gathered at the Bend. The warriors waited confidently, incited by their prophets, whose noisy incantations echoed over the river by day and night.

Jackson arrived on the morning of March 27 and surveyed the defenses that seemed so formidable to the Creeks and to Coffee. "They've penned themselves up for slaughter," he said. He sent Coffee with his mounted troops and 250 friendly Indians to ford the river 2 miles below and come into the Creek rear on the opposite bank. After some of Coffee's Indians had swum the river in the Creek rear, cut loose many of the canoes, and burned the huts of the village, Jackson opened fire with his two small field guns. The Indians shouted defiantly as the small shot disappeared in the logs and earth, but after a noisy two-hour cannonade Jackson ordered a charge on the breastworks. The 39th Regulars and the East Tennesseans ran to the wall and fired through the portholes, already ablaze from Indian rifles and muskets, and for a few moments hundreds of men exchanged volleys muzzle to muzzle.

Major L. P. Montgomery of the 39th, the first man to mount the barricade, fell with a bullet through his head, but others swarmed over him. Ensign Sam Houston climbed to the top of the works, and though an arrow pierced his thigh, leaped to the ground among the Creeks, flailing violently with his musket. The 39th and the East Tennesseans then stormed the work and drove the stubborn Creeks into the piles of logs and underbrush.

For most of the afternoon the doomed Creeks fought on, with bows and arrows, tomahawks, knives, and muskets, from the piles of underbrush, from behind trees, burning huts, and from clefts in the riverbank. The slaughter continued until near nightfall, when a number of Creeks retreated to the riverbank to the cover of a jumble of piled logs. Jackson sent one of his Cherokees to call for surrender, with the promise that Creek survivors would be spared; but the defiant survivors fired on the messenger and Jackson had his cannon brought up. When this failed, he called for volunteers to storm the redoubt. There was no response until Houston rushed forward, ordering his company to follow. He was shot twice in the right shoulder and fell with his arm useless, out of the battle at last.

After the loss of several men in attempts to storm the bastion, Jackson ordered the underbrush fired, and waiting riflemen shot down the Creeks when they darted out to escape the flames. Even now the wounded Creeks resisted until riflemen shot them down.

Some Creeks slipped through Jackson's lines during the night and one wounded chief escaped by lying in the river shallows, breathing through a length of cane, until darkness enabled him to swim away. At daylight Jackson's men rounded up sixteen warriors from hiding and killed them when they refused to surrender. Eight hundred Creeks had been killed; most of the 500 squaws and children were taken as prisoners. Only now did Old Hickory learn that William Weatherford had not been in command at Horseshoe Bend, and was still at large.

Jackson sank his dead in the river to prevent scalping, had litters prepared for the wounded, and by mid-morning had begun a southward march to the Hickory Ground at the junction of the Coosa and Tallapoosa—sacred soil in the lore of the Creek prophets, where no white man could live. Jackson's troops were busy rebuilding a ruined fort on the site when several Creek chiefs came in to sue for peace. The tribe was virtually annihilated; since October it had lost almost 2,500 dead and wounded. Some surviving warriors and many young women, expecting no quarter, had gone to join the Seminoles in Florida.

When Jackson found that Weatherford had not come in to surrender, he ordered him hunted down and brought to him in chains. Red Eagle appeared voluntarily in camp a few days later, at first unrecognized, a tall, pale-skinned figure in tattered deerskin breeches and moccasins, unarmed and on foot. He spoke to other Indians in the Muscogee dialect, and then, in hesitant English, asked for Jackson.

Old Hickory greeted him savagely. "How dare you show yourself here after murdering the women and children at Fort Mims!"

Weatherford made a brief, dignified response, saying only that he had lost control of his young warriors. Jackson invited him into his tent.

Young John Reid listened admiringly as Weatherford spoke:

"General Jackson, I am not afraid of you or of any man. I can oppose you no longer. You can kill me if you like. I am in your power."

"You're not in my power. I had ordered you brought to me in chains. But you have come of your own accord. I would gladly save you and your nation, but you do not even ask to be saved. If you think you can contend against me in battle, go and head your warriors."

"Ah, well may you say such words to me now. There was a time when

I could have answered you. I could have animated my warriors to battle, but I cannot animate the dead.

"General Jackson, I ask nothing for myself, but, I come to beg you to send for the women and children of the Creek Nation who are starving in the woods. Their fields, cabins and corn-cribs have been destroyed by your soldiers, who have driven them into the woods where they have not so much as an ear of corn. I hope you will send parties of your men to relieve them. I will tell your men where they are.

"I am done fighting. The Red Sticks are almost all killed. If I could fight any longer I would not be here. But please send for the women and children. They never did any harm. Now you can kill me if you like, or if the white people want me to be killed!"

Jackson drank a glass of brandy with Weatherford and agreed to care for the tribe's women and children. Red Eagle then rose, shook hands with the frail, stern general, and disappeared.

John Reid looked after him in wonder. "Weatherford," he wrote a friend, "was the greatest of the Barbarian world . . . all the manliness . . . all the heroism of soul, all the comprehension of intellect calculated to make a great commander. . . . You have seen his speech to Genl Jackson . . . but you could not see his looks & gestures—the modesty & yet the firmness that were in them."

With Reid's assistance, Jackson wrote a resounding order of congratulations to his army, with a hint that the war itself had only begun:

> You have entitled yourselves to the gratitude of your country and your general. The expedition . . . has, by your good conduct, been rendered prosperous beyond any example in the history of our warfare: it has redeemed the character of your State.
>
> You have, within a few days, opened your way to the Tallapoosa, and destroyed a confederacy of the enemy, ferocious by nature, and who had grown insolent from impunity. . . . The fiends of the Tallapoosa will no longer murder our women and children, or disturb the quiet of our borders. . . . The weapons of warfare will be exchanged for the utensils of husbandry; and the wilderness will blossom as the rose. . . . But before this happy day can arrive, other chastisements remain to be inflicted. . . .

Now General Pinckney arrived with fresh troops from South Carolina and Georgia and took command. After a brief rest, and a notice to the defeated Creek chiefs that he would soon call them to a treaty council, the haggard Jackson turned toward home.

Tennessee was celebrating its first truly decisive victory in more than twenty years of constant warfare, the accomplishment of a general who had begun without experience or training. Jackson's friends and supporters, including Governor Blount, took note of the general's impassioned and unswerving patriotism in the face of all odds and obstacles —and Blount in particular had observed the daring with which he had lectured his superior and threatened him with public disapproval.

Some of Jackson's critics protested that it was unnecessary to kill so many Creeks to pacify the border. But when someone asked the governor how Jackson could kill so many Indians, Blount replied, "Because he knows how to do it."

8

"There will be
bloody noses . . . "

Jackson found Rachel and young Andrew waiting for him in Huntsville, and the party moved homeward, accompanied by the Creek orphan boy, Lincoyer, the survivor of Tallushatchee. It was a slow procession, frequently halted by reception committees and orators and by the roadside crowds that gathered to stare at the iron-willed invalid who had devastated the Creek nation.

John Overton wrote to alert the general that he was returning as a hero, and that a new phase of his life had opened. "I can but imperfectly communicate to you the feeling of the people. Your standing . . . is as high as any man in America." Overton added diplomatically that Jackson should practice control of his temper, since his old enemies were waiting to test him. "There are mean people whose greatest gratification is to irritate you, and thus lessen your fame if they can." But Jackson's bitterest enemies did not dare a challenge now; even the supporters of John Sevier favored Old Hickory for governor.

Several hundred people met the general on the road outside Nashville and escorted him first to the courthouse, where Congressman Felix Grundy praised him in a roaring oration, and then to a tavern banquet, where Jackson made a brief speech. He was not immodest, but did not hesitate to point out the benefits of the campaign: "The success which attended our exertions has been very great. We have laid the foundation of a lasting peace. . . . We have conquered. We have added a country to ours which . . . will become a secure barrier against foreign invasion. . . ." He mourned the loss of his dead, "who fell contending for their rights . . . worthy descendants of their sires of the Revolution."

Jackson returned to the Hermitage in a state of collapse, ill with fever and dysentery and so racked by the pain of his wounds that he hardly stirred from bed for three weeks. He was still recuperating when he received a new commission from Washington: he was now Major General Jackson of the United States army, succeeding William Henry Harrison, who had resigned after a quarrel. The major general's pay was important to Jackson—about $6,500 a year, including allowances —and he was also assigned to a vital front of the nation's defenses, as commander of the Southern Military District, a domain that extended from Tennessee and South Carolina to the Gulf of Mexico and included Louisiana, Alabama, and Mississippi. Only eighteen months since he had left on his first military campaign dangerously wounded from the Benton brawl, Jackson had risen to the highest rank in the army.

The administration apparently reacted to Jackson's newly acquired national reputation, as well as to pressure from western congressional delegations. Newspapers in every state published full accounts of the Battle of Horseshoe Bend, and Washington's *National Intelligencer* printed Jackson's dispatches, commenting on their "modesty and vigor." Critics of the administration who had endlessly scorned "Mr. Madison's war" did not risk attacks on Jackson. Even in Tenneseee, where his enemies were most numerous and his disgruntled ex-officers still nursed their grudges, there were no further accusations. The harsh discipline of the Creek campaign was apparently forgotten; the martinet who had become a conqueror was invulnerable.

But James Madison was not disposed to entrust the conduct of the Creek peace treaty to Jackson. Instead, the President assigned to the task the aging veteran of the Revolution, General Pinckney, and Benjamin Hawkins, the paternalistic Indian agent who had been appointed by Washington. There was a spontaneous protest from westerners, who sought a harsh peace. Nine of Jackson's ranking officers petitioned the War Department to leave the treaty to "someone who knew the needs of the frontier"—an obvious reference to Jackson, who understood so well that the "needs" of the frontier included lands ripe for settlement, as well as security from Indian attacks.

Three weeks after his promotion the new major general was ordered to the Gulf, to take command of his three half-strength regiments, and on his way to conduct negotiations with the Creeks. Before he took the road, Jackson had a dispatch from a scout on the Florida border: British marines were arming Indians and inciting them to raid American settlements. The general warned Secretary of War Armstrong: "We ought to be prepared for war," and proposed a solution of his own, an immediate blow at Pensacola, regardless of the consequences:

> If the hostile Creeks have taken refuge in Florida, and are there fed, clothed and protected; if the British have landed a large force . . . and are fortifying and stirring up the savages . . . will the government say to me . . . "Proceed to _____ and reduce it!" If so I promise the war in the south has a speedy termination and the British influence forever cut off from the Indians in that quarter.*

Jackson arrived at the Hickory Ground a few days later, where he had summoned the Creek chiefs in terms that augured a harsh settlement: "Destruction will attend a failure to comply." The chiefs and sub-chiefs came, almost forty in all, most of them friendly Creeks who had sided with Jackson during the campaign. Privately, at least, the general was moved by the plight of the half-starved Indians. He wrote Rachel of their "misery and wretchedness . . . perishing from want of food and Picking up the grains of corn scattered from the mouths of horses," but he was merciless in his demands.

The War Department had instructed Jackson to seize enough Creek land to indemnify the United States for the cost of the war, to separate the tribe from the Spanish, to insist upon the right to open roads and establish U.S. military and trading posts in the new Creek territory, and to obtain the surrender of the prophets who had instigated the war.

Jackson interpreted the government's demands broadly, with the wishes of Tennessee and other western states in mind—he demanded half of the ancestral Creek lands, 23 million acres in all, one-fifth of Georgia and three-fifths of Alabama, an enormous L-shaped tract that removed the tribe from the borders of Florida, Georgia, and Tennessee. Jackson did not differentiate between the lands of friendly and hostile Creeks; all were needed, he said, to pay the costs of the war. He left the tribe about 150,000 square miles of land remote from settlements, lying between the Hickory Ground and the Cherokee

---

*Armstrong's reply to this query, so imprecise as to avoid diplomatic difficulties but explicit enough to send Jackson into Spanish Florida, was delayed for six months, apparently held up by James Madison. Jackson received the dispatch after the Battle of New Orleans and kept it "as a curiosity."

country, and bounded by the Chattahoochee on the east and the Coosa on the west—a compact territory in which, the general hoped, the Creeks would settle down to farming and ranching, and give up their nomadic life.

The outraged chiefs postponed the inevitable as long as possible. Two in particular, Big Warrior and Shelotka, made eloquent pleas, but Jackson refused to compromise. The lands to be ceded, he said, were the route of the warmakers: "Through it leads the path Tecumseh trod . . . that path must be stopped. Until this is done, your nation cannot expect happiness, nor mine security."

The friendly chiefs protested that they could not bargain away tribal lands; the hostile chiefs who had fled to Florida must be consulted. Jackson told them curtly to sign the treaty by nightfall or go to Florida themselves. The chiefs succumbed. Thirty-six of them signed Jackson's treaty on August 8, 1814, a document whose opening phrases characterized the nature of the settlement:

> Whereas, an unprovoked, inhuman and sanguinary war, waged by the hostile Creeks against the United States, hath been repelled, prosecuted and determined successfully on the part of said States, in conformity with principles of national justice and honorable warfare . . .

A few hours after concluding the most rapacious treaty in the history of Indian-white relations in North America, Jackson wrote Rachel, "A disagreeable business was done, and I know your humanity would feel for them."

While Jackson was treating with the Creeks on the remote frontier, the war in the north took an ominous new turn. Napoleon had fallen and been banished to Elba, and Wellington's army was embarked for America in overwhelming numbers. Ten thousand veterans landed at Quebec, then marched southward. Admiral Sir Alexander Cochrane's fleet burned and sacked New England towns from Eastport to Long Island Sound, then entered the Chesapeake, scattered nervous American militiamen, and occupied Washington, where he burned the Capitol and the Executive Mansion. But a thrust against Baltimore was turned back, and from the far north came the incredible news that Commodore John McDonough's little fleet had defeated the British on Lake Champlain, forcing the invading column back into Canada. Cochrane sailed for the south, bound for Jamaica, where an enormous invasion force was gathering for a blow at Louisiana.

Jackson's attention had not been diverted from Florida. As soon as he reached the Creek country he had sent John Gordon, a reliable scout, to Pensacola with a letter to the Spanish commander, Don Matteo Gonzalez Manrique, demanding the surrender of two fugitive Creek chiefs and an explanation of British activities in Florida, and threatening "disagreeable consequences" in case of an unsatisfactory reply. The Spaniard rejected Jackson's demands as impertinent, refused to surrender the two chiefs, and said that the British were in Florida under an old treaty with the Creeks. The observant Gordon returned with reports of a British outpost under construction at Apalachicola, and a rumor that Spanish and British warships were expected in the Gulf. Jackson warned Secretary Armstrong that "we may anticipate a blow" in September or October, and begged Blount to send more troops from Tennessee. "Dark and heavy clouds hang over us," he wrote.

He also wrote a bullying reply to Manrique, accusing the governor of "evasions and unfounded innuendos," imbecility, and falsehood, and closing with a challenge and a threat: "In the future I beg you to withhold your insulting charges against my government for one more inclined to listen to slander than I am; nor consider me any more as a diplomatic character, unless so proclaimed to you from the mouths of cannon."

Jackson then prepared to march for Mobile. He had already asked Governor Blount to send Coffee with a new brigade of Tennessee volunteers, requiring that these men be enlisted for six months, and insisting that the terms be read to them. "I want no more loopholes for misunderstanding on this point. I want no more scope left for the ingenuity of camp lawyers who have already done one poor fellow out of his life."

A few hours before he left for Mobile, Jackson sent his aide Colonel Robert Butler back to Tennessee to bring Rachel to headquarters. He urged her to buy a new carriage: "You must recollect that you are now a Major General's lady in the service of the U.S. and as such you must appear elegant and plain, not extravagant, but in such state as Strangers expect to see you. . . ."

The general was forced to pause at the last moment before departure to deal with mutiny once more. The men of a Tennessee regiment, under the leadership of John Harris, a Baptist preacher, had robbed and burned the army's storehouse and marched home in defiance of their officers, returning to camp only when they learned that some of their companions had been arrested. Jackson ordered the regiment marched to Mobile, where a court of 5 militia officers convicted 205 men of mutiny and sentenced 6 ringleaders to death.

Jackson arrived in Mobile with about 500 regulars on August 22, two days before the British burned Washington, and was greeted by such alarming reports that he sent a runner to intercept Robert Butler and postpone Rachel's visit: the Spanish in Florida had now dropped the pretext of neutrality. Near Pensacola, British marines occupied Fort Barrancas and began drilling some 1,000 Indians, to whom they promised $10 in bounty for every American scalp. An English fleet had anchored in the harbor, and 10,000 troops were expected within a few days, ready to occupy Mobile. "There will be bloody noses before this happens," Jackson said.

He sent out urgent calls for help, dictating letters on a day when he was so ill with fever and dysentery that he could not sign his name. Reid wrote to the governors of Tennessee, Kentucky, Louisiana, and Mississippi, pleading for troops at once, "for there is no telling when or where the spoiler will come."

A few days later the general found hope even in the British sacking of Washington. "The burning of the Capitol may be a disgrace," he wrote Rachel, "but it will give impulse and energy to our cause." He was also cheered by a change in the capital, where James Monroe had taken over for President Madison, who was in a state of nervous exhaustion. Monroe had ousted the ineffectual Armstrong, assumed the office of Secretary of War, and begun a vigorous prosecution of the struggle against England. Monroe had not only approved Old Hickory's plan for calling up troops; he had somehow found $100,000 for Jackson's war chest.

By now American and British peace commissioners were negotiating with the British at Ghent, in Belgium, and though New Englanders urged peace at any price, including cession of northwestern territory, westerners were determined to fight. Jackson saw evidence of this in small bodies of volunteers that appeared in his camp. He posted them near Mobile and continued to beg the states for more.

Coffee arrived with his horsemen in late October, 2,800 of the most reliable troops Tennessee could muster, many of them veterans of the Creek war, who rode their own horses and carried their own rifles. Jackson's faith in Coffee was boundless: "He is a consummate commander; born so, but so modest that he doesn't know it."

Coffee shared Jackson's opinion that fighting lay ahead. He wrote his wife,

I feel in my bones . . . that greater things are in store for us than ever before. There is every reason to believe the British will make an attack on our Gulf Coast this coming winter. . . .

If they do, take my word for it Old Tennessee will be heard from as she has never been heard from before. . . . My boys . . . have no pity for the redcoats, who . . . are to be held responsible for all the devilment the Indians have done. Every one of my boys wants to get within fair buck-range of a redcoat!

Jackson intended to give the Tennesseans their wish even if it involved an invasion of Spanish territory, from where newly arrived British officers were issuing provocative taunts.

From Pensacola the British Lieutenant Colonel Edward Nicholls issued a proclamation:

> Natives of Louisiana; on you the first call is made to Assist in Liberating . . . Your paternal soil. . . . American Usurpation . . . must be Abolished. . . . I am at the head of a large body of Indians, well armed, disciplined and commanded by British officers—a good train of artillery, seconded by . . . a numerous British and Spanish squadron. . . . Be not alarmed at our approach. . . . A flag over any door, whether Spanish, French or British, will be certain Protection.

Thanks to the garrulous Nicholls, Jackson was aware of the British plan to take Mobile and Baton Rouge, and then occupy isolated New Orleans. Jackson had warned Governor Claiborne to strengthen the city's defenses, but Claiborne dismissed the threat of invasion as "chimerical." In any event, the governor said, his citizens were so lacking in "ardent zeal" that he could make "but a feeble resistance": "I have a difficult people to manage . . . Native Americans, Native Louisianans, Frenchmen, Spaniards (with some English)." Claiborne had already estranged the one band whose "ardent zeal" was beyond question—the private force of the brothers Laffite, whose 5,000 men preyed upon British and Spanish shipping in the Caribbean. The Laffites controlled a fleet of more than thirty ships, operated forty warehouses on islands in the Mississippi Delta, and boldly smuggled their pirated goods into New Orleans in defiance of customs officers. The brothers had come to grief despite the clandestine aid of Edward Livingston and other lawyers, the U.S. Marshal, a bank president, and other leading citizens of New Orleans.

After the capture of a contraband cargo at Barataria by U.S. officers, Claiborne offered a reward of $500 for Jean Laffite. To the delight of Louisiana's Creoles Jean responded with an offer of $5,000 for the delivery of the governor to his headquarters. Claiborne retaliated by arresting Jean's brother Pierre on a New Orleans street, clapping him into prison, and holding him so tenaciously that not even Livingston and his influential friends could free the Baratarian leader. Thus the approach of the British armada found the government of Louisiana and the state's most effective fighting force at odds, with faint prospects of an early truce.

The Haitian-born Laffites had been reared by their shrewd, indomitable Jewish grandmother; she had instilled in them an intense hatred of the Spanish, who had killed her husband and driven the family from the country during the Inquisition. The brothers embarked on careers of smuggling, privateering, and warfare early in life. Alexandre, the eldest, who had become one of Napoleon's artillerymen and now lived under the alias of Dominique You, was the most ferocious-looking of the Baratarian pirates, a swarthy, hawk-nosed man whose face had been scarred by powder burns. He stood less than 5 feet tall, but his shoulders were so broad that he seemed to be deformed.

The younger brothers, Jean and Pierre, had learned the smuggling trade in the Caribbean from a kinsman, Renato Beluche, an adventurer of many aliases who was now one of their captains. Jean Laffite, a courtly man of thirty-two, was known for his fashionable dress, and for his brilliant red hair and mustache, which he dyed with potash and gunpowder. Pierre, a large, coarse, cross-eyed brigand, carelessly dressed, was afflicted with epilepsy and subject to occasional fits.

Among the privateers sailing from Barataria Bay to plunder merchant ships were the notorious Italian freebooters Louis ("Cutnose") Chigizola and Vincent Gambie, who frequently resorted to outright piracy in defiance of orders from the Laffites. But despite the depredations of the band, the lair of the Baratarians on the tiny island of Grand Terre—a complex of warehouses, slave pens, ammunition dumps, and boatyards—had flourished for years with immunity provided by Livingston, the most resourceful of New Orleans lawyers. The outlaws were soon to become the allies of a reluctant Andrew Jackson.

On September 3 a small British ship appeared in Barataria Bay, fired on a pirate schooner, and came to anchor near Grand Terre, flying a white flag. As 200 or more angry sailors assembled on the beach, Jean Laffite was rowed out in a pirogue to meet two British officers, who were moving shoreward in a gig. One of the newcomers hailed him.

"Is Mr. Laffite in the Bay? I have important messages for him."

"You'll have to come ashore if you want to see Mr. Laffite. Follow me."

When the British officers stepped ashore, surrounded by scowling pirates, Jean said, "I am Laffite." The British, who identified themselves as Captain Nicholas Lockyer of the navy and Captain McWilliams of the army, were hooted by the mob: "They're spies! Send 'em to New Orleans!"

"They have come under a flag of truce," Laffite said. "Let me talk to them first." He led the way to his headquarters, where the officers handed him a packet of dispatches, among which was a letter from Colonel Nicholls:

> *Sir: I have arrived in the Floridas for the purpose of annoying the only enemy Great Britain has in the world . . . I call on you and your brave followers to enter into the service of Great Britain. . . .*
>
> *We have a powerful reinforcement on its way here and I hope to cut out some other work for the Americans than oppressing the inhabitants of Louisiana.*

The British offered Laffite the rank of captain, $30,000 in cash, land grants for his officers and men—and the release of Pierre Laffite from jail. There was also a warning: if Jean did not join the assault, he must remain neutral or Barataria would be destroyed.

Laffite kept the Englishmen overnight and sent them back to their ship, promising to send a reply within two weeks, after he had dealt with his rebellious men and put his affairs in order. The Englishmen were hardly out of sight before Laffite sent the dispatches to Jean Blanque in New Orleans, an influential friend who was a member of the legislature: "Though proscribed by my adopted country, I will never let slip any occasion of serving her or of proving that she has never ceased to be dear to me. Of this you will see here a convincing proof." He ended with an appeal:

> . . . I make you the depository of the secret on which perhaps depends the tranquility of our country; please to make such use of it as your judgment may direct.
>
> Our enemies have endeavoured to work on me by a motive which few men would have resisted. They represented to me a brother in irons, a brother who is very dear to me, whose deliverer I might become, and I declined the proposal. . . . I am waiting for the British officer's good answer, and for yours to this. Be so good as to assist me with your judicious counsel in so weighty an affair.

Twenty-four hours later the dispatches reached Blanque, and then Governor Claiborne, who called a meeting of his advisers. Someone charged that Laffite's documents were forgeries, a ruse to free Pierre from prison. Commodore Daniel Patterson of the navy and Colonel

George Ross of the army, who were under orders from Washington to break up the smugglers' nest, urged a raid on Grand Terre. The Laffites were defended only by Jacques Phillippe de Villeré, a militia commander, who argued that the Baratarians were privateers rather than pirates, sailing under the flag of Cartagena and attacking only Spanish ships. "The only crime you can charge to them is illegal imports of prize goods," Villeré said. "The United States is their adopted country. They see it threatened by an enemy they despise. These documents tell the truth. We must believe them."

Villeré's advice was rejected. A majority of the committee insisted upon a raid on the Laffites' stronghold and the governor consented, perhaps swayed by wounded vanity, or by the influence of his Spanish wife. Six gunboats and the cutter *Carolina* were prepared to sail against Barataria, loaded with troops of the 44th Infantry—but the decision was only hours old when Pierre Laffite made a mysterious escape from the New Orleans jail and carried a warning to Grand Terre. Jean Laffite wrote Claiborne at once, offering all his resources in the approaching campaign:

> . . . I address Myself to you with confidence for an object on which can depend the Safety of the State. I offer to Return to this State many Citizens Who perhaps have lost to your eyes that sacred title . . . I offer . . . their Efforts for the Defense of the Country.
> This point of Louisiana that I occupy is of Great Importance in the present situation. I offer myself to defend it. . . . I am the Lost Sheep who desires to return to the flock . . .

Laffite said that he would abandon Barataria if his offer were refused, to avoid the appearance of aiding the British invasion, which, he warned, "can not Fail to take place."

Claiborne was so alarmed that he sent Laffite's dispatches to Jackson in Mobile. The people of New Orleans, the mercurial governor said, were now seized by "a much greater Spirit of Disaffection" than he had anticipated, and in this emergency, "Laffite and his associates might probably be made useful to us."

A few days later Patterson and Ross attacked Grand Terre, only to find that Jean and Pierre Laffite had fled, concealing arms, ammunition, slaves, and valuable papers on other islands. Patterson contented himself with sacking the warehouses of $500,000 worth of goods, burning the remainder, seizing eight small vessels, and carrying Dominique You and eighty men as prisoners to New Orleans. The prisoners were confined in the Cabildo, where Dominique was chained to heavy iron rings. Patterson then filed suit for himself and his men, claiming the vessels and goods as contraband prizes of war.

Jackson himself was blind to the value of the Laffites' men as allies. He wrote to Claiborne of "those wretches, the refugees from Barataria," and denounced them as "hellish banditti." Only the influence of Edward Livingston prevented the Laffites from deserting the American cause.

Livingston sought to convince Jackson that the Laffites were loyal, and that their guns, ammunition, and artillery crews would be invaluable in the defense of the city. He also sent to Mobile complete descriptions of the topography of the country surrounding New Orleans. For the first time the general began to consider in detail the strategic problem of defending New Orleans; but though Livingston pointed out the importance of waterways leading to the city, Jackson at first rejected advice on these approaches. He was convinced that the British would move overland from Mobile and march to Walnut Hills, the future site of Vicksburg, Mississippi, which would isolate New Orleans and enable the invaders to capture the city at leisure.

"A real military man, with full knowledge of the geography . . . of this country," he said, would inevitably use that route.

Jackson's persistence in this theory of the British approach delayed his development of a plan to defend the region as a whole, and time was running out. Evidence was mounting that an invasion was imminent.

Jean Laffite's warning was followed by others. On November 28 a privateer entered Mobile Bay with a British ship captured off Jamaica, a transport whose sailors gossiped of an attack on New Orleans. A week later the privateer *Warren* brought word of an armada of more than eighty British ships in Negril Bay, Jamaica, most of them loaded troop transports. The fleet was manned by 10,000 sailors, and carried 1,500 marines and 9,600 soldiers, more than 20,000 men in all. This task force was under orders to occupy Louisiana regardless of the outcome of the peace conference. Its contingent of Wellington's veterans had, in fact, sailed from England in mid-September, five weeks after the commissioners began deliberating in Ghent.

Jackson's theory of the enemy's intentions was reinforced on September 14, 1814, when a small British squadron attacked Fort Bowyer, the key to the defense of Mobile. To the general's surprise, the fort's 160-man garrison fought so tenaciously that the enemy was driven off with 240 killed and wounded and the loss of the 32-gun ship *Hermes,* which burned and exploded. One of the British wounded was Colonel Edward Nicholls, who lost an eye.

A few days later, aware that the British had returned to Pensacola,

Jackson prepared to follow into Spanish territory and drive them out. He warned James Monroe of his move in terms that would absolve the Secretary from blame in case of a diplomatic crisis:

As I act without the orders of the government, I deem it important to state to you my reasons. . . . The safety of this section of the union depends upon it. . . . Pensacola has assumed the character of British Territory. . . . I feel a confidence that I shall stand Justified to my government. . . . Should I not . . . the consolation of having done the only thing in my opinion which could give security to the country . . . will be ample reward for the loss of my commission.

Jackson marched on November 2 with 3,000 men, leaving Mobile and New Orleans virtually defenseless, and four days later appeared at Pensacola, demanding the surrender of the city and nearby forts. When his flag of truce was fired upon, Jackson ordered an assault.

He approached the town from the west, but seeing that this road was under the guns of British warships in the harbor, made a demonstration with a few horsemen there and then adroitly passed his troops through the scrub to encircle the town and approach from the east, where they faced few defenses. One of his columns charged a battery that got off a few rounds of grapeshot and the skirmish was over. Old Governor Manrique tottered into the street with a white flag, led Jackson to his house, and assured him that the forts would be surrendered. The garrisons capitulated late in the day. A few hours afterwards the British blew up Fort Barrancas and sailed away.

During the evening Jackson was entertained in the luxurious home of Don Juan Ventura Morales, a former official in Spanish New Orleans whose daughter had married a prominent Creole in the Louisiana capital, Bernard de Marigny de Mandeville. Don Juan entrusted the general with a letter to his son-in-law, and urged him to make his New Orleans headquarters in the Marigny home.

Jackson was off almost immediately, and in fear of an enemy thrust at Mobile, pushed his troops back to his base in three and a half days.

James Monroe was shocked by Jackson's reckless exposure of Mobile and New Orleans during his invasion, but the effectiveness of the assault soon became obvious—the Creek and Seminole warriors fled into the wilderness and deserted the British. And Governor Manrique was a changed man; he ended a respectful message to Jackson: "Your most faithful and grateful servant, who kisses your hands."

The nation's Federalist press denounced Jackson's raid as a violation of the territory of a friendly power, which was likely to bring war with Spain. The Spanish ambassador lodged a protest. But the west and south and the Democratic party and its press applauded. The raid also lifted the morale of Jackson's troops and stirred new enthusiasm for the war back home in Tennessee, where young men eagerly paid bonuses of up to $50 for the privilege of becoming substitutes in the militia, on the chance of joining Jackson before the fighting ended.

Soon after his return to Mobile, Jackson prepared to move to New Orleans and assume command of its defenses.

The city was torn by dissension. When the popular French consul, Louis de Tousard, urged Creoles to join Claiborne's militia, his home was stoned and the seal of the Bourbons was ripped from his doorway. Newspapers denounced the governor as a tyrant and assured the public that the call for troops was illegal. Claiborne warned Jackson that there was worse to come when the Assembly acted; though it had not yet "done anything to damp the public . . . I fear, I much fear, that they will."

Claiborne himself vacillated with every shift of the political winds: "Our country is filled with spies and traitors. . . . The natives of Louisiana are a virtuous, a gallant people. . . . The troops now in Louisiana are inadequate to our defense. . . . We are well disposed in case of attack . . . It is not believed that British are in Force anywhere in your vicinity. . . . It seems certain that the British will invade this quarter of the continent."

Jackson waited no longer. He reinforced Fort Bowyer so strongly that he felt it could withstand the attack of 10,000 troops, left 3 regiments of regulars in Mobile, and ordered Coffee's troops to Baton Rouge. On November 22 the general left on the 170-mile ride to New Orleans, still unaware of the overwhelming strength of the invasion force about to be launched against Louisiana. He was only a few miles on his way when the British fleet sailed from Jamaica.

There was a festive air aboard the ships of the invasion fleet. The wives of officers walked the decks in bright dresses, joined by numerous civilian officials on their way to establish a new British government of Louisiana. At night there were balls, and the music of army bands drifted over the calm waters of the Caribbean. Sir Alexander Cochrane, the courtly and charming veteran who had pillaged Washington, neared the coast of his dreams, irresistibly drawn by reports of $15 million worth of cotton, tobacco, and whiskey in the warehouses of New Orleans.

9

"They shall not sleep on our soil!"

Jackson and his little staff of six or eight riders arrived in the suburbs of New Orleans in the chill dawn of December 2, 1814, emerging from the fog at an old Spanish villa on Lake Pontchartrain—the home of the wealthy merchant J. Kilty Smith, who expected them for breakfast. It was the end of an exhausting ride of 11 days through the wilderness, for the general had insisted upon following a circuitous coastal route of some 350 miles, content only when he had seen for himself the points where the enemy might land.

Jackson's young aides, Robert Butler and John Reid, were saddlesore and worn, and the long-awaited saviour of the city himself was not an imposing sight. He was "more fit for the hospital than the field," and was dressed in a small leather cap, an old blue Spanish cloak with bullet buttons, and mud-spattered boots that looked as if they had never been polished. Smith and his household were never to forget the general's appearance: "a tall, gaunt man, of very erect carriage, with a countenance full of stern decision and fearless energy, but furrowed with care and anxiety. . . . His complexion was sallow and unhealthy; his hair iron grey, his body thin and emaciated. . . . But the fierce glare of his bright and hawk-like grey eye, betrayed a soul and spirit which triumphed over all the infirmities of the body."

The officers were seated at a candle-lit table spread with an elaborate breakfast; but though his aides ate heartily, the dyspeptic general took only a small bowl of boiled hominy, and was soon looking at his watch, reminding his staff that they must hurry into the city. Within a few moments they were riding into New Orleans in Smith's carriage, leaving behind a bemused host. Smith's neighbor, a Creole woman who had come to help entertain the party, now scolded him: "Ah, Mr. Smith, how could you deceive me so? You have asked me to help receive a great general. I worked myself almost to death to make your house *comme il faut* and prepared a splendid breakfast, and now I find my labor is thrown away upon an ugly old Kaintuck flatboatman. . . ." She was not to be convinced that the jaundiced countryman was a celebrated general who had been entrusted with the fate of the country.

By ten o'clock Jackson was in New Orleans and was taken to the home of another merchant, where a welcoming committee awaited him: Governor Claiborne, handsome in dress uniform; Mayor Nicholas Girod, a round and affable elderly Frenchman; Edward Livingston; Commodore Daniel Patterson, a twenty-nine-year-old veteran of war against the Barbary pirates; and Colonel George Ross of the infantry. Jackson was led through a crush of officers and politicans to the second-floor gallery of the house, where he saw that an expectant crowd had filled the street below and stood patiently, despite a steady rainfall, gazing upward.

Claiborne and Girod made speeches of welcome and Jackson moved to the iron railing. Young Charles Gayarré, a future historian, watched from the street as the general called a few brusque, direct words to the crowd, words few of the Creoles understood. Gayarré was left in no doubt as to his meaning: "His lip and eye denoted a man of unyielding temper, and his hair, slightly silvered, stood erect like quills round his wrinkled brow, as if they scorned to bend." If Jackson was not a genius, Gayarré thought, "his rock-hewn will took the place of genius."

Livingston translated Jackson's remarks into French, his vibrant voice lending excitement to the general's simple appeal: "I have come to protect the city. I will drive our enemies into the sea or perish in the effort . . . you must all rally around me, cease all differences and divisions, and join in patriotic resolve to save this city from dishonor and disaster."

The crowd shouted its approval, visibly encouraged by Jackson's air of confidence: "Countenances cleared up. Bright and hopeful were the words and looks of all who caught the heroic glance of the hawk-eyed General."

Jackson was then taken to a tall brick building at 106 Royal Street, where he was to make headquarters, and immediately rode out in the rain to the Place d'Armes to review the city's militiamen, about 1,000 gaudily uniformed troops, four-fifths of them Creoles, many of whom were drawn from the city's leading families, merchants, planters, bankers, lawyers, and physicians. There were the Orleans Volunteers of Major Jean Baptiste Plauché, 550 strong, officered by Creoles who had fought under Napoleon; the Dragoons of Captain Henri St. Gême, a 5-foot soldier who wore a foot-long plume in his helmet, and was, in civilian life, a partner of Dominique You. There were the Louisiana Blues, an "American" company led by Captain Maunsel White, all of its men of Irish birth or descent; the Francs of Captain Jean Hudri; and the Chasseurs of Captain Auguste Guibert.

Jackson inspected the ranks dutifully, congratulated officers and men, and assured them of his confidence in them. He said nothing of his need for thousands more troops, nor of the shortage of arms and ammunition and the absence of black units, which he had urged Claiborne to raise.

Free Negroes had been organized into a militia battalion some years earlier, but never mustered, and Jackson had pressed the governor to call them out, with a warning that the blacks must be treated fairly: "They will not remain quiet spectators. . . . They must be either for us or against us. Distrust them, and you make them your enemies. Place confidence in them . . . by extending to them equal rights and privileges with white men."

In a proclamation sent off earlier he had appealed to the "intelligent minds and love of honor" of Louisiana's black freedmen, urging them to volunteer for the war, offering the usual bounty of $124 and 160 acres of land and service in an independent unit: "Due regard will be paid to the feelings of freedmen and soldier. You will not, by being associated with white men . . . be exposed to improper comparisons, or unjust sarcasm. . . ."

But Claiborne, fearful of public reaction, had withheld the proclamation for more than a month, and issued it only when Jackson was expected in New Orleans. Old Hickory soon had the Negro units in the field, and enforced his promises to them despite protests by whites, who feared a repetition of the slave uprising of 1811. When a paymaster refused to pay the Negro soldiers, the general stormed, "Be pleased to keep to yourself your Opinions—It is enough for you to receive my order for the payment . . . without enquiring whether the troops are white Black or Tea."

The general returned from the review to headquarters to confer with engineers and his rapidly growing staff, to which Edward Livingston had attached not only himself but both his brother-in-law, August

Davezac, and his law partner, John Randolph Grymes. Jackson's chief adviser on the city's defenses was Major Arsène La Carrière Latour, the engineer of the Seventh Military District, a black-bearded Frenchman of forty-five who was a graduate of the Paris Academy of Fine Arts, trained as an architect and an engineer. Latour had come to Louisiana to conduct a survey for Napoleon's projected occupation, and had remained to build several of the city's notable buildings and survey the city and nearby countryside. When Latour and his associate engineer, Major Howell Tatum, spread their maps before him, Jackson began to realize for the first time the demanding problem of defending New Orleans.

The city lay between Lake Pontchartrain and the Mississippi, some 100 miles above the mouth of the great river, open to attack from the Gulf through a maze of waterways. Latour described six of the most obvious approaches in detail: west of the Mississippi were the Bayou La Fourche, narrow and easily defended, and Barataria Bay, which connected with other bayous and canals to the Mississippi at a point opposite the city.

The Mississippi itself was considered impractical for an invasion fleet because of its strong current and the confusing network of shallow branches entering the Gulf. Jackson was urged, however, to strengthen three old forts on the banks of the river and fit them with cannon.

To the east of the river lay the River aux Chenes and the Bayou Terre aux Boeufs, through which small boats could reach the bank of the Mississippi, a few miles below New Orleans.

There was Bayou St. John, leading from Lake Pontchartrain to within two miles of the city, also navigable only by small boats, and so narrow that it could be blocked by felling trees.

The single approach by land led directly into New Orleans from Chef Menteur, on Lake Pontchartrain, approaching along a ridge of high ground known as the Plain of Gentilly. Most of the city's people expected the British to come by this route, which, though unfortified, was easily defended.

Jackson discovered that the intricate terrain between the city and the Gulf was a mystery to many local people: "The numerous bayous and canals," he said, "appear almost as little understood by the inhabitants as by the Citizens of Tennessee. True every man will give you an exact description of the whole and every man will give you an erroneous one."

In any event, within a few hours after he had seen Latour's maps, Jackson had sent detachments to fell trees to block the smaller water-

ways and to sink logwork obstructions in the major channels. He also
approved Commodore Patterson's plan to send an aggressive young
lieutenant, Thomas Ap. Catesby Jones, with five small gunboats into
Lake Borgne, where he was to keep watch for the enemy.

The general made his debut in New Orleans society that night in the
home of Livingston, whose beautiful San Dominican wife had planned
a dinner party for a dozen or more young women, and was not pleased
when she learned that the "wild Indian fighter" had been invited. Mrs.
Livingston was skeptical of her husband's assurance, "He will capture
you at first sight," but she was quickly won. Even Livingston was startled by the transformation when Jackson appeared in full dress uniform—a blue frock coat with buff facings, a spotless white waistcoat,
and skin-tight yellow buckskin breeches. "I had to confess to myself,"
Livingston said, "that the new uniform made another man of him. He
had two sets of manners. One for headquarters . . . the other one for
the drawing room." At dinner Jackson was seated between Mrs. Livingston and an English-speaking Creole girl, who were both charmed by
his grave, gentle courtliness and reassured by the "easy, agreeable
manner" in which he talked of the coming invasion, his confidence of
victory, and his insistence that the young women had nothing to fear.

Livingston's sponsorship could not have failed to please Jackson,
but it accentuated the problems in the divided city, whose predomi-
nantly Creole population was still resentful of Yankee newcomers after
twelve years of American rule. As chairman of the Committee of
Safety, composed of civilian volunteers, Livingston was frequently at
odds with the legislative defense committee, whose chairman was the
aristocratic Bernard de Marigny, a spokesman for influential Creoles.

By surrendering himself into Livingston's hands, Jackson had
offended Marigny upon his arrival in the city. The general had sent
Marigny the letter he had brought from Don Juan Morales in Pensacola, and his courier had asked if Jackson might make headquarters
in Marigny's home. The Creole replied that he would "receive with
pleasure the Conqueror of the Floridas," and sent word to Jackson that
breakfast would be awaiting him the next morning. But on December
2 the general did not appear for breakfast, and there was no explanation of his absence. An apartment in the large riverside townhouse had
been prepared and, as Marigny noted in his journal, he had left "no
detail neglected so that the reception might be worthy of the guest."

Marigny was twenty-nine, the scion of a distinguished family, and
one of Louisiana's richest men. He was well known in the salons of
Paris and London and celebrated as a host in Louisiana; he was impressed by Jackson's forcefulness and was anxious to entertain him and

introduce him to the state's most influential men. At noon, when Jackson had not appeared, Marigny went to headquarters and learned that the general had changed his mind: "I was astonished . . . it would have been infinitely agreeable to receive him. . . ." But the proud Marigny gave no sign that he was offended. Instead, he joined Governor Claiborne's staff and began a shrewd and unselfish effort to help Old Hickory save the city—decisive aid that he was literally to force upon the stubborn Tennessean.

Jackson sailed down the Mississippi on December 3 to inspect the river defenses: Fort St. Philip, fifty miles from the Gulf, and an unfinished battery at English Turn, commanding a long loop in the river, only fourteen miles below New Orleans. He ordered these posts strengthened, and droves of slaves from nearby plantations were soon at work, throwing up earthworks and building gun platforms. A week later Jackson returned from his inspection to find the city in an uproar over news from Lieutenant Jones that ships of the British fleet were anchoring off the entrance to Lake Borgne. Jackson was not alarmed.

With an assurance remarkable in a commander whose army was outnumbered by five to one, the general reported to Secretary Monroe that the city's defenses were adequate; the gunboats would keep the enemy at bay, and the assault would fall upon Fort Bowyer, which was invulnerable. He wrote Coffee in Baton Rouge of the enemy's unexpected appearance, "I expect this is a faint [sic] to draw my attention to that point when they mean to strike at another—however I will look for them there and provide for their reception else where."

There was a sudden stir of activity in New Orleans. The legislature appropriated money for more defenses, the city's women organized to make clothing and bandages, a civilian street patrol was formed. Jackson then turned his attention to Lake Pontchartrain and the high ground at Chef Menteur and the Plain of Gentilly, where he spent four days, inspecting forts, ordering work on old and new defenses, and supervising as hordes of black laborers were driven to the task.

These preparations were belittled by Claiborne, whose vanity was wounded by his exclusion from Jackson's councils. The governor complained that "Those who immediately surrounded Jackson on his arrival . . . availed themselves of every opportunity to increase his sense of danger." But the city's Creole leaders were not misled. Bernard de Marigny noted that though the people of New Orleans had been eager to defend themselves, there had been "a sense of uneasiness" until Jackson took charge. Governor Claiborne was a "very honest man of personal bravery, but he had not the energy necessary to give a great impulse to the population of Louisiana." Another Creole, Pierre Fav-

rot, who thought of Claiborne as "good for nothing . . . a third rate
lawyer," observed that Jackson's presence "revived spirits . . . and
resusitated Clabo the very day he entered the town."

Jackson was badgered by nervous civilians who brought ominous
rumors to headquarters, and when he heard gossip that the British
intended to return Louisiana to Spanish control, he issued a proclamation: "Believe not such incredible tales—your government is at peace
with Spain—it is the . . . common enemy of mankind . . . that . . . has
sent his hirelings among you with this false report." Soon he had
alarming news from Lake Borgne: the enemy had overpowered Lieutenant Jones and his gunboats. The shallow lake was now undefended.
British smallcraft bearing troops could sweep within a few miles of the
city.

The panic that followed found Jackson too ill to stand. For a day and
a half, sipping an occasional brandy and eating almost no food, he lay
on a sofa in his Royal Street headquarters, sending out orders that
stirred the city to frenzied action. New troops were mustered. A battalion of black veterans who had fought in Haiti was sent to Chef Menteur, where Jackson expected an attack. He wrote William Carroll, who
had left Tennessee two months earlier with a division of recruits,
urging haste: "Our lakes are open to . . . the enemy, and I am prepared
to . . . die in the last ditch before he shall reach the city." He called
Coffee from Baton Rouge: "You must not sleep until you reach me."
He also called for troops from Mississippi and Kentucky. He ordered
commanders of forts to fight when attacked, so long as "a man remained alive to hold a gun." He requested a six months' supply of
provisions, and sent a fresh appeal for cannon to Monroe: "We have
no arms here. Will the Government order a supply?"

Jackson realized that he was on his own. He told Livingston and
Claiborne: "We can expect nothing from Washington, gentlemen. We
must defend ourselves with such resources as we have . . . at the worst
we must, can and will defend this city and State to the bitter end."

On December 16 he put the city under martial law and issued a
proclamation to make his purpose clear: "Martial law can only be
justified by the necessity of the case. The Major-General proclaims it
at his own risk and upon his sole responsibility . . ." The order forbade
anyone to enter or leave the city without Jackson's written permission.
Street lights were to be extinguished at nine o'clock each evening, and
a strict curfew was to be enforced. The general also tried to raise more
troops. Bands paraded the streets, playing *Yankee Doodle,* the *Marseil-
laise,* and *Ça Ira*; when few volunteers came out, Jackson impressed
many leading citizens and put them in ranks, among them the pictur-

esque Vincent Nolte, a wealthy cotton merchant who was partner in a prominent London brokerage firm.

He now had about 3,000 troops, a third of them regulars and the remainder Louisiana militia. Many men were poorly armed and inexperienced; the most pressing need was for artillery, guns, ammunition, flints, powder—and experienced gunners. These could be had only from the Baratarians, but Jackson stubbornly resisted all pleas that he deal with the "hellish banditti." It was Bernard de Marigny who resolved the impasse and saved the impulsive general from himself.

Marigny appeared at headquarters with the Assembly's legislative Committee of Defense and urged Jackson to set free the pirates and enlist them as gunners. After a long session Marigny reported: "The General was unrelenting. He told us these men were being pursued by United States Civil Officers, that many were in prison . . . that he did not wish, could do nothing about the matter. . . . The Committee withdrew, very much grieved at such determination."

But Marigny persisted. He took the problem to the federal district judge, Dominick A. Hall, who rose to the occasion: "I am general in these circumstances." At Hall's suggestion Marigny persuaded the legislature to pass a resolution urging suspension of prosecution of charges against the Baratarians, and a few hours later the pirates were free. Abruptly, the streets swarmed with the ex-prisoners and their companions who had been hiding in the city. Before the day was over Patterson had taken experienced crews aboard his two small vessels in the Mississippi, the schooner *Carolina* and the larger *Louisiana*.

Jean Laffite appeared, under protection of a writ from Judge Hall, and with Dominique You went in search of Jackson. They found the general on a street corner, begged him to enlist their men, and promised to supply cannon, ammunition, and equipment. Jackson led them to headquarters, where he spent an hour or more alone with Laffite, and was completely won by the pirate leader. Latour left the only record of the conference:

> Mr. Laffite solicited for himself and for all Baratarians the honour of serving under our banners, that they might have an opportunity of proving that if they had infringed the revenue laws, yet none were more ready than they to defend the country. . . . Persuaded that the assistance of these men could not fail of being very useful, the general accepted their efforts.

Laffite's Baratarians, Jackson's only battle-tested troops, needed no instructions. Dominique You and Renato Beluche formed three companies of artillery. Other pirates joined a company of marines; hundreds of others were sent by Jean Laffite into the bayou country to bring big guns and ammunition from hiding.

Jackson had been completely won by the candor and sincerity of Jean Laffite. He sent the pirate chief across the Mississippi to organize delivery of gunpowder to the army's magazine, and wrote the magazine's commander, Major Michael Reynolds: "Mr. Jean Laffite has offered me his services to go down and give you every information in his power. You will therefore please to afford him the necessary protection from Injury and Insult and . . . furnish him with your passport for his return dismissing him as soon as possible as I shall want him here."

Other troops now began to join Jackson. Coffee and 800 of his mounted riflemen arrived in a cold rain on December 20 and camped 4 miles north of the city, where they awaited several hundred of their companions whose horses had been exhausted on a forced ride through the muddy countryside. At least a fourth of Coffee's vanguard had defective rifles, and all of their gunpowder had been ruined by rains. People of the city were dismayed by the unmilitary appearance of the Tennesseans "with their long unkempt hair and unshorn faces," dressed in woolen hunting shirts and home-made copperas-dyed trousers, with hats of wool, raccoon, or foxskin. New Orleans was more impressed by the giant Coffee, "A man of noble aspect, tall and herculean in frame," a striking figure on a Tennessee thoroughbred.

Within the next two days Jackson was reinforced by the arrival of Thomas Hinds and his Mississippi Dragoons, who had marched 230 miles in 4 days, and by William Carroll's division of 3,000 more Tennesseans, who had swept down the Mississippi on unseasonable floods in 1 month, a record voyage.

The enterprising Carroll had left home with green and unarmed troops, but drilled and disciplined them on the boatdecks, day after day, until they learned to move and handle their weapons in unison. When he overtook a barge of arms bound for New Orleans, Carroll had taken 1,100 muskets and a supply of gunpowder and lead. His blacksmiths had put all these weapons in order and in addition made 50,000 cartridges, each lethally loaded with a musket ball and 3 buckshot.

Sir Alexander Cochrane's fleet had arrived at the mouth of Lake Borgne on December 10; under the eye of Major General John Keane, the invasion troops swarmed down into small boats and were rowed into the lake. The troops were among England's finest. Four of the regiments were fresh from the sacking of Washington, one brigade had

come from triumphs under Wellington in Spain, the crack 91st Highlanders had been brought from South Africa, and there were two
regiments of West Indians, chiefly Jamaicans.

When the American gunboats had been overwhelmed after a savage
two-hour battle, the army moved inland to Pea Island and camped.
The island was only forty miles from New Orleans, but it was, as a
lieutenant complained, "completely wretched," a swamp with a tiny
area of dry ground at one end, "the interior a resort of wild ducks and
. . . dormant alligators." There were no tents or huts and the men were
drenched by heavy rains "such as an inhabitant of England cannot
dream of." There was no firewood; the troops spent miserable nights
with wet clothes frozen to their bodies. A number of Jamaica Negroes
died from exposure.

For six days and nights in bitter, gusty weather the sailors of the fleet
rowed up and down the lake, ferrying troops from the ships to Pea
Island, a round trip of thirty-two miles. Some of Cochrane's crews were
at the oars four days before they were relieved. General Keane's scouts
found the waterways to New Orleans blocked, except for one, the
Bayou Bienvenu, a branch of which led westward through marshes to
the plantation of General Jacques Phillippe de Villeré, on the bank of
the Mississippi six or seven miles below the city. Keane and Cochrane
rejected the more obvious route via Chef Menteur and the Plain of
Gentilly when they learned that Americans were on guard; on the night
of December 18–19 British officers disguised as Spanish fishermen
took the course of the Bayou Bienvenu and reached the Mississippi
without detection. The troops soon followed, rowing up the narrowing
bayou as far as the boats could go, then slogging over reed-grown
marshes through freezing mud, each of them loaded with a cannon ball
carried in shirt or knapsack.

Near dawn on December 23 Keane's vanguard, some 1,700 strong,
emerged onto high ground near the Mississippi, made their way
through cypress woods and fields of cane stubble, and occupied the
Villeré plantation, surprising and capturing young Major Gabriel Villeré.

Keane halted on the narrow plain beside the Mississippi, despite the
pleas of younger officers that he push on to New Orleans before the
Americans learned of their presence. Cochrane and Keane had begun
boldly, but had been made cautious by the tale of Joseph Duclos, a
captured American picket, who reported that Jackson had 12,000 to
15,000 men in New Orleans and 4,000 more on the Mississippi. Under
questioning Duclos clung to his story with the air of a man who spoke
the truth.

Jackson was serenely confident on the morning of December 23, while the British were making camp. He assumed that approaches to the city by water had been blocked as he had ordered, though this work had been assigned to militiamen and had not been inspected by trained officers. His troops were posted within a radius of four miles of the city, with Claiborne commanding a concentration near Chef Menteur and the Plain of Gentilly, where Jackson still expected to fight. Coffee and his Tennesseans were four miles above the city on Avart Plantation; the two regiments of regulars were at Fort St. Charles, on the city's waterfront; the battalion of Jean Plauché and the gunners of Dominique You and Beluche were at Fort St. John on Lake Pontchartrain.

On the river, the *Carolina* and the *Louisiana* were carrying powder from the magazine on the west bank, whose vaults were frequently filled by Jean Laffite's men.

Last-minute preparations kept the city and the army in a stir, but though there was an air of readiness, Jackson could not predict where or when the invaders would appear. As one of the general's most astute biographers observed: "Up to this moment Jackson was hardly master of the situation. His military genius was of the kind that does one thing splendidly, hurling into it with superhuman energy both himself and all who were under him. It was not of the kind that organizes well and manages the most complex situation through mastery of detail."

Late in the morning the general wrote Robert Hays in Nashville, to report that the British had made no movements since their defeat of the gunboats, but that he hoped to check them wherever they appeared. He complained of lack of news from home, particularly from Rachel, who had been invited to visit New Orleans.

> . . . I have not received a letter or paper from Tennessee since the last of October. I am anxious to know whether Mrs. Jackson has sailed from Nashville. Under the expectation that she has, has been the reason why I have not wrote her. If she is still at home say to her the reason I have not wrote her, and say to her and my little son god bless them. . . . I hope under every circumstance, and let what will happen, you will hear that I have done my duty. All well.

A few moments later Jackson had the first warning of the approach of the enemy. Colonel Pierre Denis de La Ronde, whose militiamen were on outpost duty below the city, reported several enemy ships in nearby bayous. Jackson sent Latour and Tatum to investigate and lay down on a sofa at headquarters, enfeebled by dysentery.

Within two hours there was a more alarming report from Augustin Rousseau, a civilian who arrived with word that British were already less than eight miles from the city, on the Villeré plantation. Jackson was incredulous, but Rousseau's story was impressive—he had seen a British party overwhelm de La Ronde's pickets.

Confirmation followed swiftly. Three breathless riders arrived with news from Villeré's, one of them Major Gabriel Villeré, who had escaped from the enemy. A few moments later Tatum and Latour returned to report that 1,600 to 1,800 British troops were already making camp at Villeré's. Jackson sprang from his sofa: "By the Eternal, they shall not sleep on our soil!"

10

"The best fought action in the annals of military warfare"

The general gave no sign that he was disconcerted by the surprise appearance of the enemy, nor by the failure of Louisianans to block their approach route. Instead he astounded John Reid and his aides with his order: "Gentlemen, the British are below. We must fight them tonight." Couriers clattered out of Royal Street with orders calling for a concentration on the riverside, the regulars, the horsemen of Coffee and Hinds, the New Orleans militia brigades, and a band of Choctaw scouts led by the French-Indian half-breed Pierre Jugeat. Jackson sent William Carroll to reinforce Claiborne on the Plain of Gentilly and Daniel Patterson to prepare the heavily armed *Carolina* for action.

The general then ate a little rice and returned to his sofa for a few minutes of sleep—it was to be his last for seventy hours. Soon after 3:00 P.M. he was at Fort St. Charles on the western edge of the city, now surrounded by a growing escort of aides, staff officers, and hangers-on, including Jean and Pierre Laffite, Livingston, and August Davezac. Jackson waited for his troops, restless and intense. He swore frequently, as if obsessed by the thought of the British surprise. "I'll smash 'em, so help me God! I'll smash 'em."

An hour later the troops had passed through the fort and were below the city, the last of them Major Jean Plauché's Creoles, who had run all the way from Fort St. John on Lake Pontchartrain. Jackson led the way downstream and halted at the mansion of Augustin Macarty, a comfortable plantation house whose two-story galleries overlooked the Mississippi about six miles below the city. Here he made headquarters in the absence of the aged owner, who was ill.

Commodore Patterson reported that the *Carolina* was moving downstream, ready for action. The small two-masted schooner, fitted with naval guns, was served by a well-drilled crew of ninety, many of them Baratarians, a crew "composed of men of all nations (English excepted), taken from the streets of New Orleans." Jackson and Patterson agreed on a plan of assault: The *Carolina* would anchor off the British camp and open fire at 7:30 P.M., and after seven broadsides would send up rockets, a signal for Jackson to attack the enemy camp by land.

Patterson took the schooner downstream with its sails slack, borne by the current in the windless dusk. Jackson's troops moved toward the enemy and halted in the darkness beneath Pierre de La Ronde's avenue of great oaks, approaching so steathily that they were undetected by enemy pickets only 500 yards away. The general passed orders for the attack. When the *Carolina*'s rockets appeared, he would lead the right wing down the levée until it reached the British camp, then wheel and attack. Coffee would circle to the left flank to strike in the same fashion. Jackson's wing now formed a line from the riverside to Versailles, de La Ronde's handsome brick house: the artillery and marines, the 7th Infantry, Plauché's company, Daquin's battalion of Free Colored, Jugeat's Choctaws, and the 44th Infantry. Guided by de La Ronde and Pierre Laffite, the rest of Jackson's force moved inland— Coffee and his Tennessee horsemen, Hinds's Dragoons, and John Beale's riflemen. These men disappeared toward the edge of the swamp, ordered to circle into the enemy flank and rear.

Vincent Nolte saw a pronounced change in the ranks as the men moved into position and Jackson said a few words of encouragement to those in his line. "It was marvelous to witness the morale and elan of our men, raw militia as they were. . . . Inspired by Jackson's words . . . not one man seemed to remember that the soldiers out in front of us were . . . Wellington's veterans."

The evening was cool and raw. A light fog came off the river. The British lay about their campfires, confident of their security; this was a war in which Americans never attacked. Many of the troops at Villeré's were asleep, exhausted by a week of toil and ten weeks of shipboard confinement. They had eaten well; foragers had brought in chickens, hams, and wine from nearby plantations.

The *Carolina* approached the camp without challenge from British sentries, who watched unsuspectingly as the crew turned her into position with sweeps, dropped anchor some 300 yards offshore, and swung her broadside to the bank. A shout rolled across the water: "Now, damn their eyes, give it to 'em!"

Seven of the ship's guns opened on the British at point-blank range, raking the camp with a murderous hail of grapeshot.

British Captain John H. Cooke remembered the barrage as a devastating series of thunderbolts that blew apart stacks of arms, camp kettles, and blazing logs, a sight as demoralizing as the killing and wounding of troops: "No mob could be in a more utter state of disorganization. . . . Officers were buckling on their swords and throwing down knives and forks, and calling to their soldiers. Soldiers were looking after their arms or buckling on their knapsacks, and calling to their officers." Bugle calls rang above the bedlam.

Some of the veterans began stamping out the fires, but the gunners of the *Carolina* no longer had need of these beacons; they aimed toward the screams of the wounded. The British, helpless before this fire, were ordered to huddle beneath the dyke, where they lay listening to "the shrieks and groans of those who lay wounded beside them."

The British fired at the schooner with muskets and a few Congreve rockets, which trailed erratic yellow smears through the night and fell harmlessly into the river. Patterson's signal rockets then rose into the sky, bursts of red, white, and blue.

Jackson's men moved forward in some confusion. Troops stumbled into a rail fence and slid into a drainage ditch just as they met the British picket line, and the enemy, though driven back at first, fired several heavy volleys and charged. Frightened artillery horses reared and overturned one of the guns on the levée road. The enemy was on the point of capturing the pieces when Jackson led a few marines and a company of infantry to the spot and ordered a bayonet charge that swept back the enemy. His men remembered that the general exposed himself recklessly in the heavy fire, but he was to say years later, when someone remarked on the gracefulness of his bow to ladies, "I learned that dodging British bullets on December 23."

Major Plauché's militia blundered into a regiment of Jackson's regulars, mistook them for the enemy, and shot down several men in their confusion.

Coffee's flank attack opened with the winking of rifles across a broad front, and drove the British toward the river, from tree to tree and from hut to hut through Villeré's plantation. Men fought hand to hand in the darkness, British bayonets against musket butts, knives, tomahawks, and fists. Prisoners were taken and retaken, "the Americans were litigating and wrangling, and protesting that they were not taken fairly, and were hugging their fire arms, bewailing their separation from a favorite rifle." Both sides fired frequently upon their own men.

A British officer complained that he had not seen such a mêlée in his long military career: "an American officer, whose sword I demanded, instead of giving it up . . . made a cut at my head." And Keane's quartermaster Surtees said it was "as strange a description of fighting as has ever been recorded."

Coffee returned to Jackson after midnight, when the fighting had died away, bringing about fifty prisoners, among them Major Samuel Mitchell of the 95th Rifles, who had set fire to the Capitol in Washington. Coffee also reported losses, for the British had passed through a break in the line and captured fifty or sixty of Beale's New Orleans riflemen, most of them lawyers, notaries, and court clerks.

By 4:00 A.M., when British deserters told him Keane had been reinforced to a strength of about 6,000, Jackson withdrew behind the Rodriguez Canal, and after conferring with Latour and other engineers began fortifying the line of the ditch.

Both sides claimed victory, but though the British had held their ground, they reported a loss of more than 300 men as against about 200 for the Americans. Twenty-year-old Lieutenant George Robert Gleig of the British 85th Regiment wrote, "Our loss has been enormous, not less than five hundred men . . . many of whom were our finest soldiers and best officers." As for the effect of the *Carolina*'s fire, Keane reported that he had been bombarded by three ships. The night attack may not have been, as Jackson claimed in his journal, "the best fought action in the annals of military warfare," but he had so severely shaken the confidence of the British veterans as to influence the campaign to its end. Keane's officers were not reassured when they interrogated prisoners: "They would give but one answer—that Jackson had almost 30,000 men."

Jackson's troops built a line of campfires from the river to the swamp and beyond, circling in the rear of the plantations of Villeré and Lacoste—fires so numerous as to confirm the exaggerated reports of his army's strength.

Jackson ordered a defense line built along the Rodriguez Canal the next day; the work began at once under the direction of Major Latour, who established the line just to the rear of the canal, a dry abandoned millrace 4 feet deep and 20 feet wide running from the swamp to the levée by the Mississippi. The troops and 2,000 slaves worked in relays, deepening the canal and throwing the black muck into pens of cypress logs which formed a breastwork. When he saw that the oozing soil could not be contained, Jackson ransacked "the whole city and country" for hand tools, wheelbarrows, carts, and wagons to haul in soil from higher elevations nearby. The work went on for four days and nights without interruption by the enemy. Jackson remained on the line until it was finished, without sleeping; when he paused for a meal, he ate rice in his saddle. The strain of his sleepless nights was taking a toll. Captain Donelson wrote home: "Uncle Jackson looks very badly and has broken very much."

Each day the general toiled along on foot in his rusty cape, defying the cold rains, looking about with his hawk's eyes bright in the yellow face. His men watched him affectionately, but joked quietly about his chronic dysentery when they saw him walking down the rampart. Only the regulars had tents; other troops perched miserably amid the black mudholes, yet morale remained high. Food was plentiful. New Orleans was full of flour, cornmeal, sweet potatoes, and pork, and wagons rolled to and from the camp almost constantly, since Jackson had impressed every usable horse, mule, and wagon.

By Christmas morning the breastwork was formidable, from 7 to 8 feet high, 12 feet thick, and 1,800 feet long, and the canal was now a broad moat half filled with black water. Its first critic was Jean Laffite, who pointed out that the line might be flanked through the cypress woods, where it came to an end. Jackson agreed that the line should be extended into the swamp itself, and the work continued. Carroll's division and some Louisiana militia were called up to extend the earthworks into the swamp and turn the wing rearward to prevent a flank attack.

The enemy was next heard from in a roll of cannon fire on Christmas morning, a salute to the arrival of 3,000 fresh troops and the commander of the British expedition—Lord Wellington himself, according to rumors in the American camp.

The new commander was in fact Sir Edward Pakenham, Wellington's brother-in-law, a handsome bachelor of thirty-seven who was a veteran of the Napoleonic wars. He brought with him a commission as governor of Louisiana, and gossips said that he was to win an earldom once he had taken New Orleans. He bore orders to seize Louisiana and the Mississippi Valley regardless of any rumors of peace that might reach him from Ghent; final ratification of a treaty would find the British firmly established in the strategic region.

A complete staff of civil government officials had also arrived, ready to assume control of Louisiana—a lieutenant governor, collector of customs, admiralty judge, superintendent of Indian affairs, and many others. Their wives and children were waiting on the ships offshore in the Gulf. Pakenham brought printed proclamations claiming sove-reignty over "all the territory fraudulently conveyed by Bonaparte to the United States," a document circulated at British headquarters.

Pakenham conducted a dress review of the troops on Villeré's cane-fields, but he was not reassured by the ranks of the disciplined veter-ans, for he saw that his force was cooped up on an isthmus between a swamp and the Mississippi, a corridor some three-quarters of a mile wide, faced by Jackson's fortified position to the north, flanked by gunboats on the river, with the lake and the Gulf in his rear. His base was eighty miles away, and the army could retreat only in open boats over a narrow waterway. If Jackson should cut the twelve-mile trail from the camp to Bayou Bienvenu, the army would be helpless. In fact, Keane and Cochrane had chosen the most hazardous of all approaches open to them.

Pakenham was also disturbed by the lack of intelligence of the enemy. In the absence of cavalry, the general had expected the aid of mutinous slaves and disaffected people of New Orleans, but none of these had appeared. Pakenham had no doubt that his army could fight its way out of the cul-de-sac, overcome Jackson's "dirty shirts," and take the city, but it now appeared that his casualties might be heavy.

The first council of war added to Pakenham's sense of unease. Keane and Cochrane were at odds, and though the admiral was largely re-sponsible for the vulnerable position of the troops, he did not disguise his contempt for the infantry commander. Pakenham's critical com-ments angered both Keane and Cochrane. The admiral bristled: if Pakenham dared not risk his troops, he would storm the city with marines and sailors. Pakenham was annoyed but agreed with his offic-ers on their first objective, the silencing of Jackson's gunboats on the river. More than a dozen big guns, mortars, and a furnace to heat solid shot were dragged up over sixty miles of swampy terrain by straining sailors and horses, and by the evening of December 26 the artillery was in place on the riverbank. The two small American vessels lay tempt-ingly within range.

Otherwise Pakenham contented himself with an inspection of Jack-son's line. He was not impressed by the works, feeling confident that his troops could break the defenses and sweep across the riverside plantation fields into New Orleans.

News of Pakenham's arrival reached Jackson by a deserter, who reported the commander's boast that he would eat his Christmas din-ner in New Orleans. "If so," Jackson said, "he'll find me at the head of the table." But Old Hickory became uneasy at the British delay. He could not yet believe that Pakenham would expose his troops in a frontal assault over the open ground before the Rodriguez Canal. In the face of all evidence to the contrary Jackson persisted in his belief that a flank attack was under way, via Chef Menteur and the Ponchartrain road in his rear. He doubled the garrison there, sent Latour to strengthen the defenses, and pushed scouts deep into the enemy terrain. Jackson told Livingston that he feared this assault from the rear above all else. "It's just what I'd do, if I were in Pakenham's place."

But work did not cease on the line behind the Rodriguez Canal, where the first of an odd assortment of cannon arrived on December 27, tugged into place and expertly prepared by the Laffites and their Baratarians. Crewmen from the *Carolina* mounted a 24-pounder on the line, near the river, and an ancient 12-pound howitzer was installed nearby. Three other guns were brought in on the twenty-seventh—the last of them long after nightfall.

There had been signs of an impending British assault during the day; Jackson not only hurried the placing of his five guns, he also sent hundreds of men to begin a second line of defense, along the Canal Dupré, two miles nearer New Orleans, a precaution that increased the alarm of civilians in the city.

The schooner *Carolina* was lost that morning, the twenty-seventh, blown up by red-hot shot from a British battery as she lay becalmed in the windless Mississippi, unable to move upstream against the current. Her sister ship, the larger *Louisiana,* escaped only when 100 crewmen in longboats and ashore tugged desperately to inch her upstream, beyond reach of enemy guns. The explosion of the *Carolina* was greeted with cheers from the British camp, but one of his thoughtful officers was convinced that Pakenham was making a dangerous diversion and allowing Jackson to complete his works: "While time was lost in disposing of these annoyances, the barricade was rising out of the earth like an enchantment."

Jackson's night assault on the enemy and the rapidly growing defense line had relieved the city's civilians but did not allay their sense of alarm. Some pointed out that Jackson was as inexperienced as his troops; he had faced no other enemies than the Creeks. Gossips spread a report that the general had threatened to burn the city rather than turn it over to the British, and visions of a slave uprising amid the chaos of the burning city threatened to cause panic in New Orleans.

Colonel Alexandre Declouet, a prominent Creole militia officer who was in the city on December 27, had gone to the home of Magloire Guichard, the Speaker of the House, demanding to know why the legislature was still in session—perhaps, he felt, to make a speedy surrender of the city. The agitated Declouet left the house the next morning after a long and frustrating interview, convinced that the legislature intended to treat with the British in case of Jackson's defeat. Declouet's first thought was to carry a warning to the general, but on the street he met Abner Duncan, a New Orleans lawyer who was one of Jackson's volunteer aides, and told him of his fears. Duncan rushed off to the front to find Jackson.

Pakenham's troops moved at dawn on December 28, ready to assault the line of the Rodriguez Canal. Jackson awoke to the sound of ricebirds chattering in the orange trees. The morning was balmy, with the promise of hot sunshine. In the first light the general saw a straggling band of about forty red-shirted, bearded, and begrimed men trotting past—the gunners of Dominique You and Beluche, who had run the ten miles from Fort St. John. Infantrymen in the line cheered as the Baratarians went to work, swabbing and loading a long 24-pounder at Battery No. 3.

Jackson was soon on the ramparts, studying the front. He saw his mounted pickets falling back toward the canal, followed by British troops, who emerged from behind the buildings of Bienvenu Plantation. The enemy was in two columns, one near the river and the other moving up on the edge of the cypress woods, their files bright with scarlet, green, and gray uniforms.

Jackson's officers moved restlessly along the mud earthworks, urging the untested troops to hold their fire; like their general, most of these men were now facing their first formal battle.

The Baratarian gunners waited, with matches lighted, and in the river the *Louisiana,* anchored on the flank, lay with her big guns commanding the field in Jackson's front.

The British artillery opened with a salvo of Congreve rockets, which swooped and spluttered toward the astonished Americans, sharp iron heads on 8-foot sticks that struck the earth and writhed about, exploding at last with terrifying sharp reports and puffs of black smoke. Jackson called encouragement to the apprehensive men: "Pay no attention, boys, They're only toys to amuse children."

Pakenham's infantry moved forward steadily, but when the leading files were within 500 yards of the canal, the *Louisiana*'s guns opened and tore gaps in the British left column, forcing it to disperse. The five guns in Jackson's works joined the barrage. "Scarce a ball passed over, or fell short of its mark," a British lieutenant said, "but all striking full into the midst of our ranks occasioned terrible havoc." A single shot from the ship struck fifteen men and "tossed them into the air like old bags."

The American guns also fired the Bienvenu Plantation buildings, which Jackson's scouts had filled with gunpowder during the night. The explosions flung flaming splinters and showers of ammunition among the enemy, forcing them to take cover in ditches and behind clumps of weeds and low brush. Pakenham's field guns were dragged up to challenge the Americans, but were soon blasted. The infantry now pressed forward only on Jackson's left, under orders to overrun the unfinished defense line, "mere rudiments of an entrenched camp."

Jackson was riding toward the threatened flank when he was halted by Abner Duncan, who shouted: "The Assembly is about to surrender to the enemy!"

"Did you bring a letter from Claiborne?"

"No, General."

"Who told you this?"

"Colonel Declouet."

Jackson's thin voice rose to a scream, "Where's Declouet? He should be arrested. I don't believe his story."

The general turned toward the cypress woods, where the enemy was now firing on his line from close range.

"What shall I tell the Governor?" Duncan shouted.

"Tell him to investigate, and if they persist, to blow them up!"

Duncan spurred away.

When British riflemen neared the line, a few Tennesseans jumped over the breastwork and charged, losing their captain and thirteen men to enemy marksmen. Jugeat and his Choctaws joined this counter-attack, firing from concealment in the swamp. But though a sharp skirmish raged among the cypresses for half an hour, the British pushed ahead stubbornly, and Colonel Robert Rennie was leading a party toward Jackson's exposed flank when his troops were recalled. Rennie's men fell back in disgust to join the slow retreat of the army.

The British crept rearward under artillery fire, singly and in units, taking cover in ditches, behind fences and ruined buildings. A British captain struck by a ball from Dominique You's gun stumbled for a few paces rearward while his head, blown from his shoulders, whizzed through the cane stubble before him like a football. Jeering Tennessee riflemen clambered on their parapet and shot at the fugitives. It was noon before Pakenham's infantry was safely out of range and Jackson's artillery fell silent.

Patterson's batteries had fired 800 rounds and inflicted most of the casualties. The commodore was elated. "I never knew guns better served, or a more animated fire." But Lieutenant George Robert Gleig of the British 85th Regiment made a mournful entry in his diary that evening: "Thus . . . was a British army baffled and repulsed by a horde of raw militiamen, ranged in line behind a mud wall which could hardly have protected them from musketry, far less from round shot." Every British soldier, Gleig said, felt only "shame and indignation when he found himself retreating from a force for which he entertained the most sovereign contempt."

The American losses for the day were 9 killed and 6 wounded; British casualties, though not officially reported, were estimated at about 200. Pakenham began preparations for a heavier assault. He dismissed the futile attack as only "a reconnaissance in force," rather than an effort to break Jackson's line and sweep into the city.

Jackson returned to his headquarters to find the outraged Bernard de Marigny there, demanding an explanation of the closing of the legislature. The Creole launched an impassioned defense of the Assembly and finally asked Jackson what he planned to do in case of defeat.

"If I thought the hair of my head knew my thoughts I would cut it off and burn it," Jackson said. He told Marigny to go back to the city and tell the legislature that, "if I was so unfortunate as to be beaten . . . and compelled to retreat through Neworleans, they would have a warm session." Jackson took Marigny's hand. "It's all a misunderstanding. I was in the midst of fighting when I sent word to Claiborne to blow up the legislature if he thought it wanted to capitulate."

Marigny hurried off, apparently satisfied.

Morale in Jackson's camp was high, and his frontiersmen and Creoles were "so warm for the attack" that the general tried to restrain them with a speech—they had only to remain in their works to beat off the enemy, and Louisiana would be saved. He wrote President Monroe, "As the safety of the city will depend on the fate of this army, it must not be incautiously exposed."

But he continued to harry the enemy by night. Every evening at dusk volunteers moved toward the British lines, to raid outposts, terrify sentries, and keep the enemy troops awake, sometimes by firing a few rounds from light field guns. At least fifty British soldiers died in these night forays, and many more were wounded.

One night a Tennessean crept within a few yards of a British sentinel, shot him through the head and hid his musket and equipment, killed his replacement soon afterward, then lay in wait for his next victim. Only when he had killed his third man and the corporal of the guard left the post vacant did the Tennessean return to camp, loaded with British arms and equipment. Pakenham's officers were outraged by such unsportsmanlike tactics: "Those savages have no knowledge of how war should be fought. In Europe, when two armies face each other, the outposts of neither are molested. . . . These 'dirty shirts' entertain no such chivalric notions."

A British lieutenant complained that the troops were aroused constantly during the nights, formed into column at each outbreak of American fire, to be dispersed as silence returned, then recalled at each fresh alarm. "Thus the entire night was spent," he said, without "obtaining any sound or refreshing sleep. . . . Nothing is more trying to the spirits of an army . . . we never closed our eyes in peace, for we were sure to be awakened before many minutes by the splash of a round shot or shell in the mud beside us . . . from the first moment of our landing, not a man had undressed excepting to bathe, and many had worn the same shirt for weeks." Shells lobbed into the camp at random struck a few tents and killed or maimed sleeping men.

Pakenham sent a flag of truce to protest this barbaric warfare, but Jackson replied that he was not concerned with ethics while he was resisting an invasion of his country, and warned that he would kill British soldiers wherever he found them. "It would not be safe for our respective sentries to drink out of the same stream," he warned. The British quartermaster William Surtees saw the justice of this. "We ought not to complain, as they were defending their own country . . . I trust Englishmen will be equally zealous and bitter to their enemies should our country ever be invaded."

The backwoods guerrillas were more effective than Jackson realized. The few deserters who came from the British lines reported that many others were prevented from deserting by fear of the "dirty shirt" riflemen, who shot them on sight.

11

"All seemed apathy and fatal security"

After the failure of the first assault Pakenham moved his wounded half a mile downriver and called a council of war. "Now that the infantry has failed to scare the Americans from their line, we must bring more heavy artillery from the ships. If we fail to blast them from behind that ditch, then we must storm their little mud piles."

But the recently arrived General Samuel Gibbs scorned the plan. "And if the cannon fail, how are you going to make regular approaches in this ground where you can't dig more than two feet without making a well of water? How can parallels and zigzags be pushed in such soil?" Pakenham suggested that the troops could shelter themselves from American fire by rolling hogsheads of sugar ahead of them. Gibbs left the council in disgust.

For three days British soldiers and sailors dragged big guns and mortars from Bienvenu Canal, and during the night of December 31 dug foundations for heavy batteries "with incredible toil." Thirty guns were now in place within 700 yards of Jackson's line.

Jackson's pickets heard the rumbling of sugar hogsheads being rolled through the cane stubble, but could not guess what the enemy was doing. Pakenham's artillery now outweighed Jackson's by two to one. He could concentrate his fire on the more exposed American batteries, which were mounted above the parapet on high platforms. Once Jackson's guns were dismounted, British infantry would pour through the breaches.

Jackson had now begun new defenses across the Mississippi opposite his breastworks. Latour took 300 laborers to the site, where they
threw up a line of earth some three-quarters of a mile long, supported
by a makeshift fort in an old brick kiln and a battery of big guns placed
there by Patterson.

Jackson sent a battalion of Louisiana militia and a few sailors to man
the new defenses; he then turned to the completion of the main works
along the canal. Artillery powder and ammunition were sent from the
city under orders from Governor Claiborne, who had now joined Jackson's troops in the line.

Two batteries were added to the five that had fought so well on
December 28. Captain Enoch Humphrey of the regular artillery had
his 12-pounder at Battery No. 1 on the levée. Lieutenant Otho Norris
of the U.S. Navy had two small field guns and a 6-pound howitzer at
Battery No. 2 on the River Road; Dominique You's 24-pounder was
at Battery No. 3; crewmen from the *Carolina* manned No. 4; Batteries
5 and 6 were manned by U.S. artillerymen; and No. 7 by General
Garrigues de Fleaujeac, one of the four members of the legislature who
had volunteered for combat duty. No gunners were more impatient for
action than the Laffites' Baratarians, who had provided cannon and
ammunition from their mysterious supply; their polyglot crews were
noisy swarms of Portuguese, Greeks, Italians, Hindus, Germans, and
Swedes who spoke little or no English and understood one another
with difficulty, but worked their guns with deadly efficiency.

Someone suggested the use of cotton bales, and Jackson had scores
of them taken from one of Vincent Nolte's ships and hauled into place,
stacked about the embrasures to shield the gun crews. Afterward,
made confident by his formidable works and the inactivity of the
enemy, Jackson ordered a parade for New Year's Day. Civilians were
invited to come out from New Orleans.

January 1, 1815, dawned in a dense fog. The drifting gray curtain
thinned slowly until, near 10:00 A.M., the few men on duty in Jackson's
line saw the enemy guns and rockets, some of them within 400 yards.
Band music blared from the American rear, where officers and civilians
had gathered for the review.

Pakenham's guns opened a few moments later, a roaring volley that
fell upon the Macarty House. The fire scattered civilians gathered for
the dress review. From his distance, Lieutenant Gleig saw unsuspect-
ing Americans "dressed in holiday suits . . . mounted officers . . . riding
backwards and forwards through the ranks, bands playing and colours
floating in the air . . . then suddenly our batteries opened, and the face

of affairs was instantly changed." Jackson's officers and men scrambled to their places in the earthworks.

Latour was at headquarters, where Jackson was lying on a sofa: "In less than ten minutes upwards of one hundred balls, rockets and shells struck the house . . . bricks, splinters of wood and furniture, rockets and balls, were flying in all directions." Colonel Butler was knocked down by a falling beam, but by some miracle no one was injured.

Jackson, who reached the ramparts soon after the first shellbursts, was astonished to find his line fully manned. At the first battery he saw Captain Enoch Humphrey of the U.S. artillery puffing calmly at a cigar, waiting for his men to aim his gun. When he was satisfied Humphrey called, "Let 'er off."

Jackson found Dominique You at Battery No. 3, studying the enemy through a glass. When a cannon ball whizzed past so closely that it scorched his arms, the little Frenchman screamed curses and fired a round of chainshot and scrapiron that crippled the largest British gun and killed or wounded six men.

All of Jackson's seven batteries now opened, joined by Patterson's big guns from across the river. Major Howell Tatum, who remembered the thunderous siege of Charleston during the Revolution, said he had never known "so severe a cannonade."

During the first few moments it appeared that the skillful British naval gunners would destroy Jackson's line. Nolte's cotton bales were tossed about at the first volley, and when they caught fire, obscured the vision of gunners with clouds of smoke. Crewmen pushed them into the canal, where they steamed and smoked for hours. One of Dominique You's gun carriages was smashed, Fleaujeac's battery was silenced, the carriage of Beluche's 32-pounder was damaged. A stray rocket exploded two caissons with such a roar that British gunners stopped firing, and Pakenham's infantry, waiting in the rear, broke into cheers.

Jackson, who walked restlessly down his line, saw that You's gun was idle. "Dominique, by the Eternal! Why aren't you firing?" When You complained that his powder was defective, Jackson shouted to Claiborne—who was "so frightened he could hardly speak"—"By the almighty God, if you don't send powder and balls instantly, I'll chop off your head and have it rammed in one of those guns!" Dominique's gun was soon firing steadily once more.

After half an hour the advantage turned to the American gunners. Patterson's fire from across the river disabled a British battery on the levée. Beluche's 32-pounder, repaired by its Baratarian crew, fired repeatedly at the main British battery, and as Quartermaster Surtees said, "its shot always struck the battery at first bound," then plunged into a flimsy redoubt where waiting infantrymen had taken cover: "Any of the other guns seemed like child's play to the unceasing and destructive fire of this heavy piece of ordnance. I could distinctly see that they were sailors that worked it—one of whom, a large mulatto with a red shirt, always sponged her out after firing."

Pakenham's infantrymen, pinned down in ditches behind fences and in small earthworks at the rear, called impatiently: "What are we waiting for? What's holding us back?" But there was only one infantry movement—a British flank attack through the swamp on the left, which was beaten back by Jugeat's Choctaws and three companies of Coffee's Tennesseans. As Engineer Latour said, "Wellington's heroes discovered that they were ill-qualified to contend with us in woods where they must fight knee deep in water." This flanking party, once more led by Colonel Rennie, narrowly escaped being cut off.

Within forty minutes Jackson's artillerymen had dismounted five British guns and damaged eight others so that they could not be aimed. The bulwarks of sugar hogsheads were quickly blasted apart, upsetting many guns. With only nine guns left, enemy fire slackened. The British realized too late that they had been firing too high, that most of their shot had struck in the rear of Jackson's line, and that most of the balls that hit the rampart sank harmlessly in the mud.

Pakenham ordered a withdrawal at noon, but his troops could not pull back until nightfall because of Jackson's continuing fire. The British lay in the ditches and redoubts through a rainstorm, many of them made more miserable by eating sugar from the burst hogsheads, "A thick, sticky mass of black stuff, full of grit and little splinters of cane." Men who had breakfasted before dawn ate hungrily from the "soft, sticky and sweet mudholes," and were soon suffering from nausea and diarrhea.

British artillerymen and infantrymen began removing the guns after nightfall, but it was 4:00 A.M. before the heavy pieces were dragged to the rear. About half a dozen guns were left behind for the Americans.

Lieutenant George Gleig wrote in despair,

It was a sad day for men who, a year before, had marched through France from the Pyrenees to the sea. We retired not only baffled and disappointed, but in some degree disheartened and discontented. We knew that with small arms the Americans were foemen worthy of our steel, but we did not expect them—mostly militia as they were—to get the best of an artillery combat, pure and simple . . . something like murmuring began to be heard through the camp. . . .

Gleig feared that the army was caught in a trap from which there was no escape: "All our plans had proved abortive. . . . Even this artillery attack, upon which so much reliance had been placed, was found to be of no avail . . . provisions are scanty and coarse . . . cannon and mortar play unremittingly upon us day and night . . . nothing short of a grand assault at any cost of life can extricate us from our difficulties."

Jackson issued two ounces of whiskey to each man and congratulated the army for the second check of the British. He singled out the artillerymen who had frustrated Pakenham's attack by outshooting the veteran crews of the British navy, but failed to mention the Baratarians, whose guns had done most of the damage. The general reported to Secretary of War Monroe that he could not predict whether the enemy would storm his line once more, or attempt a flanking movement, but said confidently, "I am preparing for either event." He also complained that the arms and ammunition promised him so long before had not arrived, a "negligence" that threatened the army's defeat. When a flatboat fleet bringing arms down the Mississippi failed to arrive, Jackson sent a small party of soldiers to arrest the captain of the fleet, whom he suspected of having "halted on the way for . . . private speculations."

On January 2 Old Hickory ordered his troops to repair their battered earthworks and the big guns. Another battery was put into place, and a small outpost was begun near the river, a short distance in advance of the line. The cotton bales were hauled to the rear, where men broke them open for use as mattresses. Jackson also sent crews to strengthen his second line, and began work on a third, near the outskirts of the city. He kept watch on the enemy by day and night, but could detect no signs of a threatening movement. Pakenham's continued inactivity revived Jackson's apprehensions of an attack on Mobile, or a flanking march by way of Lake Pontchartrain. Though his scouts found nothing, the general was unable to sleep. It seemed incredible that Pakenham would plan another frontal assault on his lines.

On January 3 a rider from Baton Rouge reached Jackson with word that 2,400 Kentuckians were arriving in their flatboat fleet, but that many of them were unarmed.

"I don't believe it," Jackson said. "I've never seen a Kentuckian without a gun and a pack of cards and a bottle of whiskey in my life." But he found that at least a third of the hurriedly mustered troops had come empty-handed. He sent General John Adair with about 500 well-armed Kentucky riflemen to support Carroll; these men were veterans of fighting in the northwest, including Tippecanoe. Most of the remaining Kentuckians were placed in the rear of the line to make a show of strength. These were raw militia, many of them unarmed and the rest carrying smoothbore muskets and shotguns. They were also poorly clothed, so ragged that they had passed shivering through the streets of New Orleans "holding together their garments with their hands to cover their nakedness."

Governor Shelby had expected his troops to be armed at New Orleans, but there were no guns to be had except some antiquated Spanish "escopetas" in an old arsenal. With these and other guns found in a search of private homes, Jackson armed about 1,000 of the Kentuckians after a fashion. Many of the escopetas had broken locks, were choked with rust, and lacked bayonets; but even the worst of them "made a good club in the hands of a stalwart young Kentuckian."

By January 7, Jackson had over 5,000 men at hand, about 4,000 in the main line behind the Rodriguez Canal and about 1,000 on the west bank of the river. Almost a fifth of these troops were poorly armed.

Jackson spent the afternoon of January 6 atop Macarty's house, watching enemy preparations through Patterson's telescope, and saw heavy guns being moved as if a major assault were in the making. Three British deserters entered his lines that night and confirmed the general's suspicions. A fresh brigade of British had arrived in camp and small boats had been dragged in from Lake Borgne. At roll call, the deserters said, officers had told the troops that they would be in New Orleans within forty-eight hours.

Jackson expected an attack on January 7, but the day passed quietly except for a stir in the British camp. His pickets saw the enemy hard at work, tying bundles of green sugar-cane stalks into fascines and making scaling ladders. The decision could not be far away.

Adair's Kentucky front was about 200 yards wide, 4 lines of 150 men each. They went into place at 3:00 A.M. on January 8, an addition that put 2,000 veteran riflemen on a sector previously held by 1,400. One Kentucky battalion armed with muskets and shotguns was put in Adair's rear, and 500 more Kentuckians were sent across the river to reinforce General David Morgan, who commanded there. A regiment of Louisiana militia from the upper parishes, almost 600 strong, also came in, but many of these troops were unarmed.

Pakenham had made his own inspection through a spyglass from the top of a tall pine tree and confirmed what he already knew of Jackson's works: the heavy guns were concentrated from the American center toward the river, and the left, which stretched into the swamp, was defended only by riflemen. The parapet was lower and the ditch shallower on the left, the militia there was said to be poorly disciplined, and none of them had bayonets. Sir Edward still did not suspect that his estimate of American troop strength was exaggerated; his officers calculated that Jackson had 30,000 men in line.

Final plans for the assault were made on the evening of January 7 in Villeré's house: Pakenham planned to strike two hours before dawn, attacking simultaneously on both sides of the river. A picked force of 1,400 men, led by Colonel William Thornton, with rocket batteries and small gunboats, would cross to the west bank of the Mississippi as soon as night fell. Already Thornton's troops and hundreds of others were at work, cutting a canal to the bank of the river, to move the boats into position. Thornton was to reduce Patterson's marine battery, aid the main attack by turning its guns on Jackson's line on the east bank, and then push up the river toward New Orleans. Sir Edward was confident that Jackson did not expect an attack against his weak position on the west bank.

For the assault against the Rodriguez Canal, on the east bank, Pakenham created three divisions: General Gibbs, with 2,200 troops, would strike Carroll's front on the vulnerable American left, near the swamp; General Keane would lead a sham attack against the right flank, along the river, and with him Colonel Robert Rennie would advance along the levée and river road to seize the new American redoubt there. General John Lambert, with two regiments, would remain in reserve at Villeré's.

Officers at the briefing felt that the assault would be irresistible. The only formidable American cannon on the canal front were in the heavy batteries nearer the river, where Keane was to make his feint. Gibbs would face only the lighter guns of Batteries 7 and 8, which the British did not fear—and the Gibbs column would approach within 200 yards of the canal close to the woods, its right flank covered by a West Indian black regiment advancing through the woods.

All told, 5,300 assault troops would advance on the canal. Including Thornton's force, sailors, and troops on other duty for the day, Pakenham's strength for the attack was about 8,000 men.

A few British officers expressed reservations about the plan. The charging troops were to cross the canal on piles of fascines (bundles of green sugar cane) and climb the parapet on 10-foot scaling ladders. Lieutenant Colonel Thomas Mullens of the 44th Regiment, who was ordered to carry this equipment into battle, was asked if he understood the order: "Nothing could be clearer," he said; but a few moments later he protested: ". . . My regiment has been ordered to execution. Their dead bodies are to be used as a bridge for the rest of the army to march over."

Two officers of a British rifle regiment walked over the cane-filled stubble with growing apprehension. Quartermaster William Surtees, who remembered that commanders had gone over every foot of the battlefields of the Peninsula campaign against Napoleon, saw that Pakenham and his staff and field officers had gone to bed without inspecting the terrain. "I was sadly disappointed at our not meeting with any other commanding officers engaged in this most necessary duty . . . here all seemed apathy and fatal security, arising from our too much despising our enemy." Surtees went to sleep in the early morning so despondent that he determined to take no part in the assault of the next morning, "for I almost felt confident of its failure."

Colonel Thornton was another who feared what was to come. At 9:00 P.M., long after his boats should have crossed the river, he stood on the levée and watched sailors floundering through the deep mud of the canal, dragging the boats toward the river through a few inches of water—a broken dam had drained water from the canal, and most of his boats were hopelessly mired. He pushed on with a reduced force of 340 infantrymen and a few sailors and marines.

As British troops advanced toward the main American line during the night, Colonel Mullens halted his regiment at an outpost where engineers were to have left fascines and ladders; but though the equipment was scattered about, Mullens moved forward without it, since no engineer officer appeared to deliver it.

Artillery crews dragged guns into position about 700 yards from the canal, resting them insecurely on cypress planks when digging was halted by water at a depth of 1 or 2 feet. The batteries were in place before dawn.

12

"They're near enough now, gentlemen"

The night passed quietly on the American line. Jackson was so positive that morning would bring another British attack that half the troops stood ready at their posts while the others slept under arms nearby. Sentries were posted at plantations in the rear with orders to shoot down any men who left the lines.

The general went to sleep early, rolling in his blanket on the floor at Macarty's house. Reid, Butler, Davezac, and Livingston slept in the room with him.

Jackson was aroused at 1:00 A.M. by R. D. Shepherd, Patterson's naval aide, with a report that British boats were beginning to cross the river, and that reinforcements were "most earnestly" requested for the force on the west bank. Jackson was unaware that most of the Kentuckians sent to Morgan during the afternoon had failed to reach him.

"Tell General Morgan," he said, "that I have no men to spare. He must hold his position at all hazards."

He looked at his watch, rose from his blankets, and called to his aides, "Gentlemen, we've slept enough."

Jackson led the group of officers to the line and inspected the small redoubt 30 yards in advance of the line, whose two small guns were to challenge an enemy advance along the levée. Jackson felt that the work was vulnerable. "I don't like that redoubt," he said. "I didn't want it in the first place, but my young officers talked me into it." He had yielded against his better judgment, he said, "for the first time in my life." Jackson brightened when he saw that a company of the 7th Infantry regulars was in the post, and that Beale's riflemen were nearby.

Jackson then moved slowly down the line, halting at Battery No. 3 drawn by the smell of coffee. "It was as black as tar," Colonel Butler remembered, "and its aroma could be smelled twenty yards away." Jackson found Dominique You and his gunners drinking from a drip pot that had been immersed in a bucket of hot water over the embers, coffee lovingly made by the slow process of ladling water over the grounds with a spoon.

"That smells like better coffee than we can get," Jackson said. "Maybe you smuggled it in?"

"Mebbe so, Genéral," Dominique said. He handed a cup to Jackson, who sipped it gratefully.

As he passed down the works, Jackson told Butler, "I wish I had fifty such guns on this line, with five hundred such devils at their butts." Butler was surprised to see that Jackson called by name almost every man they met on their way down the line, and exchanged familiar greetings without a hint of relaxation of discipline. The general spent more than an hour passing along the three-quarters of a mile of his works, his alert glance noting details of the defenses and the readiness of his troops. When the group came at last to Coffee's Tennesseans and the Choctaws on the far flank, amid the mudholes of the swamp, Jackson appeared to be content.

At about three o'clock a messenger told him that pickets had reported movement in the front and Jackson said abruptly, "Yes, yes. They mean to attack in force this morning. But I think they'll wait for the fog to scale up."

About this time Jackson stopped at Battery No. 8 and ordered Adair to place his reserve troops behind the point where the fronts of Carroll and Coffee joined, in the most vulnerable spot near the edge of the cypress forest. With this addition, Jackson had 5,172 men in line. He could use no more. The units were placed, from the river down the long slope to the swamp: the 7th Infantry regulars, Plauché, Lacoste, Daquin, Carroll (with Adair's Kentuckians in support), Coffee, then Jugeat's Choctaws on the turned flank. The eight batteries were spaced along the line from the river to the edge of the woods.

Near daylight, when a trace of gray appeared in the sky above the swamps, Jackson sent for his spyglass. Vision was limited to about 40 yards by a thick fog. Fires along the earthwork smoldered and added to the haze. Latour, who knew the country, predicted that the fog would lift within an hour. There was a slight breeze from the north-west, which would blow the fog toward the enemy. Two shots echoed in the darkness. "Some of my Choctaws, I guess," Jackson said. "That's where they ought to be."

Jackson mounted the parapet with Colonel Butler at sunrise, just as the British ranks became visible. Two rockets flashed into the sky, the first rising from the field in a smear of silvery blue, the second from the riverbank. "That's their signal for advance, I believe," Jackson said.

He ordered Butler and others to leave the parapet, but remained in his exposed position, studying the enemy. His troops quietly watched the approach of the British files, apparently cool and confident. Jackson sent orders along the line: the men were to keep down, pick their targets in the British ranks by aiming for the buckles on the crossbelts. They were to hold fire until the order was given.

The British advanced in silence. One of Jackson's Kentuckians imagined that he saw in the clouds "the wings of the Angel of Death." Lieutenant Samuel Spotts, an eager artilleryman in Fleaujeac's battery, found the sight of the oncoming scarlet files irresistible, and fired his 12-pounder when they were 500 yards away. The first blast tore gaps in the enemy front, but the British did not falter. Stepping over fallen comrades, they pressed toward Jackson's works, still marching in unison.

At that moment all the American guns opened, and the British batteries fired at the flashes. Richard Ogilvy, a young Kentuckian, recalled that the enemy guns "lit up in a wonderful way, though the guns themselves could not be seen. The enemy's infantry did not fire a shot, but came on with fixed bayonets."

From the British line the roaring echoes were so fierce that "the vibration seemed as if the earth was cracking and tumbling into pieces . . . the woods seemed to crack to an interminable distance, each cannon report was answered one hundred fold. . . . The flashes of fire looked as if coming out of the bowels of the earth. . . . The reverberation was so intense towards the great wood, that any one would have thought the fighting was going on there."

The American guns soon halted. Adair and Coffee sent word that their smoke would prevent the waiting riflemen from finding their marks, and Jackson silenced the artillery.

A few minutes later Jackson spoke quietly to Carroll and Adair, "They're near enough now, gentlemen. Fire when ready."

Adair stepped to the side of one of his sharpshooters, Morgan Ballard. "Morg, see that officer on the gray horse?"

Ballard nodded.
"Snuff his candle!"
Morgan fired, and a British officer fell from his saddle.

The dead officer was Major John Anthony Whitaker of the 21st Foot of General Gibbs's brigade. A British onlooker saw the major's death from the balcony at de La Ronde's: "At a distance of nearly three hundred yards! As if to warn us of the fate in store!" Ballard's bullet entered just above the major's ear and passed through the head. From the British position it looked as if the entire army might suffer the same fate: "Instantly the whole American line, from the swamp to a point past its center was ablaze. In less time than one can write it, the Forty-Fourth Foot was literally swept from the face of the earth . . . the regiment seemed to vanish from sight—except the half of it that lay stricken on the ground. Every mounted officer was down at the first fire. No such execution by small arms has ever been seen or heard of."

Under shelter of the levée Rennie's column hurried toward the advance redoubt on Jackson's right; though two-thirds of them fell, the survivors swarmed over the vulnerable redoubt and within a minute's fighting overcame the garrison and took the post. Now only 50 feet from Jackson's main line, with only the canal in his path, Rennie ordered his men to take cover and began looking for reinforcements. With Keane's support, he could turn Jackson's flank and drive into the American rear.

But Keane had turned his column to the right in support of Gibbs, and the British opportunity was lost. Gibbs and Keane now pressed forward, the 21st Regiment marching over the casualties of the mangled 44th, its men determined to scale Jackson's earthworks though they knew that most of the ladders had been left behind. The ranks moved rapidly toward the mud ramparts—400 yards, 300, 200 . . .

At that moment, as Butler saw it, "The whole line, from Carroll's Tennesseans to the swamp was almost one solid blaze." Jackson's men stood four ranks deep, firing and loading continuously, each aiming and shooting in turn, stepping rearward to allow the next to take its place, so that the spurting of flame from the rifle and musket barrels was virtually unbroken. Every rifleman in the line seemed to find his mark. As one British officer saw it, his men fell "like blades of grass beneath the scythe."

Quartermaster E. N. Burroughs, watching from de La Ronde's house, wrote of these moments: "Never before had British veterans quailed. But . . . that leaden torrent no man on earth could face." In a few minutes the column was broken and disorganized, and units began to fall back in a retreat that became a rout. More than half of Gibbs's column had fallen, carpeting the ground in Jackson's front with dead and wounded. Every mounted British officer on this front had disappeared, "and such as had escaped death or wounds were running as fast as their legs could carry them to the rear—anywhere to get out of reach of those awful rifles." Gibbs sent 300 men rearward to bring up the fascines and ladders, and spurred forward through the panic-stricken troops, shouting, "If I live till tomorrow I'll hang Mullens to the highest tree!" Officers beat at retreating soldiers with the flats of their swords, and the column halted and rallied briefly to the attack.

Lieutenant Leavock led a few of his men of the 21st to the canal, where they looked in vain for timbers or ladders to throw across. Some who leaped into the ditch were shot from above, and only Leavock scrambled to the top of the breastwork, where he was confronted by two American officers. He first demanded their surrender, then realized his plight and gave up his sword.

A few other British soldiers made their way into Jackson's works, but were overpowered at once and killed or captured. Those who were left behind, a British officer reported, "were exposed to a sweeping fire which cut them down by whole companies. . . . They fell by the hands of men whom they absolutely did not see; for the Americans, without so much as lifting their faces above the rampart, swung their firelocks by one arm over the wall, and discharged them directly on their heads."

Colonel Rennie and his men, pinned down in their captured redoubt, were now forced to move by the riflemen of the 7th Regulars, who fired at every movement and shot several men through the head. When Rennie saw the division of Gibbs in flight and Keane's men quartering away to the right, leaving his trapped garrison to its fate, he led his survivors in a desperate rush down the walls and over a plank spanning the ditch. Some of those who fell into the ditch drowned, others were shot down, and only Rennie, clawing his way up the slippery mudbank, reached the top of Jackson's works, where one of Beale's riflemen shot him through the head and tumbled his body into the ditch.

Keane's leading files, thrown into the support of Gibbs, were struck by a hail of fire. One officer who emerged from a "little world of mist" caught a glimpse of the action: "The first objects which we saw . . . were the cannon balls tearing up the ground and crossing one another and bounding along like so many cricket balls through the air."

General Keane fell from his horse, shot through the neck, a severe but not fatal wound. His Highlanders hesitated in confusion, their ranks disordered by the fugitives of Gibbs's division, who fled in all directions, flinging down arms and knapsacks as they went. A captain who moved up with a rear rank called to a retreating soldier, "Have we or the Americans attacked?"

"The Americans!" the soldier called, racing on to the rear.

General Pakenham rode into the mêlée with his aide, Duncan McDougall, and General John Lambert, dismayed by the sight of his men crouching in ditches and among underbrush. "That's a terrific fire, Lambert," Pakenham said, and rode forward to rally the remaining troops, shouting to the Highlanders and waving his hat to cheer them on. Gibbs rode up and reported that his men were out of control and would no longer obey him.

Pakenham shouted to the crouching figures about him, "Shame! Shame! Remember you're British! Forward, gentlemen, forward!" The Scotsmen responded by dropping their knapsacks and charging toward Jackson's line. For a moment the tall Pakenham, riding in the van, was spared by the riflemen, but he was downed by artillery fire— one ball knocked his horse to the ground and another struck the general's shoulder.

McDougall sprang to his side, but Pakenham waved him away, mounted McDougall's horse, and rode forward. The commander was shot almost at once. One rifle ball struck his throat and another just below the ribs. Pakenham slid from his mount into McDougall's arms and gave a final order in a low voice. "Have Lambert bring up the reserve," he said.

A staff officer took the news to Gibbs, who was riding in circles as if demented by the disaster.

"They've killed the General, Sir. You are now in command."

Gibbs roared, "Where are the Highlanders? What's the matter with the Highlanders?"

"They can't be urged to go further. They're nearly destroyed already."

"Then get them out of the way!" Gibbs shouted. He galloped toward the American ramparts alone in a mad charge, was brought down by four bullets, and borne, cursing violently, to the rear, where he was to die a lingering, agonized death.

Along Jackson's line elated riflemen clambered on the breastworks, loading and firing while fully exposed, defying Jackson's order to take cover.

The general told Carroll, "The only thing I fear now, William, is that

those desperate boys will go over the works when the enemy breaks
—as they will any second now."

Ensign Robert Polk of a Tennessee company sprang on the parapet
with his tomahawk, shouting, "Follow me, boys! Charge 'em!"

Jackson roared, "Down, sir, down! Back to your post!"

Polk leaped into the ditch and Jackson fumbled at his waist, found
that he was unarmed, and borrowed a pair of pistols from Captain
William O. Butler. "Now," he called in a ringing voice, "I'll shoot the
first man who dares go over the works. We must have order here." No
one followed Polk into the ditch.

Within twenty-five minutes the three ranking British commanders
had been carried from the field, the cane stubble was littered with
bodies, and the British troops had fallen back in panic. Lambert made
an attempt to move up his reluctant reserves and then ordered a
retreat.

Jackson's rifles blazed until 8:30 A.M., but his cannon fired on until
2:00 P.M., blasting the field where the British bodies lay. Some of the
wounded crawled away, "but every now and then some unfortunate
man was lifted off the ground by round shot, and lay killed or mangled." A British officer who lay on the field watched a wounded man
among the corpses 200 yards to the rear, who "continued without any
cessation, for two hours, to raise his arm up and down with a convulsive motion . . . a dreadful magnet of attraction."

Men began to rise from the field. "I never had so grand and awful
an idea of the resurrection," Jackson said, "as when I saw . . . more
than five hundred Britons emerging from the heaps of their dead
comrades, all over the plain rising up, and . . . coming forward . . . as
prisoners."

Colonel Thornton launched his belated attack on the west bank of
the river only after rifle and musket fire had ceased in Jackson's front.
Old Hickory watched helplessly as the British boats blasted the Kentucky militia at close range, while Thornton's infantry charged and
drove them back into Morgan's unfinished earthwork. The Kentuckians fired, but the redcoats charged steadily on in two columns and
flanked the line, so that Patterson could not fire his big guns without
slaughtering his own troops. Caught between the hail of grapeshot and
swarming bayonets, the Kentuckians fled, exposing the Louisiana militia, who also broke. Patterson spiked his guns, dumped his ammunition in the river, and joined the flight upstream. The British chased the
fugitives for more than a mile, but it was too late. The battle had been
lost on the canefields of the east bank. Lambert ordered Thornton to
bring his men back across the river.

Jackson agreed to a two-hour truce in the afternoon and sent troops to help the British move their dead and wounded, 1,971 in all. Jackson's losses were seven killed and six wounded.

Bodies lay so thickly in the canefield that one officer said he could have walked over them for a quarter of a mile without stepping on the ground. The carnage was almost beyond belief.

The 44th Regiment, which had been within rifle range no longer than 20 minutes, had been reduced from 816 to 134 men, and ended under command of a lieutenant, 1 of 5 officers surviving from the 31 who had gone into battle. The Sutherland Highlanders had lost 876 of 1,008 men in less than half an hour—and only 3 of their 103-man color company escaped unhurt.

A British sergeant who walked over the littered field as burial parties began their work noted that almost 1,000 British bodies were gathered from an area a few hundred yards wide: "Not a single American was among them; all were English; and they were thrown by the dozens into shallow holes . . . with a slight covering of earth." The sergeant was outraged by an American officer who stood watching, smoking a cigar, "apparently counting the slain with a look of savage exultation." Again and again, to every man who came near, the American called triumphantly, "We lost only eight dead, and fourteen wounded—only twenty two of the whole shebang!"

One British corpse was that of a tall Highlander color sergeant who had been shot twice through the head, over the left eye and near the right eye. The two bullets had obviously struck simultaneously, fired by marksmen who stood almost 200 yards apart. "A little lead wasted there," one dour Tennessean said.

The British quartermaster Burroughs noted that few of these men had fallen under cannon fire. "Nearly all fell to the rifles . . . an appalling proportion . . . were shot through the head." The tiny rifle balls, about a third the size of a British musket ball, left only minute "purple spots, from which the blood oozed slowly, but life went out as the ball went in."

Jackson had 300 British wounded carried into New Orleans and placed in barracks, where civilians brought large quantities of bedding, cotton, and linen for bandages, though such materials were so scarce in the city that "not a truss of straw could be purchased."

The British buried their dead on Bienvenu Plantation. Most of the officers were buried in Villeré's garden, but the bodies of Pakenham and Gibbs were disemboweled and crammed into rum-filled casks for shipment to England.

Still wary of further attacks, Jackson held his troops in their works, and for ten days his artillerymen kept up a sporadic fire on the enemy camp. He proposed an attack across the canefields, to be led by the Mississippi cavalry, but was dissuaded by Coffee and Adair, who warned that a charge across the open plain by raw militia might end in disaster. Edward Livingston protested: "What do you want more? . . . The city is saved."

Lambert's army disappeared during the night of January 18, leaving campfires burning and dummy figures guarding the picket lines. By the time Jackson and his staff rode into the abandoned camp, the British were far away, struggling toward their fleet over a crude roadway of saplings laid across the marshy prairies.

Though he was satisfied that Lambert would not return to the battlefield, Jackson feared a blow against the city from other directions. He wrote General Winchester at Mobile:

> Major General Lambert is said to have went crazy. Should this crippled army attempt to visit you on their passage home you will give a good account of them . . . I have no idea that the enemy will attempt Fort Bowyer, or your quarter. Still you cannot be too well prepared or too vigilant. . . . They may in this situation attempt some act of madness— if their Panic does not prevent it.

13

"If we had a Jackson everywhere . . . "

Jackson hurried news of the victory northward by Billy Phillips, who galloped almost as swiftly as he had in bringing word of the war's opening to Tennessee. Billy reached Nashville on January 14, and other riders carried the tidings northward, leaving wild celebrations in their wake. In Washington a gloomy James Madison waited in Colonel John Tayloe's Octagon House, the temporary Executive Mansion, presiding over a defeated nation whose treasury was empty, its credit ruined. When the government sought to borrow $6 million, it was offered only half of that—at 20 percent interest. The President had been forced to pledge his own credit to the city's bankers to obtain money to send arms down the Mississippi to Jackson's troops, a transaction that was to impoverish him in his old age. The coast was blockaded, trade had been halted, and thousands of working men were idle. Cadets of the military academy at West Point, who were out of firewood, tore down fences and old buildings and uprooted shrubs to warm themselves. The war was a failure at best; there was every reason to believe that Madison's commissioners at Ghent must pay a ruinous price for peace and equally ominous news was anticipated from Connecticut's Hartford Convention, which had been debating the possible secession of New England. From New Orleans, Madison had heard only that the British had landed in overwhelming strength; news of disaster was expected.

Word of Jackson's victory touched off spontaneous rejoicing in Washington. From the moment that Dolley Madison illuminated the Octagon House with scores of candles, a new mood spread through the country. The nation's surging pride was reflected in newspaper headlines:

ALMOST INCREDIBLE VICTORY!!
GLORIOUS NEWS
RISING GLORY OF THE AMERICAN REPUBLIC
GLORIOUS!!
UNPARALLELED VICTORY

As swiftly as the news spread, Jackson became the most celebrated man in the country, the first genuine national hero since Washington; Americans assumed from the first that the conquest of the British was peculiarly his own. The miracle of New Orleans was not diminished by arrival of news of the Treaty of Ghent in mid-February. The nation's joy seemed the greater because the war's greatest American victory had been won after the peace treaty had been signed.

Rather than deploring lives needlessly lost, Washington exulted. The *Enquirer* said, "How fortunate it is for the U.S. that the peace did not arrive *before* the attack was made on N. Orleans. How elegantly does it round off the war! It is the last touch to the picture!" Congressman Ingersoll told the House, "The terms of the Treaty are yet unknown to us. But the victory at Orleans has rendered them glorious and honorable be what they may. . . . The nation now . . . is above disgrace." The *New Hampshire Patriot* declared that "the brilliant and unparalleled victory . . . has closed the war in a blaze of glory . . . and placed America on the very pinnacle of fame." And in Paris Henry Clay, fresh from service on the peace commission, said fervently, *"Now,* I can go to England without mortification."

In four brief engagements during his first formal military campaign, Jackson had revived American nationalism. In the words of a critical twentieth-century historian: "Through Andrew Jackson, the American people were vicariously purged of shame and frustration. At a moment of disillusionment, Andrew Jackson reaffirmed the young nation's self-belief; he restored its sense of national prowess and destiny."

The nation's almost hysterically grateful reception of the news from New Orleans was universally uncritical. It was to be many years before scholars noted that the British defeat had become virtually inevitable with their choice of the approach route and the battlefield, and that Pakenham had ensured disaster by pressing his complicated plan of assault after the dawn light had exposed his advancing infantry to Jackson's marksmen on January 8.

More than a century was to pass before critics were to find fault with Jackson's campaign strategy, to suggest that he had been surprised by the appearance of the British despite ample warning, that he had belatedly perceived the threat to New Orleans, and that he had not been prompt in ordering arms or assembling entrenching tools—or in fortifying the western bank of the river. Even later critics were to insist that Jackson owed his victory more to the skill of his artillerists—particularly the neglected Baratarian pirates—than to the legendary skill of his frontier riflemen. But it remained that Jackson was a peerless leader in battle, inspiring men to their best through the example of his indomitable spirit.

To most Americans, in any event, the stunning victory was above criticism, and it was forever linked with the name and fame of Andrew Jackson.

The engineer Latour helped to create the legend that Jackson had won the victory singlehandedly, through the sheer exertion of will: "Although his body was ready to sink under the weight of sickness, fatigue and continued watching, his mind nevertheless, never lost for a moment that energy which he knew well how to communicate to all that surrounded him . . . the energy manifested by General Jackson spread, as it were, by contagion, and communicated itself to the whole army."

The country accepted this almost literally. The *New York Evening Post* said, "If we had a Jackson everywhere we should succeed everywhere."

News of the victory reached Jonesboro, Tennessee, in a letter that was read to a crowd before the courthouse. The reader departed from the written report to add that Jackson had killed the whole British army on the battlefield, except for a few who were driven into the Mississippi and drowned; he had captured all their arms and ships, had taken his own army aboard the vessels—and was already crossing the Atlantic to conquer England herself! An old man in the crowd who remembered Jackson as a boy jockey in 1788 threw his hat in the air, jumped up and down, and shouted, "Whoopee and hoorah for Andy Jackson, hell and thunder. I knowd the day I seed him ride that horse in Greasy Cove he could whip anybody."

When he was told that the arrival of the news from New Orleans in Virginia had inspired Jefferson to preside over a Jackson celebration and offer a toast, Old Hickory said, "I'm glad the old gentleman has plucked up courage enough to at least attend a banquet in honor of a battle!"

Jackson himself came to regard the victory as miraculous, and spoke of it in some of the rare religious expressions of his life. He told Major Davezac, "Ever since the battle of the night of the 23d . . . I have had the sense that these things occurred to me before, and had been obliterated; and when I observed it, I was sure of success, for I knew that God would not give me previsions of disaster, but signs of victory. He said this ditch can never be passed. It cannot be done."

As one historian put it, Jackson accepted graciously the notion that he had served as "the right hand of God." He wrote Robert Hays: "It appears that the unerring hand of Providence shielded my men from the shower of Balls, bombs, and Rockets, when every Ball and Bomb from our guns carried with them a mission of death." And to Monroe he wrote, "Heaven, to be sure, has interposed most wonderfully in our behalf, and I am filled with gratitude when I look back to what we have escaped. . . ."

Other legends rose from the battlefield below New Orleans before the guns had ceased firing, and there were other bids for glory. Frontier riflemen were quick to lay claim to their share in victory, especially the Kentuckians, whose valor and marksmanship were celebrated in "The Hunters of Kentucky," a new ballad that swept the country:

> . . . But Jackson he was wide awake and wasn't
>   scar'd at trifles,
> For well he knew what aim we take
>   with our Kentucky rifles;
> So he led us down to a cypress swamp,
>   the ground was wet and mucky,
> There stood John Bull in
>   martial pomp, but here is old Kentucky . . .

Jackson's war did not end when the guns fell silent on the riverside battlefield. He was now caught up in a struggle with civilian New Orleans in which he was to play a less spectacular role, but one which was to expand his fame as a folk hero.

On January 21 the general led his troops from the battlefield, which rains had made into a quagmire permeated by the stench of death. British bodies had risen from the swampy soil, and arms, legs, and heads protruded from the shallow graves. American troops had become sickly; more than 500 died of fevers within 2 weeks. The troops marched into New Orleans where, at Jackson's request, the abbé Guillaume Dubourg had agreed to hold a thanksgiving service in the cathedral.

The troops were greeted with wild enthusiasm by a throng of 2,500 packed into the Place d'Armes as the tattered column swung past to the tune of "Yankee Doodle" and the roll of cannon fire. Jackson suspended the curfew and the city roared all night. The general appeared in the Place the next day, walked under a triumphal arch, was crowned with laurel wreaths, and passed slowly between two rows of singing children in white robes, who held flags and strewed his path with flowers. He was greeted warmly by abbé Dubourg: "The first impulse of your religious heart was to acknowledge the signal interposition of Providence."

The abbé followed the general's lead in attributing the city's salvation to God, and in the process all but beatified Jackson:

> . . . it is Him we chiefly intend to praise, when considering you, General, as the man of his right hand, whom he has taken pains to fit out for the important mission of our defence; we extol that fecundity of genius, by which, in a moment of the most discouraging distress, you . . . raised as it were from the ground, hosts of intrepid warriors . . . To Him we trace that instinctive superiority of your mind . . . Immortal thanks be to His supreme majesty, for sending us such a gift of his bountiful designs! . . .

Jackson responded briefly and the choir began to chant the *Te Deum*, joined at once by people who packed the square and filled windows, doors, and rooftops in every direction.

A few hours after this ceremony Jackson turned at last to the case of the six mutinous Tennessee militiamen who had defied authority at the end of the Creek war, and had been under sentence of death in Mobile for two months. He wrote a careful review of the case and approved the sentence. The men were shot in Mobile a few days later, facing death bravely and protesting their innocence to the last. Though the general was not responsible for the verdict of the court, he might have modified it, but felt that the national defense was at stake and that mutiny must be crushed at all costs.

Scouts had reported that the British had been reinforced by fresh regiments, and that Lambert's army, now 15,000 strong, was approaching Mobile aboard Cochrane's fleet. Jackson was confident that Winchester would defeat them; and if the enemy should return to New Orleans, Jackson reported, "I am ready." He had yet to reckon with the carefree people of the city.

New Orleans awoke from its brief celebration to discover that it was still under martial law and that Jackson had no intention of relaxing his rigid control until the danger of a second British assault had passed. Curfew was imposed once more. Militiamen who had expected to be mustered out were marched to new camps on the outskirts of the city and drilled daily. There was a clamor of protest. Jackson's popularity waned overnight.

The Assembly passed a resolution of praise for the saviours of New Orleans, but though it named officers down to the rank of captain, made no mention of General Jackson. The House voted Old Hickory a commemorative sword—a proposal that was killed in the Senate through the influence of Bernard de Marigny. The legislators had not forgotten Jackson's one-day suspension of their sessions in December.

The general faced more serious problems that threatened to develop into full-scale rebellion. Governor Claiborne urged Jackson to release the militia, and was not impressed when he was reminded that the enemy was only four days away. Claiborne now openly sympathized with the Louisiana militiamen, and persisted in his demands that they be disbanded even after news that the enemy had taken Fort Bowyer by assault, leaving Mobile vulnerable to siege.

At this moment Edward Livingston returned from a mission to the British fleet, bringing a rumor that the war was over, a report based on a story in a six-weeks'-old London newspaper. This was enough for New Orleans. The city forgot Fort Bowyer and turned to its own celebration of peace. Prices of cotton, sugar, tobacco, livestock, and furs skyrocketed in a flurry of speculation as merchants and traders scrambled to create new fortunes from goods accumulated on the wharves and in the bulging warehouses during two years of the war's blockade. Within less than a week the price of cotton almost trebled, from 6 to 16 cents per pound. Eager skippers prepared their ships for sea, but Jackson forbade them to sail, and issued a general order to the people of the city: "You must not be thrown into a false sense of security by hopes that may prove delusive. It is by holding out such that an artful and insidious enemy too often seeks to accomplish what the utmost exertions of his strength will not enable him to effect." The order went unheeded, and the clamor for a return to civilian control grew daily.

Livingston then apparently told some of his friends that the reports of peace were based on evidence more substantial than newspaper rumors—Admiral Cochrane had shown him a British Foreign Office bulletin announcing that a peace treaty would take effect upon ratification.

Jackson received a copy of this bulletin on February 21, and a few moments later heard newsboys selling handbills in the streets, shouting that Cochrane's boat had brought Jackson news of the treaty at Ghent. The handbills were printed by the *Louisiana Gazette,* whose editor was Livingston's intimate friend. Jackson immediately ordered the "unauthorized and improper" handbills destroyed and forced the *Gazette* to publish a retraction, saying that no truce could take place until final ratification of the treaty. Jackson added a final plea:

"The Commanding General again Calls upon his fellow Citizens and Soldiers to recollect that . . . until . . . peace is properly announced there can be no relaxation in the army under his command." It was to no avail.

The arrival of Rachel and young Andrew Jr. during the tumult diverted the grim Jackson and provided a temporary truce. Rachel was taken over at once by women of the city, who were in the midst of preparations for a ball on Washington's birthday. Rachel was becoming only slightly gray at forty-eight, and though her beauty had faded in middle age, her manners remained those of the vivacious, sensible, unaffected frontier girl of her youth. She was short, fat, matronly, and by the standards of the city's Creole society hopelessly dowdy. Vincent Nolte found her "simple-mannered and homely-gaited."

Edward Livingston's wife surveyed Rachel in her unfashionable back-country clothes and ordered cloth and French seamstresses to produce a gown fit for the wife of a new national hero to wear to the Washington's Birthday ball. A local cartoonist depicted this tableau with Rachel standing on a table while Mrs. Livingston tugged at the strings of her stays in a desperate effort to contain her bulging waistline.

Rachel was dazzled by the sights of the city: "I have seen more already than in all my life past it is the finest Country for the Eye of a Strainger but a Little while he tir[e]s of the Disipation. . . . So much amusement balls Concerts Plays theatres &c &c but we Don't attend the half of them. I herd a band of musick a few Evinings since." She was all but overcome by the pomp of the dinner and ball staged by the elegant Creoles on Washington's Birthday: "The Splendor, the brilliant assemblage the Magnificenc of the Supper and orniments of the room . . ."

A roster of American heroes, displayed in gold letters on glass, was lighted with candles: "as we Sat at Supper I was placed opposit the Motto Jackson and Victory are one on the table a most Ellegant piremid on the top was Vivi Jackson in Large Letters on the other Sed the Immortal Washington—ther was a gold ham on the table. . . ."

The highlight of the evening was the rendition of a frontier dance by Jackson and Rachel, a throwback to the days of their youth in the Donelson blockhouse. Vincent Nolte left a glimpse of the performance: "The general a long, haggard man, with limbs like a skeleton, and Madame le Générale, a short, fat dumpling, bobbing opposite each other like half-drunken Indians, to the wild melody of *Possum up de Gum Tree,* and endeavoring to make a spring into the air . . . very remarkable."

At the grand ball, so delighted gossips reported, a woman who asked Rachel how she was feeling was informed, "Poorly, thank God. The ginral kicked the kivvers off and we all kotch cold."

The ball was a brief interlude in Jackson's vigil. As Rachel wrote home, "of all men in Erth he Does the most Business from Day Light to ten at night." The general still feared that the British would strike again at any moment, that since Lambert had taken Fort Bowyer he might drive for the city through Mobile. He kept his troops on the alert, guarding all approaches.

His Louisiana militia melted away alarmingly, in response to the pleas of their women. Even the abbé Dubourg risked his uncertain English to beg Jackson to release the troops: "A Number of unfortunate half starved women of Terre Aux Bouefs fall at your feet to redemand you their husbands." French citizens in the ranks discovered that they could be discharged by registering their nationality with the French consul, Louis de Tousard, and many of them disappeared. Native Creoles who learned of this also applied for French citizenship papers, with Tousard's cooperation. Jackson retaliated by deporting the newly created aliens to Baton Rouge, and when he protested, Tousard was sent after them.

The general was faced with a city-wide mutiny when *Le Courrière du Louisiane* published a demand for an end to martial law. "It is high time the laws should resume . . . that citizens accused of any crime should be rendered to their natural judges. . . . The moment for moderation has arrived."

Louisiana militiamen posted at Chef Menteur became mutinous in the wake of this provocation, and a New Orleans company refused to march out to take their places. Jackson did not rest until he had discovered the author of the article, Louis Louaillier, a member of the legislature who had strongly supported the war. Jackson arrested him. When Judge Dominick Hall issued a writ of habeas corpus, Jackson arrested the judge and imprisoned him in the barracks with Louaillier. Excitement increased the next day with the arrival of a courier from Washington who carried a letter identifying him as the bearer of official news of peace; but though he brought dispatches for Jackson, none of them mentioned peace. Jackson was confident that the missing document was due to a clerical error—yet though he promptly notified General Lambert that the treaty had almost certainly been ratified, he delayed his public announcement until the next day, when he released the Louisiana draftees and allowed the banished Creoles to return from Baton Rouge.

At Jackson's insistence Louaillier was tried by a court-martial; when the editor was acquitted, the enraged general sent Louaillier back to his cell and had Judge Hall escorted to the city limits and set free.

Two days later, on March 13, official word of the ratification of the peace treaty reached headquarters. Jackson revoked martial law within an hour, set free his prisoners, released the Louisiana volunteers, and ordered Mississippi, Kentucky, and Tennessee troops to prepare for the homeward march. On March 16 the general reassembled the army on the battlefield and read a farewell address that undoubtedly owed much to John Reid:

> You have secured to America a proud name among the nations of the earth, a glory which will never perish. . . . Go, then, my brave companions to your homes, to those tender connections and those blissful scenes which render life so dear—full of honor and crowned with laurels which will never fade. . . . The expression of your General's thanks is feeble; but the gratitude of a country of freemen is yours; yours the applause of an admiring world!

The last of the volunteers left for home within a week, leaving a small force of regulars in the city. There were no further threats from the enemy. But Jackson was caught up in the settlement of innumerable claims for property seized under martial law, claims he was to spend six weeks in settling with characteristic disregard for the letter of the law. Though his authority was limited to certifying the validity of these claims, Jackson drew drafts for payment on the War Department, which honored them without protest despite their irregularity.

Jackson was still embroiled with these claims when Judge Hall summoned him into court on a charge of contempt. The British-born Dominick Hall, as one of his friends said, was "a magistrate of pure heart, clean hands, and a mind susceptible of no fear but that of God," and he was by no means in awe of Jackson. The general appeared in the courtroom with John Reid, who offered to read a lengthy explanation of Jackson's conduct of martial law in the city, and his suspension of Hall's writ of habeas corpus. Hall declined to hear the argument and ordered Jackson to reappear a few days later.

The hearing drew hundreds of Jackson's indignant supporters—a throng that filled the old red-tiled Spanish courthouse and overflowed into the street. Hall's courtroom was crowded "to suffocation" when Jackson made a dramatic entrance, dressed in new civilian clothing, escorted by several of his officers. The throng remained silent until the general reached the bar and stood before the impassive Judge Hall. At that moment, led by the Laffites and their Baratarians, the crowd broke into a roar: "One wild yell of defiance, which was echoed by the multitude outside, swept over the building and seemed to shake the roof and walls." Jackson turned to face the crowd "with an expression of calm and august majesty," and waved a hand. The room fell silent. Jackson bowed to the judge.

The clerk called sharply, "The United States versus Andrew Jackson." The district attorney read the charges, and concluded with a challenge: "Despotism is not martial law. It is the absence of all laws. We are compelled, therefore, to attribute the arbitrary proceedings of the defendant, not to his conviction of their necessity, but to the indulged infirmity of an obstinate and morbidly irascible temperament, and to the unyielding pride of a man naturally impatient of the least show of opposition to his will."

The prosecutor then passed a list of questions to Jackson's attorneys, Edward Livingston and Abner Duncan. Jackson stood and read a statement:

> I will not answer interrogatories. . . . You would not hear my defense. . . . Under these circumstances I appear before your Honor to receive the sentence of the court. . . .
>
> Your Honor will not understand me as meaning any disrespect to the court . . . but as no opportunity has been furnished me to explain the reasons and motives which influenced my conduct, so it is expected that censure will form no part of that punishment which your Honor may imagine it your duty to perform.

Hall made a brief, dignified response: No one could forget the general's services to the country, he said. Imprisonment would be unthinkable. Still, it was clear that Jackson had refused to respond to the queries of the court, and was in contempt. "The only question was whether the Law should bend to the General or the General to the Law." It was his unpleasant duty, Hall said, to fine Jackson $1,000 and costs.

Men rushed from the crowd, seized the general, and carried him on their shoulders into the street, where they halted a carriage in which a woman was riding, "politely" removed her, and thrust the protesting Jackson into the seat. The Baratarians then removed the horses and dragged the carriage through the streets, laughing and shouting. Vincent Nolte, who watched the scene, noted that civilians "blushed to see this procession, and the General himself seemed to dislike it." The crowd carried Jackson to a coffeehouse, where he made a speech:

> During the invasion I did my best to defend and preserve the Constitution and the laws. Today, I was called upon to submit to them under circumstances that might have justified resistance. But I believe that the first duty of a citizen is to obey the laws, even when they may be unjustly applied, and so I will not hesitate to comply with the sentence you have heard. I beg you to remember the example. . . .

Jackson sent Reid to the courthouse with a check to pay his fine, but the general's friends began a collection to raise $1,000, with individual contributions limited to $1. Jackson ended the campaign by declining to accept the purse. He asked that the money raised be given to the widows and orphans of men who had died in the battle.

The story of the general's clash with Judge Hall spread through the country in the wake of the news of victory at New Orleans, adding greatly to his fame.

14

"A triumph over the constitution"

The Jacksons left the city April 5, 1815, on a homeward journey that became a triumphal procession, halted at every town and hamlet by banquets or fanfares of welcome. It was forty days before they reached Nashville, where the weary general was welcomed once more, subjected to yet another banquet, and presented with ceremonial swords by the states of Mississippi and Tennessee. There was word that Congress had voted a medal to the hero of New Orleans.

When he returned to the Hermitage at last after an almost unbroken absence of two years, Jackson found the plantation prospering from high prices of cotton and tobacco; thanks to land sales and his army salary and allowances, he was out of debt for the first time in twenty years. He was also a man of mystery, though he was the most celebrated man in the United States at the moment. Jackson moved to supply the deficiency of information about him by turning over his carefully preserved papers to John Reid, so that he could write a biography.

Jackson had returned home in poor health, and spent the summer recuperating, enjoying himself with young Andrew, and the boy's constant companion, Lincoyer, the Creek boy who had been rescued from among the survivors of Tallushatchee. But there was a distracting air of excitement at the Hermitage. The national elections were only a year away and there were unmistakable signs that Jackson was being

seriously considered as a presidential candidate. William Carroll returned from a trip to report that "many leading characters" in Kentucky, Ohio, and Pennsylvania hoped that the general would make the
race. Arthur Hayne of South Carolina, who had served at New Orleans,
wrote: "You are the favorite . . . in the *New England* States." General
Adair, it was reported, was confident that with "proper management,"
Jackson "might be elevated to the highest office in the American Government." The general's ward, Anthony Butler, reported that he had
traveled through Pennsylvania and Virginia, talking with influential
men, and found "a strong disposition . . . to run your Name for the
Presidency." Young Butler urged Jackson "to stand a candidate."

The general was not yet tempted. He maintained a complete silence
about the campaign, and rested until October, when he set off for
Washington by carriage, accompanied by Rachel and young Andrew
and John Reid. Ostensibly Jackson went to the capital to consult with
the War Department on the reorganization of the army, but his real
purpose was to challenge a move to court-martial him for his treatment
of Judge Hall and Louaillier. Jackson sent ahead blistering letters
denouncing his critics, and threatening the impeachment of Hall, then
rode slowly through the autumn countryside, frequently halted by
committees of welcome but avoiding all reference to politics until he
reached Lynchburg, Virginia.

The general was met outside the Virginia hill city by a delegation
and escorted to an elaborate banquet in his honor attended by 300
people, among them Thomas Jefferson, now seventy-two, who had
come down from Monticello to greet the hero. It was the first meeting
of the two since the trial of Aaron Burr, but they exchanged toasts and
parted with an outward show of friendship. The Jacksons reached
Washington in mid-November, where they were entertained at a round
of dinners and banquets. They dined with James and Dolley Madison
and found the President warm and friendly, with high praise for the
general's conduct of affairs in New Orleans.

Jackson called at the War Department "fully prepared" for battle, as
John Reid reported, but acting Secretary of War George Dallas would
not so much as listen to the general's explanation of his clash with
Judge Hall. "The President and the heads of all departments are satisfied," Dallas said. No official inquiry had been considered.

The Jacksons dined twice with James Monroe, who was the leading
candidate for President. The little Virginian, described by his critics as
"a dull, sleepy, insignificant-looking man" who "hasn't got brains
enough to hold his hat on," was not an imposing figure in his rumpled
suit and carelessly tied neckcloth, "his countenance wilted with age

and care." But Jackson admired his aggressive patriotism, and during long private conversations learned that Monroe shared his views on the problems of the southern frontier: Florida was destined to become American territory; the sooner the better. Spanish control of the southern border was a constant menace. The futile negotiations of Jefferson and Madison for the purchase of Florida had dragged on too long; Jackson yearned to end them by a show of force, and Monroe evidently agreed. The planners of national expansion were also of one mind as to the Creeks and Choctaws, who were showing signs of restlessness. And there was a tacit understanding that Jackson, as commander of the Southern District, was to keep the peace and protect American settlers who had swarmed into the old Creek territory. Routine operations would be conducted from New Orleans by General E. P. Gaines, the second in command, and Jackson would remain at the Hermitage until duty called him into the field.

The Jacksons left for Tennessee in January 1816, pausing for a brief stop in Virginia to leave John Reid at his family home, where his sister was dying of tuberculosis. Soon after he reached the Hermitage Jackson was saddened by news of the sudden death of Reid, victim of an undiagnosed fever. Determined that Reid's biography should be completed, the general advanced funds for its printing and began a search for a writer to complete the book, whose proceeds were to go to Reid's widow and young children. From a number of volunteers Jackson chose John Henry Eaton, a wealthy lawyer and planter of Franklin, Tennessee, who had a local reputation as a writer and scholar.

The general was soon off on a tour of inspection to New Orleans, where he met and shook hands with Judge Hall in an amicable ending to their conflict of wills during the British invasion.

Old Hickory also succumbed to the speculative fever once more. He took options on lands on the Gulf coast and considered the purchase of a Louisiana sugar plantation. When he returned to Tennessee, Jackson joined several of his friends in land deals near the Muscle Shoals of the Tennessee River—transactions that were to be branded as corrupt by his critics. A huge tract of Muscle Shoals land was bought at government auction by the Cypress Land Company, an enterprise led by John Coffee in which Jackson owned stock. The company somehow managed to ward off all competition and acquire the lands cheaply, then prospered immediately by establishing the little town of Florence, Alabama, where it sold lots for premium prices of as much as $3,500 each. Adjoining farmland was resold for $80 an acre. Jackson acquired at least two lots and some cotton acreage, when competitors withdrew by common consent to allow the conqueror of the old Creek territory to take his choice of the property. Jackson paid $2 an acre for the farmland, the minimum bid allowed by the government.

During this time Jack Donelson, John Henry Eaton, and half a dozen other Nashville men also made large investments in and near Pensacola, Florida, obviously in confidence that Spanish control of the territory was near its end. Jackson himself did not benefit from this scheme, though he gave the group's agent a letter of introduction to the Spanish governor.

All of these schemes, and the peace of the southern frontier as well, were endangered by British agents in Florida, who armed the Seminoles and convinced the defeated Creeks that the lands seized from them by Jackson had been restored by the Treaty of Ghent.

The Irish colonel Edward Nicholls, who had remained in Florida after the Battle of New Orleans, became the leader of the Seminoles; and though he warned them not to invade American territory, bound them in a treaty to Great Britain—a military alliance "both offensive and defensive." Nicholls returned to England with several Creek and Seminole chiefs, who were received with great ceremony, but the Nicholls treaty was disavowed by the Foreign Office. Other agents replaced the impetuous Irishman in Florida.

When it became apparent that the harsh treaty with the Creeks had included 4 million acres that actually belonged to Jackson's Cherokee and Choctaw allies, Secretary of War George Crawford returned these lands to the friendly tribes. Jackson was infuriated by Crawford's action, and the chorus of protest from western states became so insistent that President Madison sent Jackson to negotiate for the return of the disputed territory, which he accomplished by offering an indemnity of $180,000.

By now James Monroe had won the Democratic nomination for the presidency and, confident of victory, had begun to choose his cabinet. It was soon evident that he had a gift for selecting capable associates, the most notable of whom was John Quincy Adams, a prim middle-aged intellectual, the son of President John Adams. Though exceptionally able, the new Secretary of State was cold and tactless, seemed to lack the capacity to enjoy himself, and confessed that he could never learn the art of conversation. Adams had been educated in Paris and Holland and at Harvard; he had gained invaluable experience in his youth as secretary to the ambassador to Russia at fourteen, then as ambassador himself to Russia, Germany, and England, and as senator and peace commissioner.

Monroe's Secretary of the Treasury was the Georgian William H. Crawford, shrewd, ambitious son of an Indian fighter, who had begun as a backwoods lawyer and risen to senator and minister to France. Monroe offered the post of Secretary of War to Jackson, who declined; the place went to the brilliant South Carolinian John C. Calhoun, an intense Yale-trained politician of thirty-five who had become prominent as a congressional War Hawk and now aspired to the presidency.

On Monroe's Inaugural Day, March 4, 1817, Jackson wrote to congratulate him, but in the course of a long letter complained that interference by the War Department was undermining discipline in his command: acting Secretary of War George Graham had ordered an engineer officer from the Southern District to New York without consulting Jackson. Seven weeks later, when the new President had not responded, the impatient Jackson issued an order forbidding his subordinates to obey any orders from the War Department unless they bore his endorsement. This act of insubordination was reported by the press, and someone sent Jackson a critical article from a New York paper, reporting that its author was Major General Winfield Scott, who had accused Jackson of mutiny.

Jackson sent Scott a restrained note, saying that he took no stock in the report but asking for clarification. Scott replied that though he had not written the article, he considered Jackson's order mutinous and "a reprimand to the President" as well. Jackson dashed off an intemperate response, branding Scott as "a hectoring bully" and one of the "intermeddling pimps and spies of the War Department." He ended with a flourish that was tantamount to a challenge to a duel: "For what I have said I offer no apology. You have deserved it all and more. . . . I will barely remark, in conclusion, that if you feel aggrieved at what is said here, any communication from you will reach me safely at this place."

Scott's reply conceded that he could not match Jackson's "billingsgate," and dismissed talk of a duel as ludicrous; he declined the challenge on religious grounds, saying he preferred to risk his life in battle.

The incipient feud subsided, but Jackson's defiant attitude toward the War Department remained unchanged. In fact, he declared, he would resign his commission before he would rescind the insubordinate order in which he had declared his independence from Washington.

Monroe, with the advice of Calhoun, responded diplomatically, urging Jackson to remain in the army so long as the Florida crisis threatened war with Spain. But he declined to grant Jackson absolute control over his army district and personnel, since the issue involved "the

naked principle of the power of the Executive over the . . . army." The
Tennessee congressman John Rhea, one of Jackson's old friends,
added an assurance that the administration was unanimous in his support, and Old Hickory remained in service. He had no intention of
resigning so long as there was a prospect of Indian warfare in Florida.

When further violence erupted along the southern border, Calhoun
ordered Gaines to cross the Florida line and attack Indians there,
unless they should take refuge in a Spanish fort, in which case he was
to halt his troops, notify the War Department, and await orders.

Jackson pointed out the weakness of the order in an urgent dispatch
to Monroe: "Suppose the Indians . . . take refuge in either Pensacola
or St. Augustine. . . . General Gaines . . . has to halt and communicate
with his Government; in the meantime the militia grows restless, and
he has to defend himself with regulars. The enemy . . . attacks him,
what may not be the result? defeat and massacre."

Jackson proposed a more effective plan, which could be accomplished by his troops, with the assistance of the congressman Rhea as
a clandestine messenger. Jackson himself offered to seize "the whole
of East Florida . . . without implicating the Government. Let it be
signified to me through any channel (say Mr. J. Rhea) that the possession of the Floridas would be desirable . . . and in sixty days it will be
accomplished."

Less than a week after this proposal was sent north, Jackson received
a letter direct from the President, intimating that Florida was to be
taken now or never, and that no risk was too great for the prize. "The
mov'ment . . . against the Seminoles . . . will bring you on a theatre
where you may possibly have other services to perform. . . . Great
interests are at issue. . . . This is not a time for repose . . . untill our
cause is carried triumphantly thro."

Jackson needed no further hint—he prepared to invade Spanish
Florida. He authorized a few of his old officers to raise 1,000 more
Tennessee troops, most of them veterans of New Orleans. Governor
Blount was out of the state, but Old Hickory did not hesitate. He swore
in about 200 of the troops himself, advanced $4,000 from his own
pocket to pay expenses of the march, and was on his way to the Georgia
frontier with the vanguard only 11 days after receiving Calhoun's
order to Gaines, leaving Blount to approve upon his return.

In mid-February he halted his column near the village of Hartford,
Georgia, where he was overtaken by a mail pouch. It was here, so he
insisted afterward, when his bare-bones diplomacy was denounced,
that Jackson received Monroe's consent to seize Florida first and leave
diplomatic consequences to others. This authority, Jackson claimed,

arrived in a letter from Representative Rhea, who assured him of Monroe's blessing. Jackson had every reason to expect support from Washington. Not only had the President spoken in unmistakable terms of "great interests at issue"; he had said nothing to restrain Jackson during his months of preparations for war.

By the same mail Calhoun sent orders broad enough even for Jackson's taste: he was to "adopt the necessary measures to terminate the conflict." In addition to troops already in the field, he was authorized to call on neighboring states for more if they were needed. Jackson realized that though few troops would be necessary to overcome the Seminoles, who had fewer than 1,000 warriors, he must have a large force to occupy Florida. His Tennesseans, though on the march, were far behind him, but he did not delay.

On March 10 he marched from Fort Scott near the Florida border at the head of 1,100 regulars and volunteers, more than half of them hungry and poorly disciplined Georgia militiamen. The troops left the fort with a quart of corn and three rations of meat per man, and floundered through a flooded countryside for five days before meeting supply boats loaded with food. They paused briefly to eat their first full meal in three weeks.

Jackson had now identified his enemies, "a motley crew of brigands, slaves enticed away from their masters . . . or stolen," fugitive Creeks and a handful of Seminoles—all incited to war by British agents. The clandestine British effort in Florida was led by Colonel George Woodbine, who had replaced Nicholls, but a more influential agent was a seventy-year-old Scots trader, Alexander Arbuthnot, who lived among the Indians, treated them fairly, deplored their exploitation by both the English and the Americans—and sold them arms and ammunition. When he learned that the Seminoles were seeking arms from the Spanish commander at the fortress town of St. Marks on the Gulf, Jackson marched promptly, fighting several skirmishes on the way. He found more than fifty fresh scalps of white victims in an Indian village, burned its huts, and pushed on, through jungle growth "as virgin forest as in the days of de Soto." Jackson's men fought a brief skirmish outside St. Marks, but found that the Indians and Colonel Woodbine had fled. The white-haired Arbuthnot, surprised in the fort, was taken without resistance; Jackson reported to Rachel that "the noted Scotch villain" was held for trial.

Jackson took other notable captives a few hours later through the simple stratagem of flying a British flag from a gunboat in St. Marks Harbor. Two Creek leaders, the prophet Francis and Chief Himollimico, were lured aboard and seized, and hanged the next morning.

Jackson then pushed his army—now grown to 5,000 men—south-eastward along the Gulf coast, in hopes of surprising an Indian band led by Chief Boleck (or Billy Bowlegs, as the invaders called him). Jackson's men covered 107 miles in 8 days, delayed only by 2 skir-mishes; but when they arrived at the Seminole town on the Suwanee, they found its huts empty. Boleck and his warriors had fled to the swamps.

After nightfall Jackson discovered why the Indians had escaped him at every turn when two Englishmen stumbled into his camp—Lieuten-ant Robert Ambrister of the marines and a civilian, Peter B. Cook. The captives carried a letter of warning from Arbuthnot to Boleck that Jackson was advancing in overwhelming force. Jackson returned to St. Marks and convened a court-martial to try Arbuthnot and Ambrister. He chose six regular officers and six from the militia, and as president of the court General Gaines, who was well versed in military law.

Arbuthnot was charged with spying, inciting the Seminoles to war, and giving aid to the enemy. The old Scot was denounced by rival traders of the Scottish house of Forbes & Company, and by young Peter Cook, who had quarreled with him. Documentary evidence against the trader was incontrovertible—numerous letters in Arbuth-not's handwriting, including appeals to the British governor at Nassau for troops and arms to fight the Americans, as well as pleas for help to the British minister in Washington and the Spanish governor in Havana. The old trader made a feeble defense. He did not disavow the letters, and said only that he had sold a mere ten barrels of powder to Boleck, a supply sufficient for hunting but not for war.

Lieutenant Ambrister, charged with commanding hostile Indians in warfare against the United States, entered a plea of guilty, with "justifi-cation," and, like Arbuthnot, made a plea for mercy.

The court found both men guilty, sentencing Arbuthnot to be hanged and Ambrister to be shot. One officer changed his mind and persuaded the court to reconsider the vote against Ambrister, where-upon the lieutenant's sentence was reduced to fifty lashes and a year's imprisonment.

The stern Jackson approved the hanging of Arbuthnot and insisted upon carrying out the original sentencing of Ambrister, on the ground that the court lacked the authority to reconsider. The two were ex-ecuted the next morning, as the army fell in for the return march northward.

At the end of the first week of May 1817 Jackson wrote Calhoun that he would next invade West Florida, and, if he found Indians there, would seize Pensacola. He left a 200-man garrison at St. Marks, with the intention of holding Florida as indemnity, and began a two-week march through the watery wilderness. After a siege of three days he occupied the Spanish capital, where he confiscated the royal archives, declared the revenue laws of the United States in force, left one of his colonels behind as governor of the territory, then marched on for Tennessee. In less than three months he had solved the troublesome Florida problem that had vexed the diplomats of three nations for many years.

Public acclaim for the easy conquest came from all parts of the country, but there was an air of crisis in Washington. "The storm is rapidly thickening," John Quincy Adams said. Don Luis de Onis, the Spanish minister, lodged an angry protest at the "monstrous acts of hostility" by the "haughty conqueror." Spain broke off negotiations for the cession of Florida. "How was it possible to believe," Onis demanded, "that at the very moment of negotiation . . . the troops of the United States should invade the Spanish provinces. . . . In the name of the King, my master, I demand prompt restitution of St. Mark's, Pensacola, Barrancas, and all other places wrested by General Jackson from the Crown of Spain. I demand . . . indemnity for all injuries and losses, and the punishment of the general."

Newspapers supporting William H. Crawford began sniping at the administration, warning that the honor and prestige of the President and the country demanded the repudiation of Jackson and all his works. The cabinet went into extraordinary session and debated for three days. At first only John Quincy Adams defended Jackson. Calhoun, Crawford, and Monroe himself felt that Jackson had acted "not only without, but against his instructions; that he had committed war upon Spain." If Old Hickory were not disavowed, the administration would be ruined. Adams noted that Calhoun "seems to be personally offended that Jackson has set at naught the instructions of the Department." Crawford and Calhoun, who were especially vehement in their denunciations of Jackson, insisted that the captured forts be restored to Spain and that Jackson's actions be publicly repudiated. Calhoun hinted that Jackson's invasion had been for the benefit of the land speculations of Eaton, Jack Donelson, and their friends. Monroe was persuaded but hesitant. The influence of the stern, popular general was much in evidence during cabinet deliberations.

Adams stood firmly against the majority, declaring that Jackson had acted out of necessity and had not violated his instructions. He charged that Monroe sought to use Old Hickory as Elizabeth had used Walter Raleigh, to enjoy the fruits of his brilliant achievements and then sacrifice him to partisan opinion. Adams failed to convince Monroe, but effected a compromise—a course the New Englander condemned as "weakness and confession of weakness." Monroe directed Adams to tell Onis that the forts would be returned to Spain, but that Jackson could not be censured, though he had taken the posts on his own responsibility. Attorney General William Wirt drafted a press release designed to satisfy the public, and the President himself turned to the delicate task of justifying the administration's position to Jackson.

Monroe's letter of pacification to Jackson was an adroit blend of flattery, cajolery, and distorted facts:

> In calling you into service against the Seminoles, and communicating to you the orders which had been given just before to General Gaines, the views and intentions of the Government were fully disclosed in respect to the operations in Florida. In transcending the limits prescribed by those orders you acted on your own responsibility. . . .
>
> It was proper to follow the Indians into Florida, but an order by the Government to attack a Spanish post would assume another character. It would authorize war, to which, by the principles of our Constitution, the Executive is incompetent. Congress alone possesses the power . . .

The President said he could appreciate Jackson's motives in attacking cities whose Spanish rulers had incited the Indians to raid American settlements, but then explained that St. Marks and Pensacola must be returned to Spain, since holding them "would amount to a declaration of war," and the President would be accused of usurping congressional authority and of "giving a deep and fatal wound to the Constitution."

Monroe was not prepared to risk war over the Florida posts: "The war would doubtless soon become general: and we do not foresee that we should have a single power in Europe on our side." He pointed out that Spain, already faced with the loss of her empire in Central and South America, was clearly unable to hold onto Florida and would soon cede the territory to the United States, "provided we do not too deeply wound her pride by holding it."

Monroe then proposed that Jackson's dispatches from Florida be altered to put the adventure in a more favorable light:

> Your letters to the Department were written in haste, under the pressure of fatigue and infirmity, in a spirit of conscious rectitude, and, in consequence, with less attention to some parts of their contents than would

otherwise have been bestowed on them. . . . If you think proper to authorize the secretary or myself to correct these passages, it will be done with care. . . .

Jackson was neither misled by Monroe's subtleties nor cowed by the prospect of being disavowed by the administration. His forthright reply made scant reference to the President's claim as to the guilt of Spanish officers, nor to the threat of war or the invitation to alter his dispatches. Jackson's chief concern was the matter of his responsibility, which he accepted fully: "I have never shrunk from it and never will . . . I have passed through difficulties and exposures for the honor and benefit of my country; and whenever . . . it shall become necessary to assume a further liability, no scruple will be urged or felt."

Jackson insisted that his conduct of the Florida invasion had been fully justified by the order from Calhoun "to adopt the necessary measures to terminate . . . the conflict"—an order which did not impose the restrictions set forth in earlier instructions to Gaines. "The fullest discretion," he said, "was left with me . . . and for the exercise of a sound discretion on principles of policy am I alone responsible."

Jackson's resentment of the administration's surrender of the captured posts, though not expressed to Monroe, was made clear in a confidential letter to a friend in Pennsylvania:

. . . Had the government held the posts until the guarantees were given stipulated in the Articles of Capitulation . . . I would have been more than willing to have taken on myself all responsibilities, but when my country is deprived of all the benefits resulting from my acts I will not consent to bear . . . responsibility that ought to be those of another. My situation is . . . delicate. I must for the present be silent.

Jackson's silence was enforced by his affection for the President: "Being a sincere friend of Mr. Monroe . . . it is not my desire to injure him unless impelled in my own defense."

Monroe's meek response to Jackson's statement succeeded only in worsening matters: "Finding that you had a different view of your power, it remains only to do you justice on that ground. Nothing can be further from my intention than to expose you to a responsibility . . . which you did not contemplate." The President suggested that Jackson write a letter explaining that they disagreed as to the extent of authority granted for the invasion of Florida. Jackson stuck to his guns: "I have no ground that a difference of opinion exists between the government and myself, relative to the powers given me in my orders."

Monroe also deliberately misled Jackson as to Calhoun's hostile attitude, saying only that the South Carolinian held "very just and liberal sentiments" about Jackson's role in Florida. Jackson's correspondence with Monroe ended as the affair burgeoned into a major issue in national politics.

A few weeks later Madrid demanded that Monroe disavow Jackson and administer "a suitable punishment," but the President clung to his uneasy peace with Jackson and directed Adams to reply to the Spanish. The Secretary of State composed a bristling defense of Jackson and the invasion: "The President will neither inflict punishment nor pass censure upon General Jackson for that conduct—the vindication of which is written in every page of the law of nations . . . self defense." Adams denounced Spanish officials who had encouraged Indian raids on American settlers and harbored British troublemakers, a "narrative of dark and complicated depravity; this creeping and insidious war . . ." He contrasted Jackson's seizure of Pensacola with its occupation by Colonel Nicholls, who had blown up one of the city's forts: "Where is His Majesty's profound indignation at that?"

Adams then declared that the inability of Spanish officials in Florida to control Indian raiders did not justify their role.

> The right of the United States can as little compound with impotence as with perfidy, and . . . Spain must immediately make her election, either to place a force in Florida adequate to the protection of her territory . . . or cede to the United States a province of which she retains nothing but the nominal possession, but which is, in fact, a derelict, open to the occupancy of every enemy, civilized or savage, of the United States, and serving no other earthly purpose than as a post of annoyance to them.

The truculent message concluded with a warning that the United States would not surrender the Florida forts if it became necessary to seize them again. The Spanish were convinced. Negotiations for Florida were resumed, just as enemies of the Monroe administration and Jackson's opponents launched an investigation of the affair in Congress.

In January 1819 the House Committee on Military Affairs approved a resolution condemning the executions of Arbuthnot and Armbrister. Thomas Cobb of Georgia, a Crawford leader, broadened the attack on Jackson by calling for laws forbidding the execution of captives taken in Indian wars, and prohibiting the invasion of foreign territory without congressional approval. Cobb also urged a House resolution declaring Jackson's seizure of St. Marks and Pensacola unconstitutional.

The House devoted itself to the issue for three weeks, in heated debate before packed galleries. After twelve days of the excitement Henry Clay, whose volatile temper had won him the sobriquet, "the Western Hotspur," descended from the Speaker's chair to deliver the major attack on Jackson; it was his first public criticism of his newly popular rival.

The ambitious, dashing Clay, a perennial candidate for the presidency, was a nonchalant figure more than 6 feet tall. He had been prematurely gray since his early twenties; his forehead was high, his small gray eyes quick and alert, and his mouth, "a long and deep horizontal cut," so large that Clay confessed he had never learned to whistle. He spoke with an actor's voice, but his crowd-pleasing performances, though brilliant, were not profound.

The Seminole war had originated in Jackson's harsh treaty with the Creeks on the Hickory Ground, Clay charged. "A more dictatorial spirit I have never seen displayed in any instrument, not even in the treaties which Rome forced from the Barbarians. It spared to the poor Indians neither their homes, their property, nor their prophets." Clay declared that the Creek treaty was void in any case, since it had been signed by a minority of tribal chiefs. He condemned the use of a false flag to capture the Indian chiefs at St. Marks, and ended by raising fears of an American military dictatorship: "Recall . . . the free nations which have gone before us. Where are they now and how have they lost their liberties . . ."

Clay said he felt no personal animosity toward Jackson, but warned the House against supporting Old Hickory. The members, Clay said, "May bear down all opposition . . . even vote the general public thanks; they may carry him triumphantly through this house. But, if they do, in my humble judgment, it will be a triumph of the principle of insubordination—a triumph of the military over the civil authority—a triumph over the constitution of the land."

Eaton, who was in the Senate when the furor broke, realized that the public approved Jackson's treaty as well as his seizure of Florida, and that Clay's protests were in vain. Eaton had urged Jackson to remain in Nashville, in hope of shielding him from congressional criticism; but Old Hickory could not be restrained. He arrived in Washington at the end of January, only three days after Clay had spoken, when the capital was still stirred by his sensational charges. The general was outraged by "the hypocracy and baseness of Clay in pretending friendship to me, & endeavouring to crush the executive through me." He confessed to Lewis: "I despise the villain," and to others announced his resolve to "defeat these hellish machinations."

Clay called at Jackson's hotel a few days later to assure him that his attack had been based on principles, and that he had a warm personal regard for him; but Jackson was out, perhaps fortunately for the peace of the capital.

Jackson felt that Clay's attack was so irrational that he sent copies to his friends and asked them to have it published: "I hope the western people will appreciate his conduct accordingly. You will see him skinned here & I hope you will roast him in the West." He also asked that Monroe, Adams, and Calhoun be praised for their support of his conquest in Florida—he was not yet aware of Calhoun's role in the cabinet debates on the affair. When Adams told the general that he had defended him on the unimpeachable grounds of international law, as set forth by the authorities Grotius, Puffendorf, and Vattel, Jackson retorted, "Damn Grotius! Damn Puffendorf! Damn Vattel! This is a mere matter between Jim Monroe and myself." As Adams's Virginia friend Henry Wise said: "Jackson cared only for his justification; but Adams was horrified at its mode. Jackson made law, Adams quoted it."

From the time of his arrival Jackson's supporters lobbied tirelessly. The general did not appear in the Capitol, but counseled, directed, and held court in his hotel room until it was over and the Clay-Crawford resolutions resoundingly defeated.

After his victory in the House Jackson left on a trip to the north, ostensibly to visit his godsons at West Point. His triumphal progress suggested that of a conqueror showing himself to the admiring multitudes. Philadelphia held him for four days of festive welcome and honors, and New York for five days. The New Yorkers presented him with the symbolic freedom of the city in the form of a gold box and Tammany honored him with a banquet—during which he stunned Martin Van Buren and other Crawford leaders by toasting their bitter enemy, DeWitt Clinton. In Baltimore, where he was given another riotous welcome, Jackson learned that the long Florida controversy was over. The Spaniards, cowed by the belligerent Adams and struck by the obvious fact that the Americans could easily seize the territory when they wished, had ceded Florida to the United States for $5 million. The English had withdrawn their protest over the executions of Arbuthnot and Armbrister. Amid celebrations of this welcome news Jackson read the report of a Senate committee, a highly critical review of his conduct of the Seminole war. Jackson hurried back to the capital in "a great rage."

The Senate committee, led by the quiet, methodical Abner Lacock of Pennsylvania, conducted its investigation undeterred by rumors that Jackson was blustering about town threatening to cut off the ears of those who opposed him. There was also a report, which Lacock and many others accepted as true (but Jackson denied), that Old Hickory had hurried to the Capitol to assault Senator John W. Eppes, Jefferson's cousin, who was a member of the offending committee. By this story, in any event, Old Hickory was deterred only by Captain Stephen Decatur, who raced across Washington in a hansom, and, intercepting Jackson on the Capitol steps, persuaded him to return to his carriage.

Whatever the nature of Jackson's protest, the Senate's report was tabled at the end of the session for lack of time to vote on the issue. Jackson returned to Tennessee in triumph.

It became apparent that the American people were weary of the marathon debates; they had long since concluded that Jackson was a brave, aggressive, and patriotic general, and was also a man they could trust in the White House. The debates, in fact, seemed to benefit rather than harm the general. Thousands of voters came to share the veneration for Old Hickory felt by his most dedicated supporters. Representative Alexander Smythe warned Clay and other detractors that they were committing sacrilege by their attacks on the hero:

> Surely there must be an overruling Providence, who directs the destinies of men and nations . . . the English sailed to New Orleans; and there they met the dire avenger: The man appointed by heaven to tread the wine press of Almighty wrath. . . . Let me assure you that the American people will not be pleased to see their great defender, their great avenger, sacrificed. . . . Had this man lived before . . . Homer sang, temples would have been raised to his honor; altars would have blazed—and he would have taken his stand with Hercules and Theseus, among the immortals.

National policy in the wake of the Florida adventure was conducted deviously within the cabinet, where an anti-Jackson movement had begun to mature. A few weeks after he had attempted to persuade Monroe to sacrifice Jackson, John C. Calhoun sought to conceal his own role and win the general's good graces. He made a point of praising the Florida campaign to Jackson's friend Captain James Gadsden, and hinted that others in the cabinet had sought to betray Jackson to further their own careers. Calhoun also wrote to Jackson, agreeing that possession of Florida was vital to the security of the southern frontier, and assuring him that there was nothing to fear from Spain. There was, however, grave danger of war with England, and "a certain degree of caution" would thus be desirable.

William H. Crawford, who saw Jackson as a threat to his presidential ambitions, shrewdly stored his knowledge of Calhoun's duplicity and thereafter played Jackson and Calhoun against each other. Crawford's alliance with Monroe also became strained. Finally their friendship deteriorated to the point that the Georgian called the President "a damned, infernal old scoundrel," whereupon Monroe whacked him with a poker.

15

"I am not fit to be President"

A new Hermitage was now rising near the site of the aging log cabins that had served the Jacksons so well. Construction began in a time when Old Hickory was recuperating slowly from another onset of his perennial ailments.

One day when he was able to leave his bed, Jackson led Major Lewis into an open field near the blockhouse and thrust his cane into the earth. Here, he said, he would build a new house. The time had come to move Rachel into a more comfortable home. Lewis suggested another site a few yards away, higher on the slope of a gentle hill, a spot favored by Jackson himself.

"No, Major," the general said. "Mrs. Jackson chose this spot, and she shall have her wish. I'm going to build this house for *her*. I don't expect to live in it myself."

The new Hermitage soon began to take shape, a square, two-story brick house of little architectural distinction, apparently designed by Jackson himself. The limestone foundation stones were quarried on the farm by slaves, the walls were built of bricks burned at the site, and poplar timbers and cedar flooring were cut nearby.

The 85-foot front of the house faced south. On the first floor, flanking a central hall, were two parlors, a dining room, and the Jacksons' bedroom. Five or six guest bedrooms occupied the second floor. Among the new outbuildings were a small brick office for the general, a kitchen and quarters for house servants.

Landscaping of the new home was supervised by William Frost, "a regular bred english gardner," who laid out a broad, tree-shaded lawn, with a 1-acre flower garden visible from Rachel's bedroom window. The new Hermitage, like the old, was almost constantly filled with guests, many of them strangers who had come from great distances for a look at the general, and were invited to stay for a meal, or overnight, or for several weeks.

The new house also acquired a permanent resident in Ralph E. W. Earl, an itinerant painter who arrived in Nashville to paint portraits and immediately won Rachel's heart. Earl married her niece, Jane Caffrey, and after the bride's premature death, Rachel took the artist into the Hermitage, where he was to remain for seventeen years, end-lessly turning out somewhat pedestrian portraits of Jackson, for which the public demand was insatiable.

Once more the general's respite from duty was brief. Despite his illness he continued to correspond widely. He revealed a growing restlessness and frustration in an exchange with President Monroe.

Though he was not anxious to remain in the army, the proud, stub-born Jackson kept his post for a few months after the congressional investigation, when there was doubt that Spain would sign the Florida treaty and there was a brief prospect of war.

Charges that he sought to profit by the Florida land deals of Eaton and Donelson distressed Jackson. He wrote Monroe, "I am wearied with public life. . . . I have been accused of acts I never committed, of crimes I never thought of, and secretly . . . charged . . . in the Senate . . . of doing acts in my official capacity to promote my private interest."

He had hoped, he said, that the Florida treaty would be settled, so that he could retire from the army, but he reminded the President that he was ready to do his duty; "you know my services is my countries," as long as the country should need them. He then asked Monroe to allow him to resign when the threat of war receded.

Monroe was at a loss as to how to handle Jackson. When someone proposed sending him out of the country as minister to Russia, the President asked Jefferson's advice. "Good God," Jefferson said. "He would breed you a quarrel before he had been there a month." Thus in February 1821, when Monroe announced the Florida treaty and Jackson prepared to leave the army, the President offered him the governorship of the territory. Jackson accepted reluctantly, protesting that he and Rachel longed to remain at the Hermitage. He took office June 1, 1821, with broad powers to govern Florida, and was soon off for his new post. He and Rachel reached New Orleans by a river steamer and rode into the festive city in an elaborately fitted carriage. Rachel was stunned by the gaiety of the sinful city: "Great Babylon is come up before me. Oh, the wickedness, the idolatry of this place! unspeakable riches and splendor. . . . Oh, farewell! Pray for your sister in a heathen land." Her husband was still a hero in New Orleans: "The attention and honors paid to the General far excel the recital of my pen. They conducted him to the Grand Theatre . . . which rang with loud acclamations, Vive Jackson. Songs of praise were sung by ladies, and . . . they crowned him with . . . laurel."

Mrs. Jackson found their next tarrying place, the village of Montpelier, Alabama, equally sinful, and the U.S. regulars who accompanied Jackson a dissolute lot: "The Sabbath entirely neglected and profaned. The regiment . . . no better than the Spaniards. . . . The General, I believe, wants to get home again as much as I do. . . . He wishes he had taken my advice. . . . Amen. Rachel Jackson." The Jacksons waited in this outpost for five weeks while the Spanish delayed sending final authority for the transfer from Havana. Jackson sent Rachel into Pensacola in advance and stayed outside the city with his troops until Spanish plans for withdrawal were complete. At last, on July 17, after a hostile correspondence with Don José Callava, governor of West Florida, Jackson entered the city, his troops took over from the departing Spanish, and the U.S. flag rose over Government House.

Jackson found the city full of officeseekers, one of whom, David Cowan, so touched Rachel's heart with a tale of his needy family that she persuaded Jackson to give him a job. Jackson made him port warden, but he was soon ousted when merchants protested his exorbitant fees. Few of Jackson's friends were to win posts in the new government, for Monroe had ignored his suggestions and sent a corps of officials from Washington and elsewhere to take the desirable offices.

The pious Rachel also found the mores of Pensacola unbearable: "The Sabbath profanely kept; a great deal of noise and swearing in the streets; shops kept open; trade going on, I think, more than on any other day." She was so offended by this wickedness that Jackson attempted to curb the sinners in the city. Stern orders worked a miracle on the city's outward manifestations of morality and Rachel's relief was immediate: "Great order was observed; the doors kept shut; the gambling houses demolished; fiddling and dancing not heard any more on the Lord's day; cursing not to be heard. . . . What, what has been done in one week!" Mrs. Jackson's reform had only begun. At her insistence the general closed theaters and gambling houses on Sunday, and reserved for Pensacola's new mayor and council the right to make any regulations they wished as to the observance of the Sabbath. The new régime did not please the local Catholic hierarchy. A Methodist missionary passed out tracts on the streets; when a priest protested, the intruder merely pointed to the new American flag over the City Hall and the priest turned away.

Jackson was increasingly restive in the city. As Rachel wrote one of her brothers, "There was never a man more disappointed than the General has been. In the first place he has not the power to appoint one of his friends, which, I thought, was in part the reason of his coming. . . ." A few days later she wrote a friend in Tennessee: "The General, I think, is the most anxious man to get home I ever saw. He calls it the wild-goose chase, his coming here . . . oh, how has this place been overrated."

There was grim news for the Jacksons from Tennessee, where a depression that had spread from the east had brought ruin to many of their friends. Plummeting cotton prices had forced sales of farms, slaves, and businesses. Trade was at a standstill. Banks were failing. Jackson blamed the wholesale issue of paper money by banks. He wrote a friend:

> I fear the paper system has and will ruin the State. Its demoralizing effects are clearly seen and spoken of everywhere . . . let every honest man take care of himself, and have nothing to do with the new rags of the State; for, be assured, it will be a reign of immoral rule, and the interest of speculators will be alone consulted during the existence of the new dynasty . . . I objected to the new State bank bills. I never had one of them, and I never will receive one of them. In this country you could not pass them, and get one dollar in specie for ten dollars in them. I therefore protest against receiving any of the trash. . . .

Jackson's relations with Governor Callava did not improve. The Spaniard, a handsome blond Castilian, was haughty and difficult, given to tempestuous outbursts, and to sudden, mysterious illnesses in the midst of negotiations. Callava and Jackson resumed their squabbles over the disposition of the cannon in the Spanish forts, which Jackson had been instructed to keep in return for furnishing provisions to the departing Spanish troops. After a few days of bickering Callava agreed to leave the guns in place and accept the provisions, with an exchange of receipts. Jackson gave his receipt for the guns; but when Callava did not respond in kind, Jackson replied in a rage, denounced Callava's "perfidy," and said he would deal with him no further.

Jackson's resolve was broken soon afterward when a young woman appealed to him for help in retrieving her inheritance, which had been withheld by conniving Spanish officials. He found himself involved in a petty squabble which sorely tried his patience.

The applicant was Mercedes Vidal, the natural daughter of Nicholas Vidal, a Spanish territorial official who had died in 1806, leaving a valuable estate which included 16,000 acres of land at Baton Rouge and properties in Pensacola. Over the years Vidal's octoroon heirs had sought in vain a settlement of the estate from its executors, Forbes & Company, the firm of Scottish merchants who had been the actual rulers of Florida. The company had evaded and defied the demands of Spanish officials to account for their stewardship of the Vidal estate even in face of accusations of fraud. In recent years the firm's manager, John Innerarity, had become friendly with Callava, and the charges had been dropped.

Now, Mercedes Vidal said, the voluminous records of the estate were about to be carried away to Cuba, leaving the heirs helpless. Jackson ordered the papers seized from Callava's lieutenant, Domingo Sousa, who refused to surrender them, and took them to Callava instead.

Sousa was haled before Jackson and then sent under guard to Callava's house, with orders to bring in the papers or go to jail. The governor—who was dining with other Spanish officials, American army officers, and several women—sent Sousa to Jackson with word that only Callava himself had authority to deliver the papers. The governor then left the dinner party, stricken with another of his sudden illnesses, an attack of indigestion. The indignant Jackson ordered Sousa to jail and sent a couple of officers and twenty soldiers to Callava's house to seize the papers of Callava himself. Callava demanded a copy of the order from the officers, who left to prepare the papers. When they returned to find the gate locked, and the house silent and dark, the troops discovered Callava in bed, fully dressed but for his coat. Having refused to produce the Vidal documents, Callava was arrested and taken to Jackson. It was about 10:00 P.M. when he was led before the glowering general, who demanded to know whether Callava had the Vidal papers. The governor erupted in a fury of protest.

Interpreters were called in—though Callava spoke English perfectly —and the Spaniard repeated a lengthy protest of the proceeding, insisting that as a Spanish commissioner he was not answerable to Jackson.

Jackson said sharply that he would hear no protest against his authority as governor, refused to recognize Callava as a commissioner, and ordered him to respond to questions.

Callava began to write in Spanish, then complained of weak eyes and began dictating to his secretary, still another prolonged challenge to Jackson's authority.

Jackson pounded the table and roared. No protest would be permitted. Callava halted in the middle of a word and remained silent when he was commanded to answer directly as to whether the papers were at his house. The governor's steward, one Fullerat, who was examined over Callava's objections, admitted that the papers were in the house and Callava was then ordered to deliver them. Callava still refused to admit possession of the records. He shouted excitedly about the terms of the treaty and Spanish rights, and appealed to his officials and the roomful of spectators. By midnight Jackson's patience was at an end. He roared a command for silence and ordered Callava to the city jail.

The Spanish version of this scene was left by one of Callava's officers:

> The Governor, Don Andrew Jackson, with turbulent and violent actions, with disjointed reasonings, blows on the table, his mouth foaming, and possessed with the furies, told the Spanish commissary to deliver the papers as a private individual; and the Spanish commissary, with the most forcible expressions, answered him that he . . . did not know what papers were demanded of him; that, as soon as he could know it . . . he would deliver them most cheerfully; and that, if papers were demanded of him which he ought not to deliver, he would resist it by the regular and prescribed means . . . that his answers were the same as he had given to every interrogatory which had been put to him, because he was not permitted to write in his own defense; and also, that he would answer for the future consistency of it, as well as what had been asked of him, and all that had been done to him; that he wished for this protection of the law to every man; and that he would never yield. . . .

In any event Callava was not cowed by Jackson. His friends flocked to the rickety little prison, where they staged a champagne party, consumed a huge meal, and spent the rest of the night singing and entertaining themselves with imitations of the apoplectic Jackson presiding over the hearing.

The next day a writ of habeas corpus for Callava was issued by Judge Elijius Fromentin, a newly arrived American official.

Jackson had retrieved the Vidal papers from Callava's house and was on the point of freeing the governor when Fromentin's writ of habeas corpus was presented. The general ordered Fromentin before him and lectured him sternly for his interference, but after a final barrage of threats released Callava.

The Spaniard left immediately for Washington, where he created a stir with his protests of the indignities he had suffered at Jackson's hands. Several of his officials, who published their version of the affair in a Pensacola newspaper, were ordered by Jackson to leave Florida within four days.

When the tempestuous affair came to an end, Mercedes Vidal and her relatives discovered that they had not only lost their inheritance —they were in debt to Forbes & Company for $157.

The episode echoed through the country for a few weeks in charges and countercharges, with Jackson's enemies loud in their denunciation of his high-handed methods. But the public and the press concluded that though he may have been hasty and ill-tempered, Old Hickory had manfully sought justice for the Vidal heirs and had properly refused to permit the arrogant Callava to defy him. Impartial observers saw nothing in the affair to Jackson's credit. "The real sinners in this business," as Jackson's biographer Parton said, were "Old Prejudice and Chronic Diarrhea."

Though Jackson's time in Florida had been brief and his mood testy throughout, he had contributed to the country's development with his plan of civil government for Florida—city government for Pensacola, the formation of counties, adoption of public health regulations, and establishment of courts. Jackson was careful to separate the territory from Georgia and Alabama, with an eye to Florida's eventual statehood.

To his enemies, who condemned him for "high crimes and misdemeanors" and for failure to abide by the Spanish constitution, Jackson responded that Spanish law was no longer in effect and that Florida was in need of a "simple and energetic" American government. In brief, he had not hesitated to violate the letter of the law in order to enforce its spirit, in Old Hickory's view a sound basis for any administration.

By now Jackson had come to suspect that he had been shunted off to the governorship through the influence of enemies in Washington, who hoped that he would disgrace himself and advance Crawford's chances for the presidency. Since Jackson felt that Monroe's disregard of his recommendations for appointments in Florida stemmed from the same conspiracy, a pronounced coolness developed between them.

Jackson left Florida with scant notice to the President—a terse letter pleading that Rachel's health was poor and announcing that "having organized the Government . . . and it being in full operation," he was bound for Tennessee. The President expressed no surprise. To his intimates he had spoken of Jackson's régime as "momentary," since "temporary" was "too strong a term"—but warned his correspondent to say nothing of this, "in consideration of the high temper of the general." Jackson and Rachel left Pensacola in the great carriage in October 1821, drawn by four white horses on the laborious return journey to Tennessee. They reached home in early November.

The Jacksons found the Hermitage filled with packing cases—new furniture bought in New Orleans and a huge shipment of liquor, wine and porter, plus a stock of cigars, for which Rachel had acquired a taste in Florida.

Now, at fifty-five, Jackson's health was again so poor that friends feared for his life; but he was restored by several weeks of rest and the stimulation of life at the Hermitage. And abruptly, though he had professed no interest in politics, he became a political addict. He subscribed to twenty newspapers, and was frequently in conference with John H. Eaton, Major Lewis, and John Overton, whose ambitions for him were boundless.

The presidential race of 1824 was well under way by the opening weeks of 1822, with three secretaries of Monroe's cabinet jockeying for leadership: John Quincy Adams of State, John C. Calhoun of War, and William H. Crawford of the Treasury. The outsiders in the race were Henry Clay, who was to intrigue for the presidency for twenty years, and Jackson, whose candidacy had been anticipated since the Battle of New Orleans.

Adams, who had served under every President since Washington, was clearly the most experienced candidate, and though he had few warm admirers, was respected throughout the country. Adams was Jackson's favorite candidate. Henry Clay said of the New Englander, "A man must be a born fool who voluntarily engages in a controversy with Mr. Adams on a question of fact. I doubt whether he was ever mistaken in his life. And then, if he happens to be in doubt about anything, he has his inevitable diary, in which he has recorded everything that has occurred since the adoption of the Federal Constitution."

In the south, where talk of Jackson's candidacy was already widespread, the prospect of an Adams-Jackson ticket inspired a ditty:

> *John Quincy Adams,*
> *Who can write,*
> *And Andrew Jackson,*
> *Who can fight.*

John C. Calhoun, the Yale-trained South Carolina champion, was intense, earnest, and dogmatic, but a man of striking presence, "a mystical something which is felt, but cannot be described." One contemporary described this manner as an air of "childlike simplicity in union with his majestic intelligence."

Calhoun had been prejudiced against a strong central government by his father, an attitude hardened by his law professors at Litchfield, Connecticut—New England Federalists who convinced Calhoun of the validity of secession as the right of oppressed American minorities.

William H. Crawford, the obese Georgian, was a resourceful politician favored by the old Virginia dynasty, and by Martin Van Buren's party in New York. His supporters, who billed him as the only true Democrat in the race, were distinctly a minority; but since they controlled the party machinery, Crawford was conceded the early lead in the race.

Henry Clay, the self-made leader of western factions centered in Kentucky, was the champion of federal spending for internal improvements, a challenger to the old Jeffersonian doctrine of states' rights. Clay was a charming but irresponsible opportunist who inspired strong feelings in his contemporaries. Calhoun said, "I don't like Henry Clay. He's a bad man, an imposter, a creator of wicked schemes. I wouldn't speak to him, but by God, I love him." Daniel Webster remarked that Clay was "no lawyer . . . no reasoner," and John Quincy Adams said of him, "In politics, as in private life, Clay is a gambler."

Though these four candidates presented themselves as heirs of Jefferson and new leaders of his old party, they were in fact embarked upon a contest of personalities in which party principles were to be forgotten.

Jackson at first rejected all overt attempts to draw him into the presidential race. When he read a suggestive comment in a New York newspaper about the political activities of his Nashville friends, Jackson flung down the paper. "Do they think I am such a damned fool? No sir; I know what I am fit for. I can command a body of men in a rough way, but I am not fit to be President."

The *New York Advocate* now wondered if his ill-considered toast to DeWitt Clinton during his New York visit had been the result of a secret alliance. Jackson responded with his first comment on the presidential campaign of 1824: "I have an opinion of my own on all subjects, and when that opinion is formed I persue it publickly, regardless of who goes with me. . . . You are at liberty to say in my name to both my friends and enemies, that I will as far as my influence extends support Mr. Adams unless Mr. Calhoun should be brought forward. . . . As to Wm. H. Crawford, you know my opinion. I would support the Devil first."

Anonymous correspondents, probably supporters of John C. Calhoun, began urging Jackson to help prevent either Adams or Crawford from becoming President. One of these letters charged that the "dull and stupid—cold & selfish" James Monroe had connived to force Jackson from the army out of jealousy, and named him governor of Florida to remove him from public attention.

Rachel was distressed by the growing signs of Jackson's political activity, and fearful that he would be lured into the race. "I do hope that they will now leave Mr. Jackson alone," she wrote a niece.

> He is not a well man and never will be unless they allow him to rest. He has done his share for our country. . . . In the thirty years of our wedded life . . . he has not spent one-Fourth of his days under his own roof. . . . Through all such trials I have not said aye, yes or no. It was his work to do, he seemed called to it and I watched, waited and prayed most of the time alone. Now I hope this is at an end. They talk of his being President. Major Eaton, General Carroll, Mr. Campbell, the Doctor and even the Parson . . . come here to talk, talk ever lastingly about his being President. In this as all else I can say only, the Lord's will be done. But I hope he may not be called again to the strife and empty honors of public place.

Near the end of the year Jackson had a visit from his old friend George Campbell, who had recently returned from a three-year term as minister to Russia. After they had reminisced for a time, Jackson said abruptly, "I'm no longer a strong man. I can't stand the fatigues and privations I used to. George, do you realize we're getting old? I'm fifty four . . . we're both getting old—towards it anyhow."

"You're only tired out," Campbell said, "and a little sick from the Florida climate and life in that filthy Spanish town. The Tennessee air will brace you this winter. You'll soon be yourself again.

Campbell paused. "You're by no means safe from the presidency in 1824."

Jackson started. "I really hope you don't think I'm damned fool enough to believe that, George." He shook his head. "No, sir. I may be pretty well satisfied with myself in some things, but I'm not vain enough for that." If there was a trace of insincerity in Jackson's manner, Campbell failed to detect it.

Jackson's physical condition worsened in the spring of 1822, in the wake of a severe cold. He wrote gloomily to one of his veterans of the Creek war, "I have been oppressed with a violent cough and have been recently visited with my old bowell complaint, which has worsened me very much, having . . . in the last twelve hours upwards of Twenty passages. . . . In short, Sir I must take a rest or my stay on Erth cannot be long."

Jackson's growing interest in the presidency was to lead to a role in a changing world of which he had a limited understanding. One of the few living Americans who glimpsed the nature of the coming era was Chancellor James Kent of New York, who had told his state's constitutional convention the year before: "We stand this moment on the brink of fate, on the very edge of the precipice. . . . We are no longer to remain plain and simple republics of farmers, like New-England colonists, or the Dutch settlements on the Hudson. We are fast becoming a great nation, with great commerce, manufactures, population, wealth, luxuries, and with the vices and miseries that they engender."

It was a nation for whose leadership Andrew Jackson seemed to be poorly prepared indeed.

16

"I mean to be silent—and let the people do as seemeth good unto them"

Rachel's growing apprehensions that Jackson would enter the race were confirmed when Senator Eaton returned from Washington with fresh gossip that raised the hopes of Old Hickory's friends, who had already banded into an informal committee to direct his campaign for the presidency. They were only a handful, but they were men of striking and diverse talents, all Jackson's friends of many years. It was the insistence of these men that made the reluctant Jackson into a candidate.

There was Jackson's old friend of the blockhouse days, John Overton, grown wealthy during a long career as a lawyer, judge, and speculator, now a profane little man with a bald, gourd-shaped skull and sunken cheeks, who had "lost his teeth and swallowed his lips." A wise counsellor who had long exerted a stabilizing influence upon Jackson, Overton was the only member of the group who was familiar with all the details of Old Hickory's marriage, which opponents would inevitably exploit as a campaign issue. He became the architect of the grand strategy of Jackson's campaign, but his contributions were destined to remain unknown in detail.

Major William B. Lewis, the former militia quartermaster, Jackson's garrulous but studious neighbor, had accumulated a sizable library and applied his scholarly habits to the problems of politics. His keen judgment of men and their motives became a decisive asset to Jackson's developing campaign. Though the tall, handsome Lewis, Jackson's most intimate confidant, had held no public office and was little known outside his neighborhood, he had already established contacts with political leaders in every state. He developed a voluminous card file of these men, probably the first such system in American political history.

Senator John Henry Eaton, whose popular biography of Jackson had made him a public figure in Tennessee, was gregarious and impulsive, a free-spending host and bon vivant with the air of a thespian about him. As the campaign developed he was much sought after because of his presumed knowledge of Jackson, but those who knew him best regarded Eaton as superficial and somewhat dull.

For all his limitations, Eaton was valuable to Jackson's cause. He had reported accurately on the intricate developments of Washington politics during the prelude to the campaign, and had created a wide circle of friendships in the capital. Eaton, who was descended from a prominent Connecticut educator, had been born on a large North Carolina plantation, and after education in law at the University of North Carolina had moved to Tennessee and settled on a family estate. He did not practice law, but lived the life of a country gentleman on his private income, from which he now gave generously to Jackson's campaign while serving informally as treasurer.

The fourth member was George W. Campbell, a capable, ambitious Scot who had been educated at Princeton, a veteran Jackson ally who had served in the House and Senate, as Secretary of Treasury and finally as minister to Russia.

Others of lesser importance who joined the group from time to time were Sam Houston, now a Nashville lawyer of growing influence; the ambitious hack politician Felix Grundy; and George Wilson, the editor of the Nashville *Gazette*. Andrew Jackson Donelson, who had completed his training in law and returned to the Hermitage, served as Jackson's secretary and aide to the group.

Though the Nashville Junto, as the group became known, was small and parochial in outlook, with little apparent influence outside Tennessee, its effectiveness was quickly established. None of these men was a national figure; but as a group they were the boldest and most adroit set of political managers that had appeared on the American scene.

The Junto planned nothing less than the destruction of the old caucus system under which party candidates had been chosen for almost twenty years—a device by which politicians controlled elections and kept them from the hands of the people. The process was simplicity itself: the majority faction in Congress met and selected the candidate; and since the only existing party was the large and formless band of so-called Jeffersonians, there was scant prospect of competition.

The first attack on the caucus was made in 1822 in the Nashville newspapers, by Judges Overton and Haywood. Overton and Lewis in particular saw that Jackson's phenomenal popularity made possible the bypassing of the party apparatus, which was firmly in the hands of William H. Crawford. The Junto's audacious plan was designed to capitalize on the nationwide clamor for a more democratic election process, and to storm the country with Jackson in a campaign whose central issue was to be Old Hickory's personality and military fame.

In the early summer of 1822 Lewis went to North Carolina, where he talked with Jackson's old friend Montfort Stokes. The influential Stokes was pledged to Calhoun, but said he would support Jackson "with great pleasure" in case Calhoun did not win nomination.

Lewis hurried home, determined to press Jackson into the race before it was too late. Jackson was absent for two or three weeks, at Mentor's Bluff, near Florence, Alabama, where four of his slaves had fled and the crops and buildings were being neglected. Jackson lectured his overseer, put the captured runaways in chains, and returned to the Hermitage. He was soon caught up in the race.

Felix Grundy wrote: "Your friends wish to know, whether there is any cause; unknown to them, which would render it improper . . . to exercise their own discretion . . . in bringing forward your name . . . for the office of Chief Magistrate of the United States. The General Assembly will meet next month. Then is the time to take a decisive step." Jackson apparently made no response to Grundy's letter, but on July 17 Nashville's *Whig* brought his candidacy into the open:

> GREAT RACING ! ! ! . . . The prize to be run for is the Presidential Chair. . . . There have already four states sent their nags in. Why not Tennessee put in her stud? and if so, let it be called Old Hickory . . .

Jackson wrote Dr. James Bronaugh, his former military physician,

> You will see from the papers that my name has been brought forward. To every application to me, I give the same answer—that I have never been a candidate for any office. I never will. . . . But when the people call, the Citizen is bound to render the service required. I think Crawford is lost sight of. . . . I am told Mr. Adams is at present the strongest in this state.

The first step, which startled Jackson's opponents, was to persuade the Tennessee legislature to nominate him for President, an unprecedented move but an appealingly democratic one. In the capital at Murfreesboro the House unanimously approved a resolution nominating Jackson as a presidential candidate:

> The members of the general assembly of the state of Tennessee, taking into view the great importance of the selection of a suitable person to fill the presidential chair . . . have turned their eyes to Andrew Jackson, late major-general in the armies of the United States. . . . The welfare of a country may be safely entrusted to the hands of him who has experienced every privation, and encountered every danger, to promote its safety, its honor, and its glory. . . .

One Jackson partisan in the Assembly interpreted the move in terms which were an augury of a stormy political future: "The commonality . . . thought him the only man . . . [to] revise what they thought a corrupt system of government, Meaning the caucus—the treasury and Bank influences."

Even now Jackson made no public acknowledgment. In a private letter he repeated that he did not seek office: "I have no desire, nor do I expect ever to be called to fill the Presidential chair, but should this be the case . . . it shall be without exertion on my part."

The Tennessee Senate was reluctant to follow the lead of the House, and it was two weeks later before Jackson's managers persuaded some of his enemies to fall into line. A unanimous Jackson-for-President resolution was adopted only after a couple of senators had walked out in protest.

Newspapers outside Tennessee ignored the legislature's action, but Jackson was apparently unconcerned: "As the Legislature of my state has thought proper to bring my name forward without consulting me, I mean to be silent—and let the people do as seemeth good unto them."

Monroe made a final effort to eliminate Jackson from the race by offering to make him minister to Mexico, which he presented as a challenging opportunity to settle the troublesome Texas question that had for so long agitated the southern frontier. Monroe approached Old Hickory through Senator Eaton in Washington, feigning an air of candor. He wanted Jackson to have the Mexican post, the President said, but hoped that he would not conclude that it was being offered "to get him out of the way."

Eaton assured Monroe that the general would harbor no such suspicions, and a few days later Jackson was appointed and approved by the Senate.

After cautious consultation with friends, Jackson refused Monroe's offer on the ground that the United States should not recognize the Mexican dictator Iturbide, and with the added excuse that "Mrs. Jackson could not be prevailed on to go." In fact, he had no intention of being eased out of the presidential race, however tempting the diversion.

After the nomination of Jackson by the Tennessee legislature, the general's managers were forced into a second step in their campaign. Though the state was overwhelmingly for Old Hickory, one of his opponents, Senator John Williams—an eight-year veteran who was committed to Crawford—had spread the report in Washington that Jackson was weak in his home state. Williams was running for reelection and the Junto felt that he must be defeated in order to refute his claims of Jackson's vulnerability. A Williams victory, they reasoned, would blight Jackson's hopes of becoming President. Several candidates to oppose Williams were considered and discarded as ineffective. The Junto concluded that only Jackson could defeat Williams, who had energetically canvassed the entire state, soliciting advance commitments from legislators. Jackson, it was said, agreed to challenge the senator only because he saw the necessity for control of his home state; but there was no lack of other motives. Williams had served as lieutenant colonel of Tom Benton's Tennessee militia regiment and had been hostile to Jackson for years. As senator, Williams had joined the attempt to censure Old Hickory's invasion of Florida during the Seminole war, and had recently ridiculed his nomination for President by the Tennessee legislature.

For whatever reasons Jackson now made a belated entry into the Senate race, and after a few hectic days of lobbying, the combination of Old Hickory's prestige and unrelenting pressure from the Junto forced most legislators to break their pledges to Williams and vote for Jackson. Those who resisted were to pay a penalty. Of the twenty-five who voted against Old Hickory, twenty-three were to be defeated in the next election.

With the added advantage of Jackson's standing as a senator, the Junto intensified its campaign to boost him into the presidency. Overton, Lewis, Eaton, Campbell, and their cohorts sensed victory, and were not to be diverted.

The Junto quickly spread the word that Jackson was available, and his national candidacy was launched—in Pennsylvania, which was thought to be safe for Calhoun. Business associates from his days as a merchant began working for Jackson in Pittsburgh, where a Jackson committee was formed, a model for many others which sprang up in the countryside, made up of riverboatmen, small farmers, and laborers. A mass meeting in Pittsburgh reported 1 vote for Crawford, 2 for Adams, 4 for Calhoun, 5 for Clay, "and Gen. Andw. Jackson upward of 1000."

Edward Patchell, a semiliterate Pittsburgh preacher, reported to Jackson: "I have reduced the Lousie party here from ten thousand to something less than fifty, and they are chiefly . . . the office holders and office hunters, and all they can do now is grin and show their teeth."

Patchell closed his letter with an outburst of fervor: "Jackson, I must repeat it, I have done no more than my duty, and I even forbid you to return me thanks: and should we fail this election I will pray my God to spare life until I see Andrew Jackson President of the United States, and then let me close my eyes in peace." Patchell founded a newspaper, the crude, forceful *Allegheny Democrat,* which did much to turn Pennsylvania from Calhoun to Jackson.

Other enthusiastic meetings were held in Harrisburg and Carlisle, where the crowds bawled for Jackson.

To H. W. Peterson, a Harrisburg barkeeper who wrote to ask Jackson's consent to use his name as a candidate, the general replied: "My undeviating rule of conduct . . . has been neither to seek nor decline public office. . . . As the office of Chief Magistrate of the Union . . . should not be sought . . . so it cannot, with propriety, be declined. . . . It was with these impressions, I presume . . . that the Members of the Legislature of Tennessee . . . thought it proper to present my name. . . ."

This letter, published in the Harrisburg *Commonwealth* and reprinted throughout the country, made Jackson a national candidate. Soon afterward, when he learned that Kentucky's Governor William Carroll, his old New Orleans lieutenant, was secretly campaigning for Henry Clay, Jackson was so incensed that he dropped all pretense of reluctance and entered the campaign openly and aggressively. He wrote John Coffee, "Should the people take up the subject of my nomination in the south, and west, as they have in Pennsylvania they will soon undeceive Mr. Clay's friends. If the people of Alabama, Mississippi, and Louisiana, follow the example of Pennsylvania, they will place Clay and Crawford . . . *Dehors the political combat.* "

Jackson's supporters now intrigued to halt Crawford by choosing Calhoun as their vice presidential candidate. The proud South Carolinian acquiesced after his defeat in Pennsylvania had rendered his cause hopeless, and summoned the humility to pay tribute to Jackson: "I find few with whom I accord so fully in relation to political affairs as yourself. . . . The noble maxim of yours, to do right and fear not is the basis not only of Republicanism . . . but of all political virtue . . . he who acts on it, must in the end prevail. The political quibblers will fail." Once Pennsylvania had fallen to Jackson, Calhoun's supporters in North Carolina, South Carolina, Maryland, and New Jersey flocked to Old Hickory, giving him a substantial lead in the race. With the Calhoun threat removed, the Nashville Junto also courted the votes of former Federalists, especially in the south—men who would accept neither Crawford nor Adams, but were so attached to Calhoun that they were drawn to the new alliance. As an added lure, Jackson's managers released his Seminole war correspondence with Monroe.

Crawford supporters had been hinting for months that Jackson was not a Democrat at heart, and that his 1816 correspondence with Monroe offered proof. When Eaton released the letters, popular sentiment was overwhelmingly in Jackson's favor. The most ardent Democrats were shocked to learn that Old Hickory had urged Monroe to place the South Carolina Federalist William Drayton in his cabinet, but the public was won by the general's forthright and sensible advice to the President-elect: "Party feelings ought to be laid out of view, by selecting those the most honest, possessing capacity and firmness." Even more to the popular taste was Jackson's declaration to Monroe that he would have hanged the leaders of New England's secession-tainted Hartford Convention if they had assembled in his military district.

There was serious talk of an Adams-Jackson ticket, a proposal made by Adams himself, who not only conceded that Old Hickory was a formidable challenger but also that he would be an honest and able President. Adams much preferred Jackson to Calhoun as his Vice President, and he saw benefits for the general—the office would assure him "an easy and dignified retirement for his old age." And, as a consideration important to the nation's peace and security, "The Vice Presidency . . . [is] a station in which the General could hang no one."

In any event supporters of Adams sought to defeat Crawford with an Adams-Jackson ticket, offering to reward Clay with the State Department and Calhoun with the Treasury. Jackson refused to bargain. Let his friends do "what was best for the country," he said, and he would rest content. Crawford's candidacy was effectively ended in August 1823, when he suffered a stroke which left him paralyzed, speechless, and almost blind. His supporters sought to conceal his condition by driving him through the Washington streets in a carriage, propped up among pillows, but it was known that he could sign documents only with the aid of a mechanical device and was in truth disabled.

Jackson's friends in the Tennessee legislature passed resolutions condemning the caucus, instructed the state's congressional delegation to vote against it, and urged other states to follow. Only Alabama and Maryland joined the movement; but the resulting condemnation of the caucus by politicians and newspapers rendered the process so unpopular that the caucus itself drew but a handful to the House on February 14, 1824. Only 66 of 261 congressmen attended, but of these 64 voted for Crawford, and for Albert Gallatin as Vice President, and the 2 were declared the official Democratic nominees, to "faint applause and a few hisses" from the gallery. Crawford had won a hollow victory, and, in fact, had even further damaged his cause with the public. As Daniel Webster observed, "The caucus had hurt nobody but its friends . . . Mr. Adams and General Jackson are likely to be the real competitors at last."

Jackson returned to Washington as senator in December 1823, and settled in the Franklin House, a comfortable, old-fashioned boardinghouse kept by William O'Neale between Washington and Georgetown, a place that had been patronized by members of Congress for many years. Two of O'Neale's sons had been appointed to West Point through the influence of the tavern's guests, and his three daughters had been endlessly pampered and spoiled. Jackson reported to Rachel his favorable impressions of O'Neale's "amiable wife and two daughters"—in particular Peggy O'Neale Timberlake, the wife of a navy purser, who played the piano "delightfully, and every Sunday evening entertains her pious mother with sacred music."

Jackson was probably unaware that Peggy, a hauntingly beautiful, vivacious, and seductive brunette, had become a favorite topic of Washington gossip. Before she was fifteen the coquettish darling of the Franklin House had provoked a challenge to a duel between two young army officers and driven the nephew of a Secretary of the Navy to suicide. An aging general had lingered on the brink of insanity for months after Peggy refused him. Peggy had planned two elopements during her sixteenth year, but both came to naught, the first when she kicked over a flowerpot while climbing from her bedroom window and awakened her father.

Peggy had been rescued from these perils by John B. Timberlake, a handsome young Virginian who won her heart in a whirlwind courtship of eight hours and married her a month later. The bridegroom, an irresponsible vagabond who drank to excess, was then on an enforced furlough from the navy, charged with delinquency in his purser's accounts. William O'Neale had established his new son-in-law as a merchant, a brief venture which cost the old man $15,000 and started him on the road to ruin. At this time John Henry Eaton had appeared at the O'Neale establishment as a boarder.

Eaton was now a twenty-eight-year-old widower, who attracted Peggy with easy, fashionable conversation, his reputation as Jackson's biographer, which had made him a minor celebrity in Washington— and his standing as one of the wealthiest men in Congress. The senator appeared at O'Neale's house with an introduction from Jackson: "You will find Major Eaton a man of acquirements, a constant scholar, and a gentleman of great private worth."

Eaton took an immediate interest in the affairs of the boarding-house. His generous financial aid enabled William O'Neale to stay in business, and his intervention with the Secretary of the Navy soon sent Purser Timberlake back to sea again. Eaton then became attentive to Peggy, courting her so openly that the resulting gossip reached the White House. Mrs. Monroe sent a note advising Mrs. Timberlake that she was no longer welcome at presidential receptions. A Virginia congressman wrote, "Mrs. Timberlake was considered as a lady who . . . dispensed her favors wherever she took a fancy. . . . Eaton's connection with . . . [her] was notorious."

O'Neale finally became bankrupt, and Eaton once more came to his rescue. The senator took over Franklin House, sold it to John Gadsby, a Baltimore hotel owner, and bought a smaller property where William O'Neale reopened his hostelry. When Lieutenant Timberlake returned, again in trouble with the navy because of fresh discrepancies in his accounts, Senator Eaton posted a bond of $10,000 and arranged a berth for him as purser on the frigate *Constitution,* which set sail on a four-year cruise around the world.

Timberlake had recently departed when Jackson joined Eaton at O'Neale's for the congressional session of 1824. One of their colleagues was Representative Richard K. Call of Florida, who had served as an aide to Jackson at New Orleans. The three friends dined in a private room, where Peggy helped to serve and entertained them during long talks at the table. One day Peggy greeted Jackson in tears, complaining that Call had "grossly insulted" her by embracing and pawing at her until she had struck him with a pair of fire tongs. Jackson immediately confronted Call, who admitted that he had made advances, but only because he had heard several congressmen say that "she was a woman of easy virtue and familiar with others."

Jackson defended Peggy stoutly: "I gave him a *severe lecture* for taking up such ideas of *female virtue* unless on some positive evidence of his own."

The general soon found himself in the thick of the maelstrom of presidential politics. He entered the Senate on December 5, 1823, to find that he was seated by Martin Van Buren, near whom sat Thomas Hart Benton, who was now senator from Missouri. The two westerners, who had not spoken since their Nashville brawl of 1813, sat for several days within a few feet of each other with no sign of recognition, refusing offers of friends to exchange seats. The solemn game was ended when Jackson was named chairman of the Revolutionary Claims Committee, with Benton as one of its members. A day or two later Jackson said, "Colonel Benton, will you inform me as to your earliest convenience for a meeting of our committee?"

"General Jackson, your convenience will be mine, you're the chairman, sir."

After a committee meeting, Benton spoke casually to Jackson and inquired after Rachel's health, and when they met in the White House a few days later, Benton gave a friendly bow and Jackson extended his hand. When Van Buren saw Jackson at a reception with Mrs. Benton on his arm, he realized that the feud was over.

Benton told a friend long afterward, "Yes I had a fight with Jackson. A fellow was hardly in the fashion then who hadn't. But mine was different from his other fights. It wasn't about Aunt Rachel . . . if it had been he would never have forgiven me." But though they were allies for the rest of Jackson's life, there was never again a warm, intimate relationship between them.

Jackson also made peace with General Winfield Scott, whom he had challenged to a duel five years before. When he heard gossip that Jackson planned to repeat his challenge, Scott set forth to retrieve his reputation by parading through the Capitol so that Jackson could hardly avoid him, but hung about the building for a week without a glimpse of Old Hickory, apparently because friends managed to keep the antagonists apart. When Scott finally sent a terse request for a meeting on terms of Jackson's choice, the senator proposed that the terms be friendly. The squabble was over. Jackson obviously saw the incident in light of his candidacy, for he wrote a friend that his reconciliation with Scott would frustrate those who expected to see him "with a Tomahawk in one hand and a scalping knife in the other."

Still, Jackson's opponents condemned him in extravagant terms. Henry Clay castigated him as "ignorant, passionate, hypocritical, corrupt, and easily swayed by the base men who surround him." And John Quincy Adams dismissed him as "a barbarian who could not write a sentence of grammar and hardly could spell his own name." Even Martin Van Buren had misgivings during his early acquaintance with Jackson, "Of his habitual self-control. . . . Many of his warmest supporters were not without lively apprehension . . ."

Daniel Webster, who visited Monticello during the year, reported Jefferson's distress over the popularity of Old Hickory: "I feel much alarmed at the prospect of seeing General Jackson President. He has very little respect for law or constitutions. . . ." Jefferson recalled Jackson's angry seizures, which had marked his attempts to address the Senate. "His passions are, no doubt, cooler now; he has been much tried since I knew him, but he is a dangerous man."

Jackson made conscious efforts to efface his reputation as a wild woodsman. Henry Clay, who was invited to a dinner arranged by Tennesseans and escorted home afterward in Jackson's carriage, found Old Hickory so friendly that he reported "a general amnesty" had been declared. Shortly thereafter, to the delight of his supporters, Jackson gave a dinner party which included his three rivals for the presidency, Clay, Calhoun, and Adams. Eaton, who was now acting as Jackson's secretary, reported to Rachel, "All his old quarrels have been settled . . . the General is in harmony and good understanding with everybody." He was also "in very fine health, and just as good spirits. . . . He is constantly in motion to some Dinner party or other. . . ." The general spruced up for the season with a new pair of stylishly cut black cashmere pantaloons and refurbished his dress coat with a set of silk-covered buttons.

Though Jackson and Clay dined together several times after that, there was no warmth between them. Clay could not have supported Jackson in any event, since he was a western rival whose popularity exceeded his own. By contrast, Adams had no great personal popularity, and with a growing tariff sentiment in the north, Clay might win powerful allies by supporting Adams. Adams and Clay agreed on foreign affairs and internal improvements and generally on the tariff. Finally Adams had led a long and distinguished career of public service, in contrast to Jackson, whose administrative experience was limited to the governorship of Florida in 1821, a performance which in Clay's mind cast doubt upon his executive abilities—or fitness for the presidency.

Jackson's new strategy for winning friends was otherwise a social and political triumph. Calhoun, Clay, and Adams celebrated the armistice with a reception in the general's honor on January 8, the anniversary of the Battle of New Orleans. A thousand guests thronged in to admire the spectacular decorations designed by Mrs. Adams—chalked drawings of flags and eagles on the floors, with the motto: "Welcome to the Hero of New Orleans." Jackson moved through the crowded rooms with Mrs. Adams on his arm, acknowledging greetings with grave, courtly bows, stared after by scores of women who climbed on chairs and benches for a better look at the conqueror from the frontier. It was Washington's social event of the season.

Jackson found time to attend a reception in Fredericksburg, Virginia, which he described in a letter to Jack Donelson, with an added warning that betrayed his intentions: "Nothing from my pen is to appear in print, whatever may be used under other names—or as coming from a friend in Virginia. . . ."

Aside from these forays and one appearance at the White House reception, Jackson refused to behave like a candidate. Though his rivals frequently visited the House of Representatives, where the election might be decided, Old Hickory kept his distance, despite the urgings of Sam Houston and other advisers. He declined an invitation to an elaborate party in Virginia with the explanation that it would smack of a campaign appearance, saying that he was determined to "take no step which may have imputed to it a disposition to recommend myself to anyone."

He wrote Rachel, "I get on pretty well amidst the intrigue for the next presidency, as I touch not, handle not of that unclean procedure." To John Coffee he reported that he refused "to intermix . . . with president makers," and said he would feel "no pain" if one of his rivals won the election, unless it were Crawford, whose victory "would be a great curse to the nation." He also wrote in this vein to Jack Donelson:

> In this contest I take no part . . . If it is intended by Providence that I should fill the presidential chair, I will submit to it with all humility, and endeavor to labor four years with an eye single to the public good, imploring the guidance of Providence in all things. But be assured, it will be an event that I never wished, nor expected. My only ambition was to spend the remainder of my days in domestic retirement, with my little family. It has turned out otherwise, to my great annoyance. . . .

To Lewis the bemused candidate protested that he was besieged by visitors every day, and repeated his insistence that he would not seek election: "I have no doubt if I was to travel to Boston, where I have been invited, that it would insure my election. But this I cannot do; I would feel degraded the balance of my life. If I ever fill that office, it must be the free choice of the people. I can then say I am the President of the nation, and my acts shall comport with that character."

In truth, Jackson was sensitive to the slightest stirring of the political winds. He sent Donelson a report that North Carolina would go for Jackson if Pennsylvania did, and offered a prediction that South Carolina, Alabama, Mississippi, Louisiana, Tennessee, Kentucky, Ohio, and Maryland "will all come out in my favor."

And when a friend sent him a copy of an attack on him in a Virginia newspaper, Jackson returned a notably candidate-like response: "General Jackson's course requires neither falsehood nor intrigue to support it. He has been brought before the nation by the people, without his knowledge, wishes, or consent. His support is the people. And so long as they choose to support him . . . he will not interfere."

Washington's perceptive veterans were not deceived by Jackson's protests of disinterest, in any case. Representative James Buchanan of Pennsylvania said, "He is a real & not a nominal candidate." Daniel Webster reported with an air of surprise, "General Jackson's manners are more presidential than those of any of the candidates. He is grave, mild and reserved. My wife is decidedly for him."

Jackson's record in the Senate revealed little of his political philosophy. He cast votes on most roll calls, but though these were watched carefully as indications of his views, the results were inconclusive. Usually he favored a protective tariff, with a notable exception in the case of frying pans—a necessity of frontier life which he championed by voting to free from import duty. He supported internal improvements in general.

Jackson spoke from the floor only four times during the session, for a total of less than twenty minutes, always on military matters. His only recorded opinion on the tariff was sent to a Virginia legislator, a letter apparently published at Jackson's suggestion. His introduction was a masterpiece of political flummery:

> . . . I wish it not to be forgotten that I have never solicited office, nor when called upon by the constituted authorities have ever declined . . . As my name has been brought before the nation . . . it is incumbent on me, when asked, frankly to declare my opinion upon any political or national question pending before and about which the country feels an interest. . . .

The letter repeated Jackson's earlier statement that he favored protection for the basic materials of national defense, minerals, hemp, and wool, so that American manufacturers could meet the nation's needs in time of war. This, he said, was "a judicious Tariff," whose dangers were "more fanciful than real." Henry Clay perceived the aptness of the phrase at once and realized that Jackson had put him on the defensive with this minor stroke of genius—"Well, by God, I am in favor of an *in*judicious tariff!"

Jackson went further. The tariff should be used to help retire the national debt. "I . . . do not believe a national debt is a national blessing, but rather a curse . . . calculated to raise around the administration a moneyed aristocracy dangerous to the liberties of the country. . . ."Thus for the first time the Tennessee capitalist and landholder responded to the radical views of the masses who supported him. By indirection he had singled out the Bank of the United States as an antidemocratic force, but his declarations apparently went unnoticed. In any event, he ended his statement with a flourish, "Believing . . . my opinions . . . correct . . . I would not barter them for any office that could be given me."

On March 15, his fifty-eighth birthday, Jackson entertained a few friends at dinner, including Adams, Clay, and Calhoun; and the next day Monroe called him to the White House and presented him the medal voted by Congress after the Battle of New Orleans. The general wrote of this to Jack Donelson, "Of all things I hate to speak of myself, and these parades and pomp are most disagreeable to me. . . ." To Rachel he commented, "You are aware of how disagreeable to me these shows, and I performed it not without a tremor which always sieses me on such occasions . . . I would to God I could now leave the city." And later, "There is nothing done here but *vissiting* and *carding.* You know how much I was disgusted with Those scenes when you and I were here."

Some Washington observers surmised that the general's popularity was fading. Daniel Webster said hopefully, "Jackson's interest is evidently on the wane." But John Quincy Adams realized that Jackson could not be judged on the basis of his response to the meaningless issues debated so hotly in Washington and hardly noted by the people at large. Jackson's supporters, Adams said, had only to shout "8th of January and Battle of New Orleans."

Though he probably grasped this truth himself, the general felt that he must remain in Washington until the Senate acted on Henry Clay's high-tariff bill, which the Kentuckian lumped with a program of federally financed internal improvements as "The Ar erican System."

Rachel added to his distress with pleas for his return to the Hermitage:

> . . . you have Been absent monthes at a tim . . . you [could] always tell when you would be at home but now . . . nothing on Erth can give me

any pleasure now But your Letters. I reade them with the tanderness and affection not to be expresst with my pen . . . as often as you find a Leasure moment from Every Public business spend that with me . . . [May God] in time of dainger send a kind guardian angel to guard your sleepe-ing hours . . . if my prayers and tears Can avail you will be well . . .

Jackson replied to Rachel as the interminable debates droned on, "I never was designed for a Legislator . . . not in the days like these whilst others are endeavouring by Log rolling . . . to defeat the Tariff Bill. . . . I shall leave here as soon as this Bill is acted on; before I cannot."

The bill passed the Senate and stirred angry protests from the agrarian south; but Jackson, who voted with the majority, had no regrets. "I cannot be intimidated from doing that which my . . . conscience tells me is right. . . ." He would not change his vote, he said stoutly, to win a seat in the "Presidential chair."

Jackson left for Tennessee in late May, obviously relieved to escape Washington. "I hope in god," he wrote Rachel, "we will never be separated again until death parts us."

With the adjournment of Congress the campaign spread throughout the country. Jackson's strategy was directed largely by Lewis, at home in Nashville, and by Eaton, who was frequently on the road. Eaton made numerous commitments without Jackson's knowledge, or perhaps, as an early biographer suggested, Old Hickory winked occasionally: "He developed a fine winking talent. He could also look away and not see what was going on."

17

"The Judas of the West"

The campaign resounded through the summer of 1824 with an ebullience new to American politics. Jackson's opposition lashed at him in savagery born of frustration. The theme had been sounded by Jesse Benton, who remained a bitter enemy despite his brother's truce with Jackson. Washington's *National Gazette* published Jesse's thirty-four-page denunciation of Old Hickory as a brawler and gambler, a promoter of shady land deals, a cockfighter and horse-racer who was at best a "mediocre politician." Jackson's military fame, Jesse charged, had been won by brave and active subordinates.

Soon afterward the Raleigh (N.C.) *Register* condemned Jackson's career as "A disgusting detail of squabbling and quarreling—of pistolings, dirkings and brickbattings and other actions reconcilable neither to regulations nor morals." The same newspaper also became the first to pose Rachel's reputation as an issue of the campaign: "I make a solemn appeal to the reflecting part of the community, and beg of them to think and ponder well before they place their tickets in the box, how they can justify such a woman as Mrs. Jackson! at the head of the female society of the U. States."

Yet the public seemed to hear nothing but the martial clamor for the aging victor of New Orleans. Crawford's lieutenants protested in vain that the "peoples ticket" of Jackson and Calhoun was a misnomer and a fraud. Privately one opposition leader confessed, "It is very difficult to electioneer successfully against Genl Jackson—his character and his services are of the kind which *alone* the people can appreciate and feel. . . ." The liquor served at Jackson rallies was a source of despair to opponents: "One cup of *generous* whiskey produces more military ardor than can be allayed in a month of reflection and sober reason."

Reflection and sober reason were not to be hallmarks of the campaign. Jackson's managers had been amused—and cheered—by a report from North Carolina that Old Hickory had a decisive advantage in the very illiteracy of his supporters, since they were "illy acquainted with the character and qualifications of the candidates"—except for "the glorious exploits which have crowned the military career of Jackson." Another Carolinian proclaimed: "Printers may puff, office men may dogmatize, politicians may calculate . . . but rely on it, the effectual voice of the people, now . . . scarcely recognized amidst the clamor will be uttered in favor of Andrew Jackson."

The general's managers capitalized on an innovation of the season, a craze for straw votes taken at militia musters, town meetings, and even among grand juries assembled for more prosaic tasks. One grand jury polled itself, announced for Jackson, and instructed the electorate: "He is a favorite of the people; he belongs to them; he has been raised with them; he has served them both in peace and in war; they feel grateful."

Jackson orators who harangued crowds in small towns and rural areas, particularly in the south and west, declaimed of their hero in ways that shut off all debate. One of his champions cried that Jackson had "slain the Indians & flogged the British & . . . therefore is the wisest & greatest man in the nation."

Another proclaimed, "Under Washington our independence was achieved; under Jackson our independence has been preserved . . ." More than one raucous crowd cheered him as "Old Hickory, last of the revolutionary patriots."

Jackson's opponents in the heart of Henry Clay's country reported ruefully from a militia muster in Ohio that Jackson had won a poll of the volunteers, a victory achieved by "The Rowdies . . . the very dregs of the community."

The pattern was repeated in every state: "In almost every company the drums were beating and the fifes whistling for the hero of New Orleans. The officers would treat the men . . . and then raise the war whoop for General Jackson. Then the poor, staggering . . . creatures would sally forth to vote. The result was always in favor of Jackson."

As summer faded, the desperation of other candidates became obvious. Van Buren began to court Clay in behalf of the stricken Crawford, holding out the promise of the vice presidency despite the nomination of Gallatin by the caucus.

The election process began on October 29 in Ohio and Pennsylvania, with general elections. Jackson took the lead from the start, and held it through the autumn as each of the twenty-four states cast its ballots. By the end of it, on November 22, when the legislatures of Louisiana and South Carolina voted, Jackson was already on his way to Washington, so confident that he took Rachel with him to help savor the victory. They began the long slow journey in the handsomely refurbished carriage that had borne them to Pensacola and back. With them rode Jack Donelson and his bride, Rachel's niece, Emily.

The final piecemeal election returns greeted them as they passed through the countryside—a victory over Clay in Louisville, Kentucky, and in Missouri. Clay was out of the running. As Jackson's carriage passed through Virginia, after almost a month on the road, he learned that Adams had won most of New York's votes, that reports of a Jackson sweep in Ohio had been premature, and that the election was certain to be decided in the House of Representatives.

Old Hickory soon had warning that he faced a fight to the finish, and that the victory won in the field might be snatched from him in Washington's secret councils. The Alexandria *Herald* predicted "a high game against gen. Jackson . . . intrigue . . . formidable opposition . . . gross dissimulation."

The general was in a mood to accept the verdict, however it was rendered. He wrote John Coffee:

> I am wearied with a public life, and if I could with propriety would retire, but my lott is cast, and fall as it may I must be content. Should it be that I can retire next March to my home I will be happy. . . . How often does my thoughts lead me back to the Hermitage. there surrounded by a few friends would be a paradise . . . and . . . it would take a write of habeas corpus to remove me into public life again.

By mid-December the final official tally reached the capital, from Louisiana, which gave Jackson three votes to two for Adams. The count in the electoral college now stood ninety-nine votes for Jackson, eighty-four for Adams, forty-one for Crawford, and thirty-seven for Clay.

Amid the suspense preceding the decisive clash in the House, the sixty-seven-year-old marquis de Lafayette arrived in the capital on a sentimental farewell pilgrimage through America. Here, as elsewhere, Lafayette was lionized. He appeared before a joint session of Con-

gress, where he was embraced by Speaker Clay and most other members, and later voted $200,000 and a township of valuable land—a
handsome token of the nation's esteem to the wealthy French hero.
The vigorous old man was accompanied by the beautiful red-haired
Fanny Wright, a young Scottish heiress who was touring America with
the hero, crusading in the cause of abolition and free love. Lafayette's
attention to his daughter, as he called her, inspired a round of gossip
in Washington.

Rachel Jackson sent home an excited report of the general's meeting
with the marquis, whom he had seen in Charleston in his boyhood, just
as the Frenchman landed in America. Rachel appeared to have overcome any reservations she had about public life in the capital. There
had been some doubt that she would be called upon by leaders of
Washington society, among whom the old gossip of adultery was still
current. One observer who heard numerous slanders about Rachel was
warned about her "awkwardness, ignorance and indecorum," but was
captivated by the unassuming air of the general's wife at their first
meeting, and praised her "unaffected simplicity of manners" and
"great goodness of heart."

Though the women of Washington called on Rachel in swarms, until
she complained to a friend back home of "this bustle . . . from fifty to
one hundred persons calling in a day," the Jacksons seldom went out,
except to church. The general and Rachel had been out to dinner
twice, and she had gone several times "to drink tea," but avoided the
dizzy rounds of Washington society. She said contentedly, "Indeed,
Mr. Jackson encourages me in my course."

Rachel was unaware of a secret warning received by the general that
documents exposing her past were reported in Alexandria. Jackson
responded to his informant, "I can assure you that whenever my enemies think it worthwhile to investigate . . . the character of Mrs. J I fear
not . . . as I know how to defend her."

The Jacksons were now given little time for social life. The general,
quite against his will, was caught up in the intrigue that swirled about
the three leading candidates. Like everyone else in the capital, Jackson
turned his attention to Henry Clay.

Jackson had hardly arrived in the city before he met Clay in the
Capitol. The lean Kentuckian was all smiles. "General, I have a *quarrel*
with you: why did you not let me know you were coming through
Lexington? I certainly should have waited for your arrival. We should
have travelled together." It was the last friendly meeting of the rivals.

Clay had realized with the arrival of the final vote that the power to
name the next President lay in his hands: "I only wish that I could have

been spared such a painful duty as that will be of deciding between the persons who are presented to the choice of the H. of R." There was an immediate rush to court Clay, who reported his amusement at being pursued by Jackson, Crawford, and Adams:

> I am sometimes touched gently on the shoulder by a friend, for example, of General Jackson, who will thus address me: "My dear sir, all my dependence is upon you; don't disappoint us, you know our partiality was for you next to the hero, and how much we want a Western President." Immediately after, a friend of Mr. Crawford will accost me: "The hopes of the Republican party are concentrated on you; for God's sake preserve it. If you had been returned instead of Mr. Crawford, every man of us would have supported you to the last hour. . . ." Next a friend of Mr. Adams comes with tears in his eyes: "Sir, Mr. Adams has always had the greatest respect for you, and admiration of your talents. . . ." How can one withstand all this disinterested homage and kindness?

"I am enjoying while alive," Clay said, "the posthumous honors which are usually accorded the venerated dead." Clay told Governor Floyd of Virginia that he was unable to make a choice. "When I take up the pretensions of Mr. Adams and weigh them . . . then take up the pretensions of General Jackson . . . I never was so puzzled in all my life as I am to decide between them."

In truth Clay endured no such torment of indecision. He apparently decided on his course immediately: a calculated bid for the presidency in 1828 by throwing his support to Adams.

Crawford was rejected by Clay not only because of his poor health, but also because of his opposition to the Kentuckian's program of high tariff and internal improvements. Jackson was scarcely less distasteful to Clay. Their acquaintance dated from 1815, when they established a cordial relationship in Washington; but when they next met in the capital, Clay was denouncing Jackson for his role in the Seminole war, and all possibilities of an alliance had vanished.

In 1817 when Jackson accompanied James Monroe on a western tour, the two called on Mrs. Clay, but missed her husband who was traveling. Clay was sitting in a tavern at Lebanon, Kentucky, one morning when Jackson and his party arrived. Clay rose and spoke but Jackson hardly acknowledged the greeting. When Clay went into the front room a few minutes later, Jackson was reading a newspaper and did not look up.

The two did not meet again until Jackson returned to the Senate and they were rivals for the presidency. Some of Jackson's Tennessee friends attempted a reconciliation, explaining that Jackson's apparent rudeness in Lebanon was due to his persistent dysentery, "which rendered necessary a quick retirement to the back yard"—though Jackson said later that he refused to shake hands because of Clay's hostile comments on his role in the Seminole war.

Clay said nothing openly of his choice between Jackson and Adams in the deadlock for the presidency; but in letters to friends, including Francis P. Blair, he pictured Adams as the lesser of two evils. The Kentuckian expressed fears that Jackson might become a dictator, and denied that his battle experience was relevant to the presidency: "I cannot believe that killing 2500 Englishmen at New Orleans qualifies for the various, difficult and complicated duties of the Chief Magistracy." Clay had told friends in Kentucky he couldn't vote for Jackson even before he came to Washington in the fall of 1824, and said as much to Benton in December, soon after arriving in Washington. In fact the self-interest of the ambitious Clay clearly lay with the election of Adams, whose influence was limited to New England; the more popular Jackson, on the other hand, was a serious challenger in the west, and was unlikely to accept the vice presidency when Clay made his race for the White House. The Kentuckian's choice was thus virtually inevitable.

Clay began a cautious approach to Adams through Congressman Robert Letcher of Kentucky, at first by means of subtle hints, since both Adams and Clay perceived the dangers of a charge of a corrupt bargain. After one talk with Letcher, Adams noted in his diary: *"Incendo super ignes"* (Walking over fires).

Adams and Clay sat together at a dinner for Lafayette on January 1, 1825, and Clay requested a private talk, to which Adams agreed. On the eve of their meeting Clay wrote Blair, dismissing Crawford as an invalid and Jackson as a mere military chief, and said Adams would probably be elected even if Clay threw his support to Jackson, since three of the four Crawford states leaned toward the New Englander.

Clay and Adams talked privately for three hours, reviewing their differences of the past, their views, and future hopes. Clay, who said he had been neutral, promised to come out for Adams but wished to postpone the announcement for a few days.

By now the capital was swept by rumors of a bargain, and tension mounted; even society women organized on Adams, Jackson, and Crawford lines. The bitterness of the rivalries in the capital was so pronounced that Lafayette had visions of his personal involvement, and since he lived at Gadsby's and had exchanged military reminiscences with Jackson, the marquis signaled his neutrality by putting aside his uniform. Clay privately declared his "really great indifference" to any office, and his uncertainty that he would accept the post as Secretary of State if it were offered.

Clay and his friends were briefly alarmed by a resolution from the Kentucky legislature, instructing the Speaker and the rest of the delegation to vote for Jackson. Clay hurriedly snuffed out the revolt, and his state was held safe for Adams. A fresh flurry of excitement passed through the city with a false report that Jackson had called on the invalid Crawford, raising the specter of an alliance that would defeat Adams and bring an end to Clay's intrigues. Though the general had made no such advance, his friends had now become so desperate that they persistently courted Crawford despite humiliating rebuffs. Louis McLane of Delaware, a firm Crawford man, declared: "They might as well think of turning the Capitol upside down as of persuading me to vote for Jackson."

By January 24 the House buzzed with talk that Ohio and Kentucky were going for Adams, and the odds shifted toward the New Englander. Even Louisiana had abandoned Old Hickory. Jackson newspapers launched bitter attacks, accusing Clay of betraying the west for the sake of a chance at succession. An anonymous congressman from Pennsylvania wrote to the *Columbian Observer* of Philadelphia, charging that Clay men in Congress had offered to sell their votes to Jackson in return for his naming Clay Secretary of State, and that when he was refused, Clay had thrown his support to Adams, and was now to be taken into the cabinet.

Clay branded the letter-writer as "a base and infamous columneator, a dastard and a liar," and challenged him to a duel. A few days later, when Representative George Kremer, an illiterate eccentric, acknowledged authorship of the offending letter, Clay abandoned his challenge and asked the House to investigate. Kremer, who said he welcomed an inquiry, refused to appear before a House committee and issued evasive and contradictory statements. He had undoubtedly been duped by shrewder Jackson men into making the charge, which posed a painful dilemma for Clay: the accusation would either bar him from the cabinet, or brand him as a corrupt bargainer if he accepted the post from Adams. The furor subsided, but the incident was not forgotten.

There was a heavy snowfall on Election Day, February 9, and Mrs. Margaret Bayard Smith, the wife of the head of the Washington branch of the Bank of the United States, was thankful, since it would keep the "lower citizens" at home and prevent violence. She had heard that an effigy of Adams had been prepared for burning. There were reports that Pennsylvania militiamen would march on Washington if Jackson were not elected.

At noon the Senate filed into the House, whose members sat without their hats, out of respect for the solemn occasion. The electoral votes were read, the President of the Senate rose and declared that there was no election, except for that of Calhoun, who had 122 votes for Vice President. The Senate then retired and the House began balloting.

Adams was certain of no more than twelve states, solid New England, plus Maryland, Louisiana, Kentucky, Missouri, Ohio, and Illinois. The House prepared for a long series of ballots.

New York held the key to the election, and her delegation stood seventeen for Adams and seventeen under the control of Van Buren, who planned to vote for Crawford on the first ballot. There was one doubtful delegate, the rich, pious sixty-nine-year-old General Stephen Van Rensselaer, a brother-in-law of Alexander Hamilton and a lifelong enemy of Adams. The general was much agitated when he entered the chamber, for Webster and Clay had led him into the Speaker's room and given him a harrowing glimpse of the dangers to the country of a failure to agree on a candidate. But McLane and other Crawford men had seized him before he took his seat, and extracted a promise that he would not vote for Adams.

The old man's bewilderment was obvious as the ballot box neared his seat. He dropped his head on his desk to pray for guidance, and as he did so, he saw a ballot on the floor bearing the name of Adams. He snatched it up as the answer to his prayer and dropped it in the box. Adams won New York by the single vote, and moments later was declared elected as the sixth President of the United States. Adams had won thirteen states, Jackson seven, and Crawford four. Hisses mingled with applause from the galleries, and the House soon adjourned.

A House committee sent to notify Adams found the President-elect in a state of shock. One committeeman feared that he would decline to accept: "Sweat rolled down his face. He shook from head to foot and was so agitated he could hardly stand." Adams stammered a few words and said he would reply in writing, as Jefferson had done.

The New Englander recovered rapidly. He wrote in his diary, "May the blessing of God rest upon the event of this day!" He and Mrs. Adams went to President Monroe's weekly reception that night, but the President-elect found himself "less an object of attention than General Jackson." Henry Clay was also there, all smiles, escorting two handsome young women. Observers who watched Jackson closely noted that he seemed to be "altogether placid and courteous," and this impression was strengthened when the two rivals met face to face.

Jackson, who was escorting "a large, handsome lady," stretched a long arm. "How do you do, Mr. Adams? I give you my left hand, for my right as you see is devoted to the fair. I hope you are very well, sir." Adams shook the big hand. "Very well, sir. I hope Gen. Jackson is well."

Jackson at first accepted defeat gracefully. He vetoed a proposed testimonial dinner the day after the election, lest it "might be viewed as conveying . . . a feeling of complaint which I sincerely hope belongs not to any of my friends," and a week later, when he gave a champagne supper for about two dozen of his supporters, the general exhibited no signs of rancor.

Three days after the election Adams offered the Department of State to Clay, who debated until February 20 before accepting. Several influential Adams men begged him to decline the post, so that the administration would be spared the reaction that was sure to follow Clay's acceptance. Though he was already alarmed by the violence of criticism from the western states, whose anti-Adams majority was crying betrayal, Clay could not resist the prize. He would weather the storm and make use of the traditional stepping stone to the presidency. His old friend Amos Kendall, editor of Kentucky's *Argus of Western America,* warned Clay to say nothing, attempt no explanations; "Passion is taking the place of reason and you have little conception of the ferocious feelings." Already the cry of "The Bargain," raised throughout the west, had become a call for revenge against Adams and a taunt that would follow Clay to his grave.

When he learned that Clay would become Secretary of State, Jackson reacted bitterly: not only had he been cheated of the presidency —"the will of the American people had been thwarted." This became party gospel despite its dubious logic. The Constitution did not provide for election by popular vote, and it was obvious that if the people had favored Jackson above all other candidates, they would have chosen electors committed to him. It was also uncertain that Jackson had won a popular majority, as his party claimed, since six states chose electors through their legislatures—and in the remaining states the popular vote stood at: Jackson, 155,800; Adams, 105,300; Clay 46,500; and Crawford, 44,200. Adding to the uncertainty was the case of Pennsylvania, in which only about one-third of the state was polled, after it became obvious that Jackson had a large majority. But Jackson's assertion made a powerful appeal to the people, who felt that corrupt political managers in Washington cared nothing for the interests of the masses.

The general himself had no doubt that the bargain had been corrupt: "What is this barter of votes for office but bribery?" To Lewis he wrote: "So you see, the Judas of the West has closed the contract and will receive the thirty pieces of silver. His end will be the same. Was there ever witnessed such a barefaced corruption in any country before?"

To the Nashville editor George Wilson, Jackson commented, "This, to my mind, is the most open, daring corruption that has ever shown itself under our government, and if not checked by the people will lead to open direct bribery. . . . Mr. Clay is prostrate here in the minds of all honest and honorable men . . . !"

And to Samuel Swartwout of New York, he declared, "No midnight taper burnt by me; no secret conclaves were held, or cabals entered into, to persuade anyone to a violation of pledges given, or of instructions received. By me no plans were concerted to impair the principles of our Republican institutions or to frustrate that fundamental one which maintains the supremacy of the people's will."

The general continued to rail against political intrigue, and to declare his own purity of motive: "I would rather remain a plain cultivator of the soil as I am, than to occupy . . . the first office in the world, if the voice of the nation was against it."

Clay's guilt was based entirely upon the inference drawn from his appointment; no other evidence was ever alleged. Jackson's managers did not challenge Clay's fitness for the post, but they saw the effectiveness of the corrupt Bargain charge as a campaign issue and had little difficulty in planting the suspicion in Jackson's mind, where it took root "like a revelation . . . with a solidity of conviction which nothing could ever shake." The conspiratorial whispers of the Junto, it was suspected, were responsible for the abrupt change in Jackson's attitude, from the "lofty urbanity" of his manner at the President's reception to the rancorous animosity he revealed a few days later.

Jackson was by no means alone in his conviction. Tom Benton, who was related to Clay by marriage and was to remain his personal friend, was positive that the Kentuckian had been bribed by Adams. "No man, in his right senses, at the public scene of action as I was, could believe otherwise."

Though it did not come to public attention, Jackson's health became a serious concern to Rachel and his friends during this time. The general suffered a fall, reopened the severe wound from the Dickinson duel, and hemorrhaged from the lungs for some time—a condition that was not improved by his insistence upon bleeding himself by opening a vein with his pen knife, often when he was alone.

The general was treated by a Dr. Sims, who had attended him for several years, and he refused to call in different doctors despite the pleas of Rachel and others. His friends persuaded Rachel to intercede, in the belief that Jackson would refuse her nothing. To their surprise, she reported failure. The general was more solicitous of the doctor's pride than for his own health, "Dr. Sims is my friend—an old and valued friend. His reputation as a physician, his feelings are all at stake. My dear, the thing is impossible; it cannot be. He shall cure me, or he shall kill me. I beg you never to speak to me again about it."

Though Clay had assured Adams that he would be approved by the Senate with little trouble, his nomination as Secretary of State passed by the narrow margin of twenty-seven to fourteen votes, with the stern-faced Jackson among those opposing. No previous cabinet nomination had been so strongly resisted as in this vote, which Adams recognized as "the first act of the opposition." Clay resigned his lucrative post as counsel for the Bank of the United States and assumed his duties as Secretary of State.

Jackson no longer spoke to Adams, but pledged to support him "When I think it useful to the country." As if he were addressing the people of the country, he added, "Mr. Adams is the Constitutional President and as such I would be the last man . . . to oppose him on any other ground than principle."

Before he left the capital for Tennessee, Jackson made it clear that he looked forward to a day of reckoning. In a personal letter that leaked to the press with notable promptness, he set forth his platform: "I became a soldier for the good of my country: difficulties met me at every step; I thank God it was my duty to surmount them. . . . If this makes me so, I am a Military Chieftain. . . . To him [Clay] I am in no wise responsible. There is a purer tribunal. . . . The Judgment of an enlightened patriotic and uncorrupted electorate." It was a challenge to battle four years hence.

Already there were plentiful signs that the Adams-Clay union had made Jackson's future election a virtual certainty. Letters poured in to the general from all parts of the country, praising his upright behavior and condemning Clay. A typical diatribe declared:

> I have not the language to express the sorrow and Mortification that I feel. . . . The West surely will not protect those men . . . nor let them go unpunished. . . .
> Louisianians!—Degraded!—Ungrateful men!! to vote against you! you!! who under God they are indebted to for the . . . Chastity of their wives and daughters! ! . .

The Pride of Kentucky like Lucifer has fallen! . . .
Your dignified conduct during the late Contest . . . and your subsequent Magnanimity has exacted praise even from those who . . . sacrificed
you.

Many who watched the inaugural parade on March 4, when Adams
succeeded James Monroe, were persuaded that Jackson would become
the next President. Adams was dismissed as a challenger: "He will
stand worse in four years than his father did," said a Crawford leader
from New York, who added, "Clay is ruined."

Jackson left Washington about March 15, and began his assault on
Clay at once, broadcasting the charge of the Bargain at every stop.
Until this time, as more than one observer commented, it was uncertain whether Jackson had been enthusiastic about the race for the
presidency; but now that it had been reduced to a struggle against a
personal enemy, he was resolved to conquer or die.

The pro-Jackson press opened the campaign with extravagant
charges. A typical editorial declared, "Expired at Washington on the
ninth of February, of poison administered by the assassin hands of
John Quincy Adams, the usurper, and Henry Clay, the virtue, liberty
and independence of the United States."

Jackson had hardly settled at the Hermitage before Lafayette and his
touring party arrived for a brief visit. The Frenchman's son-in-law,
Lavasseur, was disappointed by the stark simplicity of the house, but
impressed by the "order and most perfect neatness" of the farm, which
compared favorably with the finest he had seen in Germany. He deplored "the sad spectacle of slavery" at the Hermitage, but added,
"Everybody told us that General Jackson's slaves were treated with the
greatest humanity."

Fanny Wright appeared at the Hermitage soon after Lafayette's
departure, asking advice on the founding of a colony for free Negroes.
At Jackson's suggestion she bought land near Memphis, where she
carried a number of slaves bought in Nashville, and established her
"free love colony."

18

"May God Almighty forgive her murderers . . . I never can!"

The Tennessee legislature again nominated Jackson for President in October 1825, and he resigned at once from the Senate, offering a rare revelation of his views in an opening campaign speech—he favored a single presidential term and the exclusion of congressmen from high government office, the latter obviously inspired by the Adams-Clay bargain. Without this limitation by a constitutional amendment, Jackson declared, corruption in government would "become the order of the day."

In every state a clamorous campaign for democracy was under way, and everywhere groups turned to Jackson for leadership. Adams and Clay, supremely confident as the campaign began, might have felt a chill from the opening scene, when Jackson swept down the Mississippi in the steamer *Pocahontas* to visit New Orleans on January 8, 1828, in an effort to win Louisiana, which had failed to support him in 1824. Delegations from most states joined the throng, a fleet of steamers and small boats met Jackson and Rachel at Natchez, with the banks of the river crowded with people—a ball and dinner, then a triumphal descent upon New Orleans amid almost endless cannon salutes, to a celebration and reunion lasting four days. Louisiana was safely in Jackson's camp, and other states followed. Old Hickory returned to the Hermitage, where he was to spend virtually every day of the campaign.

Though Jackson would probably have swept to victory in any case, his election was made inevitable, and the Democratic party forged into a powerful force, through the machinations of the master politician Martin Van Buren of New York. A Jackson-Calhoun-Van Buren alliance gradually took form as the campaign progressed, and the modern American political party was born, for the first time banding together men of diverse interests whose aim was to win office and not to further specific principles.

Van Buren had begun to form a new party during the Adams administration, paying lip service to Jefferson, but in practice supporting Jackson. His party had become a national power after political leaders of several states, seeking a likely candidate, concluded that Old Hickory was unbeatable at the polls, and rallied about him with the unfailing instinct of their kind. Van Buren's new Democratic party was to become Jackson's personal party throughout his life.

The dapper Van Buren, now forty-five, was the son of a Kinderhook, New York, tavernkeeper. After brief schooling "Little Van" had entered a law office where he swept floors and performed other menial chores until he became a lawyer himself. Quickly successful, he entered politics and displayed gifts for intrigue that made him leader of the Jeffersonian party in the state. He went to the Senate, and was now running for governor of New York, to help Jackson carry the state.

Early in his career Van Buren had publicly opposed banking monopolies and the uncontrolled issue of paper money; he favored revocation of some bank charters to stimulate competition, and was one of the first to propose abolishment of imprisonment for debt in the United States. Charming, alert, and perceptive, Van Buren was cautious to a remarkable degree, celebrated as the most noncommital politician of his day, a compromiser evidently without principle. He fawned upon his enemies, frequently slapping backs, joking, and shaking hands in an effort to allay their hostility. His blond, bland face smiled easily, but his eyes remained watchful and aloof, revealing nothing. One writer who observed him closely concluded that for Van Buren language was a device for concealing, rather than expressing, thought.

Van Buren was frequently vacillating and indecisive. Though he was honest, he was lax in his control of subordinates, who sometimes betrayed him. But Van Buren's most striking characteristic was a passion for the sly secrecy memorialized in his nickname, the "Red Fox." As John Randolph of Roanoke said, he had a penchant for "rowing to his object with muffled oars."

The touring British author and noted abolitionist Harriet Martineau found him loquacious and informative, but only about trifles; he shunned candor, even with close friends. Van Buren questioned people closely but gave nothing in return. His constant flattery offended many, and, as Miss Martineau said, "his flattery is not merely praise of the person he is speaking to, but a worse kind still—a skepticism and ridicule of objects and persons supposed to be distasteful to the one he is conversing with." She feared that Van Buren would fail in emergencies since he had so little trust in others, and was so completely wrapped up in himself "as to make it the study of his life not to commit himself."

As soon as Jackson had been recognized as the leading candidate for 1828, politicians in many states had aspired to become his chief lieutenant. Van Buren succeeded by shouldering aside DeWitt Clinton and usurping the position of Jackson leader in New York, and by clever manipulation of the political processes of his state. The spoils system, in fact, was perfected in New York. Van Buren and his lieutenants developed a system of primaries, conventions, committees, and caucuses, all controlled by party bosses and designed to circumvent recent reforms that had replaced the old system of patronage. By expanding these schemes, Van Buren revamped the old caucus into a national elective process through the use of a party network. Jackson admired the strict military discipline Van Buren exerted over his New York party. "I'm no politician," he once said, "but if I were a politician, I'd be a New York politician."

The party developed other new tactics throughout the country. Jackson committees were organized to conduct propaganda campaigns, to refute accusations against Jackson, and to attack the Adams administration. Partisan newspapers were used to an unprecedented extent. Many small local papers sprang up to join the fray.

Though the Democratic party was a coalition of state and sectional interests that were often in conflict, its two leaders agreed on basic policies. Jackson and Van Buren were devoted to maintaining the Union, and agreed generally on the need for economy in government, and for restricting government activities to a minimum. Both opposed Nicholas Biddle's Bank of the United States, Jackson because of his distrust of all banks and Van Buren because he had sided with New York State banks in their struggles against Biddle's powerful national bank. Old Hickory and the Red Fox shared a "judicious" attitude toward the tariff, seeking a cautious compromise of the sectional issue which menaced party unity. Both leaders favored cheap lands in the west, and for the sake of harmony, Van Buren supported Jackson's plan for removal of the Indians from tribal lands covered by their white neighbors.

The party's power base was in the west and south, but it was also strong in the poorer farm districts of Pennsylvania, New York, and Massachusetts.

In addition to labor groups, debtors all over the country were driven to Jackson by their desire for cheap money, and these voters were hostile to the Bank of the United States and to the Supreme Court, which had invalidated new laws for the relief of debtors and bankrupts. There were also local bankers who feared and hated the Bank of the United States, and southern planters who accepted as gospel Calhoun's cry that the protective tariff was a death threat to American agriculture. Among others who flocked to the party were workers envious of the rich and intellectuals fearful of the loss of individual freedom. As an added complexity a handful of old Federalist refugees came seeking sanctuary, among them Roger B. Taney of Maryland, James Buchanan of Pennsylvania, and William Drayton of South Carolina.

Neither Jackson nor his supporters found it remarkable that the new champion of the common man lived rather grandly on a large plantation and was a leader of Tennessee's upper class. Michel Chevalier, an observant French traveler, was amused by the Jacksonian style of leadership: though Old Hickory felt that he represented the will of the people, Chevalier noted, his political method was not to respond to the popular will, but to "throw himself forward with the cry of, 'comrades, follow me!' " In any case, Jackson's cause was obviously flourishing, especially among workingmen.

Support for Jackson among the lower classes was by no means unanimous. Some of the first labor unions shunned his party. The *Mechanic's Free Press* of Philadelphia charged that the Democrats were more dangerous to the working classes because they were more deceitful than their opponents, and John Commerford of the Trades Union of New York warned members that both parties were frauds: "Stand aloof, remember we have no alliance with either of the humbugs."

The Democrats also alienated northern Negroes, since the party gave unspoken allegiance to the slave system, Martin Van Buren in New York as well as Jackson in Tennessee. Most free Negroes who were eligible to vote opposed Jackson.

Though it was not popularly recognized, the party's base of strength was in the south, whose leaders were convinced that Jackson stood with them on the issue of slaveholders' rights. The issue of slavery was actually injected only briefly, by the *New York American:*

> . . . this farmer of Tennessee eats the bread of idleness and luxury. The whip of the overseer quickens the servile labors whereby he—one of

those privileged beings, born to consume the fruits of the earth, is sustained—and men, immortal as himself, are daily "driven a field," like oxen; and their strength taxed to the uttermost, perhaps, that he, their master, may add another race-horse to his stud, or stake an additional bet upon a favorite game-cock. Of personal labor, the hands of this "farmer," are innocent; for, where slavery exists, labor is held to degrade the white man.

It may have been, as later historians were to suggest, that slavery was the all-important hidden issue. But the Jacksonians won the hearts of the American people through the adroit leadership of Old Hickory's managers, who played upon his reputation as a military hero and an incorruptible man of the people; and though the candidate himself said virtually nothing on the issues, his agents represented him as being on both sides of every question, varying their approach to please each audience. Thus, though the compelling issues of the day were raised by the press and mouthed by orators throughout the country, voters learned little or nothing of Jackson's stand on issues and he made no effort to dispel the mystery. By and large, as one critic said, the high principle upon which the Democratic party was based was its desire to remove Adams from office and install Jackson. But such considerations were of minor importance to the masses of the people, who yearned for a government more responsive to their needs. In Jackson they saw an ideal reformer, and in his race for the presidency they found unprecedented political entertainment.

For several months the resurrected cry of the Bargain rang above the furor of the campaign, and was repeated so incessantly as to gain wide currency. By 1827 there were half a dozen senators and forty representatives who declined to call on President Adams. The chief source of the noisome attack was the *United States Telegraph,* the former Washington *Gazette,* which had been purchased by John H. Eaton and a few associates and transformed into a Jackson organ. Duff Green, an energetic and eccentric St. Louis lawyer who had been imported as editor, began to assail the Adams régime and to boost Jackson so vigorously that the President scorned it as "scurrilous and abusive." Green's articles charging that Clay had sold himself to Adams were circulated throughout the country.

The Virginia orator John Randolph of Roanoke climaxed the debate with an inspired phillipic in the Senate. The sallow, wrinkled Virginia aristocrat entered the chamber booted and spurred, flicking his legs with a whip, surrounded by several dogs and a small black boy. Randolph had once caned a congressman who objected to his dogs and now, as Henry Clay said, "No one dared expel them." The black boy carried a jug of porter, from which he frequently refilled a flagon, ready to Randolph's hand.

A Randolph speech was one of the capital's genuine spectacles: the thin, frail body slouched in its chair, the beardless "young-old" face looking impassively about, then the tiny upper body heaving forward, "mounted upon a pair of high crane legs, so that, when he stood up, you did not know where he was to end." A squeaking, boylike soprano filled the chamber, now and then mounting "to a high shrill key, as if he were hallooing." His savage attacks, which had left many colleagues "bruised and sore, mortified, angry and ridiculous," had never been more telling than now, as he turned upon Clay in a diatribe that was a remarkable blend of Latin quotations, vulgar allusions, and irrelevant rambles into European history, combined in a devastating attack on Clay.

"Let Judas have his thirty pieces of silver!" Randolph cried; they might "go to buy a Potter's Field, in which to inter this miserable Constitution of ours, crucified by two gentlemen, suffering . . . under the burthen of the two first offices of this Government." The alliance between Adams and Clay he scorned as "between old Massachusetts and Kentucky—between the frost of January, and young, blithe, buxom and blooming May—the eldest daughter of Virginia—Young Kentucky—not so young, however as not to make a prudent match, and sell her charms for full value."

This union of Adams and Clay, Randolph shouted, was a "coalition of Blifil and Black George . . . the combination, unheard of till then, of the Puritan with the black-leg."

Clay was so incensed that he challenged Randolph to a duel; but though the two exchanged harmless shots on the Virginia bank of the Potomac, the clamor over Clay's Bargain did not diminish.

Senator Eaton, whose reports from Washington reached the Hermitage with regularity, sent fresh advice and assurances after the Clay-Randolph duel: "all that is necessary for you is to be still and quiet. This administration, wretched & rotten is already crumbling." Clay was a pathetic figure, who "walks alone, crest fallen, dejected and almost without associates."

By now an ill-assorted band of dissident congressional factions had combined against the Adams administration and set up an uproar of protest and controversy over every issue of substance, with the goal of discrediting the President. The "Tariff of Abominations" was an example, passed with the support of these dissidents, who hoped to embarrass Adams in the next election. By the end of the session of

1825–26 these opposition elements had begun to coalesce into Van Buren's new Democratic party, and to provide it with organized strength on a national scale. The combinations that were to elect Andrew Jackson had already been formed.

Amid the furor Carter Beverly of Virginia published a letter reporting that Jackson had been approached by Clay's friends with an offer to make him President in exchange for a promise that he would not name Adams Secretary of State. When Clay challenged Beverly for proof, Jackson supported the Virginian's charge, and said that he had declined to mention his choice for Secretary of State, and that Clay had come out for Adams two days later. Clay demanded details, and Jackson responded in a long public letter, naming James Buchanan of Pennsylvania as the congressman who had approached him.

Buchanan made a tortured and evasive statement, denying that he had been Clay's emissary when he called on Jackson—but he also sought to shield Jackson from blame. Delighted with Buchanan's response, Clay published a number of letters he had collected from congressmen who had voted for Adams. His pamphlet, *Address To The Public,* offered evidence of his innocence, based upon the claim that he had decided to vote for Adams before coming to Washington. But nothing halted talk of the Bargain.

Among the converts won by Jackson during the clamor over the issue was Francis Preston Blair, the Kentucky lawyer and editor who until recent weeks had been a bitter adversary. Blair now went over to Jackson and influenced Amos Kendall, the editor of *The Argus of Western America,* to follow him. Kendall unexpectedly opened a correspondence with Jackson, offering details of Clay's intrigue with Adams. He also congratulated Jackson on the outcome of his embarrassing exchange with James Buchanan over the Bargain. "Buchanan's statement has been received here by the Adams men with much exultation," Kendall wrote, "but their joy has very much abated. 'Sweet in the mouth,' they find this document, 'but bitter in the belly.' " This was the first offering of a master polemicist who was to become a stalwart of Jackson's administration, and one of its most influential figures.

Clay's friends in the Kentucky legislature made the mistake of moving a resolution declaring Clay innocent of the charge; but opponents called for an investigation, which turned up some discomfiting evidence, including Clay's letter to Blair of January 8, 1825, in which Clay had commented on the rival candidates. Amos Kendall published excerpts of this letter with misleading comments, and thus the clamor over the Bargain was kept at fever pitch during the final months of the campaign.

By now Jackson had come to accept his role as the leader of a crusade. He told Kendall, who was now leading his fight in Kentucky, that he intended to turn out of office all incompetents, all who opposed his election, all who had been appointed for political reasons, and all who had gained office "against the will of the people"—by which he meant Adams and Clay and other beneficiaries of Clay's "corrupt Bargain."

The campaign was the most vicious in the annals of American politics. Jackson was assailed for the murders of a dozen men, including Charles Dickinson and the six militiamen who had been executed in Mobile, and handbills picturing their coffins were circulated throughout the country. He was accused of blasphemy and land frauds and of conspiracy with Burr to betray the nation; Clay joined an attempt to obtain documents linking Jackson and Burr from Mrs. Harmon Blennerhasset, the widow of Burr's confederate. The opposition shouted incessantly of the dangers of sending a soldier to the White House. Clay told a Baltimore audience that he would prefer to see the country afflicted by war, pestilence, famine, or "any scourge other than military rule, or a blind and heedless enthusiasm for military renown."

Jackson's illiteracy was also held up to scorn. His traditional contribution of the expression "O.K." to the language, a rendition of the Cherokee "Oke," meaning "it is so," was said by his enemies to have been an abbreviation of his own spelling, "Orl korrect." Jackson was also ridiculed for his barbarous pronunciations, for example "development," which he rendered as "devil-ope-ment." As scholars were to perceive more than a century afterward, Jackson's opponents realized too late that they had aided the Tennessean's cause by attacking his scanty education: "Jackson's cause *was* his lack of training and the people supported it."

As an early Jackson biographer said: "Nearly all the talent, nearly all the learning, nearly all the ancient wealth, nearly all the business activity, nearly all the book-nourished intelligence, nearly all the silver-forked civilization of the country, united in opposition to General Jackson, who represented the country's untutored instincts." Someone asked the Virginian John Syme whether a Democrat could be a gentleman. "He's not apt to be," Syme said, "but if he is, he's in damned bad company."

Inevitably Jackson's opposition aired the old story of Rachel's adultery. Thomas D. Arnold, a candidate for Congress in East Tennessee, declared in a broadside:

"Gen. Jackson has admitted that he boarded at the house of old Mrs.

Donelson, and that Robards became jealous of him, but he omits the cause of that jealousy . . . that one day Robards surprised General Jackson and his wife exchanging most delicious kisses." Only because he was a coward, the broadside claimed, had Robards failed to shoot "Jackson dead in his tracks." As to Rachel's voyage to Natchez with Jackson on Colonel Stark's flatboat, Arnold wrote, "The Gen. omitted to tell that . . . they slept under the same blanket."

Charles Hammond, in his *Truth's Advocate and Monthly Anti-Jackson Expositor,* asked, "Ought a convicted adulteress and her paramour husband to be placed in the highest offices of this free and Christian land?" Hammond's attack was widely reprinted:

> General Jackson and Mrs. Robards . . . voluntarily and for the gratification of their own appetites, placed themselves in a situation to render it necessary that Mrs. Robards should be convicted of desertion and adultery, in respect to Robards. . . . Those indifferent to the character of the President's wife and those who conceive that a fallen female may be restored by subsequent good conduct, may conscientiously give General Jackson their support.

Eaton and others urged Jackson to make no response to the attacks. Caleb Atwater of Ohio wrote, "For Heaven's sake, for your country's sake, do remember that but one man can write you down—his name is Andrew Jackson." John Coffee also urged Jackson not to break his silence, "Control your feelings. Let nothing draw you out." Van Buren warned, "Our people do not like to see publications from candidates."

Jackson fretted under the restraint: "How hard it is to keep the cowhide from these villains. I have made many sacrifices for my country—but being—unable to punish these slanders of Mrs. J. is a sacrifice too great to be endured."

Finally he gave way to his impulse and started to draft a furious, discursive letter to Henry Clay:

> I could not at first believe that even you, sir . . . could descend so low. . . . It did not seem possible to me that the Secretary of State . . . would travel through the country for the cowardly purpose of slandering a virtuous female—one who has passed from infancy to old age in the confidence and friendship of the good and pious citizens . . . and who has received the mark[ed] and I may say honored attentions of Mrs. Clay and yourself. . . . Were all these professions base hypocrisy? . . . Sir, assassination of character in all its horrid forms and colorings is not as bad as such conduct as this. . . .

Then the general began to flounder: "Sir, One would have looked for something less degrading from a champion of the Pistol Gag Law. . . .

He started anew: ". . . I have only to add that Mrs. J. and myself hurl at you our defiance. A virtuous and well spent life has assured her a skirt which such men as you and your worthy associate Charles Hammond cannot sully."

Old Hickory could write no more. He gave up the attack, and probably never mailed the letter to Clay.

The Adams-Clay press was not content with charges of adultery. One day Rachel found the general in a chair with a crumpled newspaper in his hands and tears streaming down his face.

"I can defend myself," he said. "You I can defend; but now they have assailed even the memory of my mother."

Rachel read the accusation:

> General Jackson's mother was a COMMON PROSTITUTE brought to this country by the British soldiers! She afterward married a MULATTO MAN, with whom she had several children, of which number General JACKSON IS ONE!!!

At the suggestion of Lewis an eighteen-man committee was named to defend Jackson against these attacks. Under Overton as chairman and Lewis as the guiding genius, these leaders were introduced at a public meeting in Nashville and were promptly dubbed the Whitewashing Committee. Overton went to Natchez and elsewhere, collecting evidence to defend Rachel; but the burden of the campaign fell on the party's press.

Duff Green of the *Telegraph*, Amos Kendall of Kentucky, and Isaac Hill of New Hampshire led Democratic editors in savage counterattacks. Green branded the charge of Jackson's adultery a lie and charged that Adams himself had lived in sin with his wife before marriage. Papers in Pennsylvania charged that Mrs. Adams had been born out of wedlock.

The tales had no basis in fact, but such slanders were justified by Duff Green as counters to the attacks on Rachel: "I saw the necessity of bringing home the matter to Mr. Adams' own family . . . by threats of retaliation . . . the effect here was like electricity. The whole Adams corps was thrown into consternation . . . Jackson was denounced in the most bitter terms for assailing female character by those very men, who had rolled the slanders on Mrs. Jackson under their tongues as the sweetest morsel. . . ."

Jackson told Green that though he approved tossing firebrands into the enemy camp, "female character should never be introduced by friends unless . . . attack should continue to be made against Mrs. Jackson and that by way of *just retaliation* upon the known GUILTY. My great wish is that it may be altogether *evaded,* if possible . . . *I never war against females,* and it is only the base and cowardly that do."

In addition to the cry of the "corrupt Bargain" by Clay, the Jackson press charged that the Kentuckian had cheated two carpenters out of their wages, embezzled $20,000 from a legacy left to Transylvania University, kidnapped a free Negro in Pennsylvania, and smuggled him to bondage in Kentucky. Clay was also accused of plotting with Burr to separate the west from the Union. Pro-Jackson papers bayed after Adams, with considerable effect—the President, it was charged, lived in splendor in his palace. He wore silk drawers, and in the East Room where his mother had once hung laundry to dry, Adams had installed extravagantly expensive furniture. He had used public funds to buy a billiard table and a chess set, and to speculate in Russian stocks. Ike Hill also insisted that Adams had sought to prostitute a beautiful American woman to Czar Alexander in order to win influence at the Russian court.

One Jackson handbill depicted Adams with a horsewhip, driving off an old crippled soldier who had dared to ask for alms. Adams was denounced for having married an Englishwoman, and for having written a scurrilous poem against Jefferson in 1802. It was charged that he was rich—and that he was in debt—and that his accounts with the Treasury were not in order. He was said to have quarreled with his father, and to have been disinherited.

"King John the Second" was charged with a mania for public office which had brought him an income from the government equal to $16 a day from the day of his birth. He was also scorned as "a fit representative of a party which consisted of those who despised democracy and battened on the sufferings of the poor."

Jackson's partisans accepted these slanderous charges at face value. Lewis wrote Van Buren of the "triumph of virtue and republican simplicity over corruption and unprincipled aristocracy." The campaign was fought to its end on this level rather than on the serious issues of the day—the tariff, land policy, internal improvements, and the Bank of the United States. The campaign of personalities and slander ushered in the nation's modern political system, featuring party dominance. Despite the party's talk of the common man, his real attraction for Jackson's managers in every state was his voting rights and their exploitation. The roaring campaign of the autumn of 1828 boded ill for the United States.

Some of Jackson's South Carolina partisans originated a campaign toast: "Adams, Clay and Company! Would to God they were like Jonah in the whale's belly; the whale to the devil, the devil in hell and the door locked, key lost, and not a son of Vulcan within a million miles to make another."

Perhaps the most telling Democratic counterblow of the campaign appeared in the Jackson press during the summer, in response to the charges that Old Hickory was a killer:

COOL AND DELIBERATE MURDER—
Jackson coolly and deliberately put to death upward of fifteen hundred British troops on the 8th of January, 1815, on the plains below New Orleans, for no other offense than that they wished to sup in the city that night.

Though the authors of this and other campaign blasts from the Hermitage were anonymous, one of them was almost certainly Henry Lee, the half brother of Robert E. Lee, who had come to live at the Hermitage. Lee had fallen into disgrace after seducing his wife's seventeen-year-old sister, who gave birth to their child, and in his distress he had turned to Jackson for help. The general generously invited "Black Horse Harry" to live in the house, and encouraged him to begin a new Jackson biography. Lee remained to write reams of political tracts, among them "some of the finest campaign papers in this country."

By July it was apparent that Jackson would sweep to victory, and his supporters were concerned chiefly with the margin in key states. Several of Jackson's advisers bet heavily on the outcome. Swarms of well-wishers appeared at the Hermitage to congratulate the old man or to curry his favor—as many as fifty strangers turning up at the dining table each day.

Old Hickory had become universal. The symbol of his campaign, the hickory pole, appeared in astonishing numbers, set up in every village and on city street corners throughout the country. In the train of noisy demonstrations around the poles came new trappings of political campaigning designed to excite the electorate and appeal to its basic emotions—barbecues, ox roasts, torchlight parades, bonfires, and fireworks displays.

Though living Americans were hardly aware of it, more decisive events were changing the country during the year of this raucous chase for the presidency. Thirty thousand registered foreign passengers entered the United States. Four years later, over 50,000 aliens were to arrive, and the annual total was to fall below that figure only twice before the Civil War. All told nearly 600,000 immigrants would come to America in the 1830s, a massive influx that severely challenged the translation of the nation's democratic ideals into economic and social realities. The immigrants formed an ever-expanding supply of cheap labor to man new factories and heavy construction projects, and to fill the need for domestic servants and other menials, but they also began to congregate in growing slums like those around New York's Five Points. Though they were not discussed in the campaign, urban social problems were becoming acute. Neither party was prepared to deal with them.

Jackson may have been preordained as the victor, but Adams played into his hands at every turn. The President refused to attend private social functions and entertained rarely, contributing to his reputation as a haughty Yankee aristocrat, though in fact his spartan régime was dictated by his modest means and congressional penury. The President was obliged to pay for heating and lighting the White House, and the mansion was incomplete—the East Room was unfurnished, no portico graced the front of the mansion, and the south grounds were a tangle of unkempt thickets. The President also became known for his bizarre habits.

During warm weather Adams, who was fifty-eight, plunged nude into the Potomac, swimming a mile and a half daily without resting—a regimen he abandoned after a year or so in favor of brisk walks from the White House to the Capitol or to Georgetown.

Not only was the President cold, reserved, and lacking in personal magnetism; he refused to create a party machine, and alienated many supporters by insisting upon the merit system in government employment.

Adams supported internal improvements with an enthusiasm that startled even Clay. He regarded public lands as a national resource, whose sale would provide funds to build roads, canals, bridges, and other public works to develop the nation. He favored a national university, a naval academy, enlarged coastal forts, and an adequate army and navy—most of them popular causes, but all ridiculed and defeated by his opposition. Calhoun, presiding over the Senate, uniformly appointed committees hostile to the administration, and southerners continued to rail at the new tariff bill of 1828, on the ground that it protected New England manufacturers at southern expense. The ineffectual Adams foreign policy, especially the failure to open trade with the British West Indies, was resented by shippers, merchants, and business interests in general.

By 1827, when the Twentieth Congress opened, for the first time in the country's history the President could no longer command a majority.

The Adams régime, in short, had a barren record.

Jackson's candidacy inspired an almost religious fervor in some states. Tennessee was so strong for Jackson that it became dangerous to speak against him. A North Carolina legislator told the tale of entering a Tennessee village on Election Day and finding all the men out hunting—they were looking for two townsmen who had voted for Adams, thus ruining local hopes of giving Jackson a unanimous vote. The Democrats had trailed the culprits in vain, hoping to tar and feather them, but the dissidents could not be found.

With the south and west in solid support of Jackson, Kentucky drifted to the Democrats under the leadership of Amos Kendall, who attacked Adams incessantly in the *Argus*. When Clay took government printing contracts away from him, Kendall turned on Clay as well.

It was already apparent to Adams that Jackson could not be defeated. And the President, an ungraceful loser like his father before him, noted in his diary that Jackson men in Washington, including John Randolph and James Hamilton, were "skunks of party slander who had been squirting round the House of Representatives thence to issue and perfume the atmosphere of the Union." Of Calhoun, Adams said that though he was talented, he was mercurial and unprincipled, "and the dupe and tool of every knave cunning enough to drop the oil of fools in his ear." Clay was so depressed that he offered to resign, and remained only under persuasion by Adams, who feared that his departure would be taken as an admission of defeat. Adams said that four years of Jackson's reign would sicken the nation and that Clay would have his chance in 1832; but the Cock of Kentucky said gloomily that he would then be too old.

The election results bore out the country's expectations of a Jackson victory. Though the popular vote was fairly close—648,000 to 508,000 —Old Hickory won overwhelmingly in electoral votes, 178 to 83. He had swept thirteen states, including New York, and taken every electoral vote south of the Potomac and west of the Alleghenies. Adams had won only New England, New Jersey, and Delaware.

When the news came, Jackson wrote John Coffee, "I am filled with gratitude. Still, my mind is depressed." He seemed to sense that Rachel would not long survive the victory.

Rachel heard or read most of the campaign attacks upon her, and it was useless to attempt their concealment from one so alert and sensitive. Her only recorded comments were notable for their restraint. She wrote a woman friend, "the enemys of the Genls have dipt their arrows in wormwood and gall and sped them at me . . . they have Disquieted one that they had no rite to do." She prayed for her tormentors with a Christian forbearance, "my judg will know how many prayers have I ofered up."

Though she took little note of the campaign's furies, she sent a handsome suit to Moses Dawson, the editor of a Cincinnati newspaper friendly to Jackson—a suit woven and made at the Hermitage, some of the work done by Rachel herself. Dawson's effusive reply congratulated Rachel on Jackson's election as President. She probably responded politely, but to William B. Lewis, who delivered the letter, she spoke her mind: "For Mr. Jackson's sake I am glad. For my own part I never wished it."

One of her friends noted a depressing change in Rachel when news of Jackson's victory was received at the Hermitage: "From that moment her energy subsided, her spirits drooped, and her health declined. She has been heard to speak but seldom since."

Rachel once spoke wistfully of having lived with Jackson for nearly forty years without "an unkind word passing between them," and insisted that the only subject on which they had differed was his acceptance of public office, which she opposed from the start. She had hoped to remain at the Hermitage until Jackson had been inaugurated and the opening excitement of his administration had subsided; but Eaton wrote from Washington, insistent that she accompany the general:

> The storm has now abated—the angry tempest has ceased to howl . . . for the honor of your husband you cannot but look back upon the past as an idle fading vision. . . . The Ladies from . . . remote parts of the Union will be here . . . to manifest to you their feelings and high regard. . . . If you shall be absent how great will be the disappointment. Your persecutors may then chuckle and say that they have driven you from the field. . . .

Eaton was so sure of her acceptance, he said, that "I shall no longer speak of it as doubtful." There seemed to be no escape for her.

Henry Wise, a visitor from Virginia, feared that her health might prevent Rachel's going to Washington: "She was very plethoric and obese . . . and talked low but quick with a short wheezing breath. . . ."

Wise once heard her say quietly amid the preparations for leaving, "I assure you I had rather be a doorkeeper in the house of God than to live in that palace at Washington."

Until now Jackson's friends, and perhaps his political managers, had conspired to keep Rachel out of sight, fearing the exposure of "her dowdyfied figure, her inelegant conversation, and her total want of refinement."

An army officer who visited the Hermitage about this time was taken aback by Rachel's easy familiarity. The officer was sitting before a fireplace with the Jacksons one night when Rachel lit her pipe, drew a few puffs, and handed it to him, "Honey, won't you take a smoke?"

Several of her women friends and relatives carried the reluctant Rachel to Nashville to have her fitted for stylish new clothing worthy of the First Lady. During one visit to the fashionable seamstresses Rachel was resting in the parlor of the Nashville Inn, when she was mortified to overhear several of her friends bemoaning the impossibility of transforming her from an illiterate pipe-smoking country woman into a First Lady who could be made presentable to polite society in Washington.

During the same period Rachel discovered in a newspaper office a pamphlet printed by Jackson's friends, and realized that she had been ignorant of the most scurrilous attacks upon her, after all. Her companions returned to find her hysterical, crouching in a corner and sobbing uncontrollably. Rachel called for her carriage at last and stopped on the way home to wash her tear-stained face in a creek before she confronted Jackson.

Rachel's health had deteriorated rapidly during the past five years. A chronic bronchial complaint had been diagnosed as asthma, which became increasingly painful. Her voice had now become a low-pitched, barely audible wheeze. She also complained of heart palpitations.

On December 17, as she and her maid and companion, Aunt Hannah, were talking in the Hermitage sitting room, Rachel suffered a stroke, with severe spasms of the muscles of her chest and left shoulder, and a rapid irregular heartbeat. Doctors bled her three times during the day, and after the last operation Rachel was relieved and fell asleep. Young Dr. Henry Lee Heiskell, who had recently come to Nashville from Winchester, Virginia, noted the disappearance "of all alarming symptoms." The doctors went to bed in an adjoining room, but Jackson sat by his wife's bedside all night. She awoke rested and calm, appearing to have regained strength.

Rachel recuperated for three days, sitting before the fireplace much of the time. A few friends who were admitted found her cheerful and apparently on the way to recovery.

The end came Sunday night, December 22. She had sat up too long during the day, greeting a few friends who called, and caught a cold.

Jackson recalled the doctors and Dr. Heiskell rode out from Nashville to aid Dr. Hogg, who lived in the neighborhood. The doctors found evidence of pleurisy, put Rachel to bed, and gave her hot drinks until her face was bathed in sweat. Heiskell and Hogg assured Jackson that her condition was not serious and urged him to sleep in another room for the sake of his health. The doctors then went to bed and the house grew quiet.

Rachel was up twice during the night, helped by Hannah to her fireside chair, where she smoked her pipe. About ten o'clock she repeated again in a distant voice, "I'd rather be a doorkeeper in the house of God than to live in that palace."

A few minutes later she called out "I'm fainting!" and fell unconscious into the arms of Hannah, whose screams roused the household. Jackson rushed in to help lift Rachel onto her bed. He felt a convulsive twitching of her legs but could not believe she was dead. He clung to hope even when he saw the bleak faces of Hogg and Heiskell as they listened in vain for her heartbeat. Servants shrieked throughout the house, "She ain't dead, she's just fainted!"

"Bleed her," Jackson ordered Heiskell.

The doctor saw that the old man's agony was almost unbearable, and he lanced Rachel's arm. There was no flow of blood. Jackson urged him to try her temple, but only two dark drops welled onto the pallid skin. The doctors ordered the body laid out, but Jackson refused to leave.Rachel's side. When a table was brought in, he said tearfully to his servants, "Spread four blankets on it. Then if she does come to, she won't lie so hard on it."

Relatives and neighbors began filling the house by midnight and many stood in the cold outside. Major Lewis, who arrived at dawn, found Jackson sitting beside the corpse, his head buried in his hands. The old man stirred and absently stroked Rachel's forehead with a trembling hand. To John Coffee, who came in soon afterward, he said, "John, can you realize she's dead? I certainly can't."

Except for a few moments when she was being dressed in her white burial gown, Jackson remained at Rachel's side all day, so enfeebled and distracted that the doctors and his friends feared he would collapse. It was almost dark before he could be persuaded to drink some coffee, his first food or drink since Rachel's death.

She was buried at 1:00 P.M. on December 24 at a spot in the garden she and Jackson had chosen long before. Though news of her death had reached Nashville after midnight of December 23, word had spread throughout the region. *The Republican* had already been printed, but the editor and his staff scratched the news on the margin

by hand: "Mrs. Jackson has just expired!" Handbills were being carried through the town and nearby countryside by daybreak. On the
morning of the funeral a crowd of 10,000, twice the population of
Nashville, converged on the Hermitage by horseback, in carriages,
buggies, farm wagons, and coaches, people on foot, people of every
condition "rich and poor, white and black . . . as if impelled by instinct
to the grave prepared for Rachel Jackson." As one of Jackson's biographers, Marquis James, said, "Davidson county mourned Aunt Rachel
for reasons with which her husband's fame and station had little to
do."

Church bells in Nashville began tolling at one o'clock and clanged
mournfully for an hour. The celebration of the day before, the anniversary of the night battle at New Orleans, had been canceled, as had the
ball and banquet at the Nashville Inn. Jackson's old friends and politicians, who had assembled, some from as far away as the Gulf, put on
mourning to attend the funeral.

Sam Houston led the pallbearers into the chill drizzle under a bleak
sky, over a muddy walk covered with cotton. Jackson followed on the
arms of John Coffee and Henry M. Rutledge, staring vacantly before
him as if unaware of his surroundings. An onlooker said the old man
had aged twenty years overnight. Jackson was followed by a throng of
Rachel's relatives, with the waiting household servants in the rear,
many of them wringing their hands and moaning.

There was a delay after the funeral party had filed into place about
the grave, waiting for the Reverend Dr. William Hume to speak. The
sobbing Aunt Hannah flung herself on the grave and could not be torn
away. "She was more than a mistis to us," she cried, "she was a
mother." Jackson refused to allow her to be lifted from the mound.
The party waited in silence until Hannah permitted other servants to
lead her a few feet away, still sobbing and moaning.

Though Hume spoke for twenty minutes his tribute to Rachel was
not effusive, but praised chiefly her gentle modesty and good nature:

> While she rejoiced in the honor of a nation, yet no unbecoming elation
> of mind, no haughtiness, no overbearing conduct, could ever be seen
> . . . in this amiable lady. She was adorned with the ornament of a meek
> and quiet spirit. . . . By her kindness and affability, her husband was more
> happy in his own family than in the midst of his triumphs.

Hume spoke of the attacks upon her during the campaign by men
of "unfeeling hearts and unjustifiable motives":

... Under this cruel treatment, Mrs. Jackson displayed the temper of a disciple of Him who was meek and lowly of heart. . . . She felt the injustice of the warfare. . . . Her tears flowed, but there was no malevolence in her bosom. . . .

While we cordially sympathize with the President of the United States in the irreparable loss he has sustained . . . we cannot doubt but that she now dwells in the mansions of glory in company with the ransomed of the Lord.

In the silence that followed, Jackson looked about him, tears flowing down his long cheeks for the first time since Rachel had been stricken. He swallowed convulsively in a vain effort to control himself. "I know it's unmanly," he said, "but these tears are due her virtues. She has shed many for me." In tones that could be heard several yards away, he said, "In the presence of this dear saint I can and do forgive my enemies." His voice rose, "But those vile wretches who have slandered her must look to God for mercy."

The general tottered and would have fallen but for John Adair, who caught him. Adair and Jackson had been estranged for some time after the Battle of New Orleans, when the general had made a slighting remark about the Kentucky troops.

"John, it's very good of you to be here and comfort me now. You've been with me before when I needed you."

Adair's eyes filled with tears as he and Coffee led the general into his office, where Carroll and Lewis joined them. Jackson seemed to brighten, but his face darkened. "Oh yes, oh yes," he said absently, "we're all nothing but poor creatures anyhow. No matter what we gain there's always some loss that takes it all away!"

A few days after the funeral Jackson went to the grave with Lewis and Emily and Jack Donelson, stood at the foot of the mound, and cried, "She was murdered—murdered by slanders that pierced her heart! May God Almighty forgive her murderers as I know she forgave them. I never can!"

By popular tradition, Jackson wrote Rachel's epitaph himself, but it was also attributed to both Henry Lee and Major Eaton:

> Here lie the remains of Mrs. Rachel Jackson, wife of President Jackson, who died the 22nd of December, 1828, aged sixty-one years. Her face was fair, her person pleasing, her temper amiable, her heart kind. She delighted in relieving the wants of her fellow creatures and cultivated that divine pleasure by the most liberal and unpretending methods. To the poor she was a benefactor; to the rich an example; to the wretched a

comforter; to the prosperous an ornament. Her piety went hand in hand with her benevolence, and she thanked her Creator for being permitted to do good. A being so gentle and so virtuous slander might wound but could not dishonor; even death, when he bore her from the arms of her husband, could but transport her to the bosom of her God.

Jackson had a temporary wooden shelter built over the grave and ordered a contractor to build a marble tomb in the form of a Greek cupola. On the day of his departure for Washington Jackson wrote Coffee: "As rational beings it behooves us to live so as to be prepared for death when it comes, with a reasonable hope of happiness here-after. . . ." But he then gave way to his grief, "My mind is so disturbed . . . that I can scarcely write. In short, my dear friend, my heart is nearly broke. I try to summon up my usual fortitude, but it is in vain."

Jackson was still in a stricken mood a few days later when he began his journey to Washington. After his trunks had been packed and his coach driven to the front door, Jackson walked slowly into the garden for a final visit to the grave. He cut four shoots from a willow by the springhouse and planted them at the corners of the fresh mound, stood bareheaded for a few moments, returned to the coach, and doffed his hat to the Hermitage in farewell, "same as if it was a lady." His servant Alfred noted that the general was weeping soundlessly as the coach rolled away to the Hermitage landing, where a steamboat was waiting. He was to write John Coffee from Washington a few weeks later: "My days have been of labor and my nights have been of sorrow; but I look forward with hope once more to return to the Hermitage and spend some days near the tomb of my dear departed wife."

19

"It was the People's day, and the People's President . . . "

Jackson's steamer churned down the Cumberland to the Ohio, thence upstream toward Pittsburgh, hailed by crowds at every hamlet and city along the route.

The touring Frances Trollope, mother of the British novelist Anthony Trollope, who had a glimpse of the President-elect as he passed through Cincinnati, noted that Jackson was regarded as public property by most Americans, many of whom accosted him in the streets as if he were an old friend. Mrs. Trollope found Jackson a striking figure, "a gentleman and a soldier," despite his harsh, gaunt features, with his hair carelessly "but not ungracefully" combed. A "greasy fellow" halted the President-elect:

"General Jackson, I guess."

Jackson nodded.

"Why, they told me you was dead."

"No. Providence has spared me."

"And is your wife alive, too?"

Jackson shook his head wearily.

"Aye, I thought it was one or t'other of ye."

After leaving the boat at Pittsburgh, the Jackson party moved toward Washington over the National Road. An elaborate relay of escorts from Pittsburgh to the capital had been canceled by Jackson's friends, probably out of respect for Rachel's memory; but he had also been advised to eschew pomp and ceremony by supporters, who had flooded the Hermitage office with letters of congratulation and comment.

One admirer gave thanks to God that he had lived to see the overthrow of John I and John II and hoped that he would not see another of that race on the throne. John Brown, a Virginia countryman who said he was an "old revolutionist and one of your warmest friends," offered advice: the "court etiquette and pompous parade" of Washington should be foregone as an offense to republican principles. Jackson endorsed the envelope, "friendly letter—worth reading—private."

The waiting capital was like the bastion of a defeated nation preparing for doomsday.

Daniel Webster reported to friends in New England:

Gen. J. will be here abt. 15 Feb.—
Nobody knows what he will do when he does come. . . .
Many letters are sent to him; he answers none of them.
His friends here pretend to be very knowing; but . . .
Great efforts are being made to put him up to a
general sweep as to all offices . . .
My opinion is
That when he comes he will bring a breeze with him.
Which way it will blow; I cannot tell. . . .
My fear is stronger than my *hope.*

"The country is ruined past redemption," John Randolph of Roanoke declared. "There is an abjectness of spirit that appals and disgusts me. Where now could we find leaders of a revolution?"

Congressman Samuel C. Allen of Massachusetts dreaded the coming of the new ruler: "There is more effrontery . . . in putting forward a man of his bad character—a man covered with crimes . . . than ever was attempted before upon an intelligent people."

Henry Clay had auctioned his household goods for $3,000 and left for Kentucky to attend to his neglected farm. The Western Hotspur was in poor health, "his eyes sunk in his head"; he was unable to sleep, evidently convinced that he was near death. During a farewell banquet Clay had delivered another warning of the coming military tyranny and declared a lack of confidence in the new administration, but ended with a hopeful toast: "Let us never despair of the American Republic." He left behind a band of afflicted colleagues—the Attorney General a victim of vertigo, the Secretary of Navy confined to his room for nearly a month, the Secretary of War "almost blind from inflammation of the eyes," and the Secretary of Treasury "alarmingly ill."

President Adams still rose at 5:30 A.M., made his own fire in his bedroom, and continued his long daily walks and horseback rides, but he was gloomy in defeat, looking past the few days in the White House left to him: "I shall be restored to private life and left to an old age of retirement." His enemies, Adams wrote, were now

> exulting in triumph over me for the devotion of my life and of all of the faculties of my soul to the Union and to the improvement, physical, moral and intellectual, of my country. The North assails me for my fidelity to the Union: The South, for my ardent aspirations of improvement. . . . I can yet scarcely realize my situation. . . . My time is now all leisure, like an instantaneous flat calm in the midst of a hurricane. I cannot yet settle my mind to a regular course of future employment.

Mrs. Margaret Bayard Smith, who had seen every change of administration since Washington's, mourned the passing of a world. She had never seen the capital in such a state of despair, "so many changes in society—so many families broken up. . . . Drawing rooms in which I have so often mixed with gay crowds, distinguished by rank, fashion, beauty, talent . . . now empty, silent, dark, dismantled. Oh' 'tis melancholy!"

As the day of Jackson's arrival drew near, the city was swarmed by the masses who had come from every state, throngs of such people as the genteel capital had never known. Daniel Webster, who watched the gathering of the Jacksonians, said he had never witnessed such a scene: "Persons have come five hundred miles to see General Jackson, and they really seem to think the country is rescued from some dreadful danger." But most of the clamorous crowd of frontiersmen, war veterans, adventurers, confidence men, and Irish immigrants from seaport cities were officeseekers, whose chief anxiety was to save the nation from the incumbents of the Adams administration.

Other observers found the invasion reminiscent of the mob of Paris marching on Versailles, or of "the inundation of northern barbarians into Rome. . . . Strange faces filled every public place, and every face seemed to bear defiance on its brow." Jackson men surged through the streets, overran barrooms, and imperiled the local whiskey supplies of Washington, Georgetown, and Alexandria. Hotels and rooming houses overflowed with five or six guests to a bed, and many were forced to sleep on billiard tables and floors, in doorways or the streets. Webster felt that the office-hungry multitude were "too many to be fed without a miracle."

The Reverend Robert Little of the First Unitarian Church used as a text for a sermon: "When Christ drew near the city, he wept over it."

Jackson and his party were spirited into the city past a welcoming delegation on February 12, 1829, and the President-elect was settled at Gadsby's Tavern several hours before the mob became aware of his presence. It was a weary party that descended at Gadsby's with the old man: William Lewis and Henry Lee, Jack and Emily Donelson, and Emily's pretty young cousin, Mary Eastin. As Rachel had wished, Emily had come to serve as hostess of the Executive Mansion, and her husband was to be Jackson's secretary.

Jackson was soon beset by hundreds of job seekers who crowded Gadsby's by day and night, a roaring siege that inspired an offended observer to rechristen Democratic headquarters "the Wigwam." Jackson was delighted to find Isaac Hill of the *New Hampshire Patriot* at the Wigwam. He flattered the little editor by reciting several of his editorial quips from memory, and may have offered him a place in the administration at their first meeting. Hill, who shunned ostentation of every kind, was dressed as always in workman's clothing.

Ike Hill was a loyal party man, an embittered cripple who had made his way in the world as a printer. Though conservative by nature, he was quick to denounce the rich and powerful. Hill had supported Crawford and the caucus system in 1824, and championed a protective tariff, but had been an early convert to Jackson's cause. No one had been more effective in the campaign attacks on Adams than Hill, a gifted phrasemaker and relentless partisan who rejoiced when his barbed words struck home, "I have hit them, for they flutter." The lingering animosities of the campaign were due in some measure to Hill's influence.

Jackson refused to pay a courtesy call on Adams, and announced in the press that he would not "go near" his opponent. Adams protested to friends when he read in the *Telegraph* that Jackson was avoiding him because the President had had a hand in publishing slanders against Rachel. "This is not true. I have not been privy to any publication in any newspaper against either himself or his wife." Adams sent a courteous message to the Wigwam saying that he would vacate the White House by March 4. Jackson replied with the hope that the Adams family would remain until it was convenient for them to move.

Another problem confronting the new administration was less easily disposed of. Peggy O'Neale Timberlake, after a brief widowhood, had become Peggy Eaton, to the accompaniment of a tempest in the society of official Washington.

Lieutenant John Timberlake had died aboard the *Constitution* during a cruise of the Mediterranean, of tuberculosis, according to the official record—of drunkenness, by the gossip of crewmen. The tale was soon abroad in Washington that Timberlake had cut his throat because he knew that his wife was living with Senator Eaton. Once the election was over, the senator turned to Jackson for advice as to whether he should "snatch her from the injustice done . . . by a gossiping world." Eaton was somewhat hesitant, however. "At a *proper time,*" he added, "I will tender her the offer to share my life and prospects."

Jackson advised prompt action. "Major, if you love Margaret Timberlake go and marry her at once and shut their mouths . . . your marrying her will disprove these charges, and restore Peggy's good name."

John Henry Eaton had returned to Washington a few weeks before Jackson's arrival, and settled at the O'Neale boardinghouse once more, still postponing the date of his marriage, which he now set for the following summer after Congress had adjourned. He was prompted to action by Jackson, who had written from the Hermitage during his mourning to urge that Eaton marry Peggy "forthwith" or leave the boardinghouse.

Eaton acquiesed in an emotional outburst, declaring that the marriage would make him "a happy and contented man," and that his faith in Peggy was absolute: "Judge! General, you who have known me long and well, if I could do such an act as this apart from the belief that she has a soul above everything of crime and design. . . ."

Peggy's marriage to Eaton on January 1, 1829, by the chaplain of the Senate, was not a social triumph.

Congressman C. C. Cambreleng of New York broke the news to Van Buren, "Poor Eaton is to be married tonight to Mrs. T———! There is a vulgar saying of some vulgar man, I believe Swift, on such unions —about using a certain household———and then putting it on one's head."

Margaret Bayard Smith also reported the marriage of "the bosom friend and almost adopted son of General Jackson" to Peggy, whose reputation had been "totally destroyed" by their liaison: "She has never been admitted to good society (!!!), is very handsome. . . . The General's personal and political friends are very much disturbed about it." Mrs. Smith amused her correspondent with the suggestion "of what a suitable lady in waiting" Peggy would have made for Rachel Jackson. "His enemies . . . repeat the old adage 'birds of a feather will flock together . . .' The ladies will not go to the wedding and if they can help it will not let their husbands go."

Amid the hubbub at the tavern, working late into the nights, Old Hickory dealt with a kindred challenge, the composition of his cabinet.

The process of selection had begun before he left home, with an odd and undiplomatic approach to the Tennessee senators, Eaton and Hugh White. Jackson offered White an unspecified post in the cabinet, asking that he pass the invitation to Eaton in case he could not accept himself. White declined and Eaton at first demurred, perhaps because, as one gossipy observer remarked, "Public opinion will not allow Genl. Eaton . . . to bring *his wife* into society." When Jackson insisted that both Eaton and White should not desert him, Eaton accepted with professed reluctance the post of Secretary of War, which he had probably coveted from the start. Peggy Eaton, who felt no such restraint, shrilled a premature cry of triumph: "Dammit, I'm off !"

After Jackson reached the capital, White, Eaton, and Lewis, who were with him constantly, exerted decisive influence on the other selections, though even they handled the old man gingerly. As an astute biographer said, "Like most men of passion, his choice could be determined by some trifle of temper or accidental mood, and for this reason those who sought to direct his will were ever cautious about their manner of approach."

The remainder of Jackson's cabinet was complete within ten days after his arrival, and was announced in the *Telegraph*.

As expected, Van Buren was to be Secretary of State, and placed in line of succession to the White House.

The Treasury went to Congressman Samuel D. Ingham of Pennsylvania, a wealthy paper manufacturer who was a Calhoun man and an active anti-Adams pamphleteer.

John Branch, the Secretary of Navy, was a well-to-do North Carolina planter and socialite who had served as governor and senator. Though Branch was said to be weak-willed and lacking in exceptional abilities, he was eminently qualified in Jackson's eyes because he had voted against the confirmation of Clay as Secretary of State after his bargain with Adams.

The Attorney General, John M. Berrien of Georgia, had also won Jackson's esteem by voting against Clay. A native of New Jersey and Princeton graduate, Berrien had migrated to Georgia where he became a judge and senator; though he supported Calhoun, he was known as a strong Union man.

The Postmaster General, now raised to cabinet level, was to be John McLean, a popular and efficient Ohioan who had administered the mails in the Adams régime.

The selections came under fire at once. Despite Jackson's earlier condemnation of the practice, he had drawn four members from Congress, three of them dismissed by critics as "of the least capacity." Alexander Hamilton's son James said it was "the most unintellectual Cabinet we ever had." Virginians, who had been excluded for the first time, were bitterly resentful. John Quincy Adams rendered his judgment: "Among them all there is not a man capable of a generous or liberal sentiment towards an adversary, excepting Eaton, and he is a man of indecently licentious life."

The first formal protest came from the Tennessee delegation, which objected to Eaton out of fear of his ambition and his influence over the President. Jackson rejected the complaint with a sharp rebuke, determined to cling to his one personal friend and confidant in the cabinet. Jackson defended Eaton stoutly, "I have known him for twenty years, without a speck upon his moral character . . ." The major's character, Jackson declared, made it highly unlikely that he would compromise Peggy's reputation in any way. Jackson was prompted to a revealing expression of the traits he treasured in his personal relationships: "I have known him for twenty years and have yet to find a man or woman, white or colored, to say that John H. Eaton ever quoted me."

Jackson's party leaders were not unanimous in their praise of the cabinet. Even Van Buren was disappointed, and said that Ingham's was the only name he had heard mentioned for a post. Louis McLane complained, "By what interest that miserable old woman, Branch, was ever dreamed of no one can tell."

Though the cabinet reflected the party's uneasy coalition of rival interests, thoughtful politicians noted that it was carefully balanced, with two men each from the north, west, and south.

Jackson had made the final decisions himself, and was proud of them. His cabinet, he boasted, was "one of the strongest . . . that have ever been in the United States." His opponents, who greeted the announcement with the cry, "A millennium of Minnows," made a more accurate judgment, for the cabinet was to serve only two years and was to be of limited use to the President. But the pragmatic Congressman Cambreleng expressed the feeling of the party majority at the moment: "The Democrats are all not only satisfied but gratified with the cabinet, while the whole federal phalanx is shocked at the idea that the plebian race should have the ascendancy in the councils of the President."

The cabinet was forgotten in the excitement of the inauguration. A crowd estimated at from 10,000 to 20,000 visitors crowded the city to witness the opening of the new régime on March 4.

The morning was misty and cold, and a scattering of snow remained. The ground was mercifully frozen, firming the mud of Pennsylvania Avenue beneath the feet of spectators. The crowd that covered Capitol Hill raised a cheer when Jackson appeared from Gadsby's with a party of a dozen or more men. A salute of cannon fire rolled across the city, Old Hickory's lone concession to tradition, since he had vetoed plans for a parade. As Jefferson had done before him, Jackson walked to his inauguration, the first to be held outdoors. He alone was bareheaded and the crowd recognized him at a great distance by the bristling white shock of his hair.

The mist lifted as the President's party entered the Capitol gates and the sun burst through. Jackson sauntered up the slope with his companions, circled the crowd at a long-legged gait, nimbly scaled a stone wall, and disappeared into the Capitol basement. Cheers broke out anew when he appeared on the portico above. One observer noted that "the color of the whole mass of the crowd changed, as if by a miracle; all hats were off at once, and the dark tint which usually pervades a mixed map of men was turned, as by a magic wand, into the bright hue of ten thousand upturned human faces. . . . The peal of shouting that arose rent the air, and seemed to shake the very ground."

Jackson bowed to the applause—a commanding presence in sharp contrast to the image of the unlettered, uncouth backwoodsman caricatured in the Adams press. Some of his steadfast opponents were impressed. James Hamilton, Jr., a skeptical South Carolinian, took note of his "grace and composed dignity"; and Mrs. Smith was moved to praise: "It is *true* greatness which needs not the aid of ornament and pomp. I think I shall like him vastly when I know him."

Jackson read his speech in a voice so low that it was heard only by those at his side. The message was disappointingly bland, with none of the fire and brimstone all had expected.

Jackson spoke humbly of his new task, as if the campaign uproar of the past four years had escaped his memory and he had been summoned unexpectedly to the presidency. "I approach it with trembling reluctance. But my country has willed it, and I obey . . . "

The first concerns of his administration, he said, would be the liquidation of the national debt, "a judicious tariff," and "a Just respect for State rights." There was scarcely a hint of the storms that lay ahead.

It was said that Lewis or Lee had written the message from Jackson's ideas and that it had been much revised. It bore signs of compromise throughout, with two unmistakably Jacksonian exceptions. First, he foresaw a decisive clash between the states and the federal government: "Between the power granted to the general government, and those reserved to the States and the people, it is to be regretted that no line can be so obviously drawn as that all shall understand its boundaries. . . ." This dilemma, he said, must be resolved in a spirit of compromise "by the good sense" of the nation.

Second, he intended to improve matters in Washington: "The task of reform will require particularly the correction of those abuses that have brought the patronage of the federal government into conflict with the freedom of elections. . . ." He meant to turn the rascals out.*

He took the oath from Chief Justice Marshall, kissed a Bible, and bowed, whereupon the mob cheered, broke across the barricade on the steps, and rushed upward with outstretched hands, crushing about the President. Jackson fought his way slowly into the Capitol and passed down the hill, halted at every step. "The living mass was impenetrable," Mrs. Smith said; but a passage was opened at last and the old man reached his horse, mounted, and turned toward the White House.

Since neither Adams nor his supporters appeared, and the city's only uniformed company had declined to escort the new President, a few aging officers of the Revolution had volunteered at the last moment and now fell in behind Jackson with the mob pressing on their heels. "Such a cortege as followed him!" Mrs. Smith wrote. "Country men, farmers, gentlemen, mounted and dismounted, boys, women and children, black and whites, carriages, wagons and carts all pursuing him. . . ."

The jubilant democratic mob filled the Avenue, bound for the White House reception that was to usher in the rule of the common people. It was almost as if the aromas of the feast were wafted across the city from the laden tables in the East Room where cakes, ice cream, and orange punch were to be served.

The throng rushed through the gates into the White House, leaving congressmen, diplomats, ranking military officers, and leaders of capital society in its wake. Congressman John Floyd of Virginia and his 300-pound wife forced their way in behind their two tall, strong sons, and Georgia's Congressman George Gilmer and his wife entered by clinging to the coattails of the Floyds. Glasses and china were broken, clothing was ripped, and women fainted amid the chaotic press within. Elegant $150 chairs were "profaned by the feet of clodhoppers" from

---

*It was generally assumed at the time that Jackson was incapable of composing such an address, but the surviving rough draft of the address, undoubtedly his own work, demonstrates his ability to write clearly and forcefully; later drafts did not improve the message. Adams said of the address as delivered, "It is short, written with some eloquence, and remarkable chiefly for a significant threat of reform."

the provinces who were determined to have a glimpse of the President. The Gilmers and Floyds escaped through a window at the first opportunity.

According to one story, a small girl lost during the mêlée was found by her anxious parents as she jumped up and down on an old sofa in Jackson's private quarters. The young democrat shrieked: "Just think, mama! This sofa is a millionth part mine!"

To the disappointment of the crowd Jackson soon sank into "a listless state of exhaustion," and he too retreated, with the aid of several henchmen who locked arms to clear a path to a rear door. Guests might have lingered even then except for the removal of the punch tubs to the lawn—an inspired stroke which dispersed the mob.

The President had disappeared by the time Margaret Smith arrived, astounded by the sight of "A rabble, a mob, of boys, negroes, women, children, scrambling, fighting, romping. . . . Ladies fainted, men were seen with bloody noses." Most of those within, she said, could escape only through the windows.

"But it was the People's day, and the People's President and the People would rule. God grant that one day or other, the People, do not put down all rule and rulers. I fear, enlightened Freemen as they are, they will be found, as they have been found in all ages and countries where they get the power in their hands, that of all tyrants, they are the most ferocious, and despotic."

The "People's day" ended with an inaugural ball which provided the capital's restructured social world with its first sensation—the calculated snub of Peggy Eaton by Emily Donelson, Mrs. Calhoun, and cabinet wives.

Jackson lectured Emily with a notable lack of effect. He insisted that as his hostess, she must treat Peggy with the respect due the wife of his old friend, and assured her that the gossip about the Eatons was spread by "Clay and his minions." Emily and Jack humored Jackson by returning a call from the Eatons, but Emily would go no further.

The incident was the overture of a bizarre affair of state that would rock the administration for months to come and contribute to the unease of a régime beset by misgivings as to its social adequacy. The burgeoning Peggy Eaton scandal added intensity to the fascinated curiosity with which the capital kept watch upon the old man in the White House.

Jackson was a disappointment to those who expected the mansion to degenerate into a frontier outpost. He retained three servants who had been with Adams for fifteen years: a French chef, Anthony Vivart; and Antoine Ginusta, a steward and butler whose wife was assistant housekeeper. Among the wines served at Jackson's table were Château Margaux and Château Lafitte; supplies of gin, rum, brandy, whiskey, wine, beer, ale, and porter were generous. Jackson was to entertain so lavishly as to consume most of his $25,000 salary.

The historian George Bancroft, who had been offended by "the vilest promiscuous medley that ever was congregated in a decent house," returned later to dine with Jackson, Emily and Jack Donelson, and others, a company notable for its "perfect ease and good breeding."

The mansion itself was soon made more presentable. A portico was added, thus completing the modern exterior of the White House after nearly thirty years of use. The East Room was also furnished and made ready for its first public functions.

The capital buzzed over another of Old Hickory's innovations, "The King's Painter," Ralph Earl, who had followed the old man to Washington and was established in the White House. Earl was to spend eight years there, turning out portraits of Jackson to meet the brisk demand. Gossips were quick to report that the way to the President's heart was through an order for an Earl portrait.

The expectant nation, awaiting it knew not what at the hands of this administration, had scant conception of Jackson's true character. Aside from his fame as a soldier, little was known of his talents. He came as the dominant, though not the most able, political leader of Tennessee, a landholder and slaveowner of comfortable means, conservative by station and association, provincial in outlook, and inexperienced in statecraft and in the rough and tumble of partisan politics known to the eastern cities.

Though the masses seemed to have boundless faith in him, many feared that the general would find himself hopelessly out of his depth in Washington, where his instincts would be inadequate to the challenges of complex affairs. Some observers who were close to him in these days, however, found cause for hope in the unexpected resources of Jackson's mind. Louis McLane, his former opponent who was to serve in a later Jackson cabinet, found the general "the most rapid reasoner I have ever met with. He jumps to a conclusion before I can start on my premises." Benton agreed: "The character of his mind was that of judgment, with a rapid and almost intuitive perception, followed by an instant and decisive action." The author James Kirke Paulding was baffled by the brilliance of the untutored President: "To him knowledge seemed entirely unnecessary. He saw intuitively into everything, and reached a conclusion by a short cut while others were beating the bush for the game."

Nathaniel Hawthorne, who saw him but once, was so struck by Jackson's presence that he eagerly gathered impressions of the new President from men who knew him intimately. "Surely he was a great man," Hawthorne concluded, "and his native strength, as well of intellect as of character, compelled every man to be his tool that came within his reach; and the more cunning the individual might be, it served only to make him the sharper tool."

But it was Martin Van Buren who perceived that the secret source of Jackson's strength was an unerring understanding of the people of his country. "They were his blood relations," Van Buren said, "—the only blood relations he had." The New Yorker was also convinced that Jackson sincerely felt that "to labour for the good of the masses was a special mission assigned to him by his Creator."

Van Buren arrived belatedly in the capital, ill and exhausted after a trying journey. At every turn he had been warned by friends that he should reject the post of Secretary of State and refuse to associate himself with such an unpromising administration. Levi Woodbury of New Hampshire and Louis McLane of Delaware had forecast disaster for Jackson's régime, and even the President's old friend Edward Livingston had deplored the ineptness and confusion in Washington— above all, the lack of social dignity that marked the opening of the era of the common man. The fastidious Van Buren, resplendent in a snuff-colored coat, white trousers, morocco shoes, yellow gloves, and a lace-tipped cravat, was pounced upon by officeseekers as soon as he arrived. Scores of insistent strangers followed him to his room, making their pleas as he lay on his bed for an hour, resting before calling on the President.

He found Jackson sitting in his office with Lewis, the room lit by a single candle. The sick old man rose with a welcoming smile and an eager handshake, and when he saw that Van Buren was weary, urged him to go back to bed and begin their talks on affairs of state the next day. Van Buren did not forget the warm sincerity of Jackson's manner: "From that night to the day of his death, relations . . . official, political and personal, were inviolably maintained between that noble old man and myself, the cordial and confidential character of which can never have been surpassed among public men."

Van Buren's arrival helped to restore order from chaos. The army of officeseekers and disappointed overflowed the public buildings daily and departmental operations were at a virtual standstill. The new administration, unprepared for the crisis, milled in confusion. Jackson spent his days with Eaton and Lewis, whose efforts to reward their friends added to the disorder. At least one of Jackson's friends advised him to dismiss his counsellors in order to restore calm to the city. Van

Buren's quiet competence became obvious at once; his savoir faire and his wide circle of acquaintances made possible a more effective distribution of patronage and created a lull in the clamor of complaints. It was Van Buren who first gave the capital an inkling of what was to be expected of the new administration. His role as a catalyst measurably increased Jackson's influence and effectiveness.

Jackson's political views in general were those of a Jefferson Republican—he favored strict control of federal powers and authority, reliance on the states, frugality and economy in government. Like a majority of Americans, he believed that the central government should interfere in the affairs of the people as little as possible.

Though his administrative experience had been limited to his store, his plantation, and military affairs, and he was accustomed to the art of command rather than leadership, he adapted readily to the duties of civil administration. His training and personality made it inevitable that he would take strong positions and accept full responsibility for them. Daniel Webster was completely in error in his judgment that "Genl. J. has not character enough to conduct his measures by his own strength. Somebody must and will lead him."

Though Jackson was interested in political rather than administrative affairs, he was to bear his burdens of office routine patiently. Van Buren found him uniformly considerate of his associates in day-to-day administrative affairs, but unyielding in moments of decision:

> Although firm to the last degree in the execution of his resolution when once formed, I never knew a man more free from conceit, or one to whom it was to a greater extent a pleasure, as well as a recognized duty, to listen patiently . . . until the time for action had arrived. Akin to his disposition in this regard was his readiness to acknowledge error whenever an occasion to do so was presented and a willingness to give full credit to his co-actors on important occasions without ever pausing to consider how much of the merit he awarded was at the expense of that due to himself. . . .

Arthur Schlesinger, Jr.—a perceptive student of Jackson's political career—has concluded that though Old Hickory came to the White House with great natural gifts, he, like other strong American presidents from Washington to Franklin Roosevelt, was to be shaped by the challenges that lay ahead: "Jackson grew visibly from the day of his inauguration. His leadership gained steadily in confidence and imagination. . . . The people called him, and he came, like the great folk heroes, to lead them out of bondage."

20

"If I had a *tit* for every one of these pigs . . . "

The administration of the folk hero opened inauspiciously. The cabinet suffered its first loss within less than a week after members took office.

Jackson's plan for purifying the republic by dismissing opposition men from office met resistance from the upright John McLean. When told that he must oust postmasters who had supported Adams in the election, the Ohioan said he would dismiss all politically active postmasters in that case, Jackson men included. He was finally called to the President's office, where he repeated his firm declaration.

Jackson eyed him without comment, then paced the room, puffing his pipe in a fury. "Mr. McLean," he said, "will you accept a seat on the bench of the Supreme Court?" McLean agreed, and after a four-day reign as a member of the cabinet, stepped aside in favor of the more amenable William T. Barry of Kentucky.

There was no doubt within or without the party that the Democrats intended to reward the faithful on a scale heretofore unknown. Jackson may have had more modest goals in mind, but the militant newcomers who filled the streets and the anterooms of the House of Representatives were so noisy, importunate, and persistent as to create the impression of an imminent revolution within the federal heirarchy.

Ike Hill added to the impression with his pronouncement: "The barnacles will be scraped clean from the ship of State, most of whom have grown so large and stick so tight that the scraping process may be fatal to them."

Senator William Marcy of New York put the issue plainly in a speech that added a new battle cry to the American political vocabulary: "If they are defeated, they expect to retire from Office; if they are successful they claim, as a matter of right, the advantages of success. They see nothing wrong in the rule that to the victor belongs the spoils of the enemy."

Duff Green's *Telegraph* clamored for the dismissal of Adams men from office, and when anti-Jackson papers protested that faithful old public servants should not be turned out for political reasons, for the sake of their families, Green retorted, "No one should be continued in office who, in a country like this, cannot make an honest living."

Never before had Washington's officeholders feared the loss of their jobs at the change of an administration, and some were seized by panic, since all government workers were "tremblingly alive to what may happen." Several officials suffered nervous breakdowns and three committed suicide.

Daniel Webster was alarmed: "The army is the army of the country; the navy is the navy of the country. . . . The Post Office, The Land Office, the Custom-house, are in like manner, institutions of the country, established for the good of the people; and it may well alarm the lovers of free institutions, when all the offices . . . are spoken of, in high places, as being but 'the spoils of victory.' "

To Jackson, as it would to succeeding presidents, the spoils system brought only vexation; but once he had become convinced that as the leader of the people it was his right and duty to install his supporters in office, he was unmoved by the howls of the opposition and the press.

Though by Jackson's estimate there was about 1 office for every 500 applicants, the city was literally filled with job seekers. Amos Kendall met a sensitive Kentucky friend who confessed, "Mr. Kendall, I'm ashamed of myself, for I feel as if every man I meet knew what I came for." Kendall reassured him: "Don't distress yourself, for every man you meet is on the same business."

One Washington editor found the almost universal desire to feed at "the public crib" astounding, since government jobs paid less than mechanics could earn back home. "The great inducement," he said, "perhaps is laziness—a mortal hatred of work."

Ex-President Adams noted in his diary, "Everyone is in breathless expectation, trembling at heart, and afraid to speak." Adams conceded that many removals were appropriate because of old age, "incapacity . . . intemperance . . . irregularities of private life." But he noted that

● Rachel Jackson. *(Miniature
attributed to L. C. Strobel, Ladies'
Hermitage Association, Nashville.)*

● John Overton, Jackson's early friend in Tennessee, and personal and political advisor. (*Tennessee State Library and Archives, Nashville.*)

● Aaron Burr, who retained Jackson's loyalty despite his arrest and trial for treason. (*National Archives.*)

● John Sevier, Jackson's chief antagonist in Tennessee politics, and adversary in a celebrated duel. (*Tennessee State Library and Archives, Nashville.*)

● Sam Houston, Jackson's protégé and a founding father of Texas. (*Tennessee State Library and Archives, Nashville.*)

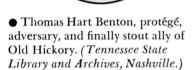

● Thomas Hart Benton, protégé, adversary, and finally stout ally of Old Hickory. (*Tennessee State Library and Archives, Nashville.*)

● John Henry Eaton, whose intimate friendship with Jackson survived the Peggy Eaton Affair. (*Tennessee State Library and Archives, Nashville.*)

● Bernard Marigny in his old age. The Creole leader forced upon Jackson the services of the Laffite brothers, who did so much to win the battle of New Orleans. (*The Historic New Orleans Collection.*)

● John Quincy Adams, Jackson's longtime political opponent, to whom he lost the 1824 Presidential election and over whom he won the 1828 election. (*Library of Congress.*)

● Andrew Jackson, Jr., Jackson's adopted son (Rachel's nephew) upon whom Jackson lavished such affection and wealth. *(Ladies' Hermitage Association, Nashville.)*

● Andrew Jackson. Portrait by Thomas Sully, 1829. *(Historical Society of Pennsylvania.)*

● Peggy Eaton in her forties. *(Library of Congress.)*

● Roger Taney, Jackson's appointee as Chief Justice in the expansion and liberalization of the Supreme Court. *(National Archives.)*

● Amos Kendall, the Svengali of Jackson's administration. *(National Archives.)*

● Francis B. Blair—"Bl-aar"—the chief publicist of Jackson's regime and an intimate adviser to the President. *(National Archives.)*

● Martin Van Buren, the Red Fox
of Kinderhook, who made
himself indispensable to Jackson
and became his anointed successor.
(National Archives.)

● Nicholas Biddle, Jackson's
antagonist in the bank crisis.
(Library of Congress.)

● John C. Calhoun, a victim of
Jackson's wounded pride.
(National Archives.)

● Henry Clay, Jackson's perennial
political rival and bitter enemy.
(National Archives.)

● Andrew Jackson, 1845, in a
portrait painted by George Healy
during the last three weeks of Jackson's
life. *(Ladies' Hermitage Association,
Nashville.)*

● General Jackson's office in the Hermitage.

● Uncle Alfred, Jackson's personal servant, who long survived his master, seated before the Jackson tomb. (*Ladies Hermitage Association, Nashville.*)

the replacements were, "on the average, much less respectable than those dismissed." Adams felt that his worst fears were to be confirmed: "The only principles yet discernible in the conduct of the President were to feed the cormorant appetite for place, and to reward the prostitution of canvassing defamers."

And a few months later Adams noted that "the removals from office are continuing with great perseverance. The custom houses in Boston, New York and Philadelphia had been swept clear, also at Portsmouth, New Hampshire and New Orleans. The appointments are exclusively of violent partisans; and every editor of a scurrilous and slanderous newspaper is provided for."

Jackson found further justification for the spoils system as evidence of government corruption accumulated. When Amos Kendall took his place as fourth auditor of the Treasury, he discovered that $7,000 had been embezzled by his predecessor, Tobias Watkins, a close personal friend of Adams and Clay. Watkins aided the cause of reform by fleeing, whereupon he was run down, convicted, sentenced, and pilloried in the Jackson press. Kendall halted subscriptions to more than twenty newspapers Watkins had bought with public funds, and also ended the practice of forwarding mail for his friends under government frank—even the letters of his wife, the latter a gesture that startled the most upright Jacksonians.

Eleven Treasury officials were found to be short in their accounts, and hundreds more in other departments were said to be chronically delinquent; some officials had taken bankruptcy oaths as often as a dozen times within the span of a few months. Jackson himself dealt with the aged register of the Treasury, one Nourse, who had been a government employee since the Revolution and was now in default by more than $10,000. Nourse begged the President for mercy and refused to resign upon request. Jackson dismissed him abruptly. "I'd turn out my own father under the same circumstances," he said. Jackson said that "a considerable number of the officers who have been long in office are old men and drunkards," and complained that he had never seen Harrison, the Treasury's first auditor, when he was sober.

After eighteen months of investigation it was found that some $300,-000 had been stolen by Treasury Department officials.

The President ordered reports from all department heads and asked for suggestions as to how jobs might be eliminated and efficiency improved. He urged the dismissal of all employees of poor "moral habits," and went further. It was his duty, he declared, "to dismiss all officers who were appointed against the manifest will of the people or . . . by subserviency of selfish electioneering purposes. . . ." He said that he was determined to preserve free elections by turning out such rascals.

Jackson was not a mere spoilsman. Not only did he seek to remove inefficient and corrupt officeholders; he insisted that the idea of property rights in government offices was undemocratic and un-American, and that rotation would give the people a sense of sharing in their government.

Though Jackson announced that he was "determined to hear with caution, examine well and grant offices to none but such as was honest and capable," he could handle but few of the horde; and he sometimes abandoned high principles and made some errors of judgment, as in the case of Samuel Swartwout. This veteran officeholder, who had helped to swing New York to Jackson, had raised the party's cry soon after the inauguration: " . . . *no damned rascal who made use of his office or its profits for the purposes of keeping Mr. Adams in, and General Jackson out of power, is entitled to the least lenity or mercy, save that of hanging* . . . whether or not I shall get any thing in the general scramble for plunder, remains to be proven; but I rather guess I shall. . . ."

He was a prophet. In the face of many objections Jackson made Swartwout collector of customs of the Port of New York, through which passed almost two-thirds of all American imports.

Van Buren warned Jackson that this appointment would "in the end be deeply lamented." Representative Cambreleng of New York protested even more positively: "Mark me—if our Collector is not a defaulter in four years, I'll swallow the Treasury if it was all coined in coppers."

Jackson rejected this advice. "Respecting Mr. Swartwout all agree, and many have spoken, that he is a warm hearted, zealous and generous man, strictly honest and correct. . . . He is reputed to be poor, but as an honest man is 'the noblest work of God,' I cannot recognize this as an objection to any man."

The headstrong Jackson also appeared at a disadvantage in the case of his old rival William Henry Harrison, a Clay partisan who had been named as minister to Colombia by Adams. Old Tippecanoe had just presented his credentials in Bogotá when Jackson replaced him.

Postmaster General Barry sought to save the conqueror of Tecumseh from Jackson's vengeance. "If you had seen him, as I did, on the Thames, you would, I think, let him alone." Jackson peered through his pipe smoke.

"You may be right, Barry. I reckon you are. But thank God I didn't see him on the Thames."

Harrison returned home.

Among the applicants was Jack Dade, one of Jackson's old friends: "Now, Andy, I don't care what it is, just so it pays well—one of those sinecures, you know."

Jackson appointed him superintendent of the District Penitentiary, where Dade made a memorable address to the assembled inmates.

"Ladies and gentlemen," he began. "No, that won't do. Fellow citizens—no, you've forfeited your right to that. Well, anyway, you people, listen. As long as you behave yourselves, you'll be well treated, but any devilment, and, I'll turn every damned one of you out!"

Jackson exhibited a growing irritation under the siege of officeseekers, who sought only "A tit . . . to suck the Treasury Pap." But he was touched by the tearful performance of one woman, "who had once rolled in wealth" and now begged him for an office he could not give, though she sobbed that her children were starving and that she had sold her thimble to buy food. Old Hickory had little cash, but impulsively gave her half the money in his pockets.

After a White House reception the President was cornered by the elderly postmaster of Albany, New York, who complained that Van Buren's henchmen planned to oust him though he had no other means of support.

Jackson said nothing, and the old man began to undress. "I'm going to show you my wounds," he said. "I fought under General Washington."

"Put on your coat at once, sir!" Jackson said quickly.

The next day, when the New York congressman Silas Wright produced a list of officeholders to be dismissed, and Jackson saw the name of the aging postmaster, he shook his head. Wright protested that the culprit had committed the unpardonable sin of voting for John Quincy Adams.

Jackson flung his pipe in the fire and cried, "By God, I won't remove the old man! Do you know he carries a pound of British lead in his body?"

The President's devotion to those who had fought the British was unwavering. David Buell, a young New Yorker who spoke for another postmaster in danger of losing his place, explained that this man, too, was a war veteran, that he had lost a leg in battle and could no longer support his large family if he lost his post. There was a problem—"I must tell you that he voted against you."

"If he lost a leg fighting for his country," Jackson said, "that's vote enough for me."

A tale that was to become one of Abraham Lincoln's favorites was revealing of the pressures upon Jackson from clamoring constituents.

An officeseeker begged Jackson to name him minister to Great Britain.

"The place is filled."

"Then, can't you make me Secretary of the Legation?"

"I'm sorry. That's also filled."

"How about Vice Consul?"

Jackson shook his head. "Too late, I'm afraid."

The caller sighed. "Well, then, would you give me a pair of old boots?"

As the tide receded and the army of disgruntled officeseekers disappeared from Washington, there were mutterings of rebellion from those who had been denied. If Jackson handed out no more jobs to his followers, one malcontent said, "the party is Ruined and the sooner we begin to build up a new one the better." Jackson was unmoved. "If I had a *tit* for every one of these pigs to suck at they would still be my friends," he said.

The constant harassment by officeseekers had left the President weary and despondent. He wrote a friend in Tennessee: "Late in the night I retire to my chamber . . . deprived of all hope of happiness this side of the grave and often wish myself at the Hermitage there to spend the remnant of my days & drop a daily tear on the tomb of my beloved wife."

Though the party was to bear the stigma of the development and ruthless application of the spoils system, the extent of Jackson's removals was much overemphasized.

Of the country's 8,000 postmasters, who held some of the most desirable jobs, fewer than 500 were replaced. The heads of all the Washington bureaus were replaced with the exception of Indian Commissioner Henry R. Schoolcraft; about half the Indian agents in the field were replaced.*

Jackson did not introduce the spoils system, though he had greatly expanded its use. He applied his high personal standards of integrity and propriety to public service, but was often in ignorance of conditions within departments, and was also blindly loyal to his friends. He thought in terms of individuals and gave few hints that he had a grasp of the administrative process in broad terms.

Jackson submitted 319 appointments for Senate approval, of which

---

*By the fall of 1830 after eighteen months of Jackson's reign, fewer than 10 percent of officeholders had been removed—919 out of 10,093, according to the *Telegraph*—and a painstaking survey by a twentieth-century scholar revealed that the 10 percent figure was probably accurate, though total removals may have been as high as 20 percent. In any event Jackson had not made a clean sweep of the federal bureaucracy.

121 were replacements for men removed from office; but he had also reappointed 62 incumbents.

Jackson's announced policy of rotation was a sensible remedy for the problem of superannuation that had grown up in forty years of government bureaucracy; yet he did not perceive its ultimate consequences. He was to leave the system largely as he found it and made no innovations in the art of administration. He was content to attempt to apply his precepts of morality and common sense to government—and his true purpose was to destroy the idea of government office as property and give all citizens an equal opportunity to participate in self-government.

Jackson undoubtedly felt that he was acting in the public interest throughout. He wrote in his private journal, "There has been a great noise about removals." He intended to ask Congress to pass a law that would terminate all government employment after a specified term. "Now," Jackson wrote, "every man who has been in office a few years, believes he has a life estate in it, a vested right, and if it has been held twenty years or upwards, not only a vested right, but that it ought to descend to his children, and if no children, then the next of kin. This is not the principles of our government. It is rotation in office that will perpetuate our liberty."

Jackson's administration was but a few weeks old when Calhoun and Van Buren began a power struggle for the right to succeed their aging chief. Their first open conflict became involved with the continuing saga of Peggy Eaton.

When the wives of leading government officials refused to call on Peggy, she made a whirlwind round of visits herself, leaving her cards at virtually every distinguished address in the city. Her calls were not returned. Peggy then declared war upon Washington society.

Margaret O'Neale Timberlake Eaton, at twenty-nine, retained the full bloom of her beauty. Her small, lithe body was voluptuously rounded, her complexion was perfection itself, her huge dark eyes sparkled with humor and the joy of living—and, it was frequently remarked, with lascivious promise. She laughed often, and immoderately, revealing the most celebrated teeth in Washington; she offended fastidious noses with the overpowering scent of her toilet water.

A sharp-eyed observer from Virginia who visited the Eatons was surprised to note that Peggy was more at ease than her husband. Peggy chattered: "Entering into conversation she talked away about anything and every thing—jumbling great and small subjects together. . . . She loves admiration and bedaubs every one almost with flattery who notices her. The gentlemen who call on Eaton, knowing this, pay her particular attention." The visitor's final conclusion was that the senator would find Peggy a burden; "Eaton can never get along with such a woman."

During Jackson's selection of the cabinet Peggy had watched every move as if her life depended upon the outcome. To a suggestion that Eaton be given a foreign ministry she said adamantly that she would remain in Washington, "in the presence of my enemies," and humble them at their own game. She won a few, and temporary, battles. Branch and Berrien, while they were intriguing for their posts, became intimate with the Eatons and paid them frequent visits, Berrien with his wife and the widowed Branch with his daughters.

When Jackson questioned John Branch forthrightly about his attitude toward Peggy, the North Carolinian denied that he knew anything disreputable about her, and declared that he believed none of the current gossip. Eaton was so high in his praise of Branch and Berrien that the general had been influenced to take them into the cabinet. John Calhoun warned the old man of trouble ahead. Whatever the makeup of the rest of the cabinet, he predicted, public opinion would be outraged if Eaton became Secretary of War. Jackson retorted, "Do you suppose I've been sent here by the people to consult the ladies of Washington as to the proper persons to compose my Cabinet?" Old Hickory relished the prospect of a battle for Peggy's honor: "This makes me well," he said. "I was born for storm and calm does not suit me."

But once Jackson had been inaugurated and the cabinet was sworn in, Peggy had been rudely rejected. The smiles, invitations, and calls ceased abruptly. She saw Mrs. Berrien and the Branch girls no more. Even Emily Donelson joined in the ostracism of Mrs. Eaton. The mistress of the White House wrote her sister, Mrs. John Coffee, that Peggy was "held in too much abhorrence ever to be noticed, The ladies here have determined not to visit her. To please Uncle we returned her first call. She talked of her intimacy with our family . . . [which] so disgusted . . . me that I shall not visit her again. Fear this is to be a source of great mortification to our dear old Uncle."

Emily's hostility to Peggy became so marked that Eaton sent her an anguished note, declaring that she had been misled by the slanders of Mrs. Branch and Mrs. Ingham, and warning: "You yourself may become a victim of those meddling gossips. Your excellent aunt . . ."

Emily replied tartly:

. . . Having drawn my attention to slanders got up for political purposes to tarnish the reputation of my lamented Aunt you will suffer me to say that the most conclusive proof of her innocence was the respect in which she was universally held by her neighbours. . . . As to the probability of my becoming a victim to the slanders . . . I hope I shall maintain my reputation as it has heretofore been . . . not only pure but unsuspected. . . .

As you say I am young and unacquainted with the world, and therefore I will trouble myself as little as possible with things that do not concern me. . . .

Jack Donelson, who had a hand in Emily's reply, enclosed a note of his own assuring Eaton that Emily actually took no stock in the gossip about Peggy. But a few days later, when Jackson and Jack Donelson called on Peggy, Emily did not accompany them.

Soon afterward, when she was publicly snubbed by Emily, Peggy protested indignantly to Jack Donelson—if his wife continued her hostility, she might as well pack to go home, for Jackson had promised that he would banish her if she refused to accept the Eatons.

Gossip in a new vein began to circulate about Peggy: she prompted Major William Lewis to remain in Washington, rather than return to Tennessee as he had planned, since she had hopes of persuading Jackson to banish Emily from the White House and replace her with Lewis's attractive daughter. To this end, it was said, Peggy conspired to have the Treasury's second auditor dismissed so that Lewis could have his place. There was also a tale that Peggy made a vain effort to intercede with Amos Kendall, when he questioned the padded account of one of her friends, a contract mail-carrier, and that she went so far as to offer the bribe of a new carriage to Kendall's wife. There were other inferences that Peggy was seeking to wield an influence of her own, actual or imaginary. A Virginian who maintained a fascinated watch upon her career wrote of Peggy, "Her Ladyship is *decidedly* the greatest fool I ever saw in a genteel situation."

Some of this came to Jackson's ears in a way that influenced the course of the Calhoun–Van Buren feud. " 'That base man Calhoun,' the president said, is secretely saying that *mrs* Eaton is the president. . . ." Jackson also believed that Calhoun had joined Clay to set off the clamor against Peggy, but he was probably mistaken. The earnest Calhoun was more likely a victim of the episode, since he could not regard Peggy's cause seriously when the country was faced with so many pressing problems. "These are not times in which the petty arts can succeed," he said. "I have ever held them in contempt, and never more than now." Otherwise Old Hickory seemed to be oblivious to the undercurrents of the affair. In a burst of naïve optimism he wrote a relative in Tennessee, "The cloud is blowing over. Satelites of Clay are falling in the pitts [they] dug for Eaton."

Martin Van Buren now entered the drama—"The Eaton malaria," as he called it. The New York widower became the first cabinet member to dine with the Eatons and he was soon joined by the new Postmaster General, John Barry, who arrived from Kentucky with his wife and cast his lot with the Eatons.

Jackson also gave Peggy official sanction, as if her social recognition had become a matter of national policy. His policy was promptly challenged by a letter from a friend of his early days in Congress, the Reverend Ezra Stiles Ely of Philadelphia, who warned Jackson that Peggy had borne a bad reputation as a girl and that she had traveled with Eaton before their marriage. The minister also quoted a guest at Gadsby's Tavern as saying that "Mrs. Eaton brushed by him last night . . . having apparently forgotten the time when she had slept with him."

Jackson's response, longer than his inaugural address, was a vigorous defense of Peggy and John Eaton. The President declared that though he would disregard all rumors and suspicions, he welcomed any "facts and proofs sustained by reputable witnesses in the light of day."

Two or three others sought to warn Jackson, among them Congressman Call, who was dismissed curtly: "My Dear Call *you* have a right to believe that Mrs. T. was *not* a woman of easy virtue."

Ely sent Jackson a second letter, recounting a story that Peggy had suffered a miscarriage during her marriage to Timberlake, at a time when her husband had been at sea for more than a year. Jackson once more demanded proof, and sent Major Lewis about town to collect testimonies as to Peggy's virtue. Some of his supporters became uneasy as signs of Old Hickory's involvement multiplied. "God knows," said one lieutenant, "we did not make him president to work the miracle of Making mrs. E———an honest woman."

Peggy's reaction when she heard of Ely's tale was strongly suggestive of her innocence. She hastened to Philadelphia, confronted Ely, and demanded the source of his information. The minister refused, until at the end of a prolonged and angry discussion Peggy said, "You pretend to be a Christian minister. You have basely wronged an innocent woman, and have got to tell me . . ."

"From the Rev. Campbell."

"It's a wicked lie," Peggy said, "and he'll suffer for it."

She returned to Washington and bearded Campbell, who reluctantly confessed that he had got the story from her doctor. John N. Campbell, the young pastor of the Presbyterian Church attended by Jackson while he was in Washington, had scoured the town for evidence against Peggy, who reported indignantly: "He had even been to my laundress and to my mantua-maker."

Campbell brought the issue to a head in September by writing Jackson to reveal that it was he who had given Dr. Ely the report of the alleged miscarriage, a story told to him by the late Dr. Craven, who had attended Peggy. The incident, Campbell said, had taken place in 1821.

A few hours later Campbell was called to face a stern Jackson, who presented documentary evidence that Timberlake had been in Washington in 1821. When the President had delivered a scathing lecture, the minister told of a recent visit he had made to Dr. Craven's widow, who said that Eaton and Peggy had also called on her in an attempt to frighten her into a denial of the miscarriage story. The Eatons, Mrs. Craven said, had spoken of duels and lawsuits in an effort to influence her—but she had told them that though she was ignorant of the miscarriage episode, she knew that Timberlake had frequently confided in Dr. Craven and had given him "impressions not favourable to the character of Mrs. T."

Jackson rejected the charges completely, and insisted that the change of dates rendered Campbell's tale incredible.

The President then called an extraordinary meeting of the cabinet to hear the evidence concerning Peggy's reputation, and summoned Ely, Campbell, John Calhoun, and Jack Donelson to appear. Jackson began by reading at length from the voluminous evidence and testimonials collected by Lewis, who had written "so many letters and statements in relation to this business that he was worn out with the nightly toil of copying." Jackson had also sent a man to New York to investigate a report that Peggy and Eaton had registered at a hotel.

The President gave the cabinet an impassioned review, defending Peggy as blameless. It was not true, he said, that Rachel had condemned Peggy; "Mrs. Jackson, to the last moment of her life, believed Mrs. Eaton to be an innocent and much injured woman." Further, he said, "Female virtue is like a tender and delicate flower; let but the breath of suspicion rest upon it, and it withers and perhaps perishes forever."

Jackson then called on Ely and Campbell to testify, and cross-examined them in the manner of a frontier prosecutor. Ely spoke of the New York hotel incident, and conceded that there was no evidence to convict Major Eaton of improper conduct.

"Nor Mrs. Eaton either," Jackson said.

"On that point," Ely said, "I would rather not give an opinion."

"She is as chaste as a virgin!" Jackson snapped.

Campbell then said rather lamely that his only motive had been to save the administration from reproach, and that he had revealed nothing publicly. The angry Jackson told the minister that he had been invited to give evidence, not to discuss it. Campbell replied, "I stand ready to prove, in a court of justice, all I have said, and more than I have said . . ."

Jackson dismissed the hearing with an air of triumph, as if Peggy's vindication were complete.

However sincere Jackson's verdict, in the eyes of the leaders of Washington society Peggy was guilty as charged. As Calhoun's biographer Margaret Coit declared, she was "guilty of social ambitions beyond her 'lowly condition,' guilty of beauty unbecoming a matron of thirty, guilty of wit and conversational charm, to which years of association with Washington leaders had given intellectual polish as well as picturesque profanity."

Peggy Eaton's position did not improve, and the war over her reputation raged on. Society in the capital was "rent in twain" and many prominent men kept their families at home rather than risk the perils of entertaining socially. Jackson's loyalty to Peggy did not waver, but the hopelessness of his cause was apparent in his appeal to John Calhoun, who replied sagely that this was a quarrel among women, whose laws, like those of the Medes and Persians, could neither be appealed nor repealed.

Numerous theories were advanced to explain Jackson's persistence in the cause: the wounds he bore from the gossip about Rachel; his limited experience with women, which had been confined to those of "the simple pioneer type"; and the volatility of his temper, once his suspicions of Clay and Calhoun had been aroused. Mrs. Margaret Smith, who had come to regard Jackson as a warm and kind-hearted but obstinate old man, observed, "In truth, the only excuse his friends can make for his violence and imbecilities, is, that, he is in his dotage." Most persuasive of all, perhaps, was the judgment of the twentieth-century Jackson scholar John S. Bassett: "There is no record that Jackson ever changed an opinion once formed, whatever the proof offered to him."

The Eaton case, in any event, continued as Washington's leading entertainment of the season. The capital laughed over Henry Clay's quip about Peggy, a parody of Shakespeare, "Time cannot wither, nor custom stale her infinite virginity." Wags spoke of Peggy as "Princess Immaculate, that delicate bone of contention," and newspapers made sly allusions to the American Pompadour. But it was no laughing matter to Jackson: "What divine right let females with a clergyman at their lead . . . establish a secrete inquisition and decree who shall, & who shall not, come into society—and who shall be sacraficed by their secrete *slanders?*"

21

"The people will put these things to rights . . . "

From the first day of his administration Jackson had been guided, and his policies allegedly set, by a handful of men who frequented the White House as his personal advisers—the men of the "Kitchen Cabinet," as they were to be known to Washington folklore. The group was at first composed of William B. Lewis, Amos Kendall, Jack Donelson, Isaac Hill, and Martin Van Buren, who preempted the roles of the cabinet and department heads and to a large extent functioned as the executive branch.

Jackson was sensitive to gibes at his dependence upon these advisers, and he occasionally belittled their influence. Tales of the potency of his Kitchen Cabinet, he declared, stemmed from "a false view" of his character: "I should loath myself did any act of mine afford the slightest color for the insinuation that I followed blindly the judgment of any friend . . ."

The President was perhaps more susceptible to manipulation by the Kitchen Cabinet than he realized. He relied particularly upon Lewis and Kendall.

Lewis was Jackson's most intimate companion and influential adviser, despite his unpopularity with other presidential aides. A few days after the inauguration when Lewis announced that he was going home, Jackson dissuaded him: "Why, Major, you aren't going to leave me here *alone,* after doing more than any man to bring me here?" The former militia quartermaster was salvaged for the Kitchen Cabinet by the offer of a subordinate auditorship in the Treasury Department, a post so desirable that a recent vacancy had drawn an army of applicants, among them five senators and thirty-five congressmen.

Moved only by his devotion to the President, Lewis gave up his library and the other comforts of his beloved Tennessee plantation to live in the White House for so long as Jackson might remain. Cautious and conservative, he was frequently appalled by Jackson's forthright moves, and he was not himself an architect of the administration's programs. Lewis spent more time in Congress than any of the Kitchen Cabinet, and almost every night, as they smoked their pipes in Jackson's White House study, the major and the President analyzed events of the day. Lewis reported and Jackson listened attentively, alert for hints of opposition skulduggery.

It was said that Jackson never went to sleep while Congress was in session, however far into the night deliberations were extended, until Lewis or Jack Donelson had brought him a resumé of the day's events.

Some critics felt that the garrulous Lewis overestimated his importance to Jackson, and held his place by shamelessly flattering the President and pandering to his prejudices. Jackson was warned by one of his friends that the egocentric major frequently boasted of his role as confidential adviser, and that Old Hickory was held responsible for this "silly conduct"; but all protests were in vain. Jackson would hear no criticism of his old companion in arms. His own appraisal of the major's talents was to be revealed in his advice to James K. Polk in 1844: "Keep . . . Lewis to ferret out and make known to you all the plots and intrigues hatching against your administration and you are safe."

But the genius of the Kitchen Cabinet was the gifted polemicist Amos Kendall, whose deadly, biting wit was to be displayed in many of Jackson's state papers.

Kendall had met the general for the first time when he brought Kentucky's electoral vote to Washington as a trophy of victory, and was rewarded with the post of fourth auditor of the Treasury.

The son of a Massachusetts farmer, Kendall had been educated at Groton and then at Dartmouth, where he stood first in the class of 1811. He had migrated to Kentucky, where he became editor and co-owner of *The Argus of Western America* in Frankfort. For more than a decade he had campaigned for democracy, championed relief laws for the benefit of debtors, and railed against the Bank of the United States. His early accomplishments hardly suggested the role of artful conspirator and vindictive partisan that Kendall was to play in Jackson's administration.

The sickly Kendall appeared to be older than his years, with his prematurely white hair and weary eyes in a sallow face. He had a chronic hacking cough and even in the heat of summer wore a great-coat buttoned to his chin; he frequently suffered from a pounding headache and bound a white handkerchief around his head. A congressman once saw Kendall riding a shambling nag down Pennsylvania Avenue, "Poor wretch . . . he looked like death on the pale horse." He was seldom seen on social occasions, and so deliberately enveloped himself in a cloak of mystery as to become the gray eminence of the new government. Kendall visited Capitol Hill so infrequently that one fifth-term congressman said he had never caught a glimpse of him.

Kendall's alter ego and effective ally was the pugnacious and loyal Ike Hill who, though by no means an intellectual, was a gifted phrase-maker, satirical and witty, and so vigorous at pillorying his political enemies that he had once been beaten by a gang of outraged Federalists in the streets of Concord, New Hampshire. Hill's ethics were not of the highest, as was demonstrated by his charge that John Quincy Adams had served as a procurer for the Russian czar—and by his advertising in the *Patriot* a quack medicine for which he was an agent. Still, the crippled editor's talents were useful, and in league with Kendall he made the Jackson press a formidable weapon.

The most independent of the Kitchen Cabinet was young Jack Donelson, whose influence was usually exerted against Major Lewis and John Henry Eaton, who was later to join the group. Van Buren, though he was frequently consulted, concentrated on matters of broad national concern rather than upon the political infighting which occupied the Kitchen Cabinet's attention during most of Jackson's régime.

In the autumn of 1829 Jackson began discussions with these men, and others, on the problem of the Bank of the United States, which he regarded as "dangerous to liberty." Jackson proposed as a substitute for the Bank an unwieldy "people's institution," which was to be owned jointly by the federal and state governments. Jackson asked Kendall, Felix Grundy, and James A. Hamilton to submit their thoughts on the Bank for possible inclusion in his first annual message to Congress. Young Hamilton took the lead in urging caution upon Jackson—his plan for a substitute bank was dangerous, an invitation to even greater concentration of financial power; and control by Congress would destroy prospects of accountability by the bank. When Attorney General Berrien and Secretary of Treasury Ingham joined the chorus of protest, the President agreed to a compromise: he would ask for a study of the feasibility of a new bank, based upon the credit and resources of the government, without offering details.

Jackson's first annual message, which went to Congress in December

1829, was couched in calm, reasoned terms as the result of the handiwork of the Kitchen Cabinet; but nothing could disguise the vigor of the document, which set forth the goals of the administration. The folk hero had outlined virtually every battleground of the seven tumultuous years which lay ahead.

In the field of foreign affairs, the time had come to demand that France satisfy American claims for damages during the Napoleonic wars, settlement of which had been evaded for twenty years; the ports of the British West Indies, closed to American vessels since the Revolution, should be opened; the disputed boundary between Maine and Canada should be resolved; and there was a growing demand for the annexation of Texas.

The tariff debate threatened disunion. South Carolina, in open defiance of the current act, had announced her refusal to pay duties and her intention to "nullify" the law. Jackson urged a spirit of compromise. South Carolinians held—as some New Englanders had held twenty years earlier—that each state had the right to reject, or nullify federal legislation it found repressive. The Carolinians, as spokesmen for the slaveholding south at large, assailed the high tariff as a device for protecting the industrial north at the expense of the agricultural south.

The problem of removing the Indians from close contact with whites was a simple one in Jackson's view—the tribes should be pushed westward. In contrast to the policy of Adams, he supported Georgia in her aim to drive the Creeks and Cherokees from lands ceded to them by treaty—in short, he could not approve an independent Indian state within Georgia's borders.

Jackson reported that national finances were strong, with some $12.5 million of the debt paid during the past year, leaving a balance of $48.5 million. When the debt was paid, Jackson said, it should be decided whether to divide surplus funds among the states for public works and end the debate on internal improvements. Any improvements, however, should be undertaken by constitutional means that would minimize discord between the states, and encroachments upon the "legitimate sphere of State sovreignty" should be avoided.

There was a muted echo of Jackson's campaign against Adams and Clay in a proposal that the President and Vice President should be elected directly by the people, eliminating every "intermediate agency." The House, he suggested, would not always reflect the will of the people in choosing a President, and if an individual held the power to decide, "May he not be tempted to name his own reward?" He also urged that presidents be limited to a single term.

Near the end of his message Jackson declared formal warfare on the Bank of the United States:

"The charter of the Bank of the United States expires in 1836, and its stockholders will most probably apply for a renewal of their privileges.

"I submit to the wisdom of the legislature whether a national one [Bank] founded upon the credit of the government and its revenues might not be devised." Congress "and the people" should consider this alternative, since the present bank had "failed in the great end of establishing a uniform and sound currency."

No one was more surprised by Jackson's challenge to the banking system than Nicholas Biddle, the patrician president of the Bank of the United States. Only recently Biddle had called at the White House, where he had been welcomed in friendly fashion. Though Jackson had questioned the constitutionality of the Bank, he had expressed gratitude for Biddle's proposal for reducing the public debt, and he had said nothing of the Bank's failure to provide a stable currency, a charge that friends of the Bank found absurd on its face. Biddle failed to realize that a struggle to the death had begun.

The Second Bank of the United States, now less than fifteen years old, had been created at the end of the War of 1812 in the image of the first Bank. As a privately owned and highly profitable quasi-monopoly, enjoying favored use of government funds, the Bank traced its birth to the final days of the Revolution, when Washington's officers were near mutiny and the bankrupt United States was drifting toward chaos. In Alexander Hamilton's view only an alliance between wealthy private citizens and government could succeed; national stability was not to be entrusted to the masses, since they were "turbulent and changing; they seldom judge or determine right." Economic inequity was thus a tenet of Bank gospel, echoed occasionally in Nicholas Biddle's scornful comment upon "men with no property to assess and no property to lose."

The Bank was a private—and in Biddle's opinion, independent—corporation, with headquarters in a Grecian marble temple in Philadelphia. Its limited monopoly was guaranteed by Congress, and states could levy no taxes upon it. Of its capital of $35 million, $7 million was subscribed by the government, which deposited public funds in the Bank without drawing interest. The President of the United States appointed five of the twenty-five directors, whose authority was nominal, since Biddle controlled the Bank as if it were a private fief—one outraged director protested that he and his cohorts were actually a Board of Directed: "We know absolutely nothing. There is no consultation, no exchanges of sentiments, no production of correspondence . . . we are perfect cyphers."

Critics complained that the Bank maintained control of the money supply, and thus of most commodity prices; but though it was the only national Bank, in practice it was by no means a monopoly. In 1830 it made only 20 percent of the nation's bank loans, circulated only one-fifth of the bank notes, and had only one-third of total deposits. Still, it was an imposing force over which the government had no effective control.

Nicholas Biddle, whose brilliant leadership had steadily expanded the influence of the Bank, had come reluctantly to the throne. This scion of a wealthy Philadelphia banking family had been a precocious Princeton valedictorian at fifteen, a lawyer, a one-time secretary of the American legation in Paris, and a dabbler in literature and the arts. Biddle had become the unlikely saviour of the government after the British burning of Washington in the War of 1812. With notable energy he had salvaged Treasury records from the ruins, arranged loans that revived the expiring government, and in face of his father's opposition, reestablished the Bank of the United States.

Quickly recognized as the most able member of the board, Biddle had become president and embarked on a program of expansion that made the Bank the central power in American economic life. In the eyes of businessmen the Bank was responsible and helpful, not to say indispensable, since it had eased the cycle of boom and depression and given Americans the most stable currency in their history.

Biddle not only conceded that the Bank was virtually omnipotent; he insisted that it was of equal rank with the government itself. He once scolded the director of his Washington branch who had consulted with the White House on the affairs of the Bank: once the President had appointed the five government directors to the Bank's board, Biddle said, "The Executive has completely fulfilled its functions . . . and no officer of the Government, from the President downwards, has the least right, the least authority, the least pretence, for interference in the concerns of the bank." The Bank's officers, Biddle added, were to carry out orders of the Board, "in direct opposition, if need be, to the personal interests and wishes of The President and every officer of the Government."

Despite this imperial attitude Biddle sought to divorce the Bank from partisan politics. Even in the raucous campaign of 1828 there were no complaints that Biddle had interfered, though it was known that he supported Adams. Biddle was not alone in his surprise, therefore, when the President raised a challenge to the Bank in his message, in terms rather vague but of unmistakable hostility. Biddle's perplexity stemmed from the ambiguities of Jackson's attitude toward public finance.

It was true, as his critics charged, that Jackson's familiarity with economics and the complexities of banking was slight indeed, and that he instinctively feared what he failed to understand. But despite his ambivalent attitude and the superficiality of his knowledge of the laws of economics, Jackson made his anti-Bank points shrewdly, in a manner thoroughly convincing to the public. As he was to argue to Congress: "The great desideratum in modern times is an efficient check upon the power of banks, preventing that excessive issue of paper whence arise those fluctuations in the standard of values which render uncertain the rewards of labor." He meant to restrict the issue of all paper money, Biddle's included.

In his attacks on Biddle and the privileged class Jackson would seldom refer to "the rich." His target was the "money power," meaning the power of paper money and of corporations. He was expressing his lifelong distrust of wealth derived from financial manipulation and special privilege—he thought of these as ill-gotten gains, as opposed to such honestly won gains as farm lands and their produce.

Congressional reaction to Jackson's plan to supplant the Bank was disappointing to him. In response to his annual message the House Ways and Means Committee reported in favor of sustaining the Bank of the United States, rejected the projected new national bank, and defeated four anti-Biddle resolutions.

The Senate, also in a rebellious mood, turned to Jackson's political appointees and rejected ten of them. Webster declared that half of the list would have been rejected, except for Jackson's "outdoor popularity." Administration opponents, professing shock that "a batch of printers" should be elevated, concentrated their fire on campaign editors and writers who had been rewarded with minor posts.

Amos Kendall, attacked because of his exposures of Jackson's enemies, was confirmed as a Treasury auditor only when Calhoun cast the deciding vote for him. Major Mordecai Noah of the *New York Enquirer* was first rejected on the ground that he was Jewish, but was approved on a second ballot, also by the margin of Calhoun's vote. Henry Lee was rejected unanimously as consul to Algiers, as the result of pleas from even his friends and relatives that the shame of his seduction of his sister-in-law be avenged.* Ike Hill was rejected as deputy controller

---

*After a year of service in Algiers the hapless Lee went to Paris, where he met Napoleon's mother and began a biography of the emperor. The first volume was published

of the Treasury, ostensibly because of his libel on Mrs. John Quincy Adams, but in fact because of his telling attacks on the Bank of the United States. With Jackson's aid Hill was soon to reappear on the scene, as senator from New Hampshire after the resignation of Levi Woodbury, for whom a place was to be made in the cabinet. Jackson at first reacted violently to the rejection of his appointees: "The people will put these things to rights, and teach them what it is to oppose my nominations!" But the mood passed quickly. He persisted with rare patience, biding his time and resubmitting the names of the men once rejected. He outlined his strategy to Lewis: when the Senate rejected a good man on political grounds, "I give them a hot potatoe, and he will soon bring them to terms, and if not . . . the vengeance of the people will fall upon them."

By now Jackson had begun secret negotiations for the annexation of Texas—an effort that he was to continue beyond his administration, almost to the day of his death. It was to end, Jackson's critics charged, as a sordid chapter in the story of American expansion. The catalyst was Colonel Anthony Butler, a speculator and member of the Mississippi legislature who had acquired large holdings in Texas, which he hoped to bring under the American flag.

Fruitless negotiations with Mexico for Texas had been opened by Adams, who offered $1 million for the lands between the Neuces and the Rio Grande. When Anthony Butler appeared in Washington with a sheaf of maps and glowing reports of the rich territory, Jackson authorized Van Buren to increase the offer to $5 million. Butler was entrusted with the confidential proposal, which was to be taken to Joel R. Poinsett, the capable American minister in Mexico City. The loquacious Butler had hardly arrived in the Mexican capital before the proposal was published in the government newspaper, which spurned the offer as degrading. Poinsett resigned, and Jackson named Butler to succeed him. It was an appointment the President was to regret.

A growing hostility between north and south threatened the unity of the Democratic party before the end of Jackson's first year in office. This sectional dispute, unchecked by the plea for compromise in Old Hickory's first message to Congress, had developed ominously before the public became aware of the issue, whose focal point was the tariff of 1828. The momentous question of the stability of the Union, which

---

in 1837, about the time of Lee's death in an influenza epidemic which swept the French capital.

lay beneath the conflict, was brought forth dramatically on the floor of the Senate in March 1830. The furor was set off inadvertently by Samuel Foot of Connecticut, who moved to suspend the sale of public lands in an effort to halt the ruinous inflation that was spawned by haphazard financing and unscrupulous promoters. The resulting debate soon veered to the question of states' rights, apparently to the surprise of both participants and audience.

Robert Y. Hayne of South Carolina sounded the southern challenge at once: "I am one of those who believe that the very life of our system is the independence of the States, and that there is no evil more to be deprecated than the consolidation of this government." Hayne was an able leader of the powerful southern bloc, a socially popular, handsome blond who was already a political veteran at thirty-eight. His challenge was the more ominous because of his substantial support in the Senate, and of John Calhoun's presence in the chair. Hayne's defiance—the first formal public statement of the doctrine of individual state sovreignty or "states' rights"—provoked violent reactions from patriotic defenders of the youthful union, whose inevitable spokesman was Daniel Webster. The New Englander, who had entered the Senate chamber while Hayne was crying South Carolina's defiance, immediately took his seat and began making notes for a rebuttal to the challenge. "I did not like it," he said, "and my friends liked it even less." The next day Webster attacked Hayne in the first of his impassioned orations in defense of the concept of the Union, and thus opened the Webster-Hayne debates, the most meaningful congressional exchange of the Jacksonian era.

At forty-eight Webster was reputedly the wealthiest lawyer in America, and one of the most avaricious. He gambled frequently and otherwise led a life of indolence and ease. Webster had become a familiar sight of Washington in his fashionably cut coats of dark blue with brass buttons, a buff vest and trousers, and a long-napped gray beaver hat.

To the visiting Englishwoman Harriet Martineau, Webster gave the impression that he was never in earnest except during his speeches on the Constitution, when he seemed to acquire a majestic and irresistible power. He was at his best in his protracted debate with Hayne.

Webster was an imposing figure during his three-day challenge of the South Carolinian. There was an air of lordly confidence in his erect, 6-foot figure, his huge head was somehow suggestive of a superior intellect, and his intense smoky-black eyes seemed to be all-seeing. Webster began to speak in a low voice, his manner subdued, with a faint suggestion of embarrassment; but his voice soon rose until it filled the chamber with rhetorical thunder, and his audience seemed to be hypnotized. He then assumed his favorite pose, left hand tucked under his coattails and the right gesturing vigorously. "At this moment," an observer wrote, "the eye rests upon him as upon one under the true inspiration of seeing the invisible."

The debates were to range widely over the sources of conflict between the agrarian south and the rapidly developing industrial north, but they were to be remembered for Webster's fervent tributes to the Union and its flag.

Webster made an eloquent defense of New England's loyalty to the Union, glossing over the lapses which had so outraged Andrew Jackson. He then struck at the heart of Hayne's argument. Consolidation, Webster declared, lent strength to the Union, and he hoped that Hayne did not share an all-too-popular tendency among southerners to belittle the value of the Union.

To the smiling approval of the presiding Calhoun, Hayne responded with a bitter personal attack on Webster, assailed New England as disloyal in several national crises, and claimed for South Carolina the right to reject any oppressive federal legislation. Hayne thus unequivocally endorsed "nullification"—a doctrine more deadly than secession, since it would dissolve the Union state by state, rather than split it in two.

Presented with the opening he sought, Webster delivered the most able speeches of his career, deriding Hayne's position as unconstitutional, impractical, and potentially ruinous to the people of the United States. "The Constitution," Webster declared, "is not the creature of the State government. The very chief end, the main design, for which the whole Constitution was framed and adopted was to establish a government that should not . . . depend on State opinion and State discretion."

The New Hampshireman outdid himself in a final triumphal outburst:

When my eyes shall be turned to behold, for the last time, the sun in heaven, may I not see him shining on the broken and dishonored fragments of a once glorious Union . . . on a land rent with civil feuds, or drenched, it may be in fraternal blood! Let their last feeble and lingering glance, rather behold the gorgeous ensign of the republic . . . not a stripe erased or polluted, nor a single star obscured, bearing for its motto no such miserable . . . words of delusion and folly, 'Liberty first and Union afterwards': but everywhere . . . that other sentiment, dear to every true American heart—Liberty and Union, now and forever, one and inseparable!

The spellbinder was halted by the exasperated Calhoun, who banged his gavel and shouted for order; but it was too late for the southern cause.

Jackson, who felt that the storm would blow over, and that the doctrine of nullification posed no serious issue, at first sided with Hayne. Major Lewis took word of Webster's first assault on the South Carolinian to the White House before the debate had ended. He found Jackson aware of the development and eager for news.

"Well, and how is Webster getting on?"

"He's delivering a powerful speech. I'm afraid he's demolishing our friend Hayne."

"I expected it," Jackson said; but he gave no indication of his feelings on the issue. Lewis, like southerners in general, apparently assumed that the President would embrace Hayne's point of view, if only out of allegiance to his supporters in the region. It was inconceivable to most southern leaders that Jackson might abandon the cause of his native section.

A few hours after the final Webster-Hayne clash in the Senate, the debaters met at a White House reception.

"How are you this evening, Colonel Hayne?" Webster said.

The South Carolinian smiled. "None the better for you, sir."

Jackson's health had failed rapidly in the summer and fall of 1829. His feet and legs were badly swollen, and by December the symptoms of dropsy were so alarming that his friends feared for his life. In facing the prospect of death, one of Jackson's first thoughts was of presidential succession. He had decided that Van Buren should be the next President, and at the suggestion of Lewis wrote a memorandum emphasizing his trust in the New Yorker, which he sent to John Overton in the form of a letter. This legacy, which was to be made public in case of Jackson's death, praised Van Buren as

every thing that I could desire him to be . . . frank, open, candid, and manly . . . able and prudent—republican in his principles, and one of the most pleasant men to do business with I ever saw. He . . . is well qualified to fill the highest office in the gift of the people. . . . I wish I could say as much for Mr. Calhoun. You know the confidence I once had in that gentleman. However, of him I desire not now to speak.

Jackson signed a copy of this letter and Lewis filed it among his confidential papers. Since the President recovered, the matter was not mentioned publicly, and Overton probably never grasped the significance of the letter.

Jackson also broke with Calhoun about this time, and though it was not to be known publicly for a year, their estrangement was complete.

Somehow the secret seeped from the White House—or Daniel Webster suffered a rare seizure of clairvoyance. A few days after Jackson had written to Overton, Webster wrote to a friend: "Mr. Van Buren has evidently, at this moment, quite the lead in influence and importance." Webster noted that the Red Fox had "a settled purpose of making out the lady, of whom so much has been said, a person of reputation. It is odd enough, but too evident to be doubted, that the consequence of this dispute in the social and fashionable world is producing great political effects. . . ." Webster hazarded a guess that Van Buren's astuteness would lead him to the White House. "He looks and acts like one having authority," Webster said, "I never saw a man more flushed with hope."

John Quincy Adams came to the same conclusion, "The Administration party is split up into a blue and green faction upon this point of morals . . . Calhoun heads the moral party, Van Buren that of the frail sisterhood; and he is notoriously engaged in canvassing for the presidency by paying court to Mrs. Eaton."

A month later Webster noted that Calhoun was "forming a party against Van Buren." Since it was obvious that Calhoun could hardly oppose Peggy without incurring Jackson's wrath, Webster hoped that the South Carolinian's indignation would increase, and precipitate an open struggle between Calhoun and Van Buren. Already there were portents that Jackson would run for a second term in 1832, and the apprehensive Webster welcomed any prospect of Democratic disunity. The development Webster feared matured rapidly. In March 1830, after prompting by Lewis, eighty-six Pennsylvania legislators wrote to Jackson urging him to run again. The letter was published with some fanfare, while the Peggy Eaton affair still raged in the White House.

After Jackson had withdrawn from the church of the Reverend John Campbell in protest of the minister's accusations, Secretary of Navy John Branch promptly invited Campbell to a dinner party. The autumn social season of 1829 degenerated into warfare. The President's traditional opening party for the cabinet, postponed until November, was a failure despite all attempts by the witty Van Buren to enlighten the occasion. The presence of Peggy Eaton rendered it "a formal and hollow ceremony."

A dinner by Van Buren which followed was even more disastrous for Jackson's cause, since Branch, Berrien, Ingham, Barry, and Eaton all attended without their wives, and the affair ended in a stag drinking bout. Van Buren won a temporary victory for his chief by enlisting the aid of the British and Russian ministers, who entertained the Eatons in a series of parties in competition with those given by Mrs. Branch, Mrs. Ingham, and the daughters of Attorney General Berrien, and which pointedly excluded Peggy and her husband. The rebellious ladies also enlisted an ally in Madame Huygens, the wife of the minister from Holland, who aided in the defense of American social standards with all the zest of a pampered aristocrat who imagined her world endangered.

Jackson remained defiant. "Eaton is the last man on earth I ought or would abandon," he said. "I would sooner abandon life." John Campbell of the Treasury Department speculated, "How Old Hickory is to get out of the Scrape I cannot say. The president . . . BELIEVES Eaton & his wife are innocent & would no longer be Andrew Jackson if any earthly consideration of popularity could induce him to give way. . . ." But it remained that Branch, Ingham, and Berrien had influential friends, "so it is an *uggly* affair." Campbell could foresee only one outcome: "Old Jackson will get thro' somehow."

Van Buren, who was once summoned to the White House shortly after dawn, found the old man drawn and red-eyed from lack of sleep, but his manner grimly composed. Jackson was ready to act. If the cabinet wives and Mme. Huygens had actually conspired against the Eatons, he said, he would dismiss Branch, Berrien, and Ingham, and send the Dutch minister home. Van Buren was hurried off to interview Mme. Huygens, and Jackson soon confronted his fractious cabinet members.

The old man read a prepared statement:

> I do not claim the right to interfere in the domestic relations or personal intercourse of any member of my Cabinet. . . . But . . . I am fully impressed with the belief that you and your families have . . . taken measures to induce others to avoid mrs Eaton and thereby to exclude her from society and degrade him. . . . If her character is such as to justify measures on the part of my cabinet . . . it is I who am responsible for this alleged indignity to public morales. . . . I will not part with major Eaton and those of my cabinet who cannot harmonize with him had better withdraw, for harmony I must and will have.

Branch, Berrien, and Ingham protested vehemently: of course their wives had indulged in no conspiracy, and their social activities, though beyond the control of their husbands, were not conducted for the harassment of Mrs. Eaton. Jackson replied with a quiet warning. Though he accepted their word, he insisted that they must work effectively with the Secretary of War or resign. Mme. Huygens added her own profuse denial, and the crisis was postponed once more. Jack Donelson declared prematurely: "The petticoat war has ended, no lives lost. The General in the goodness of his heart thinks Mrs. E. has attained a triumph."

The trivial affair was worsening the President's precarious health. His gray hair had now become white and the pale face was more deeply seamed than ever. Jack Donelson felt that the Eaton affair had "done more to paralise his energies than 4 years of the regular and simple operations of the Govt."

Jackson's relations with the cabinet did not improve and finally became so acrimonious that he sometimes roared threats against Branch, Berrien, and Ingham. Within a few months cabinet meetings became rare, and soon ceased altogether. Meanwhile Jackson and Van Buren grew more intimate. They were seen together on frequent horseback rides into the country, in animated conversation as they rode. Van Buren assumed an influential role in the Kitchen Cabinet, which was now to take over a larger role in shaping national policy.

22

"I will hang the first man I can lay my hands on . . ."

A sense of alarm spread through the nation as details of the Webster-Hayne debates trickled into the hinterlands. After painstaking revision by the senators, the speeches were printed on thousands of handbills, which were read eagerly by almost all literate Americans, inspiring fresh debates in every village, and raising a question as to Jackson's stand on nullification.

Washington gossip insisted that he supported the south. He was said to have sent a note of congratulations to Hayne after his opening speech. The South Carolina senator, a familiar figure at the White House, was one of the few admitted to Jackson's study. Hayne's brother Arthur, who had been Jackson's aide at New Orleans, remained a friend; the Hayne family was soon to leave on a trip to New York with Emily Donelson. Thomas Benton, who was thought to speak for the President, made a stout defense of Hayne in the Senate, declaring that Webster had exaggerated the threat of disunion.

Jackson himself said nothing. Since Webster's resounding Second Reply had raised the specter of civil war, there had been no hint of the President's attitude. Only Lewis, Donelson, and Van Buren knew that he supported Webster and shared his fears of the looming threat to the Union.

John Calhoun noted the continuing silence from the White House with apprehension, which was soon betrayed by his partisan, Duff

Green. The *Telegraph* criticized Webster's speeches and charged the New Englander and Henry Clay of "an unholy alliance" against the Jackson administration; and when Webster protested an interpretation of his remarks, Green accused him of sponsoring libelous attacks on Jackson during the campaign.

Amid these exchanges the Democrats prepared for the annual celebration of Thomas Jefferson's birthday with a lavish public banquet, an occasion the South Carolinians hoped to turn to their own use. A series of speeches and toasts was planned, pointedly linking Jefferson to a narrow interpretation of the doctrine of states' rights and invoking his posthumous blessing upon South Carolina's resistance to the tariff. Jackson, Van Buren, and the cabinet were to attend, and the President was invited to offer the first volunteer toast, following the twenty-four previously assigned.

Forewarned by a program published in the *United States Telegraph,* Jackson concluded that the banquet was to be "a nullification affair altogether" and composed his own toast in the privacy of his study. He showed several versions to Lewis and Donelson, who selected their favorite. Jackson put the chosen toast in his pocket and discarded the others.

Senator Benton, who was an early arrival at the banquet, found several small groups of men excitedly protesting the pro-nullification flavor of the banquet. Some of these men left, the entire Pennsylvania delegation among them; but the hall was still crowded when the diners assembled about the tables to hear an opening address by Hayne, and settled for the ordeal of the toasts. After twenty-four southern sympathizers had proclaimed their support of nullification, Jackson stood, turned his gaze on John Calhoun, and called in his high, thin voice: "Our Union: It must be preserved!"

The company was stunned by this forceful echo of Webster's speech. Ike Hill reported with satisfaction, "A proclamation of martial law and an order to arrest Calhoun where he sat could not have come with more blind, staggering force."

The old man beckoned the audience to its feet by raising his glass and the toast was drunk. Someone noticed that Calhoun drank with a trembling hand and spilled some of his wine. Jackson faced the crowd with a brief, wordless glance, then crossed the room to speak with Benton.

Senator Hayne intercepted him.

"Would you consent to the insertion of one word in your toast before it is given to the papers?"

"What is the word?"

"Federal—our Federal Union . . ."

Jackson agreed. Hayne's addition, as it happened, restored the toast to the written form Jackson had carried in his pocket, and inadvertently shortened when he stood. The Carolinian felt, for some obscure reason, that the insertion would be more acceptable to states' rights men.

The diners returned to their tables and Calhoun countered with a toast of his own.

"The Union, next to our liberty, most dear."

After a brief hesitation the South Carolinian added: "May we all remember that it can only be preserved by respecting the rights of the States, and distributing equally the benefits and burdens of the Union." Calhoun's toast may have had "moral superiority," as a twentieth-century scholar was to observe, but it was Jackson's terse battle cry that was to be remembered. The *United States Telegraph* spared Jackson only two lines of the eleven columns it devoted to the banquet, but that was enough. His toast swept the country as an anti-nullification slogan, made clear Jackson's resolve to save the Union, and marshaled widespread support for him.

About this time a South Carolina congressman, who was returning home, called on Jackson and asked if he had a message for his friends in the state. Jackson questioned him about the recent mass meeting in Charleston. "Those men who said that the Army and Navy weren't big enough to collect a penny of duties the people didn't want to pay— are they in earnest? Do they realize what their words mean?"

"I'm afraid they mean it, General."

"Well, then, tell them from me that they can talk and write resolutions and print threats to their hearts' content. But if one drop of blood is shed there in opposition to the laws of the United States, I will hang the first man I can lay my hands on engaged in such treasonable conduct, upon the first tree I can reach."

News of the President's comment soon spread through the capital. Senator Hayne expressed to Thomas Benton his doubt that Jackson would go to such extremes. Benton replied, "I tell you, Hayne, when Jackson begins to talk about hanging, they can begin to look for the ropes."

Jackson turned from the latent threat of nullification to other challenging issues which were to set the course of his administration. The choice of an opening thrust at his opposition was proposed to him by Van Buren, who urged the veto of a bill that would authorize federal financing of a turnpike from Maysville to Lexington, Kentucky. The Red Fox adroitly raised the issue of public improvements during their

long horseback rides, and convinced Jackson that the growing popularity of such projects threatened to drain the Treasury by encouraging
a congressional orgy of log-rolling and pork-barreling. If members
freely exchanged their votes to promote local schemes, the legislative
process would deteriorate and the federal government would lose
control of its fiscal affairs.

Van Buren feared a rash of federally financed projects across the
country, spawned by Clay and Calhoun and others who sought the
presidency, "operating in conjunction with minor classes of politicians
. . . and backed by a little army of cunning contractors." A veto of the
twenty-mile road, which lay entirely within Kentucky, would be a blow
at Clay, and an effective, if less obvious one, at Calhoun, who had long
championed such public projects.

At Jackson's request Van Buren collected material for an attack on
the bill, emphasizing its effect on the federal budget and its question-
able constitutionality. The industrious Van Buren assembled effective
arguments, but he was aware that his contribution was a minor one—
public clamor against the veto would be so great that it could be
countered only by the force of Jackson's popularity.

Despite all efforts at secrecy, word of the Jackson-Van Buren scheme
reached the Kentucky delegation, and Jackson's old Indian-fighting
friend R. M. ("Tecumseh") Johnson, appeared at the White House,
where he was greeted by Jackson and Van Buren. The people of Kentucky were determined to have the road, Johnson said, and a veto
would be ruinous to Jackson's supporters in the state. Johnson held up
a huge palm.

"If this hand were an anvil, and a fly were sitting on it, and a
sledge-hammer should come down on it like this"—he pounded the
palm with his other fist—"that fly would not be more surely crushed
than the democratic party would be crushed by this veto."

Jackson rose quietly.

"Sir, have you looked at the condition of the Treasury?"

"No."

"Well, I have. I was elected to pay off the national debt. How can
I do that and pay for these improvements without borrowing? It cannot be done—and borrow I will not."

Van Buren was fearful that Jackson had revealed too much. "You
mustn't think the president's mind is made up," he said. "In fact, we
were just discussing the Maysville bill when you came."

Jackson altered his tone at once and restored Johnson to "his customary urbanity"; but the Kentuckian was not deceived. He reported
to his colleagues, "Nothing short of a voice from heaven can keep the

old man from vetoing that bill—and I doubt if even that would stop him."

The House heard Jackson's Maysville veto message in grim silence, but the angry Democrats were unable to overturn it, though it obviously presaged the doom of future public projects in other states. The cleverly drawn veto appealed directly to the public, over the heads of politicians. It was the first demonstration of Jackson's uncanny ability to fire the imagination of the masses and identify their welfare with his cause. The general argued that since the road was local, it would not benefit the nation at large. He pointed out the dangers of "a scramble for appropriations" and of corruption in awarding contracts. Public projects already proposed by Congress, he said, would entail a deficit of $10 million, and could not be undertaken without increasing the public debt or raising taxes. But the industrious and intelligent American people, he added soothingly, should not be dismayed. In years to come, they could develop the country under more favorable circumstances.

Jackson's contemporaries perceived that the veto had been exercised on the grounds of expediency as well as constitutionality, a temptation avoided by his predecessors. The young French scholar Alexis de Toqueville was one who realized Jackson had made "a sort of appeal to the people," in which he could plead his cause and explain his motives quite outside the orthodox political process. The technique was to become a familiar one in later administrations. The partisan nature of this veto was to become obvious only after Jackson had gained control of both houses of Congress and then approved similar projects sponsored by loyal Democrats with the bland comment, "I am not hostile to internal improvements and wish to see them extended to every part of the country."

Observant politicians noted that Old Hickory had held the south in line during the maneuver, "with as little offense as possible to the North & West." He had also established in Washington a pattern of sound fiscal policy that was to outlive his reign.

The clamor over the Maysville veto still echoed when Jackson turned to his troubled relationship with John C. Calhoun, whom he had determined to repudiate in favor of Van Buren. He was not motivated merely by Calhoun's role in the Peggy Eaton affair, nor by the nullification controversy. For at least two years Jackson had been aware that Calhoun as Secretary of War had urged his arrest in the wake of the Florida campaign and had since encouraged the impression that his actual enemy in Monroe's cabinet had been William H. Crawford.

Late in 1829, after Jackson had entertained Monroe at the White House, Major Lewis had reported that one of the dinner guests had remarked that Monroe's cabinet had unanimously opposed his invasion of Florida.

"He must have been mistaken," Jackson said.

"I'm not so sure of that."

"Why not?"

"Because I have seen a letter in which Mr. Crawford is represented as saying that it was not he but Mr. Calhoun who was in favor of your being arrested." Lewis then told the President of a letter written by Georgia's Governor Forsyth a year earlier, which Lewis had withheld because it seemed to be inconclusive evidence.

"You saw such a letter as *that*?"

When Lewis said the letter was in New York, Jackson sent him after it at once. Forsyth declined to surrender the letter without Crawford's consent. It was only after weeks of delay that the partially recovered Crawford, now serving as a Georgia judge, wrote Jackson to acknowledge the truth of the report and blame Calhoun for opposition to Jackson within Monroe's cabinet. Jackson sent the message to Calhoun with a curt note.

"Sir . . . The Enclosed copy of a letter from William H. Crawford, Esq. . . . was placed in my hands on yesterday. . . . My object in making this communication is to announce to you the great surprise which is felt, and to learn whether it is possible that the information given is correct. . . ."

Calhoun responded immediately, professing relief that "the secret and mysterious attempts . . . to infuse my character are at length brought to light," and promising a full reply later. Jackson exhibited rare patience: "Time to explain . . . is due him. . . . *He shall have it,* but I am afraid he is in a dilemma."

Calhoun labored for two weeks before sending his explanation to Jackson—fifty-two closely scrawled pages. It was by no means an apologia. The letter demolished Crawford's charges of Calhoun's treachery to Jackson and made it apparent that the Georgian's motive was spiteful revenge. "This whole affair," Calhoun wrote, "is a political maneuver, in which the design is that you should be the instrument, and myself the victim, but in which the real actors are carefully concealed. . . . I have too much respect for your character to suppose you capable of . . . political intrigue."

For all the fervor of his defense Calhoun lacked the courage to concede that he had opposed Jackson's actions in the invasion of Florida, and that he had engaged in a deception of Jackson during the twelve intervening years. The President read the letter with growing indignation and was soon in a towering rage. He sent Lewis to show it to Van Buren, who scanned a few lines and returned the sheaf of pages. "This is going to bring a break between Calhoun and the President and it would be better if I knew nothing about it." When Lewis reported to Jackson, the old man smiled. "I reckon Van is right. I dare say they will try to throw the whole blame on him."

Old Hickory replied brusquely to Calhoun, saying that he had frequently defended him

> upon the ground that you, in all your letters to me, professed to be my personal friend, and approved *entirely* my conduct in relation to the Seminole campaign. . . . Your letter now before me is the first indication that *you* ever entertained any other opinion. . . . I had a right to believe that you were my friend, and, until now, never expected to have occasion to say of you, in the language of Caesar, *Et tu, Brute!* . . . Understanding you now, no further communication with you on this subject is necessary.

But the correspondence continued through the summer. And when Jackson attempted to end it, Calhoun dropped all pretense of civility in a savage final reply, which Jackson did not answer. He scrawled across the pages: "This is full evidence of the duplicity and insincerity of the man and displays a littleness and entire want of those high, dignified and honorable feelings which I once thought he possessed."

Crawford also turned upon the discomfited Calhoun with an eager confession that it was he who had betrayed him:

> . . . I Make no doubt that you dislike the idea of being exposed and stripped of the covert you had been enjoying under the President's wings. . . . From the time you established the *Washington Republican* for the purpose of slandering and vilifying my reputation, I considered you a degraded and disgraced man. . . . Under this impression I was anxious that you should be no longer vice-president of the United States.

Congress adjourned on the last day of May 1830, after passing three more public improvement bills in its final hours—all vetoed by Jackson. The sociopolitical season came to an end about a week later with a White House dinner. Peggy Eaton declined to attend.

She wrote the President, "It would only be another feast . . . [enabling] part of your family . . . to make me the object of their censures and reproaches."

Jackson vowed revenge against his rebellious cabinet officers. "The people shall judge," he said grimly. To Emily and Jack Donelson the President gave a final choice. They would accept the Eatons socially or return home.

When the equally stubborn Emily refused to change her stand, Jackson banished her to Tennessee with the rueful comment, "I was willing to yield to my family every thing but the government of my House and the abandonment of my friend without cause." Jack Donelson defied Peggy Eaton. He and his wife preferred to return home rather than "bow to her demands." He lamented the rupture with Jackson, "to whom I have stood from my infancy in the relation of son to Father," but remained loyal to his wife. In the end Jackson softened the blow by accompanying the Donelsons on their westward trip. By mid-June they were on their way to the Hermitage, leaving Major Lewis at the White House to guard against enemies. "I pray you," Jackson admonished Lewis, "to keep your eyes wide awake, and advise me of every occurrence." The new First Lady, "snugly recoiled in the White House," as Jack Donelson put it, was the major's daughter Mary Ann.

A more pressing reason for Old Hickory's westward journey was the prospect of new Indian treaties. Chiefs of the Choctaw tribe had requested a conference and he determined to go to them.

In contrast to the rationale offered in state papers, Jackson's actual Indian policy was rapacious and hypocritical in the view of some of his contemporaries. His theory (shared by most men of the west) was that the Indians, as mere hunters occupying a territory under U.S. sufferance, must bow before the superior civilization already flourishing in the east, "studded with cities, towns and prosperous farms, embellished with all the improvements which art can devise or industry execute, occupied by more than twelve million happy people and filled with all the blessings of liberty, civilization and religion." Before this march of progress, Jackson said, "Forests . . . ranged by a few thousand savages" must give way. The lands of the continent, as Benton proclaimed in Jackson's spirit, should be turned over to men who would use them "according to the intentions of the Creator."

No acknowledgment was made that most of the 60,000 Cherokees, Choctaws, and Chickasaws were not wandering savages, but had established an agricultural civilization of their own upon the millions of acres he had wrested from them in treaties.

The President also bewildered his critics by expressing satisfaction that "this unhappy race . . . the original dwellers in our land—are now placed in a situation where we may well hope that they will share in the blessings of civilization and be saved from the degradation and destruction to which they were rapidly hastening while they remained

in the States." As the twentieth-century historian John William Ward
has observed, the United States would "save the Indians for civilization
by rescuing them from civilization."

The Cherokees, to Jackson's dismay, retained William Wirt, a former Attorney General, to challenge the authority of states to set aside
federal treaties. Wirt's role was denounced by Jackson as "truly
wicked," perhaps because he foresaw a perplexing conflict between
state and federal governments in which he would find himself siding
with the states—and in effect approving a form of nullification.

The issue was debated warmly for months. Indian sympathizers
pointed out that the tribesmen had abided by their treaties. The Cherokees in particular had won admiration for their progress toward
civilization: the creation of a written language, the adoption of a constitution, and the provision of taverns and ferries for travelers. Numerous
groups of civilians protested the planned removal.

A delegation of Philadelphia Quakers called on Jackson to protest
the inhuman policy of driving the Indians from their ancestral homes.
Jackson bristled.

"Is Philadelphia the ancestral home and hunting-ground of the
Quakers?"

"Not exactly, but that's a different case."

"Were you born in Philadelphia?"

"We were." The Quakers said their parents and grandparents were
also natives, but conceded that most of their great-grandparents had
come from England.

"Then," Jackson said, "they left their ancestral homes and hunting-
grounds and came to the West in search of new homes."

"Well, yes. But it was a different case."

"Did your great-grandparents find Indians at Philadelphia?"

"Yes, but . . ."

"What became of those Indians?"

"Oh, those Indians moved away; but it was a different case."

"Why did they move away?"

"Because our forefathers bought their lands."

"What did your forefathers pay for their lands?"

"That was a different case."

Old Hickory dismissed the delegation. "I think you folks have taken
up quite enough of my time . . . I concede to everyone the constitutional right to be as big a hypocrite as he may please, but do deny your
right to take more of my time. . . ."

Still, though he held the conventional frontier view that it was or-
dained the Indians must give way before the westward surge of white

settlements, Jackson was uncompromisingly firm when he suspected white men of cheating their victims.

Henry R. Schoolcraft, the Indian commissioner, told the President that whites were pressing claims for damages after the United States bought Indian lands in Michigan:

"Don't pay them one dollar," Jackson said. "Pay the Indians honorably for their lands, their full value, in silver—not blankets, not rifles, not powder, but hard cash; and let their creditors collect their own debts. Don't you pay one of them, neither now nor in any future time. When white men deal with Indians, the Indians are sure to get into debt to the white men; at least, the white men are sure to say so. I won't hear of paying any of their 'claims.' The rascals are here now, I suppose. The town will be full of them, but I won't pay a dollar, and you may tell them so."

Thus it was that Jackson went westward in June 1830 with Emily and Jack Donelson, and after a brief stop at the Hermitage rode out to meet with the Choctaws. He reached the council grounds to discover that the Choctaws had not come and that only the Chickasaws were there. The President greeted the tribesmen gravely, a few of them old men who had fought against him in his first campaigns when the Indians knew him as "Sharp Knife." He met younger Chickasaws who had helped him defeat the British in New Orleans. After a ceremonial smoking of a peace pipe, Jackson addressed the chiefs; but though he hailed them as friends and brothers, his message was brief and cheerless:

> You have long dwelt on the soil you occupy and in early times before the white man kindled his fires too near to yours . . . you were a happy people. Now your white brothers are around you. . . . Your great father . . . asks if you are prepared and ready to submit to the laws of Mississippi. . . .
>
> Brothers, listen—To these laws, where you are, you must submit—there is no alternative. Your great father cannot, nor can Congress, prevent it. . . . Old men! Lead your children to a land of promise and of peace before the Great Spirit shall call you to die. Young chiefs! Preserve your people and nation. . . .

He warned that this opportunity to find "comfortable homes" might not come again. When the chiefs retired for a conference, Jackson rode away in his carriage leaving Eaton and Coffee to complete negotiations.

Peggy and John Eaton had followed Jackson to Tennessee, planning to visit Nashville, whose social leaders announced that they would not receive them. "The Malaria" had become such an issue in Tennessee politics that one stump speaker spoke of Peggy as an "abandoned" woman and was forced into a fistfight by an opponent. The old man in the Hermitage, "scowling and bemoaning the ingratitude of those for whom he had done so much," invited the Eatons to his home for a dinner party to which he summoned the most eminent families of the region. Since he was unable to persuade the divided Donelson clan to attend, even for the sake of family harmony, Jackson turned to John Coffee, who managed to restore a semblance of peace after several days of diplomatic conferences. Jackson was able to assure Eaton, "My neighbours and connections will receive you and your Lady with that good feeling which is due to you, and I request you and your Lady will meet them with your usual courtesy."

The quasi-state banquet passed with a show of peace and circumspection, though "beneath the surface there were still bitterness and war." Jackson presided over the meal with forced gaiety, joking with Eaton over the carving of a barbecued pig, and then in an abrupt change of mood, carrying the bread around the table himself, serving his guests in a grave, courtly manner.

Jackson disappeared after the party left the dining room, and Eaton asked Peggy to look for him in the garden. She found the old man lying on Rachel's grave and touched his shoulder: "Come, General, you must not do this. Please remember your company in the house. You must not come out here to grieve."

As Peggy remembered the moment many years later: "Lifting his eyes to mine, he cast on me a look I shall never forget, and said in tones which ring in my ears to this day, 'Margaret Eaton, the woman that lies here has shed ten thousand tears for my reputation and her own; and won't you allow me the privilege of shedding a few tears over her grave?' "

At the end of the summer Jackson arranged a domestic compromise, with the aid of Coffee and John Overton. Both Emily Donelson and Peggy Eaton were to remain in Tennessee when their husbands returned to Washington. The President's companions in the White House were to be his twenty-year-old adopted son Andrew Jr., Jack Donelson, and the painter Earl.

A few days after his return Jackson learned that the Choctaw treaty had been signed, and the Chickasaw-Choctaw lands had been ceded to the whites, opening up some 17 million acres in Mississippi and Alabama. There was also news of a triumph by Van Buren—a treaty opening the British West Indies to American shipping, which was to increase the value of the trade by some 2,500 percent within a year.

The party now gained a Washington newspaper of its own, as a result of the estrangement between the President and John C. Calhoun. The opportunistic editor Duff Green, alarmed by the Calhoun-Jackson break and fearful of losing his place as official spokesman and government printer, made a vain effort to restore peace, and then deserted the President. Jackson's advisers warned him that the *Telegraph* was becoming less enthusiastic, but Jackson was slow to act, out of gratitude for the editor's early support.

It was Green's association with Nicholas Biddle that finally drew Jackson's wrath: "The truth is, he has professed to me to be heart and soul against the Bank, but his idol controls him as much as the shewman does his puppits, and we must get another organ to announce the policy, and defend the administration. . . ."

As editor and publisher of the new party journal Kendall suggested Francis Preston Blair, who had succeeded him on the *Argus*. Blair had all the essential qualifications—he was an inveterate enemy of the Bank, a strong Union man who was death on nullification, and he despised John Quincy Adams.

"Bla-ar," as the President called him, in the north Irish accent of his parents, appeared in Washington in December 1830, a frail, ugly little man in cheap, rumpled clothes, whose manner betrayed no hint of his brilliance as a literary stylist. Just now his head was swathed in bandages from the effects of a stagecoach accident. Though reserved to the point of shyness, Blair regarded the President with a steady, unabashed gaze, and Jackson took to him at once. Abruptly, the President began talking of the threats of the nullifiers and Nicholas Biddle, and of troubles within the official family. "And there's my nephew, Donelson. I raised him. Let him do what he will, I love him. Treat him kindly but if he wants to write for your paper you must look out for him."

Jackson invited Blair to dinner, and led him into a room crowded with beribboned diplomats in their formal regalia, where the editor retired into a corner. Jackson summoned him to a seat at his side, engaged him in conversation, and won Blair's loyalty for life. The urbane little man quickly established himself in Washington society as a bon vivant, and endured endless rounds of sherry and champagne parties despite the formidable regimen imposed on him by his wife, who fretted over his health—he was obliged to ride horseback daily, work in his garden, and down a tumbler of rye whiskey after every meal.

The new editor-publisher began publication of the *Globe* as a semi-

weekly, soon made it into a daily, and eventually took as partner John
C. Rives of Virginia, who was business manager and a forceful editori-
alist as well. Rives was a bear of a man nearly 6 1/2 feet tall whose
favorite boast was that he and Blair were "the ugliest pair in the
country."

The *Globe* began life under control of the Kitchen Cabinet, with a
brave Jeffersonian motto at its masthead: "The World Is Governed
Too Much." The new party organ opened without visible means of
support, since there were neither advertisers nor subscribers, a situation quickly remedied by Kendall, who contracted for printing and
conjured up a horde of faithful readers—government employees who
earned more than $1,000 per year were given to understand that they
should subscribe. Jackson himself sent out a memorandum: "I expect
you all to patronize the *Globe.*" The party's papers elsewhere spread
the word that the *Globe,* and not the *Telegraph,* was now Jackson's voice.
Subscriptions and advertising poured in, and within a few weeks Blair's
Globe was prospering. The administration felt that it was ready for the
death struggle against the Bank.

The paper's style was bold and slashing, rather elegant but easily
understood by the public. Editorials by Blair and Kendall laid down the
party line for supporters in every state and served to unify the party.
Blair heightened public interest by use of a new device: he distributed
his editorials to small-town weeklies for first publication, then reprinted them in the *Globe* as expressions of popular opinion throughout the country.

Blair often appeared at the White House before breakfast to get
Jackson's views, then hurried to dash off his vitriolic editorials. The
President took Blair into the Kitchen Cabinet and gave him free rein
with the paper. When he was asked for detailed information, Jackson
frequently said, "Go to Frank Blair, he knows everything." The President came to rely heavily upon Blair as a political realist who contributed much to party stability, and Blair returned his confidence and
respect. The editor admired most the President's independent spirit:

"It is a great mistake to suppose that Old Hickory is in leading-
strings, as the coalition say. I can tell you that he is as much superior
here as he was with our generals during the war. He is a man of
admirable judgment. I have seen proof of it in the direction which he
has given to affairs this winter, in which I know he has differed from
his advisers. . . . He is fighting a great political battle, and you will find
that he will vanquish those who contend with him now as he has always
done his private or the public enemies."

After about a year of the *Globe*'s prosperity Blair bought the large brick house at 1651 Pennsylvania Avenue which was to bear his name for many years.

The *Globe* was an ideal party organ, responsive to the wishes of the Kitchen Cabinet but essentially self-sufficient because of the tact, discretion, and shrewd native ability of Blair, who also brought fresh vitality to the Kitchen Cabinet. This cabinet was now in effect the national committee of the Democratic party, with Kendall as its chairman, and was the first national committee to serve the year round for the duration of an administration. The *Globe* and the informal cabinet were also assets to party unity. Jackson's concept of party organization was military, and he insisted on a direct chain of command from the commander in chief to the lowliest private in the smallest backwoods precinct. All good Democrats followed unquestioningly the program outlined by the leader, whose edicts were handed down through the *Globe*.

23

"The Union will be preserved."

Jackson sent his second annual message to Congress in December 1830, a forthright defense of his vetoes and his positions on the controversial measures that had stirred the country.

He offered rather specious reasoning to justify the removal of southern Indians beyond the Mississippi: "Doubtless it will be painful to leave the graves of their fathers; but what do they more than our ancestors did, or than our children are now doing? To better their condition in an unknown land, our forefathers left all that was dear in earthly objects. Our children, by thousands yearly leave the land of their birth, to seek new homes in distant regions."

The actual removals of the tribes as engineered by Jackson were scenes of tragedy and national shame. The government hired private firms to move the Creeks, who were hauled and driven westward like so many cattle, under miserable conditions. One aged steamboat sank, drowning more than thirty Indians.

The migration of the Choctaws began in December 1831, with hundreds of thinly clad, barefoot Indians crossing the Mississippi in zero weather to camp at Little Rock, where they set off on a nightmare journey to their new home on the Red River. The Creeks and Cherokees were soon forced from their homes, and Creeks who refused to migrate were marched out of Alabama in chains. The Florida Seminoles were bribed, threatened, and at last duped into signing an agreement to migrate to the west. The most inhuman treatment was reserved for 15,000 Cherokees, of whom more than 4,000 died on The Trail of Tears in 1838, driven by the troops of General Winfield Scott.

The New England press denounced the removal as an "abhorrent business," and resulting criticism by Jackson's political enemies and religious groups was not without effect during congressional elections in 1830. Van Buren estimated that the party lost 8,000 votes on the Indian issue in western New York alone. But Jackson persisted, unruffled by charges that his policy was cruel and inconsistent, and the country as a whole supported him. Any real friend of the Indians, the President said, would welcome their move to the west, since there would be endless trouble so long as they remained within state boundaries. Though he expressed regret at the hardships involved, he felt that they must be borne.

Jackson's second annual message also included, despite the objections of his advisers, yet another challenge to the Bank of the United States. The President had not tempered his views in face of criticism of his tentative attack on the Bank in his first message to Congress: "I was aware the bank question would be disapproved by all the sordid and [financially] interested. . . . Although I disliked to act contrary to the opinion of so great a majority of my cabinet, I could not shirk from a duty so imperious. . . . I have brought it before the people, and I have confidence that they will do their duty"—by which he meant that he expected the public to follow his lead. A flood of White House correspondence reassured him of the nation's support. One devout Democrat urged Jackson to immediate action against the Bank: "The open mouthed million already Scorn and revile the institution. . . . It is our business to wrench from its gripe . . . a monopoly of the circulating medium . . . calculated to make the few richer, the many and the poor still poorer."

The President agreed. The annual deposits of interest-free federal funds held by the Bank were now $26 million, a pool of capital which helped to enrich stockholders. Jackson insisted that profits of the Bank should benefit "the whole people, instead of *a few monied capitalists* who are trading on our revenue."

When the second message of the reign was read to Congress, there was a repetition of Jackson's uncompromising challenge to the Bank: "Nothing has occurred to lessen, in any degree, the dangers which many of our citizens apprehend from that institution. . . ." Jackson proposed to replace the Bank by organizing a government bank of limited authority, without the power to make loans or purchase property and thus devoid of the influence that made Biddle's Bank so formidable.

Benton raised the issue in a stirring Senate speech:

I object to the renewal of the charter . . . because I look upon the bank as an institution too great and too powerful to be tolerated in a Government of free and equal laws. . . . It tends to aggravate the inequality of fortunes; to make the rich richer, and the poor poorer. . . .

Gold and silver is the best currency for a republic! It suits the men of middle property and the working people best; and if I was going to establish a working man's party, it should be on the basis of hard money; a hard money party against a paper party.

The speech, widely reprinted in newspapers and pamphlets, established Benton's fame as "Old Bullion," the champion of the downtrodden. From his North Carolina retirement the old Jeffersonian warrior Nathaniel Macon hailed Benton, "You deserve the thanks of every man who lives by the sweat of his face."

Biddle was alarmed at last: "The President aims at the destruction of the Bank." The struggle between the two most powerful men in America had entered a new phase, which was to entwine closely the destinies of Biddle, Calhoun, Peggy Eaton, Van Buren, and Andrew Jackson.

The Jackson-Calhoun feud lingered on. The Vice President busily collected letters for publication in his defense, soliciting statements from Monroe and from members of his cabinet, except Crawford. All of these supported the former Secretary of War.

The administration gave subtle hints that it sought to avoid a public rupture between Calhoun and the President. The new *Globe* pointedly refrained from giving offense to the South Carolinian, and peacemakers appeared at the White House. "Tecumseh" Johnson assured Jackson that Calhoun had always spoken of him "with respect and kindness" during the Florida controversy. Johnson also joined Felix Grundy in protesting that Lewis had gone too far in his conspiracy against Calhoun. Samuel Swartwout came from New York to urge Jackson and the Kitchen Cabinet that the party must foster harmony at all costs. Calhoun soon realized that Jackson sought reconciliation, but he was hesitant. "Every opening was made for me to renew my intercourse with the President, which I have declined, and will continue to do so, till he retracts what he has done. His friends are much alarmed. . . . Those who commenced the affair are heartily sick of it."

There was a brief and rather mysterious armistice. Samuel Swartwout appeared in the White House study one day for a private talk with Jackson, from which the President emerged to tell Van Buren that the whole affair had been settled. His hostile correspondence with Calhoun was to be destroyed, the new amity was to be publicly proclaimed, and Calhoun had been invited to dine at the White House. The imperturbable Van Buren displayed none of his dismay, but managed to congratulate Jackson on the healing of the breach as if eager to sacrifice his career and advance that of his arch rival, in the name of party harmony.

But Calhoun had second thoughts. Friends persuaded him that publication of his correspondence with Jackson would expose the conspiracy against him and discredit Van Buren, whose role as a source of party dissension would be made obvious. With the aid of Duff Green, Calhoun prepared the letters for publication.

Felix Grundy took Calhoun's long manuscript to Eaton and asked him to suggest changes that would make it acceptable to Jackson. Eaton proposed several alterations, and Grundy returned to Calhoun, with the understanding that the major would obtain Jackson's consent to publication. When Eaton did not report the President's reaction, Grundy and Calhoun assumed that Jackson approved. Calhoun published the material in February 1831—a pamphlet of fifty pages that disclosed for the first time the serious rift within the party.

Jackson stormed. "I was thunderstruck," he said. And as for Calhoun and Green, "They have cut their own throats."

The *Globe* condemned the exposé as "a firebrand wantonly thrown into the . . . party. . . . Mr. Calhoun will be held responsible for all the mischief which may follow." The uproar in 100 Jackson newspapers throughout the country doomed Calhoun's hopes of succeeding to the presidency. The aroused President attacked Calhoun at every opportunity, endorsed Van Buren, and determined to run for a second term as a means of installing the Red Fox in the White House. It was assumed that he meant to make Van Buren his Vice President and place him in line for normal succession, but privately he planned to resign after reelection, giving way to Van Buren. Jackson persisted in this scheme for some time, and was dissuaded only by the Red Fox, who realized that a violent public reaction would follow, since the American people would interpret it as a cynical political maneuver rather than a selfless sacrifice by Old Hickory.

It was only now that Calhoun learned that John Eaton had not shown his manuscript to Jackson—Peggy had been avenged.

The distraught Calhoun, abruptly isolated from the party at large and deprived of his national stature, had been limited to the support of the south. It was a major step in the evolution of the party; Jackson and the Democrats were no longer to be dominated by southerners to whom the security of the slaveholding system was a vital concern.

OLD HICKORY: A LIFE OF ANDREW JACKSON

At this juncture Peggy Eaton unexpectedly returned from Tennessee. She resumed her offensive against Washington society with a notable lack of success, and cabinet social functions, as usual, were staged without the Eatons. When Jack Donelson pleaded for the return of his wife from banishment, Jackson agreed, but only if she were willing to accept Peggy Eaton. Donelson proposed as a compromise that Emily be asked to receive Peggy only within the White House, and not in public. Jackson refused. The President and his secretary lived together in the mansion as if they were sworn enemies, sharing the same table but refusing to speak. They communicated only in writing.

Donelson resigned after a few days of this, leaving Jackson so shaken and tearful that his friends were alarmed. Emily wrote to urge Donelson to remain at his post, and offered to return to Washington herself, "to please our dear old Uncle," even if she must visit Peggy officially. Jack Donelson was not dissuaded. He returned to his family in Tennessee, leaving the old man alone.

Many of Jackson's friends deplored his blind loyalty to Peggy. "Public opinion does not sustain him in relation to Mrs. E.," one young Tennessean wrote. "This is a game too insignificant for a President." There were more forceful suggestions. John Overton's nephew William H. Overton told Samuel Bradford of Tennessee, "Eaton must be removed, or a hundred Congressmen will go home dissatisfied."

When Bradford reported the remark to Jackson, the old man's eyes blazed. "Let them come—let the whole hundred come on—I would resign the Presidency sooner than desert my friend Eaton."

It was Martin Van Buren who performed the miracle by which the administration's sociopolitical dilemma was solved. During one of his horseback rides with the President the Red Fox launched the most ingenious scheme of his career, a master stroke designed to restore harmony, to still the clamor of the Calhoun quarrel—and above all, to oust John Eaton from the cabinet. Van Buren planned his approach with care, and waited for several days for the propitious moment. When Jackson spoke of his loneliness in the White House and his grief over the break with his family, Van Buren said, "General, there is but one thing that will give you peace."

"What is that, sir?"

"My resignation."

Jackson glared indignantly. "Never, sir! Even you know little of Andrew Jackson if you suppose him capable of consenting to such a humiliation of his friend by his enemies."

Van Buren argued through a long afternoon in an effort to convince Jackson that his departure would solve many of the administration's problems, but Jackson would not hear of it. Old Hickory's attitude hardened overnight in a way that threatened Van Buren's entire scheme.

The President greeted the Secretary frigidly the next morning: "Mr. Van Buren, I have made it a rule thro' life never to throw obstacles in the way of any man who desires to leave me." Van Buren protested that only his loyalty had prompted him to resign, and that he had thought only of his devotion to Jackson and the party. Jackson grasped his hand impulsively, "Forgive me. I've been too hasty." The President asked time to consider the suggestion and promised to talk with Postmaster General Barry. Van Buren suggested that he talk with Eaton and Lewis as well. Jackson gave his consent the next day and his advisers met at the White House to discuss the plan. After the conference, as Van Buren, Eaton, Lewis, and Barry left the mansion, Eaton halted suddenly and uttered the words the Red Fox longed to hear: "Gentlemen, this is all wrong! I am the one who ought to resign." There was no response, but when he repeated the suggestion, Van Buren asked quietly, "What would Mrs. Eaton say to this?"

Eaton was confident that Peggy would agree, but the solicitous Van Buren insisted that nothing should be done until she had expressed herself, and was not content until Eaton reported that his wife "highly approved" of the decision. Only then did Eaton take his resignation to Jackson, who accepted it.

The *Globe* soon published news of the resignations of Van Buren and Eaton, and within a few days Jackson requested the resignations of Ingham, Berrien, and Branch, who departed at once, thus removing Calhoun's influence within the cabinet. The lone survivor was the inoffensive John Barry. The Red Fox had triumphed.

Jackson had no intention of abandoning his friends. Eaton was to return to the Senate as soon as the President could provide a vacant seat for him, and Van Buren was to be appointed minister to Great Britain.

Jackson and Van Buren made a call on Mrs. Eaton shortly before the new minister left for his post. Peggy gave them a greeting that was far from friendly, "a coolness directed mainly to the General," Van Buren said. Jackson was baffled by Peggy's changed attitude. He shook his head as he left the house. "It's strange," he said. But the more perceptive Van Buren realized that the self-centered Peggy had turned on the President because she felt that he had abandoned her for the sake of political expediency.

Public astonishment at news of the cabinet's departure was shared by some who were close to the President. The role of the Secretary of

State was most baffling of all. Van Buren's motive for resigning, so it was said, was "of so perplexing a character that he was sincerely embarrassed himself when he sat down to the task of explaining it."

Clay's paper, the *National Journal,* greeted the cabinet upheaval with delight: "Thus is the pie bald Administration dissolved. . . . To what a state have we been brought by the infatuation which was so successfully wielded for the purpose of placing General Jackson in the chair of the Executive. . . ."

For weeks Americans of the hinterlands regarded the shakeup of the cabinet as a mystery, since it was some time before the press dared identify Peggy as the cause of the furor. The *National Journal* at first proclaimed that "The President and his Secretaries have completely mystified the nation."

The mystery was soon dispelled. Branch published a provocative query in a Raleigh, North Carolina, newspaper: " . . . Dismissed officers have faithfully discharged their respective duties (but that was not enough). . . . *The American people have a right to know the whole truth:* from whence the alleged discord originated. . . ." Branch continued with such broad insinuations that Eaton challenged him to a duel, which Branch declined with a notice in Duff Green's *Telegraph.* Green then joined the quarrel, prompting Eaton to challenge Ingham.

The *Connecticut Herald* posed—and answered—the fateful question, " . . . what motive could have induced the president . . . to cast aside his whole Cabinet . . . wonderful as it may seem, it was a *woman.* The Hero, whom the veterans of Waterloo could not conquer . . . has been . . . debased to most ignoble purposes by one of those courteous pieces of mortality whose 'name is frailty!' We can therefore expect no 'explanations' from the President upon this subject."

The final disclosure was brought on by Peggy herself. The *Globe,* ostensibly speaking for Eaton but certainly with Peggy's guidance, demanded that Branch cease his "injurious intimations" and come out openly and name names. "Why does he not act like a man?"

The *Journal of Commerce* finally brought out Peggy's name on June 8 and the country was stirred anew by the scandal.

The *Globe* charged that the exposé was the work of the *Journal's* Washington correspondent, "a poor, irresponsible scribbler, who for five dollars a week, does all the dirty work of defamation." The *Journal* replied smugly that its circulation had doubled and that it was still unable to print enough papers to supply the demand.

The *Telegraph* and the *Globe* squabbled over the exposure in Washington, "raging" as the *National Journal* said, "like two bull dogs in *la petite guerre.* . . ." And though details of the scandal "poured through the press, the still more shocking ones . . . spoken of in private conversation are enough to pollute the public mind. A dangerous stab has been inflicted upon the morals and taste of the community. A new era has arisen in our history."

The era opened with another bizarre scene of the Peggy Eaton drama. The irate Eaton demanded an explanation and apology from the departing Samuel Ingham, who replied, "You must be a little deranged, to imagine that any bluster of yours could induce me to disavow what all the inhabitants of this city know, and perhaps half of the people of the United States believe to be true." Eaton then issued a challenge to a duel, and when Ingham declined, Eaton put a pistol in his pocket and prowled the streets in search of his reluctant adversary. One day, so Ingham said, Eaton, Major Lewis, and two other men waited for hours before his house in an attempt to waylay him. Ingham remained in hiding for a day or so, wrote Jackson to say that he feared for his life, then fled the city at 4:00 A.M. When Ingham wrote defiantly from the safety of New Hope, Pennsylvania, Peggy Eaton said tartly, "all he needs is petticoats."

Peggy defended herself fiercely to the end. She and Eaton threatened the Reverend Campbell with a suit for slander, and made things so unpleasant for him that he left the city, saying that he could no longer live "in fire." Peggy vowed that her female critics would crawl to ask her forgiveness "on their marrow bones" before Jackson's term had ended. She offered a theory to explain the origin of the crusade against her:

"To tell the truth Mrs. Donelson, Mrs. Calhoun, Mrs. Branch and Mrs. Ingham were a very indifferent set . . . none of them had beauty, accomplishments, or graces in society . . . and for these reasons—I say it without egotism—they were jealous of me. Mrs. Branch was particularly noticeable as a first class dowdy, and it was a great relief not to be obliged to entertain any of the set a good deal. Mrs. Ingham was a large, coarse, brawling creature raised too suddenly into a position she little knew how to fill. . . ."

Jackson maintained a discreet silence in face of press comments on the affair, but privately denounced the "treachery" of Branch and the "disgraceful flight" of Ingham. And when Berrien also declined an Eaton challenge, Old Hickory said scornfully, *"What a wretch!* this *southern hotspur* will not fight—My Creed is true—there never was a base man a brave one."

Eaton and his wife lingered in their large house opposite the British legation for a few months, bitter and lonely. The White House mail was filled with advice that the President should send Eaton away, but Jackson probably saw few of these letters and did not discuss the matter with his advisers. Lewis confessed to Van Buren that he dared not raise the subject with the President. At last, in September 1831, Eaton called at the White House to report that he was going back to Tennessee. The old friends shook hands, with an understanding that Jackson would use his influence to return Eaton to the Senate, an effort that was to fail.

Eaton's departure gratified, but did not satisfy, Jackson's loyal friends, some of who also urged the banishment of William Lewis. The candid R. G. Dunlap wrote the President from Tennessee,

> While the nation may admire the firm friendship by you manifested for Mr. Eaton, they cannot but rejoice at . . . his retirement. Mr. W. B. Lewis, almost too small to write about, occupies a position before the nation . . . which merits little attention. Send him home and no longer hold yourself accountable to the . . . people for the arrogant follies of such a small but busy man. . . . To speak plain, the opinion prevails at large that W. B. Lewis is one of your most confidential councillors. This fact, whether it be true or false . . . raises a suspicion of your fitness to rule. . . .

The President clung to Lewis, but in this case offered no defense of him.

Jackson undertook the selection of a new cabinet at once, and made short work of it, despite two refusals. He first asked his old Tennessee friend Senator Hugh White, and then the South Carolina Federalist William Drayton, to become Secretary of War; when both declined, Jackson chose Lewis Cass, a transplanted New England lawyer who had served as governor of the Michigan Territory for almost twenty years.

Edward Livingston was called from the Senate to become Secretary of State, a move protested by some states' rights men within the party who were wary of Livingston's strong nationalistic views. Louis McLane of Delaware, the former Federalist who had opposed Jackson, was recalled from his post as minister to London to become Secretary of the Treasury. Levi Woodbury of New Hampshire became Secretary of Navy, after leaving his Senate seat to Ike Hill; and Roger B. Taney, the gifted but little-known Baltimore lawyer, was named Attorney General. Barry remained as Postmaster General.

In response to a few critics who were fearful that these more independent men might fail to hew to the party line, Jackson offered the assurance that it was he, and only he, who would "give the rule," and that the cabinet as a whole was expected to carry out his wishes. As

Frank Blair put it, Jackson was still a general, and his administration was an army: "Old Hickory . . . is to his cabinet here what he was to his aids."

General public reaction to the new cabinet was one of relief. It was praised as more able than the first, and though apparently loyal to Jackson, included three men who were friendly to the Bank of the United States. Public interest centered on Taney, the most unexpected of Jackson's choices. The Marylander was a stooped, near-sighted man of fifty-one who looked more like a country store clerk than a future Chief Justice of the Supreme Court, but he had a keen vigorous intelligence and an enormous capacity for work.

The reorganization also brought new faces to the Kitchen Cabinet. Van Buren and Eaton were replaced by Amos Kendall and Frank Blair, and Roger Taney, who joined them, soon became one of the most effective members of the group. Major Lewis, who opposed the President on the Bank issue and was shortly to move out of the White House, was said to be losing some of his influence.

Jackson's White House advisers also assumed new roles. With the growing maturity of the Democratic party the President's personal staff evolved into an arm of the party; for the remainder of Jackson's administration it was to serve more effectively than ever as the Democratic National Committee. With the end of bitter factional strife the party's goals became more clearly defined, patronage was increasingly left to members of Congress, and the role of the Kitchen Cabinet became more palatable to the public. Even so, there was a lingering air of almost diabolical mystery about Amos Kendall, who was thought to be the author of most of Jackson's letters and reports, and of telling thrusts of propaganda.

A visiting British writer said of Kendall:

> He is supposed to be the moving spring of the whole administration; the thinker, planner and doer; but it is all in the dark. Documents are issued of an excellence which prevents their being attributed to persons who take the responsibility of them; a correspondence is kept up all over the country for which no one seems answerable; work is done, of goblin extent and with goblin speed, which makes men look about them with a superstitious wonder; and the invisible Amos Kendall has the credit of it all.

Jackson's persistent critic, Philip Hone of New York, saw Kendall as the "head devil of the Administration, the actor of all dirty work, at once the tyrant and the slave of the President." And Henry A. Wise later castigated Kendall in the House: "He was the President's *thinking* machine, and his *writing* machine,—ay, and his *lying* machine! . . ."

But though Kendall was the genie, Jackson's was the master hand in the composition of state papers and attacks on the opposition. They frequently worked in Jackson's bedroom, where the President lay with Rachel's miniature by his side, puffing at his pipe and blurting his ideas in rough, staccato fashion until Kendall left to cast the material in polished form. When he returned and read the result, the old man would shake his head and dictate a new version, then another and another until he was content; in the end even Kendall was astonished by the vigor and power of the reasoning accomplished in these collaborations.

Friends noted changes in the President himself with the restoration of harmony to the cabinet and the strengthening of his Kitchen Cabinet. Frank Blair declared, "Old Hickory is as full of energy as he was at New Orleans." Jackson had embarked enthusiastically on a new building project back home in Tennessee, where a contractor had begun a major reconstruction of the Hermitage. The new mansion concealed the simple lines of the house beneath two new wings, a colonnade, and a sweeping two-story portico whose elaborate ornamentation seemed to the contractor expressive of Old Hickory's eminence.

The new dining room would seat 100 guests in comfort, the opposite wing included a large library and an overseer's room, and 10 towering Doric columns were spaced along the facade of 104 feet. The log cabin Hermitage of the early years was reduced to the status of a homely outbuilding.

Jackson was also gratified by the return of his family to the White House. Jack and Emily Donelson came back, bringing with them two of Emily's girl cousins. Andrew Jr. and the President's ward, Andrew Jackson Hutchings, also moved into the mansion; the old man was no longer lonely.

The summer of 1831 brought fresh challenges from the south. Two South Carolina merchants tested the validity of the tariff laws by refusing to pay bonds which guaranteed their payment of duties, and the federal district attorney, himself a nullifier, resigned his office rather than prosecute the case. Jackson found it impractical to impeach the attorney, but he sent to Charleston as his secret agent Joel R. Poinsett, now returned from his post as minister to Mexico. Poinsett began making regular reports to the White House on developments in South Carolina.

Soon afterward, Senator Robert Hayne sought to have one of his friends appointed district attorney. Jackson refused, saying that he was unwilling to appoint a prosecutor who openly avowed his defiance of a federal law. It was one of Jackson's most tactful letters, but it did not signal a weakening of his resolve. On the back of Hayne's letter Jackson scrawled, "I draw a wide difference between State Rights and the advocates of them, and a nullifier. One will preserve the union of the States. The other will dissolve the union. . . ."

Groups of Union men and nullifiers staged competing celebrations in Charleston on July 4. The Unionists triumphantly read a letter from Jackson denouncing nullification. He hoped, the President said, that the challenges to the Union from South Carolina were no more than "momentary excitement," and he assured the loyal people of the state that the Union would be maintained "at all hazards." In response the nullifiers turned to John C. Calhoun, who had been covertly advising leaders of the movement while clinging to his old friends among the nationalists, men whose confidence he had won as a War Hawk in 1812. Calhoun realized that the time had come for him to declare himself on the divisive issue, and he did not hesitate. Less than a month after Jackson's reassuring message to the Unionists had been acclaimed in Charleston, Calhoun published an extended statement called *Address on the relations which the States and General Government Bear to Each Other.*

Calhoun's fine-spun intellectual argument in behalf of nullification was so subtle, as one scholar remarked, that "few of those who tried to explain it gave evidence of understanding it."* With this publication Calhoun assumed leadership of the nullification movement—the fateful cause to which he was to devote his energies for the rest of his life. Though the South Carolinian had only now publicly transferred his allegiance from his nation to his region, he had never altered his view of the basic issue of the recurrent tariff controversy: that the triumph of industrialization would bring in its train "misery to those who live on the land." The tariff, Calhoun said, was in effect a 45 percent levy on southern exports, imposed for the benefit of "a moneyed aristocracy" in the north. He intended to fight for the agrarian south with all his powers. "Were my head at stake," he said, "I would do my duty, be the consequences what they may."

---

*In response to requests for clarification Calhoun wrote his Fort Hill Letter in 1832, the last of the three documents upon which the nullification theory was based. The heart of the argument: "that the general government emanated from the people of the several states . . . acting in their separate and sovereign capacity, and not from all the people forming one aggregate political community; that the constitution of the United States is, in fact, a compact, to which each state is a party . . . and that the several states . . . have a right to judge of its infractions. . . ."

Calhoun acknowledged that the ugly reality that lay beneath the tariff struggle was slavery: "The truth can no longer be disguised, that the peculiar domestic institution of the Southern States and . . . [their] soil and climate," had brought them into conflict with the Union majority. If the autonomy of the southern states was not to be guaranteed by the Constitution, he argued, "they must in the end be forced to rebel, or submit to have their permanent interests sacrificed, their domestic institutions subverted . . . and themselves and children reduced to wretchedness."

Hotheaded leaders of South Carolina's legislature, inspired by the emergence of their champion, passed resolutions of defiance, declaring that secession was the inherent right of every state, and that withdrawal from the Union would entail neither treason nor rebellion. As to the obstinate Jackson, the Carolinians protested, they could not be expected to "legislate under the sword of the Commander-in-Chief."

The President said nothing publicly, but sent James Alexander Hamilton in New York an assurance couched in unmistakable terms, *"The Union will be preserved."*

24

"the house of Have and the house of Want"

Henry Clay returned to the Senate in the fall of 1831, after an absence of almost three years in Kentucky. He came as the dominant figure of the new Congress and Jackson's obvious opponent in the approaching presidential campaign. The Western Hotspur still managed an air of urbane dignity and grace, but he had aged since his nervous collapse of 1829, and he was saddened by four recent deaths in his family and by the tragic collapse of his son, who had been declared insane. Clay's body was almost emaciated; his thin face, seamed and weathered, peered from beneath a crown of long white hair combed back from his temples. His voice, once richly resonant, was thin and cracked, and his manner was subdued.

Harriet Martineau found the Kentuckian changed for the better: "Mr. Clay is a man of an irritable and impetuous nature, over which he has obtained a truly noble mastery. His moderation is now his most striking characteristic."

The astute Clay saw a gloomy political career ahead of him. The narrowness of his reelection to the Senate offered scant hope of victory over Jackson, whose national popularity increased daily. Still, though there was no promising issue upon which Old Hickory could be attacked, Clay did not abandon hope. "Something," he said "might turn up to give a brighter aspect to our affairs." The Senate of this session was an ideal forum for him. With Calhoun, Webster, and Robert

Hayne, Clay led a powerful anti-Jackson coalition which included John Tyler of Virginia, George Poindexter of Mississippi, and Theodore Frelinghuysen of New Jersey. And there were dependable supporters in the House—John Quincy Adams, Rufus Choate, Edward Everett, John Branch of North Carolina, and George McDuffie of South Carolina.

Clay made a brave show of vigor and optimism. Soon after his arrival in Washington he greeted John Quincy Adams, who had returned to the House out of need for the income, "How does it feel to be a boy again?" With a resolute show of his own youthfulness Clay joked with his friends and entertained them in his characteristic fashion. In masculine society he displayed the manners of "a regular Kentucky hog drover," sprawling in a chair with his feet on the mantelpiece, constantly chewing, drinking, and spitting, though he was "all gentleness, politeness and cordiality in the society of ladies." In the Senate Clay lounged in apparent indifference, read during debate, sucked sticks of peppermint candy, or wandered to the snuffbox in the center of the chamber.

With the aid of discomfited southerners under Calhoun's leadership, Clay moved to embarrass Jackson by rejecting Van Buren as minister to Great Britain. The Senate promptly confirmed all members of the new cabinet, without debate, and then executed a carefully laid plan. Clay and Webster, who had assured themselves of a majority, contrived a tie vote by dismissing several of their allies from the chamber, then sent the Senate into executive session. Webster and others attacked Van Buren as a spoilsman, and Clay, against the advice of wiser friends, led the final assault by condemning Van Buren's role in the negotiations which had opened the West Indies to American trade. Clay ludicrously exaggerated Van Buren's surrender of earlier claims pressed by the Adams administration as "prostrating and degrading the American eagle before the British lion," and his rhetoric carried the day. After an extended and bitter debate the vote ended in a deadlock; Calhoun then cast the decisive ballot that recalled Van Buren. The session was opened and the speeches of Clay and Webster were offered for publication.

The vote was reported to Jackson as he sat with friends before a fireplace in the Red Room, relaxing after a White House dinner party. A messenger whispered the news in his ear and the old man sprang from his chair, "By the Eternal! I'll smash them!"

Jackson's surprise was genuine. He had considered the possibility of a defeat, but concluded that his enemies would not risk the consequences. About a month earler he had written Van Buren, "The opposition would be glad to reject your nomination as minister if they dared, but they know it would make you too popular." Calhoun was ecstatic over the rejection of his rival. "It will kill him, sir," he cried, "kill him dead. He'll never kick, sir, never kick."

Tom Benton was more realistic. He told Senator Gabriel Moore of Alabama, who had joined the anti-Van Buren forces, "You have broken a minister, and elected a vice president." Moore was aghast. "Good God!" he said. "Why didn't you tell me that before I voted, and I'd have voted the other way." The New York congressman G. C. Verplanck peered even further into the future: "That makes Van Buren President of the United States."

The news reached Van Buren in London, where he had been moving through the Court of St. James's in his ingratiating way, forming pleasant friendships with Palmerston and Talleyrand. Young Washington Irving, the secretary of the legation, breakfasted with Van Buren the morning the word of his recall was received. The Red Fox was so elated that he immediately revived from a minor illness, and offered his own prediction that he would now become Vice President. Van Buren appeared at Queen Victoria's afternoon reception and in the evening dined with Talleyrand. After a delay to time his arrival at the most favorable moment, the Red Fox returned to America in triumph.

Henry Clay's search for an issue with which to challenge Jackson was none too promising. The President was invulnerable on the controversy over nullification, and Clay saw no opportunities in foreign affairs, Indian removal, the tariff, or internal improvements. Old Hickory's annual message to Congress provided the Kentuckian with his issue. After reporting on the generally satisfactory state of the Union, Jackson commented briefly that his opinion of the Bank of the United States was unchanged, but that he was willing to leave its fate to "an enlightened people" and their representatives in Congress.

This activity alarmed anti-Bank Democrats. C. C. Cambreleng reported that Jackson stood almost alone, with most of his advisers favoring Biddle. "Woodbury keeps snug and plays out of all the corners of his eyes. Taney, strange as it may seem, is the best Democrat among us . . . McLane has burnished all his satellites with the Bank gold and silver. Somehow or other they all begin to think the Bank must be re-chartered."

The ailing John Randolph wrote Jackson from Virginia, "I see that with your arch enemy the grand Nullifier working in the Senate . . . and his *clientele* dependent upholding the Bank in the other house and all working against you that you have Sisiphean labor to perform. I wish

I were able to help you roll up the stone, but I cannot. I am finished." Jackson replied, "Never fear the triumph of the Bank while I am here."

Biddle offered major concessions in an attempt to woo Jackson. If he would consent to recharter, the Bank would accept restrictions of its power—it would no longer lend money on merchandise nor issue branch drafts, it would maintain no more than two branches in each state, and states would be empowered to tax and sue the corporation. These were major concessions, but though he had given them close attention and supervised the drafting of several proposals, Jackson withheld his approval. In the end he had publicly revived the Bank question in his message.

McLane went to Philadelphia to reassure Biddle that he could influence the President's actions and prevent a full-scale attack on the Bank —since Jackson knew that his own bank proposal could not be adopted, he would accept the old charter with modifications. But McLane ended their discussion with a warning: Biddle should not petition Congress to recharter the Bank before the election of 1832, since Jackson would almost certainly be so aroused by the direct challenge that he would veto the bill. Biddle should wait until Old Hickory had been reelected. McLane said, "What I see of Gen'l Jackson I think he would be more disposed to yield when he is strong than when he is in danger."

Jackson admired McLane's candor and independence and liked him despite his support of Biddle. "It is an honest difference of opinion," he said, ". . . he acts fairly by leaving me free and uncommitted. . . . Mr. McLane and myself understand each other." McLane's clever manipulations delayed Jackson's final decision against the Bank, but could not sway him.

Clay joined McLane in advising Biddle to bide his time until after the election. A financial panic had raged in the Western states for several months, stimulated by Biddle's ill-advised liberalization of credit to farmers and land speculators of the region. After a disappointing harvest in 1831, when borrowers extended and increased their loans, the drain on the Bank became so serious that Biddle was forced to draw on his balances in state banks and foreign banks. When this failed to stem the tide of currency flowing to the West he pledged his full credit to obtain loans of $2,000,000 in London. For some months the Bank was in danger, and during the crisis thousands of western voters came to its aid at the polls—since they feared that their loans would be recalled if Jackson denied the Bank a new charter, many of these men turned against Old Hickory.

Clay concluded that the complex Bank issue, as yet indecisively handled by Jackson, offered the only feasible basis for his campaign. He reversed his stand on the timing of the demand for recharter and began to urge Biddle to an early attempt. Biddle found it difficult to resist, since he feared that a postponement might cost him the support of both Clay and Webster. By December 1831 when he was nominated for President by the newly formed National Republican party, Clay had maneuvered Biddle into full support of his cause, and the Bank's fate was delivered into the hands of the Western Hotspur. The Baltimore convention of the National Republicans, the first by a major national party, nominated for its vice president John Sergeant of Philadelphia, another of Biddle's lawyers.

The convention's Address, which passed as a platform, praised the Bank as a "great and beneficent institution," and charged Jackson with plotting its destruction. The Clay-Biddle manifesto challenged voters: "Are the people of the United States . . . ready to destroy one of their most valuable establishments to gratify the caprice of a chief magistrate who reasons and advises upon a subject, with the details of which he is evidently unacquainted, in direct contradiction to the opinion of his own official counselors?"

Five months later the Democrats met in Baltimore and, as expected, nominated a Jackson-Van Buren ticket virtually by acclamation. The party issued no platform.

The two major parties were challenged by the Anti-Masons, a splinter group formed in reaction to the abduction and apparent murder of William Morgan, of Canandaigua, New York, who had written an exposé of Masonry. Morgan, who had been imprisoned for a debt of $2.69, was freed when his fine was paid by an unknown benefactor, and was then seized, bound, and gagged by a band of men as he stepped forth to freedom. Morgan's disappearance near Niagara Falls caused a national sensation and a storm of protest against the Masons. The new party was of limited influence, but staged its own convention and nominated William Wirt of Maryland, the former Attorney General, for President and Amos Ellmaker of Pennsylvania for Vice President.

On January 9, 1832, Biddle surprised the White House and many of his own friends by petitioning Congress to recharter the Bank. Jackson realized that the banker could muster the votes for victory in both houses, but he said firmly: "I will prove to them I will not flinch." The President counterattacked at once. Thomas Benton prompted the friendly Representative Augustin Clayton of Georgia to demand an investigation of the Bank, and Biddle was forced to yield in order to allay suspicions that the Bank had engaged in corrupt practices. The Jacksonians launched a probe. After six weeks of hearings a House committee reported on numerous alleged abuses by the Bank, all challenged and rebutted in a minority report, and the findings were published in a volume of almost 600 pages.

The most serious charges involved generous loans to newspaper editors and congressmen, but John Quincy Adams of the committee, for one, was convinced that Biddle's hands were clean, and that the Bank's affairs had been conducted "with as near an approach to perfect wisdom as the imperfection of human nature permitted." Soon after the "microscopic" probe ended, Biddle arrived in Washington to direct the passage of his bill.

Clay was confident of victory, and declared that Jackson would be faced with a dilemma: he must veto, or concede victory to his enemies. And a veto, in Clay's opinion, would ruin Jackson's chances for reelection. He would lose the west, as well as Biddle's home state of Pennsylvania. Clay's friend Peter B. Porter observed that Jackson "would rather see a shoat enter the palace than such a Bill," and agreed that a veto would kill the President politically, if not physically. Clay rejected all suggestions of compromise on the bill: "Should Jackson veto it, I'll veto him!"

The prospect of a hard-fought campaign animated Jackson, and a minor operation improved his health. In January 1832 one Dr. Harris, a Philadelphia surgeon who visited the White House, convinced the President that the bullet fired into his arm by Jesse Benton in 1813 could be removed without dangerous shock, and that an operation would eliminate a chronic source of infection. Jackson rolled up his sleeve, grasped his cane, and said, "Go ahead." Harris swiftly made a long incision, squeezed the flesh of the scrawny arm, and the pistol ball fell to the floor. Jackson attended a dinner party that evening and his health seemed to improve immediately.

Washington gossips were soon embroidering the story: Frank Blair, it was said, had taken the bullet to Senator Benton, who declined to accept it. "The General has acquired clear title to it in common law by twenty years' peaceable possession."

"Only nineteen years," Blair said.

Benton laughed. "Oh, well, in consideration of the extra care he has taken of it—keeping it constantly about his person, and so on—I'll waive the odd year."

A few weeks later John Campbell of the Treasury Department reported the President in fighting trim:

> The evening before last I spent with him. When I went in there were some 20 or 30 ladies & gentlemen seated and standing. He was in the

midst of the ladies in as fine a humour as I ever saw him. He took me by the arm in his usual gallant style and introduced me to all the Ladies with whom I was not acquainted. . . . He then handed a young lady to the piano and stood by her while she play'd several airs. . . . He paid her some pretty compliments and then handed her back to her seat again. . . .

When most of the party went off to a ball, Campbell and a friend sat before the fire with Jackson, who said that he had recovered the use of his arm since his operation and that he could now manage a horse without pain. Old Hickory also retold the story of his duel with the Bentons, and of his subsequent suffering. Not only had the arm remained in a sling for six months during the Creek war—Jackson had torn "the broken bones of the arm to pieces again" at the Battle of Enotachopco in an attempt to kill a retreating officer with his sword.

The Senate passed the Bank recharter bill on June 11, 1832, by a margin of 8 votes, and the House approved it three weeks later, 107–85. A smiling Biddle strode onto the floor, besieged by members who offered congratulations. His headquarters roared most of the night with a victory celebration.

Roger Taney was in Annapolis when the bill passed, but Jackson assembled the rest of the cabinet and announced his intention to issue an uncompromising veto. His advisers were unanimously opposed. McLane, Livingston, and Cass in particular renewed their pleas for a message that would permit a modified Bank charter in the future. Jackson dismissed them. Taney returned to the city and urged Jackson to strengthen his veto with a positive, unyielding statement. Jackson needed little persuasion. Amos Kendall had already begun work on the veto message.

Martin Van Buren, who was just now returning from London, arrived during the crisis. He reached the White House at midnight to find the frail old man propped on pillows in his bed. Jackson seized his hand, "The bank, Mr. Van Buren, is trying to kill me, *but I will kill it!*"

For three days Jackson directed work on his veto in hectic and almost endless sessions. In one corner of the room Ralph Earl dabbed away at one of his numberless presidential portraits, oblivious to the hubbub, as Jackson wandered in and out to have passages read to him and suggested changes. When Kendall finished his draft, the President asked Jack Donelson to revise it, and when he floundered, sent for Taney. Donelson and Taney were busy with their revisions for another day, and Secretary of the Navy Woodbury then appeared, announced a change of heart, and helped with the alterations until Jackson was satisfied. The final draft was largely the work of Taney.

The veto, sent to Congress on July 10, resounded throughout the country, its most memorable passages reminiscent of Jefferson's rhetoric—an oddly eloquent expression of Jackson's theories of the basic economic rights of the common man:

> It is to be regretted, that the rich and powerful too often bend the acts of government to their selfish purposes.
>
> Distinctions in society will always exist under every just government. Equality of talents, of education, or of wealth cannot be produced by human institutions. In the full enjoyment of the gifts of Heaven and the fruits of superior industry, economy, and virtue every man is equally entitled to protection by law; but when the laws undertake to add to these natural and just advantages artificial distinctions . . . to make the rich richer and the potent more powerful, the humble members of society— the farmers, mechanics and laborers—who have neither the time nor the means of securing like favors to themselves, have a right to complain of the injustice of their Government.
>
> Its evils exist only in its abuses. If it would confine itself to equal protection, and . . . shower its favors alike on the high and low, the rich and the poor, it would be an unqualified blessing. In the act before me, there seems to be a wide and unnecessary departure from these just principles.

The message then turned to specific arguments against the Bank, which was not only unconstitutional, Jackson said. Its vast power, concentrated "in the hands of a few men irresponsible to the people," was also a constant threat to the American future.

Jackson offered a radical extension of the precepts of the Constitution:

> It is maintained by the advocates of the bank that its constitutionality . . . ought to be considered as settled by precedent and by the decision of the Supreme Court. To this conclusion I can not assent. Mere precedent is a dangerous source of authority. . . .
>
> . . . The opinion of the Supreme Court . . . ought not to control the coordinate authorities of this Government. The Congress, the Executive, the Court must each for itself be guided by its own opinion of the Constitution. Each public officer who takes an oath to support the Constitution swears that he will support it as he understands it, and not as it is understood by others. . . . The opinion of the judges has no more authority over

Congress than the opinion of Congress has over the judges, and on that
point the President is independent of both. . . .

Nicholas Biddle was outraged by Jackson's veto but also exultant. A
declaration so repulsive, so un-American, he thought, would be the
President's ruin. He wrote Clay: "It has all the fury of a chained
panther, biting the bars of his cage. It is really a manifesto of anarchy
. . . and my hope is, that it will contribute to relieve the country from
the dominion of these miserable people. . . . You are destined to be
the instrument of that deliverance."

Confident that the country would reject Jackson's reasoning, Biddle
printed 30,000 copies of the veto for use as a Clay campaign document. And though it was obvious that Congress would not override the
veto, he urged Daniel Webster to a final attack in the Senate. Webster's
assault was precisely what Biddle had in mind: the veto "manifestly
seeks to influence the poor against the rich. It wantonly attacks whole
classes of the people, for the purpose of turning against them the
prejudices and resentments of other classes. It is a State paper which
finds no topic too exciting for its use, no passion too inflam-
mable. . . ."

Webster also assailed Jackson's spurious reasoning as to the right of
each elected official to interpret the Constitution for himself. Jackson's
attitude toward the Constitution, Webster declared, would lead to
"general nullification, and end in the complete subversion of the government." As to practical matters, Biddle's sound money policies had
been a blessing the country could not surrender; further, the Bank
could not close out its affairs in so brief a time without wrecking the
nation's economy.

The senator from Massachusetts undoubtedly spoke his convictions,
but he could hardly have spoken without prejudice. Not only was he
one of the Bank's counsel and a member of its board of directors. By
now he had outstanding loans of $22,000, and was to receive another
for $10,000 a few days after his speech. Webster's acknowledgment of
his role as a partisan of the Bank was made clear in his message to
Biddle when his annual payment was delayed: "I believe my retainer
has not been renewed or refreshed as usual and if it is wished that my
relations to the bank should continue, it would be well to send me the
usual retainer."

Henry Clay and Thomas Benton offered a brief diversion during the
debate. When Benton defended Jackson and charged Clay with a lack
of courtesy and decorum, Clay said he was puzzled as to Benton's true
feelings toward the President, and made an allusion to their duel.

"Certainly," he said, "I never complained of the President beating a brother of mine after he was prostrated and lying apparently lifeless. The Senator from Missouri needs no more specific indications. . . ."

Benton roared. He conceded that he and Jackson had fought, but said they had become good friends years before and had remained so. He revived the charge of Clay's "corrupt Bargain" with Adams. Between Jackson and Benton there had been no question of an "adjourned veracity remaining on the public mind. No sir!" After the chair finally restored order, the Senate sustained Jackson's veto by a vote of twenty-two to nineteen. Friday July 13, 1832, was not a lucky day for Henry Clay and Nicholas Biddle—but that was not yet apparent to the victims.

Biddle agreed with Clay that the President's defiance of Congress had won countless friends for the Bank, and that the veto and the presence of Van Buren on the Democratic ticket would "finish the work." Biddle broadcast 140,000 copies of Webster's rebuttal throughout the country.

But the veto was more than a campaign document, and the people took it to heart. Remarkably enough, over the signature of a prominent frontier landholder, merchant, and speculator, it was a thrust at the heart of the established order Jackson had helped to erect—a thrust delivered in behalf of the common man who had turned to him for leadership. Despite its dubious economic and political theories, the message was to become a document by which Old Hickory's turbulent administration was to be remembered. Throughout the summer of 1832 the veto was debated by rich and poor, "the house of Have and the house of Want," as George Bancroft said, both of whom recognized it as the central issue of the presidential campaign.

Frank Blair hailed the veto as "a Second Declaration of Independence"; but critics saw the message as a piece of unabashed demogoguery, charging that it resorted to fantasy in its allegation that poor Americans would benefit from the suspension of the bank's charter, and that Jackson had struck a blow against "the rich and powerful" as a class.

The shock of the veto splintered but did not shatter the Democratic party. Meetings of outraged Jackson supporters, many of them conservative businessmen, were held in almost every city, to announce their defection from the party and predict Old Hickory's ruin. Only a minority of the business community remained faithful, chiefly those who feared the Bank's power. Newspaper support for the Bank was overwhelming.

The *New York American*, for example, decried the veto: "It is indeed and verily beneath contempt. It is an appeal of ignorance to ignorance, of prejudice to prejudice. . . . No man in the cabinet will be willing to share the ignominy of preparing or approving such a paper." The *Boston Advertiser* declared, "For the first time, perhaps, in the history of civilized communities, the Chief Magistrate of a great nation . . . is found appealing to the worst passions of the uninformed . . . and endeavoring to stir up the poor against the rich."

Three-fourths of the press, by Van Buren's estimate, joined Biddle's chorus, and there was evidence of pressure on publishers from advertisers and from the Bank itself. Some of Biddle's notorious loans to newspapers wrought miracles, as in the case of New York's *Courier and Enquirer,* a Jackson organ abruptly converted to the Bank's cause after receiving loans of more than $50,000. James W. Webb and James Gordon Bennett of the *Courier* defended themselves vigorously against these charges, and Webb explained why he had switched his allegiance after supporting Jackson through all previous controversies: "I feel called upon to proclaim to the people that Andrew Jackson is not their president." Old Hickory was enfeebled by age, Webb said, and was controlled by the "political gamblers" around him.

25

"I thought I would have to hang some of them . . ."

Jackson left for Tennessee in mid-August 1832, his saddlebags heavy with gold coins. He paid for all his travel expenses in gold and missed no opportunities to make his point with tavernkeepers, toll bridge tenders, and ferrymen. "No more paper money, you see, if only I can put down this Nicholas Biddle and his monster bank." His shrewd campaign tactic inspired in his wake slogans of: "Clay and rag money! Jackson and gold!"

Biddle's excessive expansion of credit and hasty retrenchment had virtually driven hard money from circulation in western states, and as a remedy Jackson had ordered the mint to turn out gold eagles at the rate of $20,000 per day. He had then seized the opportunity to propagandize against Biddle on his long ride to the west.

The President wrote Van Buren: "I found on my whole journey everything to cheer us; prosperity everywhere and all gratified and happy on the prospects of a circulating and stable metallic currency, and particularly the gold coin, which many had not for years seen a piece of before we presented them in payment of our bills."

Jackson settled at the Hermitage, confident that the people would stand behind him. "The veto works well. . . . Instead of crushing me it will crush The Bank." He wrote to Hill in New Hampshire, "Isaac, it'll be a walk." Benton and Old Hickory's other friends placed substantial election bets.

Alarming reports reached the Hermitage as the threat of nullification intruded once more. Senator Robert Hayne and most of the South
Carolina congressional delegation had sent their constituents an inflammatory call to determine whether the liberties of South Carolinians should be "tamely surrendered without a struggle or transmitted
undiminished to posterity," and a state convention had adopted a
resolution with ominous overtones: "The State looks to her sons to
defend her in whatever form she may claim her purpose to *Resist.*"

South Carolina's hotheads had obviously resolved to press the issue
despite all efforts at compromise. They were not deterred by a new
tariff bill passed late in the session of 1831–32, and signed by Jackson,
a modification of the schedules that had so offended southerners in the
Tariff of Abominations.

The Carolinians had been encouraged by Georgia's persistent defiance of the federal government. A few months earlier, after the
United States Supreme Court had denied Georgia's jurisdiction over
adjoining Cherokee lands and forbidden the state to punish Corn
Tassel, an Indian murderer, the state had defied the edict and hanged
the prisoner. Jackson had taken no action. Georgia then ordered
whites living in Cherokee territory to take an oath of allegiance, and
imprisoned two New England missionaries who refused to comply.
The Supreme Court once more declared that Georgia had no jurisdiction and ordered the missionaries freed. The Georgians refused to
obey. Jackson gave them at least tacit support, for he took no action
in this case of challenge to federal authority.

Old Hickory wrote John Coffee in a most un-Jacksonian spirit, "The
decision of the supreme court has fell still born, and they find it cannot
coerce Georgia to yield. . . . If a colision was to take place between them
[the Indians] and the Georgians, the arm of the government is not
sufficiently strong to preserve them from destruction." It was a far
different attitude than that he bore toward the rebellious South
Carolinians.

But the President left no doubt of his prejudice in favor of white
rights over red, even in a conflict involving states' rights. He was heard
to say grimly, after the Supreme Court's admonition to the Georgians,
"John Marshall has made his decision, now let him enforce it." Since
Jackson had yielded to the demands of greedy and land-hungry Georgians without a qualm, many of his anxious constituents concluded
that he would face the crisis in South Carolina with the same benign
indulgence. For the moment, these fears appeared to be justified.

Jackson passed off a warning from McLane that "Nullification continues to rumble like distant thunder in the South." He wrote Van Buren, "Calhoun is prostrate. I heard one of his best former friends say . . . he ought to be hung." But the mood of euphoria was short-lived. The President was stirred to immediate action by news that South Carolinians were preparing for an open conflict. In September, when he heard that the navy commander in Charleston was in sympathy with the South Carolina rebels, Jackson alerted Secretary of Navy Woodbury. A squadron of ships based at Norfolk was ordered to make ready to sail. A few days later, after nullifiers had swept South Carolina's state elections and Jackson was told that army officers of the Charleston garrison were disloyal, he ordered the troops replaced and hurriedly left the Hermitage for Washington.

Old Hickory was hailed joyously at every stage of the journey. A thousand men rode out to meet him near Clay's hometown of Lexington, Kentucky, singing a campaign song popularized in the *Globe*:

> *Here's a health to the heroes who fought*
> *and conquered in Liberty's cause;*
> *Here's health to Old Andy who could not*
> *be bought*
> *To favor aristocrat laws . . .*

They bawled out the chorus:

> *Hurrah for the Hickory tree*
> *From the mountain tops down to the sea*
> *It shall wave o'er the grave of the Tory and knave*
> *And shelter the honest and free.*

In the capital Jackson learned that South Carolina's preparations for open rebellion were far advanced. A convention to proclaim nullification of the tariff had been called, and troops were being raised to defend the state from federal "aggression." U.S. customs officials in Charleston had gone over the rebels. The President was assured that the navy was ready for action; a small federal fleet lay off Charleston. Fresh, loyal troops manned the city's garrison. Major General Winfield Scott was sent southward to take command.

Jackson directed the Secretary of War to send secret orders to commanders of Fort Sumter and other posts "to prevent a surprise in the night or by day. . . . *The Attempt* will be made . . . by the militia, and must be . . . repelled with prompt and exemplary punishment." Soon afterward Joel Poinsett wrote from Charleston requesting more arms for the garrison, grenades, and small rockets, said to be "excellent weapons in a street fight." Jackson hurried the arms southward.

In South Carolina the secessionists prepared for war. Volunteer military companies sprang up, drilled heroically, and offered themselves as volunteers. Thousands of men and women wore blue cockades bearing Palmetto buttons, the symbol of South Carolina rebellion. Medals were struck with the inscription: "John C. Calhoun, First President of the Southern Confederacy." Senator Robert Hayne was elected governor and Calhoun resigned the vice presidency to fill the vacated Senate seat.

The presidential campaign raged throughout the summer and early fall, taking little account of the nullification crisis and hardly pausing for an epidemic of cholera that swept most of the nation and claimed 2,500 lives. Henry Carey, a Philadelphia publisher, wrote of the plague: "If it could only carry off Jackson and few other of our politicians . . . I would submit to all the inconveniences of it for a month or two." Campaign pamphlets flooded the country in record numbers, most of them pro-Bank and many of them scurrilous. The Peggy Eaton scandal was revived. Ike Hill's *New Hampshire Patriot* listed twenty-one reasons why Clay should not be President; Number 20: "Because . . . he spends his days at the gaming table and his nights in a brothel."

Democratic orators cried that the major issue was "Czar Nicholas" and his "hydra of corruption." Cartoons in the Clay press depicted Jackson as "King Andrew I." One of the most popular of these depicted Jackson receiving a crown from Van Buren and a scepter from the devil. Others rendered Van Buren as an infant in Jackson's arms, with the devil feeding him with a spoon. Another showed Jackson, Van Buren, Benton, Blair, and Kendall, all dressed as burglars, attacking the Bank's door with a battering ram. The eminent lawyer Horace Binney warned a Philadelphia audience that the fall's free election might well be the last in American history.

The National Republicans echoed the cry: "Our liberties are in danger . . . if by your votes you concede the powers that are claimed, your *President* has become your monarch."

The opposition condemned Jackson's program as the opening of a class war designed to abolish the American élite. Spokesmen of the National Republican party preached both the blessings of poverty and the unfitness of the lower classes to govern.

William Ellery Channing, the celebrated Unitarian divine, assured poorer Americans that their lives were much easier than those of doctors, lawyers, and merchants. Channing conceded that a few of the indigent died of hunger, "but vastly more . . . die from eating too much than from too little." The masses were also assured by an upper-class spokesman that "many of our daughters are victims of ennui, a misery unknown to the poor, and more intolerable than the weariness of excessive toil!" The Boston *Courier* advised workingmen to keep their places: "A farmer never looks so well as when he has a hand upon the plough. . . . With his hand upon the statutes what can he do? It is as proper for a blacksmith to attempt to repair watches, as a farmer, in general, to legislate." And a popular reform lecturer, R. C. Waterston, declared that low wages were inevitable: "Legislation can do nothing; combinations among the working classes could probably effect no permanent remedy. It must be left to the justice and mercy of the employer."

In strident counterattacks on Jackson and Democratic principles, conservative leaders dinned their socioeconomic mythology into the public consciousness. Daniel Webster now insisted, in contrast to his earlier view, that there were no class distinctions in America, no "clear and well defined line, between capital and labor." The orator Edward Everett declared that any American might rise to wealth, "The wheel of fortune is in constant motion, and the poor in one generation furnish the rich of the next." American workers were assured that they were actually capitalists, and warned that any attack upon the moneyed classes "strikes over the head of the laborer, and is sure to hurt the latter more than the former."

But the major thrust of the attack on Jackson was the economic issue of the moment. The Bank frightened borrowers by calling loans, and the shock spread waves of panic. A Pennsylvania manufacturer laid off hundreds of workmen until after the election. A Cincinnati wholesaler offered $2.50 per 100 pounds for pork in case of Clay's victory, and $1.50 if he lost. A Pittsburgh Republican newspaper reported dolefully that steamboat building along the Ohio was at a standstill. Other stories in the press alarmed the country: thousands of mechanics were jobless and hungry; the price of bricks had fallen from $5 per 1,000 to $3; real estate values had shrunk by 25 percent. It was also said that Jackson's supporters were deserting, that the veto was being denounced at mass meetings in every state, and that the Irish voters were defecting, "thousands of them at one meeting."

The British actress Fanny Kemble, who was on an American tour, was assured by friends that Clay, "the leader of the aristocratic party," was sure to be elected. (Miss Kemble was unaware that half the American electorate was unable to read Biddle's campaign pamphlets.)

The youthful Alexis de Tocqueville, who arrived to inspect the American democracy, said he was positive that "all the enlightened classes are opposed to General Jackson."

In every city, town, and village, Jacksonians danced about their hickory poles in the revived spirit of 1828. Once more they paraded and sang and bawled slogans about bonfires, staged barbecues and ox roasts and fish fries, and turned revivals into rites celebrating Old Hickory. One Jackson torchlight parade in New York was more than a mile long, alive with banners, and candle-lit transparencies of Old Hickory's portrait. The uproar was nationwide.

Old Hickory's hold on the affections of the people was still phenomenal, and was evidently stronger than ever among the less sophisticated, a vast majority. To his admirers Jackson was not merely the hero of New Orleans. He was also the irreproachable leader who had risen from a frontier cabin to the White House through his own efforts, the honest patriot, the first true friend of the American masses, carrying their fight against government corruption and extravagance foisted upon them by grasping politicians.

His enemies, oblivious to the lessons of 1828, attacked Jackson as a ruffianly, immoral, and untutored backwoodsman, whose administration threatened the future of the nation and disgraced its honorable past by delivering the government to the control of the dregs of society.

In fact few of his contemporaries of any persuasion grasped the basic implications of Jackson's administration. He had created a tradition of dynamic, aggressive presidential leadership. As Daniel Webster charged, Jackson had claimed for the presidency not merely the power of approval, "but the primary power, the power of originating laws." A permanent new balance of power had been created by his vetoes alone, because of his refusal to limit himself to matters of constitutionality, and acting for reasons political, economic, social, or merely practical. Thereafter Congress would be forced to consider presidential preferences in advance of passing laws. Though the people may have perceived the significance of Jackson's reign but dimly, they approved overwhelmingly.

Early returns indicated a Jackson landslide of such proportions that the pro-Bank editor of the *Vermont Journal* said he had "no heart to publish election returns," and Rufus Choate wrote mournfully to Edward Everett: "The news from the voting States blows over us like a cold storm."

The mandate of the people was unmistakable: in electoral votes, 219 for Jackson, 49 for Clay, and 7 for William Wirt. In the popular vote, Jackson had defeated Clay by 661,000 to 300,000, and had swept a 40-man Democratic majority into the House.

The Boston *Courier* expressed the bitterness of the defeated: "Who doubts that if all who are unable to read or write had been excluded from the polls, Andrew Jackson could not have been elected? . . . Yet there is one comfort left; God has promised that the days of the wicked shall be short; the wicked is old and feeble, and he may die before he can be elected. It is the duty of every good Christian to pray to our Maker to have pity on us." The *Globe* reported a rumor that "minions of the bank" planned to save Biddle by assassinating Jackson, and that the Bank would gladly pay a reward of $50,000.

Several newspapers foresaw a third term for Old Hickory, and William Wirt said, "He may be President for life if he chooses."

The climax of the campaign found Jackson so preoccupied with South Carolina's defiance that he sometimes brushed aside fresh reports of his triumph to condemn the nullifiers. Frank Blair saw that the strain was telling on Jackson, that the lines in the old man's face were "hard drawn, his tones full of wrath and resentment."

The distracted President seemed to take scant notice of his triumph. "What would I not give to be free . . . and in retirement at the Hermitage," he wrote. Of his decisive plurality he told Blair and Kendall, "The best thing about this, gentlemen, is that it strengthens my hands in this [nullification] trouble."

Sam Dale, Jackson's old dispatch bearer in New Orleans, who had now become a general, visited the White House one evening and found the President, Benton, and several others discussing South Carolina's defiance. "Dale," Jackson said, "if this thing goes on, our country will be like a bag of meal with both ends open. Pick it up in the middle or endwise, and it will run out. I must tie the bag and save the country."

Dale and Johnson reminisced of the war in Louisiana after the others had gone. Jackson, who was pacing the room restlessly as he talked, paused and said abruptly, "Dale, they're trying me here . . . but by the God of heaven, I will uphold the laws."

"I hope things will go right."

"They *shall* go right, sir," Jackson said. He shattered his clay pipe on a table, but then turned calmly to show Dale his pipe collection—scores of pipes of all kinds sent to him from admirers in many parts of the world. "I still smoke my corn cob, Sam," he said. "It's the sweetest and best pipe."

The President emphasized his resolve to subdue the rebels at every opportunity. One day he faced a grim delegation of South Carolina Unionists in his study, visitors who begged him not to use force against their state. Only 9,000 South Carolinians were loyal to the Union, they said, and these would be slaughtered if fighting broke out.

"Gentlemen, there will be no bloodshed," Jackson said. He pointed to the desk. "I have in that drawer the tender of one hundred and fifty thousand volunteers. . . . We shall cross the mountains into . . . South Carolina with a force . . . so overwhelming as to render resistance hopeless. We'll seize the ringleaders, then turn them over to the civil authorities, and come home . . . there will be no bloodshed."

The Union men were little comforted by Old Hickory's belligerent assurances, for they sensed, as Fanny Kemble noted soon afterward, that "the old General is spoiling for a fight," and they feared a bloodbath in the wake of a federal invasion of their state.

In November 1832 South Carolina tested Jackson's will before Congress could convene, by declaring the tariff acts null and void after February 1, 1833. If the federal government sought to collect duties by force, the state would secede. Jackson awaited an official copy of the South Carolina ordinance, and prepared to respond with a proclamation. He wrote Joel Poinsett, "No state or states has a right to secede. . . . Nullification therefore means insurrection and war. . . . I am assured . . . that I will be sustained by Congress. If so, I will meet it at the threshold, and have the leaders arrested and arraigned for treason. . . . In forty days I can have within the limits of So. Carolina fifty thousand men, and in forty days more another fifty thousand."

Congress convened in the tense capital, but Jackson's opening message reflected little of the nation's concern. In a further effort at conciliation, he proposed more tariff reductions. He made no mention of his plans to force South Carolina to her knees.

The message depressed strong Union men. John Quincy Adams feared that it would dissolve the Union. Jackson, he said, had made "a complete surrender to the nullifiers." Once more he had misjudged the grim old man in the White House, who was already at work on his proclamation. Jackson left the writing of the document to Livingston, but insisted that it bear an unmistakable message: he would preserve the Union at all costs. Jackson had a habit of dashing off stray ideas for his messages to Congress on scraps of paper, margins of newspapers, or sometimes a page or so of foolscap, which were stored in his big white hat until Jack Donelson transcribed and revised them. It was probably from such materials that his Nullification Proclamation evolved.

He sent Livingston a partial draft with a plea, "I submit the above as the conclusion of the Proclamation for your amendment and revision. Let it receive your best flight of eloquence to strike to the heart, and speak to the feelings of my deluded countrymen of South Carolina." Livingston was inspired to a supreme effort.

Though its stern tone was softened by the entreaties to the people of South Carolina, the meaning of the proclamation was clear, and the decisive tone was obviously Jackson's:

> . . . The Constitution of the United States, then, forms a government, not a league . . . each State, having expressly parted with so many powers as to constitute, jointly with the other States, a single nation, can not, from that period, possess any right to secede. . . . To say that any State may at pleasure secede from the Union is to say that the United States are not a nation.
>
> . . . Fellow citizens of my native State . . . the laws of the United States must be executed. I have no discretionary power on the subject. . . . Disunion by armed force is treason. Are you really ready to incur its guilt? If you are . . . on your unhappy State will inevitably fall all the evils of the conflict you will force upon the Government of your country. . . .

The proclamation electrified the nation, north and south. John Quincy Adams, his fears swept away, hailed it as a "blister plaster." The New Yorker Philip Hone felt that the proclamation would "take its place in the archives of our country, and dwell in the memory of our citizens alongside the Farewell Address." Among Union men only Henry Clay withheld approval, for fear of alienating states' rights voters.

South Carolinians roared their defiance, and for a few weeks it seemed that the mutinous spirit might spread. Virginians were stirred by old John Randolph, who toured counties of his district to assail Jackson's proclamation. In the isolated village of Charlotte Courthouse, Virginia, the frail aristocrat spoke from a chair, unable to rise; he was only lately recovered from a bout of insanity, alcoholism, and heavy dosages of opium. Yet his stirring voice filled the crowded hall from 11:00 A.M. until nightfall as he harangued, in his brilliant, quixotic, rambling fashion. He wore three dress coats as he began but shrugged out of two of them as he warmed to his topic, a denunciation of Jackson and all his works. He halted frequently to sip from a glass of whiskey, which an attentive black boy replenished from time to time.

His audience saw that Randolph was in dead earnest today, and that his wit was as quick as ever; even the dark eyes rolling in the melancholy face were all "nimbleness and fire." The old man presented a sheaf of resolutions against nullification, most of which he had written himself. He spoke of Jackson's betrayal of the party that had carried him to the White House, and condemned the Kitchen Cabinet of subservient flatterers who had warped Jackson's judgment. His voice rose near the end:

Jackson did not write the Proclamation. Not that he does not possess the requisite intellectual ability, but that he has not the literary culture. I know who did write it, and I will prove to you I am right. . . . The man who wrote that Proclamation wields a pen such as no man in the United States but himself can wield; Edward Livingston of Louisiana, the present Secretary of State . . . wrote the Proclamation. Fellow-citizens, he is a man of splendid abilities but utterly corrupt. He shines and stinks like rotten mackerel by moonlight.

Governor Hayne responded to Jackson's proclamation with a flourish, declaring that he would defend South Carolina's sovreignty or die "beneath the ruins." He entertained hundreds of offers of volunteers, and local militia companies clamored for arms and ammunition. Hayne aided the arming and training of 2,500 cavalrymen, "mounted Minute men" who could be swiftly concentrated to meet a threat. By night Joel Poinsett's handful of loyal Union volunteers drilled with the new weapons sent by Jackson.

John C. Calhoun left home amid this excitement to take his seat in the Senate. He returned to Washington a subdued man. He smiled at the fears of his friends in Columbia that Jackson planned to arrest him. "It will not be done. My opponents are too politic to attempt it." Privately he was apprehensive; he expected to be arrested. As he passed through Virginia, Calhoun had a message from his old enemy John Randolph, who said he would help the nullifiers to resist "the usurpations of the Federal Government."

In the capital Calhoun found his mail filled with threats illustrated with drawings of skulls and coffins. But he took his oath in the Senate on January 4, 1833, pale and apparently calm, and though he was shunned by men who had once been his friends, the ceremony passed without incident.

Representative Robert Letcher of Tennessee burst into Calhoun's rooms one night, fresh from the White House, to say that Jackson had threatened that if South Carolina took one more step toward division, "he would try Calhoun for treason, and if convicted, hang him high as Haman." One witness reported: "There sat Calhoun, drinking in eagerly every word . . . pale as death and . . . trembling like an aspen leaf."

Jackson confided his plans to Van Buren—he would wait until he was certain that South Carolina was raising troops, and then ask Congress for power to call out volunteers to crush the rebellion. He was already preparing to arm and supply an army of invasion, and was being overwhelmed by offers from volunteers. Van Buren urged Jackson to move slowly. "You will say I am on my old track—caution—caution—caution: but . . . I have always thought that considering our respective temperaments there was no way perhaps in which I could better render you service."

Van Buren argued that the raising of troops in South Carolina was not treasonable, and that the southerners would not secede—but if they did, the method of their return to the Union should be left to Congress. Jackson fully realized that there was no precedent for presidential initiative in such a case, but he flatly rejected the advice of the Red Fox, protesting that it "would destroy all confidence in our government both at home and abroad." He repeated his determination to invade South Carolina if she persisted in her course.

But late in December, though the deadline set by the nullifiers was hardly a month away, Jackson made good the promise in his proclamation and had a compromise tariff bill introduced in the House, once more substantially reducing rates. He relented no further. On January 16, when only two weeks remained before the threatened confrontation, the President tired of delay and asked Congress for authority to collect the customs by force of arms.

In response John Calhoun harangued the Senate with such passion that he was soon near collapse. For merely daring to assert their constitutional rights, he said, South Carolinians were "threatened to have our throats cut, and those of our wives and children." He paused and looked about with a distracted air. "No, I go too far. I did not intend to use language so stormy." But in the end he surpassed it: "I proclaim it, that should this bill pass . . . It will be resisted at every hazard—even that of death." A newspaper man noted, "His whole frame was agitated. . . . It is seldom that a man of Mr. Calhoun's intellectual power thus permits himself to be unmanned in public. . . ."

Calhoun's colleague, Representative George McDuffie, performed more spectacularly in the House, shrieking, stamping, thumping his desk.

> Sir, South Carolina is oppressed. A tyrant majority sucks her life blood from her. Yes, sir, a tyrant majority unappeased, unappeasable, has persecuted us . . . we appeal to them, but we appeal in vain. . . . They heap coals of fire on our heads—they give us burden on burden; they tax us more and more . . . the tyrant majority has no ears, no eyes, no form, deaf, sightless, inexorable. Despairing, we resort to the rights which God and nature has given us. . . .

Jackson was not deterred.

In case Congress failed to act in time, he was prepared to assume full responsibility. He told Poinsett: "I can if need be, which god forbid, march two hundred thousand men in forty days to quell any and every insurrection that might arise." Once more he sent the message that the Union would be preserved.

Old Hickory's final proclamation of the existence of a rebellion was averted at the last moment by the arrival of a weary courier from South Carolina. Awed by the gathering of forces in Charleston Harbor and about their borders, the nullifiers had succumbed to Jackson's will. The ordinance of nullification had been suspended, pending a satisfactory outcome of the congressional debate on the tariff.

Jackson was not content. He insisted upon the passage of the bill authorizing his use of the army and navy to put down rebellion, known as the "Force Bill."

On February 16, 1833, Calhoun attacked once more, but he was not the Calhoun of old. Now bitter, melancholy, and lonely, the South Carolinian wore an "intense, introverted" look, and his former brilliance in debate had become "meteoric and eccentric." Harriet Martineau spoke of him as "the cast-iron man, who looks as if he had never been born, and could never be extinguished." "I have no purpose to serve," Calhoun cried, "I have no desire to be here." He had sacrificed everything, he said, for the "brave gallant little State of South Carolina." Then, in a rising doomsday voice, glaring about the hall with burning eyes, he called: "Sir, I would not turn upon my heel to be entrusted with the management of the Government." Miss Martineau observed that Calhoun failed to realize how he had betrayed himself in those few words. "His mind has lost all power of communicating with any other. I know no man who lives in such intellectual solitude."

Yet Calhoun stirred himself to meet the challenge of the Force Bill. He spoke sorrowfully of "the decay of that brotherly feeling which once existed between these States . . . to which we are indebted for our beautiful federal system." Today the South Carolinian was hoarse and his delivery abrupt and harsh. He began by pushing several chairs to the ends of a long desk before the rail, enclosing himself within a cage, which he then paced endlessly. He declared that he was exhausted and uncertain whether he could muster the strength to complete his remarks. To one observer he seemed "the arch traitor . . . like Satan in Paradise"; to another he was an "austere patriot," battling alone for the nation's liberty.

The Force Bill, Calhoun said, not merely declared war on South Carolina. "No, It decrees a massacre of her citizens." It enabled the President to subject every man in the United States "to martial law . . . and under the penalty of court martial to compel him to imbrue his hand in his brother's blood.

"It has been said to be a measure of peace! Yes, such peace as the wolf gives to the lamb. . . . Should this bill pass . . . it will be resisted at every hazard . . . even that of death . . . thousands of her brave sons . . . are prepared to lay down their lives in defence of the State. . . ."

The Force Bill, he cried, was "a verbal repeal of the Constitution." It was to be passed only because Jackson had decreed that the laws must be enforced. "Does any man in his senses believe . . . this beautiful structure can be preserved by force? . . . Force may indeed hold the parts together, but such union would be the bond between master and slave. . . . It is madness to believe that the Union can be preserved by force."

As his voice rose, an onlooker screamed in the crowded gallery, "Mr. President, I'm being squeezed to death!" Calhoun stood somberly amid the laughter that filled the chamber and after a few more words lamely acquiesced to Webster's motion to adjourn. He spoke briefly the next day, and Webster followed immediately, ignoring the grim South Carolinian's speech and attacking the resolutions Calhoun had introduced in January.

In reply Calhoun tore at Webster's logic by quoting his own phrases in his debate with Hayne. How could the New Englander maintain that the states could not alter the Constitution, when three-fourths of them were granted the right to abolish it? Power, Calhoun cried, had not been delegated to the people—the people, through the states, had delegated power to the federal government. Old John Randolph, listening delightedly, found his view of Webster blocked by a hat on a table. "Take away that hat," he said. "I want to see Webster die, muscle by muscle." But the southerner's abstractions were lost on his audience. The galleries cheered as Webster shouted that nullification meant the end of the Union and American freedom.

Jackson was exultant. "Many people believe Calhoun to be demented . . . Webster handled him like a child."

When the Force Bill came to a vote on February 24, 1833, Henry Clay complained of the "bad air" and left the chamber. Calhoun and the rest of the southern senators walked out, except for John Tyler, who remained in his seat to cast the lone nay vote.

Jackson sent orders to the House to give final approval to the bill before his compromise Tariff Bill could be passed. But he was outmaneuvered by Clay, who hurried to passage a tariff measure of his own, retaining protection for manufacturers but reducing tariff rates by 20 percent over a period of ten years. Calhoun, whose enmity for Van Buren and Jackson outweighed his distaste for Henry Clay's policies, met secretly with Clay at night and agreed to support his modified bill, though he opposed some of its sections. The Jackson press ridiculed his bargain. "A single night," Frank Blair's *Globe* said, "was sufficient to change Mr. Calhoun's constitutional scruples."

The South Carolinians rescinded their ordinance of nullification, after Calhoun had paid a hurried trip home to dissuade the hotheads; and though they made an anticlimactic gesture of defiance by nullifying the Force Bill, the dangerous national crisis had been averted. Only the intervention of Henry Clay had prevented a complete victory for the President. The affair cost Jackson the support of the last of the states' rights men within the party, but the nation acclaimed him. His popularity seemed to be greater than ever. There was praise even from Webster and Marshall. When it was over, Jackson said almost wistfully, "I thought I would have to hang some of them & would have done it."

Though Jackson expected no further challenge from nullifiers and secessionists in his administration, he feared for the future: "the coalition between Clay and Calhoun, combined . . . with a few nullifiers in Virginia . . . portends no good, but much evil." Not even John Calhoun perceived more clearly the next act in the fateful drama: "The nullifiers in the south intend to blow up a storm on the slave question. . . . This ought to be met, for be assured these men would do any act to destroy this union and form a southern confederacy bounded, north, by the Potomac River."

26

"I will not bow down to the golden calf"

A heavy snow lay on the ground for Jackson's second Inaugural Day and the capital shivered in a temperature of 11 degrees. Old Hickory took his oath in the House after Martin Van Buren had been installed as Vice President in the Senate chamber. Since no parade or reception was scheduled, the sickly President went home to bed. Two inaugural balls were staged during the evening without the stimulus of his presence.

Jackson's health was again in decline. He clung to his simple diet during the trying winter in a futile effort to alleviate his chronic indigestion; his old wounds from the Dickinson duel troubled him. A painful attack of neuralgia was treated by Dr. Robert Dunglison, who had been at the bedside of the dying Jefferson seven years earlier. Dunglison persuaded Jackson to forego his usual remedy of bleeding, since the loss of a quart of blood might weaken him, and recommended instead a counterirritant, composed of dried beetles, "a warm plaster, *animated* by cantharides." The treatment was a success, but Dunglison felt that Jackson's recovery owed more to his "energy of character" than to the remedy.

The presidential recovery was aided by the neighborly generosity of Frank Blair and his wife, who kept cows on their nearby lot. When he learned that Jackson's doctor had prescribed milk, the diminutive editor appeared on the White House porch at seven o'clock the next morning with a pail of fresh milk, and continued the deliveries daily.

Two of Jackson's oldest friends, Overton and Coffee, died during the spring of 1833. Of Overton's death the President said, "It is useless to mourn. He is gone the way of all the earth and I will soon follow him. *Peace to his manes,* let us weep for the living and not for the dead." When he learned of Coffee's death, the President was unnerved, his "philosophy fled," and he was forced to wait several days before acknowledging the news. At the request of Coffee's children he wrote an epitaph for his old comrade in arms: " . . . A disinterested and sagacious patriot, an unpretending, Just and honest man." Jackson was frequently depressed during these days: "I want relaxation from business, and rest. But where can I get rest? I fear not on this earth."

A foreign visitor who dined in the White House about this time noted that the frail, stooped President appeared to be much older than his years. "His countenance bears commonly an expression of melancholy gravity: though when roused, the fire of passion flashes from his eyes, and his whole person then looks formidable enough. His mode of speech is slow and quiet; and his phraseology sufficiently betokens that his time has not been passed among books. . . ."

Though Jackson seemed to take scant notice, Washington and the White House were being transformed. Pennsylvania Avenue and the square before the White House were macadamized at a cost of $115,000. The macadamized strip was only 45 feet wide, less than half the width of the Avenue, but was to be widened the following year in the continuing struggle to make the streets passable in all weathers. Water was piped into the Capitol, the White House, and departmental buildings at last—a major project powered by some 1,000 newly arrived Irish immigrants. No longer would congressmen and their aides be forced to use pumps in the Capitol yard.

The water was piped into the White House from springs in the square bounded by 13th, 14th, I, and K Streets, property bought by the government after prolonged debate, at a cost of 4 cents per square foot. The luxurious new plumbing system supplied the kitchen and pantry, and cold showers and water closets elsewhere in the mansion. The old frame stable at the end of the East Wing was removed and a new ten-horse stable was built 100 yards to the east.

Life in the White House was not idyllic, despite the new amenities. When Jackson prepared to return to Washington after a vacation, he wrote Major Lewis, who was again living in the White House: "Have the House in readiness to receive us; and say to the chamber maid to have all our beds clear of bed buggs."

Less than a month after the inaugural the Treasury Building was destroyed by fire. A single watchman, who made a round of the building at ten o'clock, had gone to sleep for the night. No firemen were on duty, but an enterprising passer-by saw the flames, got the engine house key from a nearby hotel, and hitched horses to an engine—all in vain. The water supply was so limited that the old building burned to the ground. Most of the Treasury papers, saved by civilian volunteers, were stored in nearby houses. One Richard H. White was charged with burning the building to destroy fraudulent pension records, but though he was subjected to four successive trials, White was acquitted when the statute of limitations expired.

The Treasury was to operate for six years from rented houses across the street, and from a number of other houses and buildings scattered throughout the city. When he wearied of the vacillation and bickering of officials over the site for a new building, Jackson, it was said, led the way down the Avenue, thrust his cane firmly into the earth, and commanded that it be built on the spot. By an enduring tradition, at any rate, it was he who decreed the new location which forever obstructed the vista from the White House to the Capitol and violated the integrity of Charles L'Enfant's classic city plan.

The weary Jackson expressed the hope that he and the country might "enjoy at least some repose" from the tumults of his administration; but within less than a month of his inaugural he was impelled once more to an attack on the Bank. Calhoun and Clay were conspiring to revive Biddle's charter, and Jackson had no doubt that they were inspired by "the corrupting influence of the Bank of the U.S."

So long as the Bank existed, Jackson reasoned, it would endanger the country. He determined to withdraw the government deposits on the ground that they were unsafe. A few months earlier, when the Treasury had notified the Bank to redeem $6 million worth of 3 percent government bonds, Biddle delayed on the pretext that the transaction would shock the economy; in fact, since he lacked the funds to redeem the issue, Biddle secretly negotiated with British bankers to buy up the bonds and withhold them from government hands, a subterfuge that failed when exposed by a newspaper.

Jackson interpreted the move as an indication that the Bank must be destroyed as quickly as possible. He told Blair, "He shan't have the public money! I'll remove the deposits! Blair, talk with our friends about this, and let me know what they think of it."

The President's mood was not improved when he learned that Biddle had begun the systematic bribery of influential men in Washington. Duff Green, for one, had been permitted to overdraw his account by $10,000. Jackson may also have known of Biddle's recent loans to

Representatives Watmough and Gilmore of Pennsylvania, Verplanck of New York, and Clayton of Georgia—loans urged upon him by a congressman "as the only means of preventing the terrible mischiefs which such men have in their power to perpetrate."

Jackson was fully convinced that the Bank bought and sold congressmen at will: "When I came into the administration . . . I had a majority of seventy-five, since then . . . it has been bought over, by loans, discounts etc. . . . until at the close of last session, it was said, there was two-thirds for re-chartering it. It is believed that in the last two years, that it has loaned to members of congress and subsidized presses, at least half a million of dollars, the greater part of which will be lost to the Bank and the stockholders. . . ."

When Jackson asked members of the cabinet for advice, it was again Roger Taney who strengthened the presidential resolve with a shrewd appeal to Jackson's fighting instincts, by predicting that Biddle would make "a fierce and desperate struggle." Taney was opposed by Van Buren, who advised against the withdrawals—undoubtedly with the presidential campaign of 1836 in mind—and by Louis McLane, who agreed that Biddle's Bank should not be rechartered, but argued that it should be replaced by a new national bank subject to federal control. McLane also warned Jackson that the deposits should not be removed until the new bank was ready to receive them; to transfer federal funds to unstable state banks was to invite disaster.

It was not an unreasonable argument, as Jackson noted (he also tacitly acknowledged the soundness of Biddle's Bank by keeping all of his money in its Washington and Nashville branches). But though he gave the divided cabinet the impression that he sought advice, he was by now so irrevocably committed to Biddle's destruction that no arguments could have swayed him. As he wrote a friend, "I long for retirement & repose on the Hermitage. But until I can strangle this hydra of corruption, the Bank, I will not shrink from my duty . . . I think a system can be arranged with the state banks."

The decision on the deposits was postponed for several weeks, by further changes in the cabinet and by an extended presidential tour of New England. The cabinet shift was set off by Edward Livingston, who was sent to Paris as minister to France at his request—and scandalized his friends by borrowing $18,000 from Biddle's Bank before he left. McLane succeeded him as Secretary of State, and as the new Secretary of the Treasury Jackson chose William J. Duane, the Philadelphia lawyer. Duane had already declined Jackson's offer to become a district attorney and one of the government directors of the Bank of the

United States, and came to the cabinet only under Jackson's insistence. The little-known Duane was not the most capable man available. Harry Lee described him as "that other Darling . . . fished up from the bottom of the Philadelphia Bar, to put in the seat which was once filled by Alexander Hamilton."

Duane's initiation into the world of Jacksonian statesmanship began on his first day in office, when he was told of the President's plans to remove the deposits. Duane's opinion was not solicited. Instead he was also told, without preliminaries, that Old Hickory had determined "to take upon himself the responsibility of directing the Secretary of the Treasury to remove the public deposits."

"I was mortified," Duane said, "at the low estimate which had been formed of the independence of my character." He was not reassured by an interview with Jackson, in which he resisted the order for removal of the deposits. The President said that though he admired candor in his subordinates, he was convinced that "unless the bank was broken down, it would break us down." Duane's suggestion that the matter be left to Congress or the courts was dismissed by the President—reliance on either, he said, would be "idle."

Jackson explained that he was leaving Washington for several weeks, and would expect to have Duane's opinion on the Bank problem when he returned.

The tour opened in Alexandria, where Jackson was to lay the cornerstone for a monument to Mary Washington.

The presidential party left the capital by steamer. At Alexandria a handsome young man boarded the ship and approached Jackson, whose chair was wedged between a berth and a table. "Excuse my not rising, sir," the President said.

The visitor began to strip off a glove. Jackson stuck out a welcoming hand, "Never mind your glove, sir." The young man pawed savagely at Jackson's face as if to pull his nose.

"What, sir! What, sir!" Jackson kicked away the table, seized his cane, and lunged after his assailant as McLane, Livingston, and Washington Irving grappled with the young man, who eluded them and dashed through the door. Someone slammed the door in Jackson's path, leaving him pounding furiously.

The assailant escaped with several confederates who had posed as passengers, but he was recognized as Robert B. Randolph, a former navy lieutenant and purser of the frigate *Constitution,* who had been cashiered for embezzlement in the case involving Lieutenant Timberlake. A bystander offered to pursue and kill Randolph. "No," Jackson said, "I want no man to stand between me and my assailants. If I'd been on my feet when he attacked me, I'd have killed him in his tracks." Thereafter Jackson refused to avenge himself upon Randolph, declined to testify against him when he was brought to trial, and asked that any sentence be revoked. "I have to this age complied with my mother's advice to indict no man for assault or sue him for slander," he said.

On the way to Baltimore the presidential party was met in the countryside by a delegation aboard cars of the Baltimore and Ohio Railroad, and Jackson was sped twelve miles into the city in the wake of a wood-burning locomotive, the first President to ride on a train. Jackson left Baltimore with a severe headache after three days of noisy celebrations in his honor.

At the next stop, in Philadelphia, Jackson rode a prancing white horse along the streets before a huge welcoming crowd and remained in the blazing sunshine for five hours, acknowledging applause. He was painfully sunburned. A newspaper reported that many Philadelphians were shocked by Jackson's appearance: "How old, how very old he looks." The President was feeling his age. He wrote his son from the city, "I sincerely wish my trip was over. Except to my Hermitage or to the watering places I think it is the last journey I shall undertake."

The country's most celebrated doctor, Philip Syng Physick, examined Jackson during his stay in the city and was captivated by his patient, who exhibited such "gentleness . . . peculiar and indescribable charm." But the famous healer did not escape a presidential lecture: "Now, Doctor, I can do any thing you think proper, except give up coffee and tobacco."

New York greeted Jackson with the most tumultuous welcome in its history. He estimated that he bowed and waved to 200,000 people. One onlooker was the young Walt Whitman, who never forgot the sight of the upright and dignified old man with his grim, weathered face, his shock of snow-white hair and hawklike eyes. Philip Hone, a newly rich social leader of the city, was forced to reluctant admiration. Jackson, he said, was "certainly the most popular man we have ever known. Washington was not so much. . . . He has a kind expression for each—the same to all no doubt, but each thinks it intended for himself. His manners are certainly good, and he makes the most of them. . . . Adams is the wisest man, the best scholar, the most accomplished statesman; but Jackson has the most tact. So huzza for Jackson."

The sensation of the day was the collapse of the bridge between Castle Garden and the Battery, which flung Cass and Woodbury, Jack Donelson, and a half dozen others into the water.

Jackson refused an open carriage in which he was to lead the procession up Broadway to Union Square. "I want to ride horseback," he said, "and I want a horse that it takes a man to handle." The stallion that was brought to him was too much for Jackson, who fought the animal constantly to keep him off the sidewalks, and as he complained, "out of the houses." Since Jackson had no spurs and his bit was ineffectual, he suffered a painful strain of his chest and shoulder muscles during the long ride.

When he escaped the public eye that night, in his rooms at the American House, Jackson turned once more to the banking problem. He conferred with Van Buren, who had been warned by Amos Kendall that Jackson planned to press the issue of withdrawal, but to make the change gradually, in the normal course of business. To minimize the shock, Jackson planned to begin by making only new deposits in the state banks. Kendall hoped that all the money could be withdrawn before Congress convened in December, so that Biddle would be driven to the wall. Van Buren was not enthusiastic, and McLane, who abandoned the party in New York, left a memorandum with Jackson, urging him to delay action on the deposits until Congress met. Undeterred, Jackson began a letter to Duane, outlining his plan for new deposits and withdrawals, and continued work on these instructions as he crossed Connecticut and Rhode Island and neared Massachusetts. At the border he was greeted by Josiah Quincy, Jr., who was to be his guide through the state.

Jackson visited a huge textile mill in Lowell, whose manager, Kirk Boott, had campaigned for Clay in 1822: "Elect General Jackson and the grass will grow in your streets, owls will build their nests in the mills, and foxes burrow in your highways." But now, when they learned that the President was coming, company directors had spared no expense to prepare a welcome. "We will feed him on gold dust, if he'll eat it," said the wealthy Boston entrepreneur Amos Lawrence.

A crowd of thousands saw Jackson ride in an open barouche with Van Buren and two of Lowell's leading stockholders. The carriage rolled between two hickory trees laboriously transplanted for the occasion and beneath banners commemorating his victory at New Orleans and his defiance of nullification. After a few speeches the guest of honor was led to a hotel balcony to witness a parade which featured 2,500 girls marching in Lowell-made white muslin dresses with blue sashes, carrying blue or green parasols. These girls were factory operatives, representative of a new labor force which was already world renowned. "Very pretty women, by the Eternal!" the general said, bowing from his balcony. Afterward he toured one of the mills where some of the prettiest of the girls, still in their festive costumes, were tending the machines, a picture of pleasant, progressive labor—the very antithesis of the traditional image of downtrodden workers. Jackson left Lowell with "a more positive attitude toward manufacturing."

In Boston, during a military review on the Common, cannon fire frightened the saddle horses of the party as Jackson reviewed the troops, but the President controlled his mount with ease and galloped along the lines of troops in advance of his escort. Van Buren had disappeared.

"Where's the Vice President?" Jackson asked.

Young Quincy smiled. "About as nearly on the fence as a gentleman of his positive political convictions can get."

Jackson saw that Van Buren's horse had backed against a fence, and could not be moved. The general laughed. "And you've matched him with a horse even more non-committal than his rider."

Jackson was ill for two days with a severe cold and a slight hemorrhage of the lungs, and remained in his Boston hotel room, prompting John Quincy Adams to remark that the illness was "four-fifths trickery," and a mere play for sympathy.

While he lay in bed, Jackson completed his long message to Duane on the bank deposits and had it copied by Jack Donelson. The President asked Duane to begin depositing government funds in state banks on September 15, and suggested that he send Amos Kendall to inspect banks in Boston, New York, Philadelphia, and Baltimore, where five "primary banks" should be chosen. Smaller banks would be selected later to create a national network, which would supplant the Bank of the United States as a depository.

The highlight of the tour was the hurriedly arranged award of an honorary degree of Doctor of Laws by Harvard. Adams, who was against this, asked Harvard's President Josiah Quincy if the award could be avoided, and was told: "Why no, as the people have twice decided that this man knows law enough to be their ruler, it is not for Harvard College to maintain that they are mistaken." Adams refused to attend the ceremony, declaring that his alma mater had disgraced herself in honoring "a barbarian who could not write a sentence of grammar and hardly could spell his own name."*

---

*Though the comment of Adams was obviously unfair, since Jackson expressed himself with remarkable force, the criticism was based upon plentiful evidence. The presidential spelling offended Adams—"parsomony," "confidents," "vissit," "betalions," "youthood." Parton suspected that *The Vicar of Wakefield* was the only book Jackson ever read, and a member of Jackson's family reported that "the General did not believe the world was round."

Francis Bowen, president of the class of 1833, welcomed Jackson with a scholarly address in Latin, to the applause of students. Woodbury translated: "Harvard welcomes Jackson the President. She embraces Jackson the Patriot."

Old Hickory made a brief response, a few words of which were whimsically reported by the popular newspaper humorist Seba Smith, who wrote under the name of Major Jack Downing: "I shall have to speak in English, being unable to return your compliment in what appears to be the language of Harvard. All the Latin I know is 'E Pluribus Unum.' " Applause rocked the hall. The students filed by afterward, gravely shaking the President's hand and calling him "Dr. Jackson."

By a more realistic account Jackson "submitted graciously" to the address, bowing occasionally, sometimes at inappropriate moments that drew snickers from the audience, and finally accepted his parchment "in eloquent silence." If the President made any comments they were, as an aide said, "a few modest words" couched in the vernacular, and in any event inaudible to most of the applauding crowd.

Jackson moved on to a reception at President Quincy's home and then to a day of ceremonies that left him exhausted. He climbed the incomplete monument at Bunker Hill and endured an address by Edward Everett, and in Cambridge visited the spot where Washington had taken command of his army almost sixty years earlier. Here Jackson made an impromptu plea for perpetual defense of American liberty of such eloquence that John Quincy Adams, who was watching unseen from a distance, was moved to tears.

Five dinners and receptions in Boston suburbs were scheduled for the day and young Quincy pled with the worn President to return to his hotel. Jackson refused. "These people have made their arrangements to welcome me, and so long as I am not on my back I will gratify them." He was forced to give up soon afterward, taking a nap at Lynn while his entourage endured the fourth dinner of the day, and collapsing in Salem just before the fifth banquet. Jackson was shaken by a severe hemorrhage during the night; yet he appeared at breakfast the next morning, wan and weak but with "an immaterial something" flashing in his eye, a signal, young Quincy said, "that the faltering body was again held in subjection."

A final gesture of goodwill was made by Commodore Jesse D. Elliott, the new commandant of the Boston Navy Yard, who proposed that a figurehead of Jackson be placed on the recently restored U.S.S. *Constitution.* Elliott, who had served as senior officer of the U.S. fleet off Charleston during the nullification crisis, was a fervent Jackson admirer who carried a lock of the old man's hair in his wallet. The commodore's proposal was greeted with enthusiasm, and a Boston woodcarver began work on a full-length figure of the President, complete in his huge white hat, a flowing cloak, and pantaloons.

From Boston Jackson moved northward, bound for Portland, Maine, but could go no farther than Concord, New Hampshire. Ike Hill had assembled aged veterans of the Revolution in the town, and Jackson met with them. He had several of the old men feel the long saber scar on his skull. "That's my certificate of service," he said. "Proof that I refused to black a British officer's boots when I was a prisoner of war." A few hours later he collapsed completely and was soon taken aboard a steamer for Washington, where, for two days and nights, it was feared that he might die.

But within days the President had returned to his attack on Biddle's Bank, badgering Duane to begin the process of withdrawing the deposits. Duane resisted, with the support of McLane and Cass, though he promised Jackson that when the time came, he would obey orders or resign. Kendall went off belatedly on his tour of inspection of state banks, and the weary President left for a rest at Rip Raps—a tiny island at the mouth of the Chesapeake where the army was building a fort.

Young Nicholas Trist, who was the husband of one of Thomas Jefferson's granddaughters, and was now acting as Jackson's private secretary, saw the old man in a revealing moment during the brief vacation. One night Trist knocked at Jackson's bedroom door to ask instructions about some correspondence, and found him undressed, seated at a table, reading Rachel's worn prayer book with her miniature propped before him. It was the picture he usually carried next to his heart, and his last act each night, Trist said, was to read from the prayer book "with that picture under his eyes."

Trist's intimate relationship with Old Hickory over several months provided a unique estimate of the old man's character: "There was more of the woman in his nature than in that of any man I ever knew —more of a woman's tenderness toward children, and sympathy with them . . . more also of woman's patience and uncomplaining, unnoticing submissiveness to trivial causes of irritation . . . a womanly modesty and delicacy, as respects the relations of the sexes."

Jackson spent almost a month at the Rip Raps, ostensibly to enjoy bathing and sunning himself, but he could not remain idle. He and Blair worked on a memorandum to the cabinet, detailing the plan for bank withdrawals. Jackson managed to occupy himself even during moments of leisure.

Robert E. Lee, a young engineer officer in charge of building Fort Calhoun on the Rip Raps, complained that Jackson imposed his own ideas upon the builders. Lee protested to his superior officer, "The President has played the Devil with the plan of Fort Calhoun."

Jackson felt an interest in Lee, as the son of Lighthorse Harry Lee, a revolutionary hero. He paid a call on Mrs. Lee at Fort Monroe and held her first child, G. W. Custis Lee, then less than a year old. The baby gazed into the pale, seamed face, grasped Jackson's nose, and stuck a finger in one eye. The old man handed him Rachel's picture to play with, gave him a half-dollar, and told Mary Lee, "He's a fine boy. You must take off his shoes and let him run barefoot."

Jackson returned to Washington in September for a showdown with the stubborn Duane, who resisted to the last. The Secretary refused to obey the President's orders, but also refused to honor his promise to resign, arguing that his control of the bank deposits was made clear by the law: "The deposits of the money of the United States . . . shall be made in said bank or branches thereof, unless The Secretary of Treasury shall at any time otherwise order and direct. . . ." In face of this Jackson continued efforts to win Duane over; but after many exchanges a heated final conference brought the matter to a climax. "A secretary, sir," Jackson said, "is merely an executive agent, a subordinate."

He solved the problem by banishing Duane, and wrote Van Buren, "In his appointment I surely caught a tarter in disguise, but I have got rid of him."

The embittered Duane felt that Jackson had been corrupted in Washington:

I consider the President intoxicated with power and flattery. . . . When he came into office, the President supposed that he would find much purity . . . among his supporters. . . . Instead of that, he found the leaders at the head of factions, each desiring to drive the coach of state. He found his tables groaning under the weight of petitions for office. . . . He heard adulation from every body; plain truth from nobody. He came into office to be the friend of a whole people, but he became the mere purveyor for the hungry expectants of discordant factions. . . . He is changed, or else we knew him not.

McLane and Cass also threatened to resign, to the dismay of Jackson's friends, who feared another cabinet explosion. Jackson at first said that they might go if they wished, and began a search for more tractable men who were willing to conduct their departments with an eye to what "the Executive believes to be the good of the country." Meanwhile, he said, "I hope for the best; but let what will come, the sun will continue to rise in the East and set in the West, and I trust in a kind Providence to guide and direct me. . . ." But when McLane and Cass did submit their resignations, Jackson declined to accept them, and the cabinet assumed an appearance of unity during the last great struggle with the Bank.

Roger Taney became Secretary of the Treasury and Biddle was notified that no government deposits would be made in the Bank after the end of September. Biddle had prepared for the emergency. The Bank was in a highly liquid condition and had a number of state banks in its debt. "When we begin," Biddle said, "we shall crush the Kitchen Cabinet at once." Discounts were reduced, interest rates rose, bills of exchange were limited to sixty days, private loans and debts of state banks were called in. Biddle had resolved to force Jackson's hand by making the public suffer and arousing a storm of protest. The process began in Boston but soon concentrated in the south and west, as Biddle moved to draw capital to the east.

"Nothing but the evidence of suffering abroad will produce any effect in Congress," Biddle said. "My own course is decided—all the other Banks and all the merchants may break, but the Bank of the United States shall not break."

Money all but disappeared from circulation, businesses failed, thousands of men were unemployed. Congress was overwhelmed with petitions and protests, and Jackson's supporters were pressed to prevail upon him to restore the deposits.

Alarmed Congressmen and frightened businessmen everywhere clamored for relief in vain. Jackson was unyielding. "I care nothing about clamors," he said, "I do precisely what I think just and right." He seemed to relish this controversy above all others. Delegations of businessmen who flocked to the White House with complaints were cowed by the old general's firmness. "The failures that are now taking place," he told a group from Maryland, "are amongst the stock-jobbers, brokers, and gamblers, and would to God, they were all swept from the land!" To others he said, "Go to the monster. Go to Nicholas Biddle. I will not bow down to the golden calf."

He startled a delegation from Philadelphia: "Andrew Jackson will never restore the deposits! Andrew Jackson will never recharter that monster of corruption! Sooner than live in a country where such a power prevails, I would seek asylum in the wilds of Arabia."

To a party of New Yorkers Jackson cried, "Go to Nicholas Biddle.

We have no money here, gentlemen. Biddle has all the money. He has millions of specie in his vaults, at this moment, lying idle, and you come to *me* to save you from breaking." After the group had gone, he chuckled to an aide, "Didn't I manage them well?"

When apprehensive congressmen told Jackson that a Baltimore mob threatened to camp on the Capitol grounds until the deposits were restored, the President smiled grimly. "Gentlemen, I shall be glad to see this federal mob on Capitol Hill. I will fix their heads on the iron palisades around the square to assist your deliberations. The leaders I will hang as high as Haman to deter forever all attempts to control . . . Congress by intimidation. . . ."

A respectful Baltimore delegation appeared a few days later and provoked a presidential explosion when its leader explained that they had come seeking relief.

"Relief, sir!" the old man cried. "Come not to me, sir! Go to the monster! It is folly, sir, to talk to Andrew Jackson."

"Sir, the currency of the country is in a dreadful situation."

"Sir, you keep one-sided company. Andrew Jackson has fifty letters from persons of all parties daily on this subject. Sir, he has more and better information than you, sir, or any of you."

"The people, sir . . ."

"The people! The people, sir, are with *me.*"

Jackson finally refused to hear protests, on the ground that the panic had been artificially created by Clay and Calhoun: "The executive branch has nothing to do with petitions, except for pardon pleas of convicted criminals. Take these petitions to the Senate, to Henry Clay and John C. Calhoun. Pray them to cease lying to you and misleading you."

The hostile press howled for Jackson's scalp. Who, cried the *New York American,* would have believed that "All the powers of our national government would be usurped by a single man, possessing no one qualification for any single trust, and who, like a maniac or a driveller, should make it his daily pastime to tear our constitutional charter into rags and tatters, and trample the rights of the people under his feet?" And *Niles' Register* proclaimed: "THE NATION STANDS ON THE VERY BRINK OF A HORRIBLE PRECIPICE."

Leading judges denounced the President. Chancellor James Kent said, "I look upon Jackson as a detestable, ignorant, reckless, vain & malignant tyrant." Justice Joseph Story of the Supreme Court declared, "Though we live under the form of a republic we are in fact under the absolute rule of a single man."

Public indignation was so violent in New England that handbills appeared in Boston denouncing the "desecration" of the U.S.S. *Constitution* with the figurehead of Jackson. The woodcarver reported a proffered bribe of $1,000 to allow the figure to be removed from his shop, and Commodore Elliott took it to the navy yard for completion. Anonymous protesters threatened to tar and feather the commodore. One handbill declared:

> Let us assemble in the "Cradle of Liberty.". . . . Shall this Boston built ship be thus disgraced. . . . Let this wooden God, this Old Roman, building at the expense of 300 dollars of the People's money, be presented to the Office Holders who glory in such worship, but for God's sake SAVE THE SHIP from this foul disgrace.

One night someone sawed the head of the figure from the *Constitution*'s bow and escaped detection despite Elliott's offer of a $100 reward. It was rumored that Nicholas Biddle appeared in Boston for a Whig banquet in a coffeehouse, that servants were banished, doors locked, and: "Bostonians! blush while the revolting story is told—THE HEAD OF THE IMAGE WAS BROUGHT IN, LAID UPON THE TABLE AND BACCHANALIAN ORGIES WERE HELD OVER IT!!!"

Unfortunately for Boston's claim to fame, similar tales were told of such a scene in Philadelphia, and a Cape Codder, one Dewey, who claimed to have severed the head, presented it, much the worse for wear, to Secretary of the Navy Mahlon Dickerson. By one report, Dickerson showed the head to Jackson, who laughed and rewarded Dewey with a postmastership for having destroyed so unflattering an image. Dewey, it was said, used calling cards bearing the drawing of a saw and the words: "I came, I saw, I conquered."

In any event a derisive cartoon appeared, entitled, "The Decapitation of a Great Blockhead . . .", in which Jackson's head was severed from the *Constitution* by a bolt of lightning.

Anti-Jackson sentiment in the new Congress that convened in December 1833 was overwhelming, but the old general greeted it as if the Bank question had been laid to rest. "I am happy to know," his annual message declared, "that through the good sense of our people the effort to get up a panic has hitherto failed. . . . No public distress has followed the exertions of the bank."

Biddle pressed the attack through Clay, who called on the President to reveal to the Senate the memorandum he had read to his cabinet on the removal of deposits—a document that had been published in almost every newspaper in the country. When Jackson refused, Clay made a violent attack on the President reviewing his entire presidency, charging him with highhanded and unconstitutional tactics, and concluding, to the wild applause of the galleries, with a resolution of censure.

Clay's resolution was based on the grounds that Jackson had endangered American liberties by his dismissal of the Secretary of the Treasury, and by removal of deposits.

In the course of his three-day speech Clay cried, "We are in the midst of a revolution, hitherto bloodless, but rapidly tending towards a total change of the pure republican character of the Government, and to the concentration of the power in the hands of one man." By removing the deposits, Clay said, Jackson had "proclaimed an open, palpable, and daring usurpation." At stake, he declared, was "a question between the will of one man and that of twelve millions of people . . . between power—ruthless, inexorable power on the one hand, and the strong, deep-felt sufferings of a vast community on the other."

The Kentuckian thundered:

> We behold the usual incidents of approaching tyranny. The land is filled with spies and informers. . . . People . . . no longer dare speak in the fearless tones of manly freedom, but in the cautious whispers of trembling slaves. The premonitory symptoms of despotism are upon us, and if Congress do not apply an instantaneous and effective remedy, the fatal collapse will soon come on, and we shall die—ignobly die! mean, and abject slaves—the scorn and contempt of mankind—unpitied, unwept, and unmourned!

When Clay reached the climax of his melodramatic appeal to galleries packed with Bank men and their families, he begged Van Buren to intercede with Jackson to save "his bleeding country . . . helpless widows . . . unclad and unfed orphans," and erupted in soaring rhetoric: "Tell him that he has been abused, deceived, betrayed, by the wicked counsels of unprincipled men around him. . . . Entreat him to pause and to reflect that there is a point beyond which human endurance cannot go, and let him not drive this brave, generous, and patriotic people to madness and despair."

Women in the galleries burst into tears, but Van Buren, who had watched with an expression of respectful innocence as Clay sank exhausted into his seat, beckoned a senator to take his chair and walked solemnly down the aisle to Clay's side, asked for a pinch of his fine maccoboy snuff and inhaled it derisively. The chamber roared with laughter.

Clay's censure resolution passed the Senate by twenty-six votes to twenty, and Old Hickory raged in the privacy of his study: "Oh, if I live to get these robes of office off me I will bring that rascal to dear account." Jackson sent the Senate an indignant protest of the censure, warning the nation of a senatorial oligarchy, and mentioning his war wounds and long service to the country. The Senate refused to enter the President's protest in its Journal.

Clay returned to his denunciation. The administration, he said, was expiring in agony. And as for Jackson, if a phrenologist examined his head, he would find "the organ of destructiveness excessively developed. Except an enormous fabric of Executive power, the President has built up nothing. . . . He goes for destruction, universal destruction."

The attack on Jackson continued into the spring of 1834, prolonged by the woes that followed the revival of wildcat banking and a surplus of paper money, and by the panic the Bank had helped to create. The debate was the longest in congressional history.

Throughout the country, meanwhile, a partisan debate on the panic was raging. The "aristocratic" Senate was denounced in Democratic mass meetings. Opponents cried that Jackson's tyranny was destroying the country—and that only the Bank could save it.

Some of Pittsburgh's leading citizens blamed the lack of streetlights on the removal of the deposits. More threats appeared in Jackson's mail. One irate man from Cincinnati wrote, "Damn your old soul, remove them deposites back again, and recharter the bank, or you will certainly be shot in less than two weeks, and that by myself!!!"

When the country's distress was most intense, the Democratic press broke its silence and charged Biddle with the deliberate creation of the panic, charges so effective that Daniel Webster and others advised an easing of the Bank's pressure; but Biddle was adamant. He felt no obligation "to redress the wrongs inflicted by these miserable people. This worthy President thinks that because he has scalped Indians and imprisoned Judges he is to have his way with the Bank. He is mistaken." And again: "Rely upon it that the Bank . . . will not be frightened nor cajoled from its duty by any small driveling about relief to the country."

Clay persisted for weeks, confident that the depression would force the President to give in; but public resentment turned against the Bank rather than Jackson. The impasse was broken with startling suddenness in Pennsylvania, where Biddle assumed that his control was absolute. When the Bank's loan policy was so rigidly enforced that the state of Pennsylvania was refused a loan of $300,000, Governor George Wolf abandoned his support of Biddle and denounced his attempt to extort a new charter from the government "by bringing indiscriminate ruin on our unoffending community." The Pennsylvania Senate passed angry resolutions urging Congress to reject Biddle's demands. Two days later the state of New York moved against Biddle with the creation of a $6 million emergency fund to help ease state banks through the panic.

The Bank's congressional supporters deserted, and James K. Polk of Tennessee, chairman of the House Ways and Means Committee, was able to pass resolutions against recharter and restoration of the deposits as well. Polk also launched another investigation of the Bank, and persisted in face of Biddle's blatantly corrupt offer of a $2 million loan to Louisianans, in exchange for votes, an attempt that failed. Biddle then retreated. In July 1834, when he restored the normal flow of Bank credit, business revived almost at once and the financial crisis vanished as swiftly as it had come.

It was scarcely noted, in the uproar attending Jackson's triumph, that the administration was far from achieving its proclaimed goal. For while this war against monopoly had raged in Washington, Democratic legislatures of the states approved monopolistic charters "as if propelled by steam power," and the character of American economic life changed steadily, directly counter to Jacksonian ideals.

In his final gesture of the congressional session, Clay mustered the votes to reject Roger Taney's nomination as Secretary of the Treasury. Jackson fumed, but named Levi Woodbury to the post and resolved to find a higher place for Taney. Jackson also provided a new post for John Henry Eaton during the year, sending him to Florida as governor to satisfy Peggy, who was bored with her long residence on a plantation in Tennessee.

Changes continued within the cabinet. The new Secretary of the Navy was Senator Mahlon Dickerson of New Jersey. Van Buren's law partner Benjamin F. Butler had become Attorney General and the astute John Forsyth of Georgia was soon to become Secretary of State. Amos Kendall was persuaded to become Postmaster General, replacing John Barry, whose negligent management had reached the proportions of a scandal. Barry was named minister to Spain, but died on his way to Madrid.

Though he had no experience to qualify him as Postmaster General, Kendall was an intuitive politician, energetic, ambitious, and his efficiency quickly manifested itself. He revised slipshod methods, auditing books that had not been balanced for twenty years. Within five months he had paid off Post Office debts, built up a surplus of $100,000, and announced that his department would have no need of the deficit

appropriation of $450,000 which Barry had requested. Kendall's over-
haul of the postal system made it one of the most effective operations
in the government.

Visitors to the White House in these times continued to express
astonishment at the refinement and luxury of the old frontier hero's
private life. A Pennsylvania lawyer who attended an impromptu dinner
for more than a dozen guests retained a vivid impression of the meal
in the candle-lit dining room; sherry, port, madeira, claret, and champagne were "constantly poured out by the servants" through numerous courses.

"The first course was soup in the french style; then beef bouille, next
wild turkey boned and dressed with brains; after that fish; then chicken
cold . . . slices of tongue garnished with dressed salled; then canvass
back ducks and celery; afterwards partridges with sweet herbs and last
pheasants and old Virginia ham. . . . The first dessert was jelly and
small tarts in the turkish style, then blanche mode and kisses with
dryed fruits . . . preserves of various kinds, after them ice cream and
lastly grapes and oranges—As soon as all had taken what their appe-
tites could possibly endure, we left the table and returned to the
drawing room. . . . We were at the table until nearly 9 o'clock and were
eating and talking all the time."

General Robert Patterson, who dined with a small party at the White
House on another evening, was impressed by the unaffected elegance
of the occasion: "The dinner was very neat and served in excellent
taste, while the wines were of the choicest qualities. The President
himself dined on the simplest fare; bread, milk and vegetables."

Jackson's open-handed hospitality in the White House consumed
not only his $25,000 salary, but also his savings and the profits of his
plantation. His personal accounts for October 1834 reflected his generosity as a host:

> Oct 1: Forty-nine pounds of beef, twelve pounds of veal, "nineteen
> cents' worth of hog fat," three gallons of brandy, two gallons of Holland
> gin, one gallon of Jamaica rum.
>
> Oct. 2: Forty pounds of beef, eight pounds of mutton, "twenty-five
> cents' worth of sausages."
>
> Oct. 3: Twenty-two pounds of mutton, twenty pounds of beef.
>
> Oct. 4: Sixteen pounds of veal, six pounds of sweetbreads.
>
> On October 13 Jackson was charged with a barrel of ale, half a barrel
> of beer, twelve bottles of London porter, and three bottles each of Châ-
> teau Margeau and Château Lafitte.

Personal afflictions continued to grieve the old man. There was a fire at the new Hermitage in October 1834, but since its massive walls were left standing and his papers and much of the furniture had been saved, Jackson was not despondent: "The Lords will be done. it was he that gave me the means to build . . . my dwelling house and he has a right to destroy it." He urged Andrew, Jr.'s, Sarah not to mourn. He would rebuild—this time a taller, simpler, more dignified house lacking the ornate finish of its predecessor. Jackson declined to accept voluntary contributions raised in New Orleans at the rate of 50 cents per donor, discouraged a similar effort in Tennessee, and sent young Andrew $1,500 for the reconstruction. He could spare no more, he said. Further funds needed must be borrowed against the cotton crop.

Andrew Jackson, Jr., also added to the President's burdens. He was a negligent manager of the plantation, incurred mounting debts, carried on an illicit love affair, and persistently disregarded the advice of the old man in the White House—advice offered tirelessly and with unfailing patience. "My son, I regret to see that we are without seed wheat and that the negroes are without shoes in these heavy frosts . . . economy must now be used . . . to pay for the land, meet my other engagements and rebuild my house." "I am fearful you have been dealing too loosely . . ." "Be careful . . . seed the pastures, have the cotton picked, ginned and sent to market."

I now address you with the fondness of a father's heart. how careful then ought you to be to shun all bad company, or to engage in any dissapation whatever and particularly intoxication . . . You must, *to get thro' life well*, practice industry with economy. . . . You must assume energy, and command our concerns . . . or we will soon be in a state of want and poverty.

27

"The French . . . won't pay unless they're made to"

Jackson's administration had been marked by substantial progress in the field of foreign affairs. Claims against the Kingdom of Naples and Denmark had been settled. Colombia had ceased its depredations against American ships, a suspended treaty with Mexico had been revived, Turkish ports had been opened to U.S. shipping. A treaty with Siam in 1833 was the first between the United States and an Asiatic nation. Most gratifying of all had been the opening of the British West Indies to Yankee trade, to the benefit of shipping firms from Maine to Georgia.

Old Hickory's emotional patriotism was a hallmark of his conduct of foreign relations, and he took an active part in most negotiations. Though he urged his diplomats to pursue objectives with tact and patience, the President was apt to threaten reprisals against stubborn governments when other methods failed. His favorite diplomatic technique was the dispatch of American frigates to foreign ports to lend force to the arguments of his ministers, a method that aided the collection of more than $12 million in claims against various nations for damages inflicted on United States shipping during the Napoleonic wars. Jackson was particularly anxious to collect damages from the French themselves.

The quarrel with the French was more than twenty years old. A succession of presidents had sought in vain to collect the claims of

American citizens for losses suffered during the Napoleonic wars, chiefly claims for French seizures of ships. Though the French had paid similar claims of other nations, they had delayed and evaded responsibility until Jackson took office. His firm stand had prompted a change of attitude in Paris, and in 1832 France had signed a treaty, agreeing to pay damages of $5 million in return for lowered duties on French wines shipped to America.

When the French failed to meet the first installment, Jackson ordered the Treasury to draw a draft for the amount due. The draft was purchased by the Bank of the United States, which was unable to collect.

Jackson ordered Edward Livingston in Paris to insist upon payment, but the Chamber of Deputies defeated the appropriation. Livingston reported, after a hint from the king, or from Lafayette, that Jackson could obtain results only through firmness, since the Chamber had refused three times to act.

Jackson then prepared an inflammatory message to Congress and sent it to a printer; but some of his cabinet, fearful that the President's strong language would offend the French, persuaded Major Donelson to modify his protest. Jackson was incensed by this interference. When John Rives, Frank Blair's partner, took a proof of the document to the White House, Jackson asked Donelson to read it to him. Old Hickory paced the floor, puffing at his pipe, and halted when Jack mumbled a passage. "Read that again, sir." Donelson repeated the words. "That, sir, is not my language." The President took up the proof and scrawled in his original phrases. Then, at least according to Washington gossips, the President snapped, "I know the French. They won't pay unless they're made to."

Louis Sérurier, the French minister to Washington, appeared at the State Department to express the hope that Jackson would follow a discreet course. But Secretary John Forsyth, though calm and courteous, explained that the President was "deeply mortified," and felt an obligation to report to Congress on the breakdown of negotiations.

Sérurier was alarmed. "What do you wish, Monsieur, a collision between us or the execution of the Treaty?"

"The execution of the Treaty," Forsyth said, but added that Jackson was determined to explain the French attitude to the American people. Soon afterward, when Forsyth turned aside his pleas once more, Sérurier warned Paris to prepare for a "very painful" turn in relations with America.

It was expected throughout the country that Jackson might resort to the tactics he had used to collect claims from the reluctant king of

Naples, when he had sent five men-of-war to lend weight to his demand for the money. Jackson's forthcoming message was awaited as if it might be a declaration of war.

The message began as a reasoned recital of the facts, but in the end halted little short of a threat of war. After so many delays, Jackson declared, it was time to "take redress into our own hands," and added, "it is not to be tolerated that another quarter of a century be wasted in negotiation about the payments." In view of continued French subterfuges Jackson urged Congress to authorize reprisals—he would seize French property if the Chamber of Deputies did not honor the treaty at its next session. As a salve to French honor Jackson added, "such a measure ought not to be considered by France as a menace. Her pride and power are too well known . . . nothing partaking of the character of intimidation is intended by us. She ought to look upon it as the evidence only of an inflexible determination on the part of the United States to insist on their rights."

Acclaim for this stand united anti-Jacksonians and Democrats for the moment. The Senate Committee on Foreign Relations, including Clay and two other anti-Jackson men, supported the President, and the Senate then voted unanimously to await the action of the French Chamber.

Two weeks later, during the tense period of waiting for word from Paris that might bring war, a would-be assassin attempted to shoot Jackson, the first such attack on an American President.

Jackson had dismissed the possibility that he might be murdered. He had received more than 500 letters threatening his life, but said he felt no concern: "I try to live my life as if death might come at any moment." His fatalism was very nearly put to the ultimate test on the cold, foggy morning of January 31, 1835, when the President went to the House chamber to attend funeral services for Representative Warren R. Davis of South Carolina, who had died in office. A bystander saw Jackson there, "looking scarcely able to go through this ceremonial," and at the end of the service watched him creep through the crowd, supported by his cane and the arm of Levi Woodbury, past the open casket, and down the stairs to the portico.

Among the spectators was a well-dressed, black-bearded young man who remained motionless until Jackson was only 6 feet away, then whipped a small pistol from his pocket and fired. Jackson was unharmed. As the report echoed, the young man drew a second pistol and fired again. Jackson lunged toward him with his cane raised, but Woodbury held him. Congressman Davy Crockett and other men leaped upon the assailant. Harriet Martineau, who was some distance away, saw the white hands of the would-be assassin flailing above the heads of the crowd as he was toppled and thrown to the floor.

Jackson was hurried to the mansion looking "very ill and weak," but as he went he profanely condemned Calhoun and Senator George Poindexter of Mississippi, who, he insisted, had inspired the assassination attempt. Jackson quickly recovered his aplomb. When Van Buren rushed to the White House to congratulate him on his narrow escape, he found the old man with the Donelson children in his lap, talking to General Winfield Scott of some other matter.

The President had escaped by a miracle. Only the caps of the pistols had fired, leaving the charges intact, though they were loaded with the finest dueling powder. An expert reported that the odds on two consecutive misfires were 1 in 125,000. When Jack Donelson recapped one of the weapons and tested it, he found that it fired perfectly.

Jackson's friends concluded that the humid atmosphere had caused the misfires and saved his life.

Davy Crockett expressed the outrage of the President's admirers: "I wanted to see the damndest villain in this world—and now I have seen him."

The assailant identified himself as Richard Lawrence, an unemployed English house painter who had been in the capital for several years. Lawrence at first insisted that Jackson had killed his father; but after it was learned that his parents had never been in America, the young man said he was an heir to the British throne, and that Jackson stood in his way to the claim. Lawrence was declared insane and put in the city jail, since there was no asylum.

The President rejected the idea that his assailant was insane but insisted that he had been hired by George Poindexter, who, Jackson said, "would have attempted it long ago, if he had had the courage." The President sent out agents to seek evidence of Poindexter's guilt, whereupon the indignant Mississippian demanded that the Senate appoint a special committee of investigation, which found him innocent. Jackson clung to his suspicions, and his hostility toward his former friend was unabated.

Duff Green also scoffed at the theory of Lawrence's insanity. He charged in the *Telegraph* that the administration had staged the scene to win public sympathy for Jackson and that one of the President's men had prepared the pistols so as to cause the misfires. Reactions in the House were proof that the incident had aroused sympathy for the President. John Quincy Adams was moved to proclaim his loyalty in a speech, and Calhoun, incensed by hints of his complicity in the attempted murder, rejected the charge on the floor of the Senate, white-faced with anger, crying that Jackson had become a dictator. Frank Blair's comment in the *Globe* apparently reflected the sentiments of loyal Democrats concerning the incident: "Providence has ever guarded the man who has been destined to preserve and raise his country's glory and maintain the cause of the people."

But Jackson's intimates were concerned about his lingering suspicions of Calhoun and Poindexter, and his impatience with those who failed to agree with his theory of the attempted assassination. Nathaniel Niles, a shrewd observer, commented that Jackson's closest friends were those who shared his hatreds. "This is not meant as a libel on the General," Niles said, "but merely the expression of an opinion founded upon careful analysis of his conduct and the emotions which govern it. For his whole course in life has been dictated by emotion in contradistinction to reason."

Old Hickory's emotions were variously tested during these weeks while the capital awaited anxiously the arrival of official dispatches from France with their burden of peace or war. With a flourish he announced the retirement of the public debt and the presence of a surplus in the Treasury, an achievement unparalleled in the modern world. As the Biddle depression faded, prosperity returned, and though the President was at first elated, he became uneasy as speculation and inflation reappeared. New banks chartered by the states flooded the country with large issues of their own notes, which drove the gold coinage of 1834 into hiding, as prudent Americans hoarded "Jackson's yellow boys" against better days. The new banks were shaky ventures from the start, and those in Kendall's network of depositories were none too sound; for though Jackson spoke piously of high standards for these banks, in practice the money usually flowed to loyal Democratic banks, rather than to those whose resources were unquestionably sound. Kendall stated the policy succinctly: "Those which are in hands politically friendly will be preferred." A later study revealed that about 80 percent of the presidents, cashiers, and directors of the favored banks were Democrats.

The greatest impetus to the wave of speculation came from the sale of public lands in the vast western domain, which had been set aside by the government for purchase by homesteaders at a minimum rate of $1.25 per acre. These lands were snatched up by speculators and sold at fantastic prices, with payment in the cheap new paper money. As imaginary cities and railroads in the west lured thousands of investors, real estate and commodity prices skyrocketed, the stock market entered the American consciousness, and the terms "bulls" and "bears" became part of the gamblers' lexicon.

The inflationary spiral gave fresh impetus to the radical movement in the United States. In New York a band of rebellious Democrats, some of them veterans of the Workingmen's party, took over Tammany Hall for a boisterous meeting; and when party officials turned out the gaslights to quell the mutiny, the renegades struck some of the recently introduced friction matches, known as "locofocos," and lighted the hall with candles. The new party formed that night—launched as a challenge to old-line Democrats—gave aid to the union movement, and contributed to the general sense of unease among American conservatives as the year 1835 dawned. This group, known as the Locofocos or Equal Rights party, was led by radical neo-Jeffersonians and socialists, hard-money men who were opposed to banks and corporations and favored unlimited liability for corporate stockholders and free trade, foreign and domestic. The party was also hostile to slavery, though it did not embrace Abolitionism. The Locofoco party was to be short-lived indeed; but it left a legacy of radical American political thought to its successors.

Abolition became a national issue as the boom inflated cotton prices and the value of slaves. William Lloyd Garrison launched his crusade against slavery in Boston, and soon afterward Calhoun and Jackson clashed over the issue of Abolition pamphlets in the mails. Jackson had proposed that Abolitionist pamphlets be delivered only to those who demanded them, and declared that "the postmaster ought to take the names down, and have them exposed thro the publick journals as subscribers to the wicked plan of exciting the slaves to insurrection. . . ."

In July 1835 a mob raided the post office in Charleston, South Carolina, and seized and burned a sack of Abolitionist pamphlets. The Charleston postmaster notified the New York postmaster to forward no more Abolitionist material and the problem was laid before Amos Kendall.

Supported by Jackson, Kendall would neither order the New York postmaster to forward the pamphlets nor the Charleston postmaster to receive them—on the ground that a citizen's responsibilities to his home community were more sacred than the law. In his next message to Congress, in December 1835, Jackson denounced the Abolitionists as plotters of a civil war and urged Congress to pass a law excluding "incendiary publications intended to instigate the slaves to insurrection."

Northern liberals were outraged, and this invasion of the right of freedom of the press was too much even for Calhoun, who proposed to keep Abolitionist tracts out of the south by subterfuge. He sought to persuade Congress to pass no law excluding material from the mails, but to forbid postmasters to circulate material forbidden by state and local laws. Both Calhoun and Jackson were defeated after a three-month debate, and northern congressmen passed a law providing fines and imprisonment for postal officials who impeded the passage of any material through the mails.

Though Jackson's position on the issue was equivocal, and he was generally regarded as a supporter of slavery, he did not go so far as Calhoun, who argued that slavery was "a good—a positive good" for blacks as well as whites.

At this point Jackson made another effort to reward Roger Taney for his support in the war on Biddle's Bank by nominating him for a seat on the Supreme Court, but his enemies in the Senate foiled him once more, rejecting Taney on the last day of the session of 1835 by a margin of three votes. Once more Jackson was forced to bide his time.

The aging President also faced an embarrassing revolt within his party. The first challenge to his leadership was launched by Tennesseans who refused to accept Martin Van Buren as Jackson's successor. Many of Jackson's old friends, including Major Lewis, joined the rebellion; the Tennessee delegation formally presented Hugh L. White as a presidential candidate and planned to back him at the approaching Democratic National Convention. Old Hickory denounced the traitors, charging that they were victims of a conspiracy by Henry Clay, who sought to divide the party. When the revolt spread to other states, Jackson's resistance stiffened. He would, he said, assume the burden of naming the party's vice presidential candidate as well. Delegates to the convention were stunned by his choice of Richard M. Johnson.

Johnson had won the hearts of workingmen during his persistent campaign to abolish imprisonment for debt, which had finally borne fruit near the end of Jackson's first term. The handsome, genial Kentuckian—a dapper figure who seldom appeared in public without a scarlet waistcoat—was also a genuine military hero who had led a charge of Kentucky cavalrymen in the Black Hawk War and was said to have killed the Indian chief Tecumseh. Johnson still bore the scars of that battle, including a badly mutilated hand.

Johnson's domestic life deprived the party of support in the slave states, for he had lived with his mulatto housekeeper, Julia Chinn, and sought to introduce their light-skinned, attractive, and well-educated daughters into society. After the death of Julia, Johnson lived with another mulatto, who ran away with an Indian in 1835. According to the gossip of the day, Johnson sold the girl once he had captured the fugitives, and took up with her sister. Despite the resentment he aroused in the south, Johnson's popularity was so great that he was a rival to Jackson for the affection of the masses. Though it was not apparent to other Democratic leaders, Jackson had made a shrewd choice. He halted a boom for Johnson as a presidential candidate, attracted labor votes, and offered a haven within the party to most radical groups except for the intractable Locofocos of New York.

Jackson's long-delayed message on the French debt reached Paris at 2:00 A.M. one February day in 1836. Edward Livingston was stunned, but felt that the protest would be effective; he passed it to the Minister of Foreign Affairs with the remark that since it was a message from one branch of the American government to another, it should not be interpreted as addressed to the government of France. The French press and politicians roared. "The long sword of France can reach far," one deputy said. Another threatened that if the Senate supported Jackson, French army veterans would find their way to Washington just as the British had.

The excitement over the assassination attempt by Richard Lawrence was at its height when the French response to Jackson's message reached Washington—a cry of Gallic outrage. Louis Phillipe had notified the Chamber that diplomatic relations with the United States had been broken. Sérurier was recalled, and as he departed, protested to the State Department that Jackson had leveled charges against the French which he knew to be untrue.

Opponents, led by Clay and Webster, exulted at the insults heaped on Jackson, and newspapers made it clear that the President had acted on his own, without popular support or that of the Senate. The Clay-dominated Committee on Foreign Affairs passed a resolution denying Jackson the right to make reprisals, and had 20,000 copies printed for use as anti-Jackson propaganda.

But before the controversy reached the House, offers of military service were pouring in to Jackson, and old John Quincy Adams came to his support once more. Though he was not on speaking terms with the President, Adams favored continued negotiations, and if they failed, he was ready to risk war: "This Treaty has been ratified on both sides of the ocean . . . it has been sanctioned by Almighty God; and still we are told that . . . the arrogance of France . . . the insolence of her Chamber of Deputies, must be submitted to, and we must come down to the lower degradation of reopening negotiations to attain that which has already been acknowledged to be our due! . . . Reopen negotiations, sir, with France? Do it, and you will soon see your flag insulted, dishonored, and trodden in the dust by the pigmy States of Asia and Africa—by the very banditti of the earth."

To the dismay of Clay men Adams also praised Jackson's message: "Whatever may be said of that recommendation, the opinion of mankind will ever be that it was high-spirited and lofty, and such as became the individual from whom it emanated. I say it now, and I repeat, that it is the attitude which the Chief Magistrate will bear before the world, and before mankind, and before posterity."

A French war fleet was reported en route to America. Diplomatic relations had all but ceased. Congress was on the point of adjournment when Jackson asked the House to amend the fortification bill by adding $3 million to be used at his discretion in case of war. The House passed it at once, and the measure went to the Senate; but Clay and Webster filibustered it to death, leaving the coast vulnerable to attack.

In response to a wave of public indignation, Webster said that he "would rather see a foreign foe battering down the walls of the Capitol" than have agreed to the amendment. Adams came to Jackson's aid again with an attack on Webster: "For a man uttering such sentiments there would be but one step more, and an easy one to take, and that would be, with the enemy at the walls of the Capitol to join them in battering them down." Jacksonians on the floor and in the gallery leaped to their feet and cheered the old man so vociferously that Speaker Polk restored order with difficulty. When quiet returned, Adams said, "Thank God the people of the country have done homage to the spirit" of Andrew Jackson.

By now the French saw that the American people supported Jackson, and offered payment—though this was conditional upon an apology by Jackson. Livingston had warned the French government that an attempt to force an apology would be resisted "by the undivided energy of the nation," but the French were immovable. They refused to pay. Jackson recalled Livingston, who left behind his son-in-law, Thomas P. Barton, as chargé d'affaires. Jackson told Congress that "the spirit of the American people, the dignity of the Legislature and the firm resolve of the Executive Department" forbade an apology, and called on Congress to support him. The *Globe* declared: "France will get no apology, nothing bearing even a remote resemblance to one."

England now offered mediation, and Jackson accepted, but with a characteristic directness that stunned British diplomats: his acceptance was to be with the clear understanding that the money due would be paid, and that he was to make no apology. Thus, after extended negotiations, the case was settled. Critics declared that Jackson had been inexcusably harsh; admirers retorted that he had merely enforced foreign respect for American rights. In any event he had rattled the saber with success, and established the United States as a respected force in international relations, offering evidence to Europeans that the young republic was not to be trifled with. American prestige had reached a new height.

At the end of the French imbroglio Biddle's Bank presented a bill of some $170,000, most of which was for damages, protest costs, interest, and losses due to exchange rates. Though the claim was within the law, Jackson refused to pay damages, declaring that the Bank had profited sufficiently from the use of surplus government funds, interest-free. When the President took advantage of the government's immunity from suit to withhold payment, Biddle deducted his bill from dividends due the government as a stockholder. Jackson was furious but helpless. The squabble was a swan song of sorts for Nicholas Biddle. Already he had begun to sell his branches, preparing to wind up the affairs of the Bank at the expiration of its charter in March 1836.

28

"A bright star . . . gone out of the sky"

The final months of Old Hickory's administration were haunted by the alluring, menacing challenge of Texas—a challenge met by the one-man diplomacy of the aging expansionist, whose ambitions for his country were sporadically tempered by his professed ideals of honor and justice.

Jackson shared with most Americans of his day a heady sense of the country's boundlessness, an underlying source of optimism that lay in the beckoning west. Since his young manhood the President had been convinced that the United States would eventually extend to the Pacific and fulfill its destiny as a continental power. An exuberant and perhaps legendary Kentuckian proclaimed a credo Old Hickory might have embraced: "Why, sir, on the north we are bounded by the Aurora Borealis, on the east by the rising sun, on the south by the procession of the Equinoxes, and on the west by the Day of Judgement."

Jackson had begun negotiations for the purchase of Texas in something of this spirit. He repeated to Van Buren the conviction he had held since his days as a boy solicitor in Tennessee, that no foreign power should control any tributaries of the Mississippi, since "the God of the universe intended this great valley to belong to one nation." In common with most southwesterners, he envisioned a westward expansion of this domain, and his first instructions to Joel Poinsett in Mexico City had included his offer of $5 million for the Texas territory, extending to the "great prarrarie or desert." Jackson pointed out the advantages of the offer for the suspicious Mexicans: a natural border with the United States, with reduced danger of conflict, and a war chest to help them resist reconquest by Spain.

Poinsett, who had become ineffectual through his involvement in Mexican politics, was recalled before Jackson's offer could be made; and the ubiquitous Anthony Butler, who replaced him, mishandled Mexican-American relations during "a seven years' period of cheap trickery." Butler continually raised false hopes of a settlement until Jackson denounced him as a "scamp" and called him home, rejecting his proposal to pay a $500,000 bribe to a priest whose claim to influence was his role as confessor to the sister of Santa Anna, the Mexican dictator. With the payment of the bribe, Butler said, Texas could be purchased for $5 million. Jackson responded indignantly, "Nothing will be countenanced by the Executive to bring the Government under the remotest imputation of being engaged in corruption."

But though he rejected this blatant attempt at bribery, Jackson was not above the practice in principle. The $5 million purchase price, he told Butler, might be used by the Mexicans "as they deem proper to extinguish *private claims* and give us the cession clear of all incumbrances. . . ." Butler returned home, but the labyrinthine saga of Texas continued to unfold in Washington's secret councils. Negotiations as conducted by Old Hickory revealed a marked conflict between his personal hopes and convictions and his official pronouncements.

When the Mexican bribery scheme became known in the capital, Butler charged that Jackson had instructed him to distribute $800,000 of the purchase price where it would accomplish the most good, with $200,000 of it to be paid to Santa Anna. Jackson denounced Butler as a liar, and the controversy remained unresolved. The invasion of Texas by increasing numbers of Americans opened a new phase of the conflict and ended Jackson's hopes of purchasing the territory.

The growing pressure of inflation and feverish speculation in lands beyond the Appalachians finally forced Jackson to intervene. Land sales rose from $4 million in 1834 to more than $24 million in 1836, and most of the valuable lands had disappeared into private hands, paid for in "land-office money" issued by banks. Once this money was deposited in the banks, it was lent out again immediately to speculators, who used it to pay for land, and so on in ever-swifter rounds as the banks became more vulnerable and the government was left with dwindling security. Largely as a result of these speculations, the currency expanded from $124 million to more than $200 million. Already the absence of the stabilizing influence of the Bank of the United States was being felt.

Jackson first urged Congress to suppress bank notes of less than $20, on the theory that the use of hard money would "revive and perpetuate those habits of economy and simplicity which are so congenial to the character of republicans." His leadership was effective to the extent that thirteen states prohibited their banks from issuing notes of less than $5, but Congress adjourned without acting to ward off the inevitable crash.

The President then issued a specie circular, ordering land commissioners to accept only gold and silver in payment. As Thomas Benton explained his purpose, "The President saw the public lands fleeting away—saw that Congress would not interfere. . . . It was a second edition of the removal of the deposits scene, and made an immense sensation. The disappointed speculators raged. Congress was considered insulted, the cabinet defied, the banks disgraced."

Jackson had served notice on speculators that the government would no longer be a silent partner in their schemes, and forced public attention on the dangers inherent in the land-office excesses. But the circular was too late by more than a year and actually hastened the inevitable panic. One effect of the policy was to draw gold and silver to the west and increase pressure in the money markets. This played into the hands of some speculators, since most purchasers had little specie, could no longer buy land from the government, and were forced into the clutches of promoters. Even so, Jackson's firm step helped to halt wild inflation and enabled prudent businessmen to take precautions before the storm broke in May 1837.

Jackson had not followed an orderly course in his efforts to control inflation. His distribution of the federal surplus to the states had helped to set off a spiral, and it was some months before he saw the approaching peril. Though opponents in the House failed to repeal the President's emergency measure, they persuaded many Americans that his policy was not only painful but based upon reckless expediency. Critics from Jackson's day to our own have considered his theories on currency and finance as bizarre and unrealistic, but it remained that the specie circular, like Jackson's other efforts to control fiscal policy, was aimed at what he saw as an abuse of privilege and the exploitation of the people. His emergency remedy was based on a simple idea, crudely expressed; yet it was rooted in the President's deep intuitive sense that in economic democracy lay the future security of the country.

Chief Justice John Marshall died in 1835, and Jackson nominated Roger Taney as his successor. It was not a popular appointment. Marshall himself had wished Justice Joseph Story to succeed him, but though Story was an able veteran of the court, he was also an old Federalist, and Jackson was resolved to change the outlook of the Court. Jackson praised Marshall as one of the great men of the time, while saying he had almost uniformly disagreed with his interpretations of constitutional law, which generally placed property rights above human rights. The Senate, in which the Democrats now had a majority, approved Taney's appointment on party lines. In naming Taney, Old Hickory gave new direction to the Court, which was to set precedents in American law, and except for its decisions concerning slavery, to exhibit an enlightened social philosophy. Taney, whose life ambition had now been realized, was soon presiding over an expanded Court of nine, of which six members had been named by Jackson. This expansion also hastened the trend toward the liberalization of the Court.

The country was tense as the election campaign of 1836 opened, and Jackson's enemies played upon public fears that the old man planned to keep his party in power in perpetuity.

Many of Jackson's associates were also alarmed. The Tennessee senator Hugh White, though he supported Jackson in his battle against the Bank, was disturbed over the expansion of the President's power, perhaps because he had accepted the mandate of his Tennessee friends and became a candidate himself:

> No matter who is President of the United States, I firmly believe executive power ought to be limited within the narrowest limits compatible with an administration of the government; otherwise all *efficient agency of the people*, in their affairs, will soon be lost. If . . . we should ever have a popular Chief Magistrate willing . . . to use his influence and . . . patronage for the purpose of designating and electing his successor. Then will this tremendous power be felt. . . .
>
> I was born under a king, but raised and educated in a Republic. To secure to our posterity the same freedom for which our fathers fought, it is essential that executive favor and patronage should be limited by law; otherwise the day may not be remote when we will have in fact a monarchy, and it the more odious because a deceptive form of a republic may be continued.

Henry Clay, who had seen the state of the nation as a revolution "hitherto bloodless," wondered how long it would remain so. Calhoun prophesied catastrophe under a government grown corrupt: "The time has arrived when reformation or revolution must go on." An epidemic of robberies, murders, riots, and other crimes swept the country.

Niles' Register proclaimed that "the time predicted seems rapidly approaching when the mob shall rule . . . society seems everywhere unhinged, and the demon of 'blood and slaughter' has been let loose upon us."

The mood of violence was so pervasive that Van Buren wore a brace of pistols while he presided over the Senate.

The election found Democrats divided, but the rival Whigs so torn by dissension as to offer little effective resistance. Henry Clay felt that the cause was hopeless and declined to make the race, with the result that regional candidates appeared, hopeful of splitting Democratic strength: William Henry Harrison of Ohio, Daniel Webster of Massachusetts, and Hugh White of Tennessee. South Carolina further complicated the race by refusing to affiliate with either party. Whig hopes that the election would be thrown into the House centered on Harrison, the decrepit hero of Tippecanoe.

Nicholas Biddle issued a statesmanlike proposal for the conduct of Harrison's campaign: "Let him say not one single word about his principles, or his creed—let him say nothing . . . about what he thinks now, or what he will do hereafter. Let the use of pen and ink be wholly forbidden as if he were a mad poet in Bedlam."

The Whigs launched a vicious campaign against the Van Buren-Johnson ticket reminiscent of Jackson's first race. Young William H. Seward of New York denounced the Red Fox as "a crawling reptile, whose only claim was that he had inveigled the confidence of a credulous, blind, dotard old man"—a theme echoed by Webster and Calhoun in the Senate, and by the now anti-Jackson Davy Crockett, whose name appeared as author of a biography of Van Buren in which the Red Fox was held up to scorn: "When he enters the Senate Chamber in the morning, he struts and swaggers like a crow in a gutter. He is laced up in corsets, such as women in a town wear, and, if possible, tighter than the best of them. It would be difficult to say, from his personal appearance, whether he was a man or woman, but for his large *red* and *gray* whiskers!" Newspaper cartoonists depicted Van Buren as the cunning manipulator of the senile puppet Jackson. Johnson was attacked in the south as an "amalgamationist," and in the north as a slaveholder.

Hugh White made a surprisingly strong race in the western states, by proclaiming that he was an original Jacksonian, faithful to the principles the west had assumed Jackson espoused in 1828 and 1832. White was supported by several young western leaders of the future, among whom were Abraham Lincoln and Andrew Johnson.

To Jackson's chagrin White carried Tennessee, including even the Hermitage polling district, and also took Georgia, whose cause Jackson had embraced during the controversy with the Cherokees. William Henry Harrison also ran well, and carried seven states of the northwest. Webster carried Massachusetts. But nothing could prevail against Jackson's influence in the west and Van Buren's firm control in the east, and the Red Fox won 170 electoral votes as against a combined total of 124 for his opponents. There was a delay in Tecumseh Johnson's ascension to Vice President, for the electoral college displayed its independence by failing to give him the necessary majority, and he won the office only because a Jackson majority in the Senate supported him. "The Jacksonian revolution," as its foremost twentieth-century interpreter said, was entering its third term.

Once more, and for the last time, Jackson responded to the ambitions of Peggy Eaton, who had tired of the provincial life of Pensacola, Florida. The President sent John Eaton to Madrid as minister to Spain, and was soon troubled by reports that his old friends had succumbed to temptation—Eaton drank too much rum, and Peggy, still the center of gossip, smoked cigars in public and generally scandalized leaders of Madrid society.

The Texas question again demanded Jackson's attention. He had consistently sought to prevent border adventurers from dragging the nation into an episode of naked conquest. When he was told that Sam Houston had boasted that he would conquer Texas or Mexico, he sent orders to the governor of Arkansas: ". . . if such illegal project should be discovered to exist to adopt prompt measures to put it down and give the government the earliest intelligence of such illegal enterprise with the names of all those who may be concerned therein."

Houston appeared in Washington, dressed in the tribal regalia of a chief of the Cherokee nation, among whom he now lived in the Oklahoma Territory, variously known as the "Raven" and the "Big Drunk." To the dismay of the capital's society matrons, Jackson welcomed his old friend to the White House. He also provided him with new clothing and sent him back to Texas as a War Department agent, ostensibly to hold talks with Indian tribes along the Red River.

The impulsive Houston at once joined the large band of land-hungry speculators in Texas, became attorney for the Galveston Bay and Texas Land Company, whose investors included several wealthy New York Democrats, and also emerged as a leader of a revolutionary movement for Texas independence. When the Mexicans denounced these interlopers, Jackson publicly disavowed the Raven. For the record, at least, the administration's hands were clean. Events in Texas now moved to a crisis.

By 1835 armed Americans had swarmed into Texas in such numbers that they clashed with Mexican troops in a series of skirmishes, and under Houston's leadership drove them south of the Rio Grande. Jackson maintained a stern show of official neutrality in face of a wave of popular support for the invaders. He forbade General Edmund P. Gaines to march to Houston's aid with his regulars, whereupon Stephen Austin addressed a stirring appeal to Jackson, the cabinet, and Congress. "Oh, my countrymen, the warm-hearted, chivalrous, impulsive West and South are up and moving in favor of Texas. The calculating and more prudent, tho' not less noble-minded North are aroused. . . . Will you turn a deaf ear?"

Jackson scrawled on the back of the document, "The writer does not reflect that we have a treaty with Mexico, and that our national faith is pledged to support it. The Texans before they took the step to declare themselves Independent which has aroused and united all Mexico against them ought to have pondered well. It was a rash and premature act, our neutrality must be faithfully maintained."

Soon afterward there was news that Santa Anna had raised an army of 7,000 and marched into Texas, where he annihilated isolated bands of Americans at the Alamo and Goliad and swept on, scattering other parties in his path.* Houston retreated before the Mexicans with a band of fewer than 400 men.

James Buchanan was in Jackson's study when this report came from Texas. He found the President tracing Houston's movement across a map of Texas. The old man's finger halted at San Jacinto, near Galveston Bay. "Here's the place," he said. "If Sam Houston is worth one *bawbee,* he will make a stand here, and give them a fight."

A few days later Jackson received the incredible news of Houston's victory at San Jacinto on April 21, 1836, a complete rout of the Mexicans, and the capture of Santa Anna. Lieutenant Hitchcock, the messenger, noted Jackson's nervous reassurances. "That's his writing,"

---

*Among the dead at the Alamo was Davy Crockett, who fled the United States after the election of Van Buren, saying that he preferred "the wildes of Texas" to the prospect of life under the régime of the Red Fox.

the old man said again and again. "That's Sam Houston's writing. I know it well. There can be no doubt about what he says."

Elated by news of the victory, Jackson discarded all pretense of neutrality. He contributed liberally to a fund collected for the Texas army, whose aim was now to conquer Mexico itself. He wrote Houston, "I hope there may be no delay or discord in organizing a stable government to make the best use of the Independence you and your men have so bravely won." But when the fever of conquest swept the south and west, and more thousands of armed men reinforced Houston, Jackson's presidential caution overcame his personal sympathies. General Gaines, who was posted just inside the Mexican border with a small force, was inspired by San Jacinto to call on nearby states for reinforcements. Jackson countermanded the order and sent to Governor Newton Cannon of Tennessee a stern reminder of the necessity for respecting "the obligation of our treaty with Mexico . . . to maintain a strict neutrality."

John Calhoun stirred the Senate with a demand that Texas not only be recognized as independent, but that it be admitted to the Union. Jackson understood that Calhoun's "powerful reasons" for these steps included the extension of slavery into the southwest; and though he made no response, he was resolved that Texas should not become another divisive issue to threaten the Union.

Jackson's annual message to Congress in December 1836, his last, made scant mention of the Texas question. It said nothing of annexation,. and of the newly proclaimed Republic of Texas, only these guarded words: "Recognition at this time . . . would scarcely be regarded as consistent with that prudent reserve with which we have heretofore held ourselves bound to treat all similar questions." The Texans were not long content with that. Late in the month, when the end of Jackson's term was little more than two months away, the transplanted Tennessean William H. Wharton arrived in Washington as minister from the infant republic, and opened a siege of Congress and the White House.

Jackson welcomed Wharton warmly but refused to sponsor recognition of the Texas Republic. That, he said, was the responsibility of Congress. When Wharton protested that Congress would not act in face of Jackson's disapproval in his annual message, the President declined to issue a second message on the subject. Wharton reported his failure to Houston, but promised to persist. "Night and day I shall . . . [present] every argument that can operate on his pride and sense of justice."

In later conversations Jackson confessed to Wharton that he still hoped, as he had for many years, that the sparsely settled Texas Territory would become American, but he was determined that its coming would not endanger the Union by rekindling sectional animosities. He could not annex Texas unless the north and south could be reconciled to it. There was one way to make annexation palatable, he said. Northern fishing interests were eager to establish a harbor on the Pacific coast, and if they were given one, the south would hear no more of the protests against the extension of slavery into the southwest. "Texas," he said, "must claim the Californias." Old Hickory's grasp of the imperial vision was firm, but his sense of caution told him that the reckless and immediate Americanization of Texas would endanger the nation for years to come.

Jackson planned to deliver a farewell address to Congress during his final days in office, and assembled ideas which he asked Taney to "throw on paper." The old man was seized by a fit of coughing as he began his work and hemorrhaged massively from the lungs. Doctors added to his danger by draining 60 ounces of blood from his veins. His family despaired for his life for two days, but on the third day found him sitting up against his pillows, pale and worn, busily dictating a letter, apparently indestructible. Jackson still smoked and chewed tobacco constantly, bled himself whenever he felt the approach of a spell of weakness, and dosed regularly with calomel as a remedy for diarrhea. He continued this regimen to the end of his term, though he was so ill that he left the upper floor of the White House only three or four times in the interim.

An Englishman who visited the White House during this period found the old man still astonishingly vigorous. A stranger, he thought, would at once recognize Jackson as a soldier,

his frame, features, voice, and action, have a natural and most peculiar warlikeness. He has . . . *a gamecock look* all over him. His face is unlike any other: its prevailing expression is energy; but there is . . . a lofty honorableness in its thin worn lines . . . a penetrating and sage look of talent, that could single him out . . . yet a caricature of him would make an admirable Don Quixote . . . an old iron-gray knight invincible and lionlike, but something stiff in his courtesy. . . . In his mouth there is a redeeming suavity as he speaks; but the instant his lips close, a vizor of steel would scarcely look more impenetrable. . . .

Jackson's farewell was a rather modest review of his annual messages, stressing the sanctity of the Union and the perennial perils of sectional quarrels, surplus revenue, high tariffs, extensive public works, and paper money. Like a good Jeffersonian, he warned of the evils of big government and extolled the advantages of "plain and inexpensive institutions." Though the phrases were Taney's, the thoughts were Jackson's own, including those in a spirited passage recalling the Bank war. Jackson warned Americans that if they failed to check the "spirit of monopoly and thirst for exclusive privileges you will in the end find that the most important powers of the Government have been given or bartered away."

The final expressions certainly owed little to Taney. "My own race is nearly run; advanced age and failing health warn me that before long I must pass beyond the reach of human events and cease to feel the vicissitudes of human affairs. I thank God that my life has been spent in a land of liberty, and that he has given me a heart to love my country with the affection of a son. And filled with gratitude for your constant and unwavering kindness, I bid you a last and affectionate farewell."

The old man's admirers on the floor and in the galleries blinked back tears, but opponents ridiculed him for his presumptuousness in delivering his farewell in imitation of Washington. The *New York American* scorned the address: "Happily it is the last humbug which the mischievous popularity of this illiterate, violent, vain, and iron willed soldier can impose upon a confiding and credulous people."

In January 1837, after almost three years of effort, Benton finally mustered a Democratic majority and forced through a resolution to expunge Henry Clay's censure of Jackson from the Senate Journal. Before a packed gallery, and with an anteroom liberally stocked with food and wine to sustain his supporters, the Missourian took the floor, prepared to fight until the President's enemies succumbed. He refused to compromise by having the censure "abrogated" or "rescinded," and insisted that it must be literally expunged.

Daniel Webster challenged the constitutionality of the Journal's defacement, and Henry Clay, who carried the burden of the opposition, attacked Jackson himself:

> He has swept over the Government, during the last eight years, like a tropical tornado. Every department exhibits traces of the ravages of the storm. . . . What object of his ambition is unsatisfied? When disabled from age any longer to hold the sceptre of power, he . . . transmits it to his favorite! What more does he want? Must we blot, deface, and mutilate the records of the country, to punish the presumptuousness of expressing an opinion contrary to his own? . . . Black lines! Black lines . . .

The debate lasted thirteen hours before Jackson's opponents finally surrendered, at midnight, and Benton roared in triumph: "Solitary and alone . . . I put this ball in motion." He then called for the Journal of 1834, and despite protests that the permanent records of the body were being illegally defaced, the Secretary brought in the Journal, drew heavy black lines around the offensive words, and wrote across them: "Expunged by order of the Senate this 16th day of January, 1837." A fury of hissing burst from the galleries, and continued until the ringleader was dragged before the Speaker's chair.

The Whig leader William C. Preston of South Carolina retorted defiantly, "It is not in the power of your black lines to touch us. Remove us. Turn us out. Expel us from the Senate. Would to God you could. Call in the praetorian guard. Take us—apprehend us. March us off."

Jackson was so pleased by the incident that he invited the "expungers" and their wives to a White House victory dinner. Though he was too weak to attend, he greeted the company, ordered Benton into his chair, and then returned to his bed. For the rest of his life Jackson took delight in displaying the pen used by the clerk in expunging the Journal—a symbol of victory over the combined forces of Biddle, Clay, Calhoun, and Webster, nullifiers, and all other enemies.

Soon afterward, when the Senate voted to rescind the specie circular in hope of staving off a growing economic depression, Jackson killed the bill by pocket veto.

The closing days of his administration brought Jackson a number of bizarre gifts from admirers. Hundreds of donors in New York State contributed a 1,400-pound cheese, a mammoth wheel 4 feet in diameter and 2 feet thick. Old Hickory had it served to White House guests at a reception on Washington's Birthday, but the formidable cheese was to endure well into the reign of Van Buren. Not long before, the king of Morocco had sent Jackson a Numidian lion, which was sold at auction for $3,500 for the benefit of two orphanages in the capital.

Among other gifts was a wagon made entirely of hickory wood, with the bark still in place, an ungainly vehicle Jackson left behind when he returned home. There was also a handsome phaeton made from the wood of the frigate *Constitution,* which Jackson admired so much that he ordered it shipped home by water, after it had been used in Van Buren's inauguration ceremony.

As the end of the congressional session neared, the resourceful Texas envoy William Wharton hung about Capitol Hill, pleading and cajoling until he managed to slip into an appropriations bill a provision for sending a U.S. minister to Texas. When watchful friends of the administration deleted that amendment, Wharton persuaded the House to approve a minister in the event that Texas became "an independent power." With that encouragement Wharton set upon Jackson once more, and after three days of his arguments, the old man succumbed. He asked the Senate to approve Alcée La Branche, a Louisianan, as "chargé de Affaires [sic] to the Texas Republic." It was the final act of his administration.

The throngs that gathered in Washington for Van Buren's inaugural on March 4, 1837, came to witness the closing scene of a remarkable era. "For once," Thomas Benton said, "the rising was eclipsed by the setting sun." In the late morning Van Buren left his house on nearby Pennsylvania Avenue and drove to the White House in the phaeton built of oak from the *Constitution*, its natural wood gleaming under varnish, its panels decorated with paintings of the ship under full sail. The old man climbed into the seat at Van Buren's side and they rolled to the Capitol behind four matched grays that were descended from old Truxton. An escort of cavalry and infantry followed. Crowds along the Avenue broke into brief cheers at first sight of the old President, but ceased abruptly and fell silent as he approached. Men removed their hats and watched somberly as he went up the hill to the Capitol.

Jackson looked on benevolently as Chief Justice Roger Taney, twice rejected by the Senate for lesser offices, administered the oath to Van Buren, once rejected as minister to England. The Red Fox delivered his address in a loud, clear voice, after which the crowd fell quiet and stood briefly in the pallid noon sunlight, with all eyes fixed on Jackson's frail figure. There was hardly a sound until the old man began moving down the steps toward the waiting phaeton. At that moment the crowd broke into a spontaneous roar, as if it had been waiting for years to pay tribute to its beloved leader. The general paused halfway down the steps, removed his hat, and made a curiously graceful bow. The crowd fell silent once more. Benton, who watched from a window, was moved almost to tears. The cry raised by the people, he said, was a tribute such "as power never commanded, nor man in power received. It was affection, gratitude and admiration. . . . The acclaim of posterity breaking from the bosoms of contemporaries. . . . I felt an emotion which had never passed through me before." Years later, when he recalled other inaugural days during his tumultuous years in Washington, all would fade when compared to this moment—all "empty and soulless, brief to the view, unreal to the touch, and soon to vanish."

The dedicated Democrat William Leggett spoke for many Americans: "This day completes a period that will shine in American history with more inherent and undying lustre, than any other which the chronicler has yet recorded, or which perhaps will ever form a portion of our country's annals."

Philip Hone, the former New York auctioneer who had risen to high estate, offered quite another interpretation: "This is the end of Gen. Jackson's administration—the most disastrous in the history of the country."

Daniel Webster, who had little reason to feel affection for the old man, paid tribute: "General Jackson is an honest and upright man. He does what he thinks is right, and does it with all his might."

William Cullen Bryant felt that Old Hickory had been indispensable —"Faults he had, undoubtedly, such faults as often belong to an ardent, generous, sincere nature—the weeds that grow in rich soil. Notwithstanding this, he was precisely the man for the period . . . and he well and nobly discharged the duties demanded of him by the times."

And a German nobleman said, "He called himself the people's friend and gave proofs of his sincerity. . . . General Jackson understood the people of the United States better, perhaps, than any President before him . . . whether or not all his measures were beneficial to the people, they were in unison with his political doctrines and carried through . . . notwithstanding the enormous opposition that wealth and talent could put in the way of their execution."

The aging John Randolph of Roanoke had foreseen disaster after Jackson's departure: "I can compare him to nothing but a sticking-plaster. As soon as he leaves the Government all the impurities existing in the country will cause a disruption, but while he sticks the Union will last."

Randolph's fears were shared by many of Jackson's thoughtful contemporaries, friends and foes alike, men who were baffled to the last by the enigma of the old man who had changed the course of the country's history. The contradictions of his fierce, unyielding spirit were inexplicable. His "exasperating tendency" to regard issues as opportunities for personal combat conflicted with his habitual inclination to study problems in exhaustive detail; his native caution was frequently overcome by his impetuosity—and his characteristic gentleness of spirit was betrayed by his violent outbursts.

His biographer James Parton, who talked with many of Jackson's contemporaries, described him as a

democratic autocrat. An urbane savage. An atrocious saint . . . a patriot and a traitor. He was one of the greatest generals, and wholly ignorant of the art of war. A writter brilliant, elegant, eloquent, without being able to compose a correct sentence, or spell words of four syllables. The first of statesmen, he never devised, he never framed a measure. He was the most candid of men, and was capable of the profoundest dissimulation. A most law-defying, law-obeying citizen. A stickler for discipline, he never hesitated to disobey his superiors.

Whatever was said of him, Jackson was to be remembered fondly for generations by a nation destined to know few leaders of such resolution. As the tumultuous reign neared its end, there were already those who sensed that the era dominated by Old Hickory would endure as a landmark. The Chicago *Democrat* prophesied that children of the day would boast in years to come, "I was born in the Age of Jackson."

A day after the inaugural, as he talked with Frank Blair and young senator-elect William Allen of Ohio, Jackson reminisced about his life and his presidency. The great achievement of his administration, he said, was his defeat of the Bank of the United States, though there were still hard times ahead until a stable currency could be established. The problems of Texas and Oregon would be solved.

As to his regrets, Old Hickory had only two—his inability to shoot or hang Henry Clay and John Calhoun.

Jackson remained in the White House only three days longer before leaving for Tennessee, abandoning to Van Buren the place he now described as "a dignified office of abject slavery."

He was off on March 6, 1837, riding in the *Constitution* phaeton from the White House to the Baltimore and Ohio Railroad Station. By his side was Dr. Thomas Lawson, the Surgeon General of the United States, whom Van Buren had detailed to make the journey despite the old man's protests. Jackson first saw the crowds as he neared the depot —the city was thronged with people lining the streets, pressed about the station, and along the tracks. As far as he could see, Jackson was surrounded by the silent onlookers. The old man clambered to the rear platform of the little train and removed his hat, staring about at the people with his white hair bristling above the weary, thin face. He bowed as the train began to move, but the crowd did not stir. The people watched until he had disappeared before they began to move away. One man in the throng felt, he said, "as if a bright star had gone out of the sky."

Jackson left the cars a few miles away, where the tracks ended at Ellicott Station, and boarded a coach. He visited Taney in Maryland for a few days, then went by coach to Wheeling, where he boarded a river steamer down the Ohio. He spent two weeks in Cincinnati as guest of Congressman Robert Lytle, and went on to face a riotous homecoming welcome in Nashville.

Another, smaller crowd met him on the road, in a cedar grove near the village of Lebanon, the old men in front, with a number of boys crowding in the rear. Jackson climbed slowly from his carriage, listened gravely to Judge George Campbell's speech of welcome, responded briefly, and shook hands with his friends. He then turned to the boys, one of whom, Andrew Ewing, stepped forward. "General," he said, "the children of your old soldiers and friends welcome you home, and we're ready to serve under your banner."

The old man's head shook and tears flowed down his face. "I could have stood all," he said, "but this. It's too much, too much!" Several men gathered about him, also weeping, to pat his shoulder and see the general back into the carriage. A few moments later he dismounted at the Hermitage, home at last.

Epilogue:
"I'm dying as fast as I can . . . "

The old man had returned with $90 in his pocket, all that was left of a fortune dissipated during his years in the White House. He divided his small store of cash with Jack Donelson, who had no money to buy corn for his livestock. Jackson found the Hermitage horses and mules lean and hungry, supplies of corn and bacon low, the house roof leaking, fields unkempt and Andrew, Jr., under freshly made debts. The general's first move was to have a large field plowed and sown in Egyptian wheat. He then turned to the daily chores of plantation management, resolved to restore his fortunes without plunging more deeply into debt. His efforts were so effective that by the end of the year he paid $7,000 in bills—mostly incurred by Andrew, Jr., who had endorsed notes for friends despite Jackson's warnings. The Hermitage animals were soon fat and healthy, and despite an unusual drought, Jackson sold seventy-four bales of cotton in New Orleans the next spring.

Jackson had seen alarming signs of a national financial crisis on his way home. After months of a feverish boom, inflation was destroying fortunes based on new paper money. Desperate speculators were borrowing at the rate of 30 percent in hopes of saving themselves. Bankers, real estate traders, and gamblers in commodities were going bankrupt in Nashville and their fall threatened ruin to the community.

In Washington, victims of the panic besieged Martin Van Buren, urging him to rescind Jackson's specie circular, arguing that public confidence would return if the government would accept paper money in payment for public lands. From the Hermitage, the general advised the Red Fox to stand firm.

Jackson urged Van Buren to "take care of the currency or the administration will be shook to the centre," but predicted that the panic would wane as soon as speculators and "gamblers in stocks and bonds" had been bankrupted. Even now he saw the nation's bankers as the chief menace to a democratic society and free economy: "You know I hate the paper system, and believe all banks to be corruptly administered. Their whole object is to make money and like the aristocratic merchants, if money can be made all's well . . . people are everywhere becoming more aroused against the . . . Banks and will sustain the Executive Government in any course . . . that will hereafter secure them from . . . the corrupt paper credit system."

He wrote Blair a few months later that he hoped to live long enough to see the government divorced, *"a mensa and a thora, from all Banks."*

As the panic increased in the country and businessmen increased pressure on Van Buren to abandon Jackson's plan, the old man wrote more urgently to the President: ". . . The Treasury order is popular with the people everywhere I have passed. But all the speculators, and those largely indebted, *want more paper.* the more it depreciates the easier they can pay their debts. . . . Check the paper mania *and the republic is safe and your administration must end in triumph. . . . I say, lay on, temporize not, it is always injurious."*

It was late April before Van Buren replied—and even then the President made no mention of the fate of the specie circular: "You cannot form an adequate idea of the dreadful state of the money market in New York. . . . My situation has been one of peculiar delicacy and difficulty. . . ." Jackson began to fear that Van Buren was weakening, and his apprehensions grew when he learned that Nicholas Biddle had gone calling at the White House.

Old Hickory begged the Red Fox to keep the faith. "Mind not the clamour of . . . Biddle and Co . . . the demogogues, the Bankmen and gamblers. . . . Recollect the former panic and pressure; the present will soon blow over. . . . Be ye therefore steady, firm and unwavouring in your course and all is safe."

Van Buren stood firm. He called Congress into special session and asked for passage of a law proposed by Jackson, which would enable the Treasury to retain government revenues and issue its own currency, gold and silver coins and notes for $50 and higher denominations.

This bill was defeated in the House after passage in the Senate, but Jackson urged Van Buren to fight on. "The eyes of the people are fast opening," he said. The old man threw himself into the struggle with all the fierce energy he had displayed in his campaign against Nicholas Biddle.

Amos Kendall arrived at the Hermitage for a visit on a cold, blustery October day in 1837 and found Jackson a quarter of a mile from the house, without an overcoat, awaiting the mail carrier, eager for news of the Independent Treasury Bill. Kendall noted that Old Hickory looked as well as he had during his presidency, but that he did not move "with the same elasticity." The old man's hearing had failed, his right eye was virtually blind, and his memory was unreliable, but he was as erect as ever, and bore himself with the air of one accustomed to command.

Jackson now sensed the gaze of history upon him. Soon after reaching home he sent Van Buren a summary of his own administration, an estimate of the triumphs of the stormy years in Washington couched in terms of unconscious egotism.

> The approbation I have received from the people everywhere on my return home on the close of my official life, has been a source of much gratification to me. I have been met at every point by numerous democratic-republican friends, and many repenting whigs, with a hearty welcome and expressions of "well done thou faithful servant." This is truly the patriot's reward, the summit of my gratification, and will be my solace to my grave. When I review the arduous administration through which I have passed, the formidable opposition to its very close, of the combined talents, wealth and power of the whole aristocracy of the United States . . . I am truly thankful to my God for this happy result. . . . It displays the virtue and power of the sovereign people, and that all must bow to their will. . . .

The general was also beset by visions of the hereafter. In his second summer at home Jackson joined the small Presbyterian church he had helped to build for his wife. The general said he would have kept his promise to Rachel and joined earlier, except for his fear that political enemies would charge him with hypocrisy.

The simple brick Presbyterian church that stood near the Hermitage was remodeled during the year, and the congregation was asked to pay for this work. Jackson assumed control. When it was suggested that a committee raise the funds and oversee the work, Old Hickory said firmly, "When the Lord wanted the Ark built he gave the job to one man. If He had appointed a committee, the Ark wouldn't have been built yet."

By 1842, when Jackson was seventy-four, visibly weaker with each passing month, the Hermitage began to show the signs of hard times. The house was in need of paint and repairs. Jackson had been forced to sell his favorite saddle horse, and the plantation's food supplies were still limited. The old man had paid $15,000 of Andrew, Jr.'s, debts during the past year, and even that was not enough. The Negroes of Halcyon Plantation were starving, and the overseer was suing for back wages. Bankruptcy seemed to threaten the impoverished general.

Reports of Jackson's financial troubles were published in newspapers and were greeted with delight by the old man's enemies, who found it appropriate that he should suffer in the panic he had brought upon the country. But Jackson's financial woes were not of his making; they were due entirely to inept management by Andrew, Jr., who continued to incur debts, and to conceal some of them from the old man. The general maintained that young Andrew's misfortunes were caused by a conspiracy of his enemies, and resolved to pay the debts at all costs, though the effort would take everything he owned except the Hermitage itself.

Frank Blair learned of his plight and offered the general a loan of $10,000, which was accepted gratefully. Jackson's cotton crop had been a failure, he had lost several of his thoroughbred horses, and was unable to meet payments due on Halcyon, which Andrew, Jr., had badly mismanaged. Over Blair's protest Jackson gave as security a mortgage on Halcyon, a bill of sale for thirty black plantation hands, and a note signed by him and by Andrew, Jr. He also added a codicil to his will, specifying that the debt to Blair be paid before any other obligations.

Jackson declined offers of aid from several other friends but did accept a loan of $6000 from Jean Baptiste Plauché, who borrowed the money to help his old commander of the New Orleans campaign. In return Jackson offered a mortgage on the Hermitage as security. Plauché refused it, but accepted a note signed by Jackson and his son. The old man added a provision to his will to ensure that the Creole, too, would be repaid.

Jackson's distress was eased by the government's refund of the fine levied by Judge Dominick Hall in New Orleans.

The bill providing for a refund of the New Orleans fine was introduced by Jackson's friends in March 1842, and was bitterly opposed by the Whigs, who forced its postponement for almost two years.

After several weeks of House debate, the original refund bill was amended. Under Whig insistence the government's payment was to be tendered as a gratuity, rather than as restitution for an injustice to General Jackson.

Jackson raged. "I would starve," he said, "before I would touch one cent of the money under that odious & insulting amended bill." He refused to accept repayment unless it came as a vindication of his conduct in New Orleans. When Whigs cited François-Xavier Martin's *History of Louisiana* in support of their opposition to the refund, Jackson scorned the book's treatment of his New Orleans campaign: "A greater tissue of falsehood never before eminated from a wicked and corrupted heart." .

The old man had his way at last. The new Congress passed an acceptable refund bill in February 1844, the fine with interest now swollen to $2732.90. Jackson agreed to accept the refund in the interest of future national security, since he felt that the threat of civil interference should not handicap military commanders in time of danger. The government draft came to the Hermitage in a letter from the President himself. News of the congressional gesture set off a number of celebrations across the country.

A streamer across New York's Broadway greeted the news:

JUSTICE TO THE BRAVE
Judge Hall's
Sentence on
GENL JACKSON
Repudiated by the
Nation
Feb. 14th 1844

The draft arrived at a time when Jackson did not have a dollar in cash, but he sent $620 of it to Blair, to pay interest on his loan. Blair generously extended the term of repayment of principal due on the $10,000 loan for another year—the loan was to remain unpaid long after Jackson's death.

To the old man's gratification the United States Bank of Pennsylvania failed in the winter of 1839–40 and Nicholas Biddle went into retirement, a ruined man. A few months later Congress passed the Independent Treasury Bill, ending the federal government's dependence upon private banks. Old Hickory's final victory revived his popularity to such an extent that Van Buren, with an eye on the approaching election, urged him to visit New Orleans for a celebration of the twenty-fifth anniversary of his greatest victory.

Jackson's friends protested the cruelty of asking the old man to travel so far in the bitter winter weather, and Jackson himself said, "Again I am out of funds, and I cannot bear to borrow or travel as a pauper." But in the end, spurred by Andrew, Jr.'s, worsening financial problems, the general borrowed against his cotton crop, made plans to sell his old Hunter's Hill Plantation, obtained a $3,000 loan to aid his son, and made the long voyage to New Orleans down the ice-filled Ohio and Mississippi. He suffered a serious hemorrhage during the trip, but insisted upon continuing. After enduring ten days of banqueting and parades, he rode out to the old battlefield beside the Mississippi, where he limped to the weathered rampart on his cane and stood for a few moments, his dimmed eyes staring for the last time over the canefields where Pakenham's army had been destroyed.

On his way home Jackson wrote young Andrew, ". . . I have taken this trip to endeavour to relieve you from present embarrasments and if I live to realize it I will die contented in the hope that you will never again encumber yourself with debt that may result in the poverty of yourself and the little family I so much Love." The old man hoped—also in vain—that he had aided the cause of Van Buren.

The Whig party nominated William Henry Harrison and John Tyler for the campaign of 1840, to oppose Van Buren and his running mate, Tecumseh Johnson. Jackson urged Van Buren to drop Johnson in favor of Governor James K. Polk of Tennessee, who would help to carry the south and west, but Van Buren sought to compromise by leaving the vice presidential choice to the states, and when Polk rejected the scheme, Johnson took his place on the ticket.

The Whigs conducted a campaign reminiscent of Jackson's own sweep of 1824, dramatizing the wealthy Harrison as a log cabin candidate who was content to drink hard cider and to wear a coonskin cap, in contrast to the fastidious Van Buren. Harrison's military career was echoed in the Whig war cry of "Tippecanoe and Tyler Too," which was taken up in every state, and became a part of American political folklore.

Jackson scoffed at the raucous Whig campaign, confident that the public could not be "led by hard cider, coons, Log cabins and demagogues. I have a higher opinion of the american people than this. I think Tennessee will give Mr. Van Buren a good majority."

Despite his frail health, the general left the Hermitage on a speaking tour for Van Buren, an outing which exhausted the old man and accomplished little for the Red Fox. Though Jackson appeared with

Polk at several towns in the state, and harangued crowds at barbecues, Tennessee was lost by 12,000 votes, and Harrison carried the country. Van Buren won only seven states. The bitterly disappointed Jackson took the defeat philosophically, saying that the republic was sound enough to survive even the disaster of four years under Harrison.

The old warrior continued to roar defiance at his enemies in Washington, his judgments harsh, angry, and sometimes capricious. He disdained the military talents of "the Mock Hero," Harrison: "May the Lord have mercy upon us, if we have a war during his Presidency."

He also turned on his old friend John Henry Eaton, who had betrayed the Democratic cause.

Eaton not only opposed the reelection of Van Buren, but campaigned openly for the Harrison-Tyler ticket. When Jackson heard that he had praised Harrison before a crowd in Philadelphia, he said bitterly that Eaton was "the most degraded of all the apostates fed, clothed and nourished by the administration." The break was complete.*

Jackson denounced Harrison in bitter terms, "The Republic . . . may suffer under the present imbecile chief, but the sober second thought of the people will restore it at our next Presidential election." Old Hickory was unashamedly gratified when Harrison died after a month in the White House: "A kind . . . providence has interfered to prolong our glorious union and happy republican system which Gen'l. Harrison and his cabinet was preparing to destroy under the direction of the profligate demogogue Henry Clay. . . . The Lord ruleth, let the people rejoice." He lost no opportunity to excoriate Clay as "a swaggering, unprincipled demogogue, boldly stepping into difficulties, but meanly sneaking out."

Jackson placed his hopes in John Tyler: ". . . surely Tyler . . . will stay the corruptions of this clique who has got into power by deluding the people by the grossest of slanders . . . and hard cider."

John Tyler won Jackson's heart by his energetic efforts to annex Texas, whose affairs had reached a new crisis in January 1844. Antonio Lopez de Santa Anna, the Mexican dictator, was massing troops along the Rio Grande. Indian tribes raided the territory at will. The Texas Republic's currency was worthless.

Sam Houston, who continued to rule Texas despite his retirement

---

*After Eaton's death Peggy, still vivacious at sixty, married her granddaughter's nineteen-year-old dancing master, who relieved her of her fortune and eloped with the granddaughter.

from its presidency, shrewdly played upon American fears of foreign intervention. When the U.S. Senate had twice rejected annexation, Houston rebuffed Tyler's plea for new negotiations. His European friends, he said, had helped to make a truce between Texas and Mexico —and the republic could not risk another rejection by Washington. Tyler warned that the United States would not tolerate the presence of a European power on her southwestern border, and asked Houston what he hoped to gain by fostering a war over the territory.

The President realized that his efforts might fail, and turned to Jackson for help in a message to the Hermitage: ". . . the annexation of Texas depends *on you.* May I request you to write by the first mail to President Houston?"

Jackson sent two hasty pleas to Houston:

> . . . Some of your enemies have been & are circulating at the City of Washington that you are endeavouring to athwart the wishes of an over-whelming majority in Texas to become annexed to the United States— that you are desirous to become closely allied to Great Britain . . . I have denied . . . the slanders . . . confident that you could never become the dupe of England. . . .
>
> . . . if you will achieve this annexation your name & fame will become enrolled among the greatest chieftains. . . . Now is the time to act . . . with promptness & secrecy & have a treaty laid before the United States Senate where I am assured it will be ratified. . . . It will be an unfailing laurel in your ploom. . . . I am scarcely able to write—The Theme alone inspires me with the strength. . . .

Houston's secretary, William D. Miller, soon arrived at the Hermit-age with the Texan's reply, a long, equivocal letter that Jackson read with mounting apprehension. Houston's first concern, he said, was the security of Texas, which he had tried to safeguard from the start. Now, he declared, the independent state of 30,000 settlers was untroubled by the threat of the slavery question which was dividing the United States into hostile factions. Texans almost unanimously approved of the slave system. Further, Houston added, "Texas with peace could exist without the U. States; but the U. States cannot, without great hazard, exist without Texas."

Houston revealed that Miller was on his way to Washington, where he was to join a "Secret Legation of Texans with authority to negotiate an annexation treaty." Houston warned that the Texans, twice spurned by the United States, would turn to some other nation if they were rejected once more.

Jackson assured young Miller that the Senate would approve annexation, and sent him on to Washington with letters of introduction to Tyler and others. He then wrote Houston in the same vein, but added a warning that if Texas turned to Great Britain for protection, the United States would go to war to prevent their ancient enemy from forming "an iron hoop about the United States." Americans, Old Hickory said sternly, would oust England from Texas and Oregon though it might "cost oceans of blood & millions of money."

The struggle reached a climax in the spring of 1844, when Henry Clay published an attack on annexation as "a measure compromising the national character, involving us certainly in a war with Mexico . . . dangerous to the integrity of the Union, inexpedient in the present financial condition of the country, and not called for by any general expression of public opinion." Jackson read the statement in early May and pronounced Clay "a dead political Duck."

A mass meeting of supporters of annexation in Nashville on May 4 heard several confirmed Whigs denounce Clay. James K. Polk took the good news to the old man of the Hermitage. Clay's downfall was certain, once Van Buren had declared himself in favor of annexation.

But on May 6, two of his old friends, Willoughby Williams and General Robert Armstrong, brought Jackson news that the Red Fox had failed him. "It's a forgery," Jackson said. "Mr. Van Buren never wrote such a letter." Williams handed the old man a copy of the *Globe* and left him to read the eight-column statement by Van Buren. Van Buren had been forced to declare himself on the Texas question, and had said that the territory should not be annexed at present. Though he predicted that the American people would not permit Texas to fall into the hands of Great Britain, he said that the nation must honor its position of neutrality, and avoid evils rising from a lust for power. If the issue were forced upon him as President, Van Buren added, he would exercise the will of the people as expressed in Congress. Jackson no longer doubted. Frank Blair would print only the truth.

"Mr. Van Buren must write a second letter explaining himself," the old man said.

Armstrong pointed out that it was too late. The Tennessee delegation was on the point of leaving for the Democratic Convention in Baltimore. Would Jackson have it support Calhoun, or Lewis Cass, or Silas Wright? The old man blinked tears from his eyes. He would have none of these. A few hours later, after a small crowd of his friends had gathered and conferred quietly, Jackson sent for James K. Polk.

Though the old man agonized over his abandonment of the Red Fox, he hesitated no longer. He wrote Frank Blair, "I am quite sick really, and have been ever since I read V. B. letter. Political matters out of the question, Texas is the key to our future safety . . . we cannot bear that Great Britain have a Canedy on our west as she has on the north . . . some good democrat must be selected. . . ."

Jackson sought a place for Polk on the Democratic ticket as the vice presidential candidate, but by mid-May Polk's adroit maneuvers had begun his metamorphosis into a serious challenger for the presidency. Polk's letters to influential friends played shrewdly upon Jackson's support: "The Genl . . . speaks most affectionately of Mr. Van Buren but is compelled to separate from him. . . . Genl. J. says the candidate for the first office should be an annexation man . . . from the Southwest. . . . I aspire only to the 2nd office. . . . I am however in the hands of my friends and they can use my name in any way they think proper."

Polk also reported to friends that he was "the most available man" in light of Jackson's insistence upon Van Buren's withdrawal. Jackson himself still clung to the hope that Van Buren would reverse himself on annexation, but was obviously elated when the Democratic Convention in Baltimore broke a deadlock between Van Buren and Lewis Cass to nominate Polk and George Dallas of Pennsylvania, who were to run on the slogan, "Polk and Dallas! Oregon and Texas!" Once more the old man of the Hermitage had imposed his will upon the country. Polk was presented to the voters as "Young Hickory," the heir to the Jackson mantle. Jackson sent the candidate his congratulations and a forecast of overwhelming victory.

The campaign of 1844 was hardly begun when the Senate rejected the annexation of Texas once again, and Jackson redoubled his efforts to assure the election of Polk, as the only hope of safeguarding the southwestern border. His voluminous correspondence with state and national leaders included several urgent letters to John Tyler, who was running as an independent. Jackson persuaded the Virginian to withdraw and leave the field to Polk and his rival, Henry Clay.

Despite charges by Clay and his supporters that the extension of slavery was the secret issue behind the demand for annexation, public opinion in all sections of the country supported Jackson. The general urged Polk to keep the issue alive, "Lash Clay on Texas"—advice that became the focus of Young Hickory's campaign. In November, though Clay won Tennessee itself, Polk squeaked into office with an electoral margin of 65 votes, and a popular majority of a scant 38,000 out of 2.6 million votes cast.

Polk visited the Hermitage soon after his victory, and the general reported that their two-day consultation was "a full and free discussion." He predicted that Congress would promptly pass a bill annexing

Texas. Once more the old man urged Sam Houston to resist British blandishments, and the Texan replied with assurances of his devotion, proclaimed that he owed everything to Jackson, and promised to return to the Hermitage in the spring, so that the general might bless his young son.

The campaign for Polk had sapped Jackson's strength. "I await with resignation the call of my god," he wrote. The victory had also strained some of his friendships. Thomas Hart Benton, who had favored annexation until he realized that John Calhoun was using the issue for the extension of slavery, abandoned the cause and opposed the treaty with Texas. Benton wrote Jackson to explain that his chief objection to annexation was Calhoun's conspiracy for "the dissolution of the union and the formation of a Southern confederacy to include California." He charged that the lure of Texas lands had made "fearful havoc among our public men."

Benton went so far in his opposition to annexation as to make an emotional appeal to his old adversary, John Quincy Adams: "We are both now old men, we must unite now and save the Constitution." Jackson winced when he read Benton's remark. Even now he would brook no challenge to his will. Those who differed with him were traitors or insane. He wrote Frank Blair of Benton's defection, ". . . inform me if this can be true. If it is I want no better proof of his derangement, and it politically prostrates him."

Benton's accusation that politicians who favored annexation were moved by greed of land was made in ignorance of Jackson's ownership of a substantial claim near the town of Washington, Texas. The old man apparently acquired these lands in 1844—whether by gift or purchase was to remain a mystery.

Though he had now become an invalid, Jackson continued his battle for annexation by correspondence into the early spring of 1845, when the opposition surrendered. "The pressure of two presidents and an ex-President is too much for us," one Senator wrote. Congress passed a pro-Texas resolution, which Tyler signed on March 1, 1845, the last important act of his administration.

Frank Blair sent Jackson congratulations from Washington and the general responded fervently, "I congratulate my beloved country."

Convinced that the Union was safe once more, the old man prepared for death. He took a walk every afternoon which ended at his granddaughter Rachel's tomb, where he sat quietly for a few moments. Sometimes little Rachel went with him, but the child soon sensed that he wanted to be alone, and she left him at the garden gate. Even in his last year, after he became bedridden, Jackson asked his servants to carry him out in his chair, and sat for hours beside the tomb, staring dreamily over the garden and pasture.

Jackson's health had declined during the past year. Each of his periodic hemorrhages seemed to leave him weaker, and now, in an advanced stage of consumption, he was tormented by coughing day and night. One lung was useless and the other severely affected. He was almost blinded by frequent headaches. He continued to have himself bled during each attack, and to dose himself with calomel for diarrhea. Though Jackson had been a semi-invalid for more than thirty years, he still drove himself to limited activity each day. He still smoked and chewed tobacco and drank coffee freely. The old man now sang almost incessantly, and his high, shrill voice frequently echoed through the house as he chanted "Auld Lang Syne" or a favorite hymn.

Symptoms of dropsy appeared late in 1844, and at times Jackson's body was swollen to almost twice its normal size. During the worst of these attacks, he complained, he was "one blubber" from head to foot. He obtained relief from dropsy only when he was prostrated by diarrhea, and was forced to lie quietly in bed until the swelling subsided.

Isaac Hill of New Hampshire, who visited the Hermitage one day in March 1845, noted that the old man's feet and ankles were greatly swollen, and that since he could no longer take exercise, he bathed himself in some liniment each evening in an effort to improve his circulation. Hill feared that Jackson would live no more than a week:

> For the last four months he has not attempted to take his customary meals with the family. He sits through the day in a well constructed easy chair, with his writing materials, his miniature bible and hymn book before him. As soon as the mail arrives his first inquiry is for the daily Washington newspapers and the letters bearing the postmark of the capital. The absorbing topic with him is Texas.

A few days after Hill's visit, on March 15, some of Jackson's old friends celebrated his seventy-eighth birthday in Washington, an occasion made memorable by Auguste Davezac, his companion of New Orleans, who toasted the old hero: "There are craven hearts who would have refused the boon of an empire lest . . . it should lead to War: a war, they said, to be dreaded by a nation having no army, no leader to match the great commanders of European nations. No leader! They forget that Jackson still lives. Even if the hero were dead, go to the Hermitage, ye men of little faith; Go! ask for that old *cocked hat*; it is still there; take it; raise it on the top of a long hickory pole! One hundred thousand American horsemen, rallying around that standard, will tread down Europe's or Mexico's mercenaries like the grass of the Texas prairies."

Word spread through the west Tennessee countryside that Jackson was near death, and drew hordes of pilgrims to the Hermitage. The stream of callers was virtually endless. More than thirty came on May 29. Jackson allowed them to enter his room two or three at a time, and they came and went, day after day. Visitors who were forced to wait while others made their pleas stared curiously about the room, at the dueling pistols on a table, swords on the wall, and a log with a spear stuck in it, a souvenir from the Creek war.

With the officeseekers and political intriguers came admirers clamoring for autographs or locks of the bristly gray hair. Requests for locks of hair were so frequent that he had the clippings saved when he was given a hair cut. He bore most of the intrusions good-naturedly, lying quietly, sometimes smoking a small silver pipe while a black boy fanned the air to keep flies away. Jackson signed autograph albums, smiled and patted young boys on the head, occasionally passing out a snipping of his hair. Once, at least, he lost his patience.

One of his visitors remembered the scene, a hot spring noon, when he and another stranger entered Old Hickory's room: "The feeble old man was lying upon a sofa . . . clad in an old-style, snuff-colored coat, with a high stiff collar . . . a coverlet was thrown over him. . . ." The visitor saw that the old man was now emaciated, his chest sunken, his face hollow and wan, his eyes dull.

One of the visitors had brought a letter from Jackson's old lieutenant, General Robert Armstrong, a recommendation to President Polk. The stranger asked Jackson to sign the letter. The old man cried, "No, no! I'll do no such thing! They'll say I'm dictating to the President!"

He was now fully aroused. "I'm dying as fast as I can. And they all know it, but they will keep swarming upon me in crowds, seeking for office—intriguing for office."

Many who besieged the old man hoped to benefit from his influence with Polk. One of these was Amos Kendall, who was in financial difficulty. Kendall asked Jackson's aid in removing Washington Irving as minister to Spain, so that Kendall could be appointed to the post. Jackson obliged by writing to Polk, but his memory was so unreliable that he confused Irving with G. W. Erving, who had been minister to Spain during Jackson's invasion of Florida almost thirty years earlier. The general advised Polk that there should be no trouble in removing Irving, since "he is only fit to write a book, and scarcely that, and he has become a good Whig."

The general soon subsided. To a minister who came to ask about his health and his faith, he said, "Sir, I am in the hands of a merciful God. I have full confidence in his goodness and mercy. My lamp of life is nearly out, and the last glimmer has come. I'm ready to depart when called. The Bible is true." He said the Bible had been his guide through life and that he had tried to live by its teachings. He kept his Bible beside him, and read brief passages from time to time.

Jackson was not slow to offer the new President advice on sundry matters. When Jackson objected to the selection of James Buchanan as Secretary of State, Polk said, "But General, you yourself appointed him minister to Russia in your first term."

"That I did! It was as far as I could send him out of my sight, and where he could do the least harm. I'd have sent him to the North Pole if we'd kept a minister there!"

On May 2, five weeks before his death, the old man wrote Polk, urging firmness in the face of British bluster about the northwest boundary: "This bold avowal . . . of perfect claim to Oregon, must be met as boldly, by a denial of their right, and confidence in our own. . . ." He reminded Polk that he had vouched for his courage during the campaign, and warned that aggressive British diplomats were testing his nerve as a new President. He added sternly, "Dash from your lips the councils of the timid on this question, should there be any in your council. No temporizing with Britain on this subject now—temporizing will not do."

One of his visitors in late May was George P. A. Healy, a young artist who had been living in France. Healy, who had been commissioned by Louis Phillippe to paint a portrait of Jackson for the royal gallery, arrived at the Hermitage unannounced, to find there only the sick old man and a few servants. Healy was led into Jackson's room and saw the general peering at him from his wan, sallow face. By now the swelling of his body was so severe that Jackson could no longer lie down, and he was propped up in bed amid pillows, or carried to his great chair beside a window. The artist was so overcome by the hero's presence that he fell to his knees and blurted, "I have come to paint your picture."

Jackson would have none of Healy's Old World homage.

"Get up," he said. "Get up! Kneel to no one but your maker!"

Healy explained that he wanted him to sit for his portrait, but was unable to persuade the old man.

"Can't sit, sir, can't sit."

"But, General, the King of France has sent me all this way . . ."

"Can't sit, sir, not for all the kings in Christendom!"

Healy returned to Nashville, where he was advised to talk with young Andrew's wife. She was dubious but offered to try. Jackson refused her bluntly. "Can't sit, child. Let me die in peace." At last, after she had exhausted her arguments, she said, "Father, I'd so like you to sit!" and broke into tears.

"My child, I'll sit."

The general greeted Healy politely the next morning. "Sir, you made a *faux pas* yesterday. You should have shown me the King's letter." He submitted patiently to numerous sittings while Healy worked near his sickbed, amid the coming and going of doctors and servants. The lower part of his face was so grotesquely swollen that Healy could use only Jackson's forehead and the eyes, one of them completely blind by now. Healy copied the rest of the face from a portrait by Ralph Earl.

The painter worked under difficult circumstances in his race against death, and completed the portrait only ten days before Jackson died.

At about this time Dan Adams, a Nashville photographer, visited the Hermitage to make a daguerrotype of Jackson. The sick old man was carried to the back porch in his chair and sat for the camera. Old Hickory scowled when he was shown the picture. "Humph!" he said. "Looks like a monkey."

The family admired Healy's completed portrait, and the general praised it as the best likeness ever made of him, and asked for a copy for his children. Healy said a copy would be inferior to a painting from life, but agreed to paint another for Louis Phillippe and let the family have the first one, if Jackson could endure more sittings. Old Hickory summoned the strength to sit a day or so longer.

Healy had also been commissioned to paint a portrait of Henry Clay, who was passing through Nashville at the time. When Healy mentioned this to Jackson the old man gave him a piercing look, but he said only, "Young man, always do your duty."

Soon afterward, when he arrived at Clay's home, Healy was accused by the Kentuckian. "I see that you, like all who approached that man, were fascinated by him."

Jackson's thoughts turned increasingly to the past. He asked one of his doctors what act of his administration would be most severely condemned by future Americans.

"I don't know," the doctor said. "Perhaps the removal of the bank deposits."

"Oh, no!"

"Then maybe the specie circular?"

"Not at all!" Jackson rose in his bed, eyes flashing. "I can tell you.

Posterity will condemn me more because I was persuaded not to hang John C. Calhoun as a traitor than for any other act in my life!"

During the spring Jackson was offered for his tomb an ancient marble sarcophagus that had once held the remains of the Roman emperor Alexander Severus, a relic brought from Palestine by Commodore J. D. Elliott, the skipper of the *Constitution.*

The old man declined the offer of the imperial coffin. "My republican feelings and principles forbid it," he wrote. "The simplicity of our system forbids it . . . true virtue cannot exist where pomp and parade are the governing passions. . . . I have prepared an humble depository for my mortal body beside . . . my beloved wife."

On Sunday, June 1, Jackson asked his family to leave his bedside and go to church. "This is the holy Sabbath," he said, "and apparently the last one I'll be with you." He spent a restless night and by morning his abdomen had become so swollen that a messenger was sent into Nashville for Dr. Esselman, a surgeon, who drained fluid from the old man's body. Jackson's pain was eased for a time, but he suffered throughout the day and repeatedly prayed for relief. Esselman increased his dosage of opiates, with little effect. Two other doctors from Nashville, Robinson and Walters, examined the patient on June 3, but approved Esselman's treatment and said they could do nothing more than make Jackson as comfortable as possible and await the end.

The general rallied on Thursday to write a business letter, another request for an advance to cover debts incurred by Andrew, Jr., a plea that ended valiantly, "You may rest assured that Andrew Jackson Jnr will never again draw unless covered by assets."

During the night, while Sarah sat beside his bed, the general rambled deliriously, praying and singing snatches of hymns. It was near midnight when he stirred into consciousness.

"How do you feel, Father?"

"Pretty comfortable," he said, "but I cannot be long with you all. When I'm about to go, send for Major Lewis and Judge Campbell to make arrangements for my funeral. I want to be buried without display or pomp." He added weakly: "Or any superfluous expense."

His mind wandered. The high-pitched voice filled the room as he spoke of the annexation of Texas, "All is safe at last." His old friend Houston had "recovered" Texas for the Union, he said. And he trusted Polk to protect the country's right to Oregon, and hoped that he could do so without war. His voice rose, "If not, let war come. There'll be patriots enough to repel foreign aggression. . . ." He became so excited over the prospect that he wrote a letter. Andrew, Jr., proposed that he wait until the next day. "Tomorrow," the old man said, "I may not be here."

Jackson took a pen firmly and wrote slowly, his words clearly formed but with occasional errors. He offered advice to Polk about the Treasury, and a warning to resist efforts by Robert J. Walker, the new Secretary of the Treasury, to redeem depreciated Texas script. He added a large, bold signature and asked Andrew to fold and address the letter. "I'm too exhausted, my son, to do it."

On Sunday, June 8, 1845, Dr. Esselman entered the room and saw that death was near. Young Andrew sent for Major Lewis, as the old man had requested.

The doctor had Jackson moved to his bed, but he fainted in the arms of his servants, who thought he was dead. The word spread and wails of grief echoed through the house. Jackson opened his eyes and spoke quietly. "My dear children, don't grieve for me. I'm going to leave you . . . I've suffered so much pain."

Esselman gave him a spoonful of brandy and Jackson revived. He said emotional farewells to his servants and kissed each member of his family.

"My dear children, and friends and servants, I hope and trust to meet you all in heaven, both white and black. Both white and black." He could speak no more, but gazed at Little Rachel for several seconds, then closed his eyes.

By now the yard and portico had filled with people of the neighborhood, drawn by the swiftly spreading report that Jackson was dying. Peggy and John Henry Eaton were among the crowd. Negroes from the plantation fields began to pray and sing hymns.

When Lewis arrived at noon, the old man said in a feeble voice, "I'm glad to see you. You like to have been too late." For most of the afternoon he lay quietly, propped up amid his pillows, speaking to Lewis occasionally. He sent farewell messages to Benton, Blair, and Houston and several other friends, then fell silent.

At last young Andrew took his hand and whispered in his ear, "Father, how do you feel? Do you know me?"

The general stirred. "Know you?" he said clearly. "Yes, I know you. I would know you all if I could see. Bring me my specs."

When he heard the moaning of servants at the windows, he said, "Please don't cry. Be good children and we'll all meet in heaven." He closed his eyes and lay for half an hour, breathing shallowly.

Someone asked black Hannah to leave the room. She refused. "I was born and raised on this place, and I belong here."

At six o'clock, the old man's head fell forward abruptly. He was gone.

Lewis removed the pillows, slipped the frail body flat upon the bed, and closed the eyes.

At nightfall, a few hours too late, a dusty coach rolled into the yard, bearing Sam Houston and his young son. Houston took the boy into the room where Jackson lay, knelt sobbing beside the general's body, and said, "My son, try to remember that you have looked upon the face of Andrew Jackson."

He was buried two days later, before a crowd of 3,000 that pressed about the house.

There was an awkward pause as the mourners gathered on the shaded lawn—a withering blast of profanity and obscenity came from the gallery above, where the parrot, Old Poll, the general's favorite of many years, stood sentry on her perch. The Reverend Dr. Edgar, who had received Jackson into the church, read the burial services from the stone-paved portico, a few of Old Hickory's beloved hymns were sung, and after a brief prayer the casket was carried from the hall into the garden. The rattle of a firing squad's salute echoed across the fields and black smoke hung in the gleaming foliage of the magnolias.

At last Jackson was at rest beside Rachel, of whom he had so often said, "Heaven will be no heaven for me if she is not there."

Notes

Prologue

The opening scene is based on an account by T. D. Faulkner, a cousin of General Jackson whose narrative, published in the Fort Mill (S.C.) *Times* on Oct. 8, 1931, details and reinforces local traditions. The author's search for other, purported accounts of the remarkable funeral were unsuccessful.

The claim that Andrew Jackson's parents landed at Charleston, long accepted by historians, was impressively if not conclusively challenged by the late A. S. Salley, Jr., secretary of the Historical Commission of South Carolina. Salley and Jackson's biographer, J. S. Bassett, concluded that the Jackson family reached the Waxhaw settlement via the well-traveled wagon road from the northern colonies. In the Walter Clark Manuscripts of the North Carolina Department of Archives and History (vol. III, p. 332), the Memoir of James D. Craig states that the Jacksons landed in Pennsylvania at Conowingo Creek (on the Susquehanna) and "came Straight to the Carolinas."

The involved controversy over the birthplace of Andrew Jackson began in 1815, with his rise to fame at the Battle of New Orleans. Of Jackson's several statements that he was born in South Carolina, the most emphatic was in response to a query in 1824: "I was born in So. Carolina, as I have been told at the plantation whereon James Crawford lived about one mile from the Carolina road (crossing) of the Waxhaw Creek" (Bassett, *Correspondence*, III, 265).

North Carolina's belated claim to Old Hickory dates from 1858, when Samuel H. Walkup, a lawyer in the Waxhaws region, told another Jackson biographer, James Parton, that the hero was born in the McKemey cabin—which then stood in South Carolina, but became a part of North Carolina by a survey made four years after Jackson's birth.

Marquis James, in his one-volume biography, pp. 791–797, discussed the matter at length and concluded that South Carolina had "a little the better" of it on the basis of Jackson's testimony.

Accounts of Jackson's youth on the frontier owe much to tradition. Parton, the only biographer to investigate at the scene while traditions were still fresh, accepted testimony uncritically. The problem has been compounded by later writers who retold Parton's tales. Augustus Buell, for instance, seems to have embroidered the Jackson legends for his own purposes, and may have originated the story of Jackson's role as a public reader. Buell's methods are revealingly analyzed in the *Pennsylvania Magazine of History & Biography* (October 1956) by Milton W. Hamilton: "Buell, Fraudulent Historian." The most that can be said for Buell is that his interviews with Jackson's contemporaries added a stock of colorful anecdotes to the story of Old Hickory's career. James made full use of Buell's stories, and made only two or three corrections.

The most reliable account of Jackson's life in this period was given by Jackson to Francis P. Blair. His recollections of his experiences during the Revolution, detailed and persuasive, appear in Buell, I, 51–53.

A thorough search by J. S. Bassett in the 1920s revealed no records of Jackson's early practice in North Carolina, and Marquis James, on a visit to Salisbury, managed to uncover little more than a tradition as to the identity of Jackson's critics in the town. Catherine Hoskins of Summerfield, North Carolina, provided details of Jackson's brief career in Guilford County.

Chapter 1

Jackson's arrival in Jonesboro is described in John Allison's *Dropped Stitches in Tennessee History*, pp. 2 ff.; the same work details his later exploits in the town.

Marquis James (p. 45) renders a different version of Jackson's affray with Waightstill Avery, citing a newspaper article by the North Carolina historian Archibald Henderson. The present narrative follows the version given by Avery's son Isaac, as printed by Allison.

Details of Jackson's early law practice in Tennessee, which mark the true beginning of Jackson's documented career, were gathered by Parton chiefly from Colonel A. W. Putnam, who was president of the Tennessee Historical Society around the middle of the nineteenth century.

The unsatisfactory version of Jackson's early relationship with Rachel Robards that has come down to us rests on the testimony of Jackson's lifelong friend, John Overton, who could not have been without bias. Other witnesses, including Mary Donelson Wilcox and Elizabeth Craighead, were unwilling or unable to offer definitive versions. Jackson's own view of the affair is apparently embodied in Amos Kendall's biography. The incompleteness of the recorded story contributed to its later use and distortion by Jackson's political enemies, and to its persistence through generations. Overton's statement, which appeared in the *United States Telegraph* on June 22, 1827, thirty-seven years after the fact, was actually prepared by a committee of Jackson's friends in response to attacks on Rachel Jackson's character, and must be regarded as a campaign document.

Jackson's rather naïve maiden venture into the power politics of the Mississippi Valley region, made in his letter to Daniel Smith of February 13, 1789, is in Bassett, *Correspondence*, I, 7.

Chapter 2

Modern readers may fail to understand how Jackson could have assumed for two years that the Robards divorce was final when the most cursory investigation would have revealed the truth. But as James has pointed out, this was certainly the case. Eighteen prominent Tennesseans officially vouched for the fact that neither Jackson nor Rachel suspected that no divorce had been obtained in 1791, and even Jackson's enemies stopped short of charging him with deliberate bigamy.

The preliminary attempt of Robards to obtain a divorce is documented in *Acts Passed at a General Assembly of the Commonwealth of Virginia* (1790), p. 155.

Records of the Robards divorce have been missing at the courthouse in Harrodsburg, Kentucky, since 1891, about the time of their publication in the St. Louis *Post-Dispatch*. A draft of the court's findings, written three years after the second marriage of the Jacksons, is in the *Jackson Papers* (Library of Congress).

Jackson's financial involvement with David Allison, endangering his holdings of Tennessee land, is detailed in Bassett, *Correspondence*, I, 13 ff., and II, 427.

The tradition that Jackson gave the state of Tennessee its name is recorded in J. G. M. Ramsey's *Annals of Tennessee* (1853), p. 655. Details of Jackson's service in the state's constitutional convention are from Parton, I, 170–173.

Chapter 3

Gallatin's sketch of Congressman Jackson's arrival in Washington is from Hildreth's *History of the United States,* IV, 692.

The hostile response of congressional Democrats to President Washington's address appears in Parton, I, 206–207. Jackson's comment on his vote against the address is in Buell, I, 116, citing Governor William Allen of Ohio. Jackson's correspondence with Stevens T. Mason, Henry Tazewell, and Nathaniel Macon is in the *Jackson Papers* (Library of Congress, Jan. 17, 1796; April 27, May 25, and July 20, 1798; Feb. 14, 1800; and Jan. 12, 1801).

Jackson's comment on his admiration for Edward Livingston was recorded by an anonymous writer in *The Democratic Review,* vol. VIII, p. 368, cited in Parton, I, 223–224.

The account of the Jackson-Sevier duel is based on the narrative of Isaac T. Avery, Parton, I, 164. Jackson's challenges are in Bassett's *Correspondence,* I, 71–73. The duel itself was described by Andrew Greer, whose affidavit is in *American Historical Magazine,* vol. V, p. 208.

Chapter 4

Jackson's letter of congratulation to Jefferson concerning the Louisiana Purchase is in Bassett's *Correspondence,* I, 67. His protest that he would not pay court to Jefferson for the governorship of Louisiana was made to George W. Campbell, April 28, 1804, *ibid.,* I, 90. His failure to win the post was probably due to Jackson's friendship with Nathaniel Macon and John Randolph; his opposition to Jefferson was strengthened by the incident.

The duns from Jackson's creditors, John Morrell & Son and John Smith & Son, are in the *Jackson Papers* (Library of Congress, Jan. 8 and June 5, 1805).

The training and racing career of Truxton at Clover Bottom are described by Balie Peyton in *The Rural Sun* (1873), and in James D. Anderson's *Making of the American Thoroughbred* (1916), p. 242.

Details of the challenge race, and of the developing hostility between Jackson and Swann and Dickinson, are in Bassett's *Correspondence,* I, 124 ff. The account of the Dickinson duel itself is drawn from official documents and from *The Impartial Review,* whose accounts are reprinted in Bassett's *Correspondence,* I, 144–149. Parton, I, 289–301, based his full account on interviews with men of the community who offered the versions of deceased witnesses. Buell, I, 167–182, offers a strongly pro-Jackson version, but does add the testimony of Thomas Hart Benton as to Jackson's comments just before the duel. Ben Truman's *Field of Honor* (1884), pp. 280–284, offers a reliable summary.

Chapter 5

Some aspects of Jackson's association with Aaron Burr are puzzling. No one ever suspected Jackson of disloyalty to the United States, but it is clear that he was fond of Burr to the end, and defended him stoutly against Jefferson's charges. Not the least bizarre detail of the record was the visit of "Capt. Fort," who first revealed Burr's intentions to Jackson. The account rests on a manuscript in vol. III of the *Jackson Papers,* which James concluded to be the work of Henry Lee. This account did not name Jackson's visitor, but identified him (erroneously) as Burr's illegitimate son. Jackson wrote George Campbell (Bassett, *Correspondence,* I, 167) revealing the caller's name as Fort. His identity had baffled historians for more than a century before this letter was discovered and published. The letter also made clear Jackson's distaste for any scheme that would divide the Union.

The historians McMaster and Beveridge, who contended that Jackson aided Burr's escape from Nashville after the arrival of Jefferson's proclamation, were in error. *The Impartial Review* noted Burr's departure on Dec. 27, 1807, and reported the proclamation on Feb. 3. General James Robertson made it clear in a letter to Daniel Smith, Feb. 2 (Bassett, *Correspondence*, I, 164), that Burr had been gone for some days when Jefferson's proclamation reached Nashville.

Jackson's denunciation of Jefferson after the arrest of Burr is in Buell, I, 202–203, citing a letter from Jackson to Francis P. Blair.

Secretary of War Dearborn's remarkable letter to Jackson, cited in Marquis James, pp. 125–126, was owned by Emil Edward Hurja of New York as of 1932. Jackson's fiery response is in Bassett's *Correspondence*, I, 172.

Jackson's brief contemplation of a westward move during a period of depression was revealed in a letter to Senator Jenkin Whiteside, Feb. 10, 1810 (*Jackson Papers*, Library of Congress).

Chapter 6

The sketch of Thomas Hart Benton is drawn from William Nisbet Chambers, *Old Bullion Benton* (1956).

Jackson's role in creating an effective Tennessee militia before the War of 1812 is made clear in Scott's *Laws of Tennessee*, I, 559, and his belated rise to command is detailed in correspondence between Governor Blount and General James Robertson in *American Historical Magazine*, vol. I, p. 193, and vol. II, pp. 84 and 231. Jackson reported his selection as major general to David Campbell in a letter of Jan. 25, 1802 (*Jackson Papers*, Library of Congress).

Jackson's ringing call to arms may be found in Bassett's *Correspondence*, I, 220.

The passage of the news of war through the country is described in P. Perkins to Jackson, July 5, 1812 (*Jackson Papers*, Library of Congress). Governor Blount's urgent recommendation of Jackson to the Secretary of War is also in the *Jackson Papers*, dated June 25, 1812.

Parton, I, 361, reports Aaron Burr's comment on Washington's reluctance to send Jackson against the enemy, and Jackson's impatience is revealed in his letter to Blount of Nov. 11, 1812 (*Jackson Papers*, Library of Congress).

The departure of the Tennessee militia for the front is described in Parton, I, 368, and in *Correspondence*, I, 271 ff.

Jackson's controversy with James Wilkinson during the wait at Natchez is documented in *Correspondence*, I, 274 ff., and 290, 296, 304.

The origin of the nickname "Old Hickory" is reported in Parton, I, 382, and though traditional, has been accepted by biographers and historians.

Jackson's brawl with the Benton brothers is described in detail by several witnesses and participants in *Correspondence,* I, 309–318.

Chapter 7

The account of the Creek war in this work is based largely on those of Parton and Buell, with the valuable addition of Mrs. Dunbar Rowland's *Andrew Jackson's Campaign Against the British . . . in the War of 1812,* which made copious use of documentary records in Mississippi and Tennessee. The biographies of Eaton and Reid, and Eaton add details furnished by Jackson. Jackson's correspondence covers the campaign in detail, as if he had become aware of his status as a historical personage.

The fierce determination of the wounded Jackson to lead his men to the front was reported some years later by Enoch Parsons (Parton, III, 610), and contemporaneously recorded by George S. Gaines (Pickett Ms., Alabama State Library). The general's order to his troops, dated Sept. 24, 1813, is in the *Jackson Papers.*

David Crockett recorded incidents of the campaign in his *Life,* and detailed Coffee's massacre at the village of Tallushatchee, p. 75.

Reid and Eaton (p. 60) describe Jackson's feeble health in the field, but though they wrote from the general's recollections, may have occasionally drawn a long bow, as in their report that Jackson subsisted on acorns. John William Ward, *Andrew Jackson—Symbol for an Age,* pp. 70–71, remarks on the effectiveness of this story during Jackson's presidential campaign. In 1824 and afterward the story was widely published in American newspapers.

The execution of John Wood is documented in Jackson's correspondence, but the general's whereabouts when the boy faced the firing squad are in doubt. He gave conflicting versions of the incident in letters to Blount (Buell, I, 325) and to General Pinckney (*Correspondence,* I, 481).

The most reliable accounts of Weatherford's surrender to Jackson are by John Reid, who was present, and by Albert J. Pickett in his *History of Alabama,* which is based on interviews with witnesses. Reid's version is in an undated fragment of a letter in the Tennessee Historical Society, Nashville.

Chapter 8

John Overton's admonition to Jackson that he had become a national hero, and should govern his behavior accordingly, is in *Correspondence,* II, 1.

Jackson's warnings of the approaching British invasion of Louisiana date from June 27, 1814 (*Correspondence,* II, 12), and continue through the months of waiting, growing more insistent as President Madison and Secretary of War Armstrong rejected his advice and declined to take action. By Aug. 22 (two days before the British sacked Washington) Jackson had reached Mobile, was calling up troops from the southern states, and preparing for battle on his own (Aug. 28, 1814, to Robert Butler, in *Correspondence*, II, 35).

As a result of the harsh treaty imposed on the friendly Creek tribes by Jackson, claims against the United States remain an active issue. Indian Commissioner Luke Lea told Congress in 1853 that these claims were just, and though a successor challenged this view in 1930, there are prospects of renewed efforts by the tribe's descendants to reclaim vast tracts in Georgia, Alabama, and Mississippi.

The role of the Laffites and their pirates in the New Orleans campaign is documented by Jane L. de Grummond in *The Baratarians and the Battle of New Orleans*, which is based on numerous documents in the Bibliotheca Parsoniana, New Orleans. Among these sources is the *Journal* of Jean Laffite.

British expectations of loot from New Orleans were confirmed by Lord Wellington, "The expedition originated with that colleague [Cochrane] and plunder was its object . . . this evil design defeated its own end." (*Louisiana Historical Quarterly*, vol. IV [January 1926], p. 8). General Ross and Admiral Cochrane contested a law suit over American booty after the war.

Chapter 9

The narrative of the Battle of New Orleans is based chiefly on previous works by Bassett, Parton, and James, who in turn made use of Jackson's letterbook (*Jackson Papers*, Library of Congress); and on the authoritative account by Alexander Walker, *Jackson and New Orleans* (1856). Frequent use was also made of Major A. Lacarrière Latour's *Historical Memoir of the War in the West* (1816), Major Howell Tatum's *Journal* (*Smith College Studies in History*, vol. VII), and from the British side, George R. Gleig's *A Narrative of the British Campaigns . . .* (1821). John William Ward's *Andrew Jackson—Symbol for an Age* (1955) offers valuable analysis and commentary, though I do not accept all of its conclusions. A colorful guide to the battle is a recent work in popular style, *Blaze of Glory*, by Samuel Carter, III, which, though the product of much research, lacks annotation.

Jackson's proclamation to the free Negroes of Louisiana appears in Parton, I, 614–615, and his striking remonstrance to Governor Claiborne that black and white troops be given equal treatment, dated Sept. 21, 1814, is in the *Jackson Papers*.

Jackson's astonishment at the ignorance of residents of the city as to the topography of the New Orleans region was expressed to James Brown, Feb. 4, 1815 (*Jackson Papers*). Bassett's biography of Jackson offers (pp. 144–146) a clear, concise summary of the military topography of the region and its implications for Jackson's defense of New Orleans.

Jackson's unstudied insult of Bernard Marigny and its consequences are detailed in *Louisiana Historical Quarterly*, vol. VI, pp. 82 ff. Marigny left a remarkable work, *Reflections on the Campaign of General Andrew Jackson in 1814 and '15*, in which he stated the French claim to a share of the glory of the victory at New Orleans.

Glimpses of Jackson's activities and of life in the city preceding the Battle of New Orleans were recorded by Vincent Nolte in *Fifty Years in Two Hemispheres*. Nolte became an international speculator after the war. His memoirs became the basis for Hervey Allen's popular novel of 1933, *Anthony Adverse*.

Despite a lingering controversy over the identity of the man who took Jackson word of the British landing, James awards the credit to Gabriel Villeré, whose claim was substantiated by Walker (p. 151). Villeré wrote his own memoirs of the event in his old age, but contemporary evidence seems to corroborate his story. Reid and Eaton, however, credit Jackson's old friend Howell Tatum, who modestly refrained from mentioning his own name in his *Journal*, and gave credit to Latour instead.

After the war Latour joined Pierre and Jean Laffite in the Spanish secret service. As a spy, Latour was known as John Williams, and the Laffites as operatives 13–A and 13–B.

Chapter 10

Though this abbreviated narrative does not consider the incident, Jackson suspected that General Jacques Phillippe de Villeré had betrayed him by failing to block the water approach to his plantation, in order to save damage to his own property (Jackson–Governor Holmes, Dec. 25, 1815, *Correspondence*, II, 124). Young Major René Villeré, in fact, was arrested by Jackson and was later tried for neglect of duty and harboring the enemy. He was acquitted (General orders, Headquarters 7th Military District, March 3, 1815; Louisiana State Museum.)

Jackson's exact strength for the night attack of Dec. 23 is unknown. Reid and Eaton (p. 503) recorded it as 2,167 and Latour (p. 105) as 2,131, excluding the staff. But Jackson reported to Secretary of War Monroe on Dec. 27 (*Correspondence*, II, 127) that he had no more than 1,500 men.

The events of the night were recorded by Jackson in a manuscript narrative before the end of 1815. This account, now in the *Jackson Papers*, offers a concise summary of the period Dec. 23, 1814, to Jan. 19, 1815, except for several pages which have been lost, covering the crucial period between Dec. 28 and midmorning of Jan. 8.

Vincent Nolte, also a participant, left an account of the night action. Parton (II, 106 ff.) describes the American attack, and cites *"Recollections of an Artillery Officer,"* I, 311, for details in the British camp. The fullest British account is in Gleig's *Narrative*, pp. 220–227.

Jackson's defense line along the Rodriguez Canal was conceived by Major Latour and built under his direction, but except for Jean Laffite's suggestion that the left flank should be extended into the cypress swamp, the British would almost certainly have turned the line and may have driven its defenders. Livingston passed Laffite's suggestion to Jackson on Dec. 25 (*Correspondence*, II, 125).

Earlier students, including James and Charles Gayerré, concluded that leaders of the Louisiana legislature planned to cooperate with the enemy and save the city despite Jackson's announced scorched-earth policy. A legislative committee investigated the charge after the battle and exonerated the accused. The *Louisiana Historical Quarterly*, vol. VI, p. 68, and Gayerré's *History of Louisiana*, IV, 534–577, illuminate the controversy.

British outrage at the tactics of the American "savages" was expressed by Gleig in his *Narrative*, pp. 313–314.

Chapter 11

Dissension within the British command is described by Henry Adams in *History of the United States of America During the Second Administration of James Madison* (1921), II, 357. For Adams's account of the entire campaign, with emphasis on British problems, see pp. 311–385.

Jane de Grummond's *The Baratarians . . .* , pp. 130 ff., describes Pakenham's preparations and the composition of his assault force. Her account also makes clear the decisive contribution of the Laffite gunners to the American victory.

The role of Colonel Mullens and his 44th Regiment is described fully in William James, *Military Occurrences . . .* , II, 374–380.

Jackson's neglect of his defenses on the west bank of the river is made clear in his exchange with Commodore Patterson on Jan. 7 (*Correspondence*, II, 132, and Walker, p. 319). Only the completeness of his victory on the east bank on Jan. 8 saved him from disaster on the front defended by Patterson and Morgan.

Buell, II, 8 ff., recorded most of the details of Jackson's inspection of his line on Jan. 7.

Chapter 12

Jackson's concern over the vulnerable advanced redoubt was recorded in his *Manuscript Narrative* (Library of Congress). The general's prediction of the coming attack was recounted to Buell by William D. Butler (Stanley Clisby Arthur, *The Story of the Battle of New Orleans* [1915], pp. 181–182).

The exact strength of Jackson's line on Jan. 8 remains unknown. Bassett, after a close study of Latour's detailed presentation, calculated it at 3,989. The *Louisiana Gazette* of June 15, 1815, estimated it at 4,698. Marquis James, who is followed here, combined unit totals from morning reports on the day of the battle for his total of 5,172. John William Ward more recently surmised that the total on the line itself was 3,569. In any event the line was fully manned and at some points overcrowded.

Jackson's own description of the British charge, written to Monroe, expressed admiration for the brave troops of the enemy and wonder at his good fortune (*Correspondence*, II, 136 and 142).

The account of the effects of American fire in British ranks is from John Henry Cooke, *Narrative of Events in the South of France and the Attack on New Orleans* (1835), pp. 234–235 and 240–241.

Estimates of British casualties of‚the battle vary widely. This narrative accepts Bassett's figure of 1,971 (an official report to London on January 10 listed 291 killed, 1,262 wounded, and 484 missing; many of the wounded died before reaching the fleet). Total British casualties from Dec. 23 to Jan. 8 were 3,326, as against Jackson's loss of 71 men during the campaign.

A controversy as to whether rifle or cannon fire accounted for most British casualties has persisted since the battle. John William Ward, for example, concludes that most of the carnage was caused by artillery. However, the British medical director stated that 3,000 of 3,326 killed or wounded had been struck by "the small bullets American sharpshooters used in their rifles" (Buell, II, 33 ff). Ward contends, probably accurately, that the story of the Highlander color sergeant shot twice in the head is apocryphal. The story appeared in various newspapers, including *Liberty Hall*, March 11; *Spirit of the West*, March 25; and *The Albany Argus*, March 21, 1815. The death of Major Whittaker at the hands of the rifleman Morgan Ballard, however, was observed from both lines, and the British observer, Quartermaster E. N. Burroughs, noted the range at almost 300 yards (Carter, *Blaze of Glory*, p. 254).

The hapless Colonel Mullens was cashiered for his role in the battle, charged with disobedience of orders, "scandalous and infamous misbehaviour," and "scandalous conduct" in having declared the attack to be hopeless (*Louisiana Historical Quarterly*, vol. IX [January 1926], pp. 34–110).

Chapter 13

The swift spread of Jackson's fame in the wake of the battle is effectively shown by John William Ward (*op. cit.*, pp. 5 ff.), who cites quotations from the several newspapers mentioned in this text. Henry Clay's expression of gratification is from Epes Sargent, *Life and Public Service of Henry Clay* (1848), p. 19.

Latour's contribution to the Jackson legend is from his *Historical Memoir* . . . (Appendix, p. xvii).

Jackson's wry remark on Jefferson's reception of news from New Orleans is in Buell, I, 208. The general's striking revelation from God that he would defeat the British is from Ralph W. Emerson's *Journals*, VI, 350–352. His acknowledgment of divine intervention in the battle was made to Monroe on Feb. 17, 1815 (*Jackson Papers*).

"The Hunters of Kentucky," written by Samuel Woodworth (the author of "The Old Oaken Bucket"), circulated first as a broadside, and in 1822 was sung in New Orleans by Noah Ludlow, to the tune of "Miss Baily" from the comic opera *Love Laughs at Locksmiths*. Thus was launched one of the most popular songs of the nineteenth century (Ward, *op. cit.*, pp. 13–15).

Rachel Jackson's reaction to the spectacle of New Orleans was confided to her relative, Robert Hays, March 5, 1815 *(Jackson Papers)*.

Jackson's controversy with Judge Hall is described in Gayarré's *History of Louisiana*, IV, 611 ff. Jackson's response to Hall's charge and details of the sentence imposed are in *Jackson Papers* (Library of Congress).

Chapter 14

First reports of a boom for Jackson as President, from Carroll, Hayne, Adair and Butler, are reproduced in *Correspondence*, II, 215 ff.

The meeting of Jackson and Jefferson in Lynchburg is described in Parton, II, 334.

Jackson later reported that Madison approved his part in the Hall controversy and gave him "chart blank, approving my whole preceedings" (Jackson–Kendall, June 18, 1842, Cincinnati *Commercial*, Feb. 5, 1879).

Jackson's Alabama land speculations are revealed in *Correspondence*, II, 241, and in Thomas Perkins Abernethy's *From Frontier to Plantation in Tennessee* 1932, p. 271. Bassett, in his *Life of Andrew Jackson*, p. 292–293, demonstrates the falsity of charges that Jackson profited from Florida land deals after his conquest of the Seminoles.

Jackson's stern order forbidding subordinates to obey War Department directives without his approval is a Division Order, April 22, 1817 (*Correspondence*, II, 275). The exchange of hostile letters with Winfield Scott is in *ibid.*, II, 325 ff.

Monroe's tactful settlement of the issue of control of army personnel is in *Correspondence*, II, 329.

Jackson's proposal for his Florida invasion, which secured the southern border and instigated a lingering controversy, is in *Correspondence*, II, 345. The dispute over the responsibility for the invasion of Florida was postponed until 1830, when Jackson and Calhoun were at odds. Most historians have concluded that the record is too fragmentary to assign blame, but in recent years Jackson's role has been condemned as fraudulent, as well as one of naked, almost unprovoked aggression. See Richard R. Stenberg, "Jackson's Rhea Letter Hoax," *Journal of Southern History*, vol. II (November 1936), pp. 480–496. Marquis James (pp. 827–828) discusses the issue fully, and though he comes to no firm conclusion as to whether Jackson or Monroe told the truth about the affair, he favors Jackson, and accepts his statement that the Rhea letter had been accidentally burned.

This brief narrative of Jackson's campaign against the Seminoles follows Bassett's lucid account, which cites the pertinent documents (Bassett's *Life*, pp. 233 ff.)

The protest of de Onis over Jackson's seizure of Florida is found in *American State Papers, Foreign Relations*, IV, 486–495.

Monroe's somewhat agonized explanation of his Florida policy to Jackson is in *Jackson Papers*, dated July 19, 1818. It is one of the most remarkable letters in the annals of American diplomacy. Jackson's reaction, in *Jackson Papers*, Aug. 19, 1818, was written to the Pennsylvania politician Thomas Cooper.

The spirited and able reply to Spanish protests by John Quincy Adams is in *American State Papers, Foreign Relations*, IV, 539 ff.

Clay's anti-Jackson speech in the House, which inaugurated the lifelong feud between the two men, is found in *Annals of Congress*, 15th Congress, 2nd Session, vol. I, p. 653.

Henry A. Wise's observation on Jackson's amoral approach to international law is in Wise's *Seven Decades of the Union*, pp. 151–152.

Representative Smythe's fulsome praise of Jackson, in a vein which was to become familiar, appeared in *The National Intelligencer*, Feb. 9, 1819. A typical expression of the nation's general approval of Jackson's role in Florida was Colonel Robert Butler's toast when Old Hickory returned to Nashville from Pensacola: *"The Floridas*—Ours without 16 years of negotiation" (*The Nashville Whig* and *The Tennessee Advertiser*, July 18, 1818). The brawl between Crawford and Monroe is described in Margaret Coit's *Calhoun*, p. 126.

Chapter 15

Jackson's new mansion is described by Stanley F. Horn in *The Hermitage*, pp. 22–23, citing a letter from the contractor, D. Morrison.

In 1820 Ralph Earl sold an equestrian portrait of Jackson to the City of New Orleans, aided by the general's comment that the canvas was "a more correct likeness of myself than perhaps you have seen." John James Audubon saw the portrait in 1821, *"Great God* forgive me if my Judgment is Erroneous—I Never Saw A Worst Painted Sign in the streets of Paris." Earl improved as he worked, but there is no evidence that Jackson's artistic taste did so.

Jackson reluctantly accepted the Florida governorship, he admitted, so that he could dispense offices to his friends (see *Jackson Papers*, Monroe–Jackson, Jan. 24, 1821; Jackson–Bronaugh, Feb. 11, June 9, 1821; Jackson–Monroe, Aug. 4, 1821). Jackson's distaste for public office was expressed to Monroe Nov. 6, 1819 (*Correspondence*, II, 439).

Jefferson's warning to Monroe that Jackson should not be sent to Moscow is cited in Henry Adams, *History of the United States*, IV, 76.

Rachel Jackson's report on sinful New Orleans, obviously revised from the original, appears in Parton, II, 595, and her letters from Montpelier, Alabama, and Pensacola, Florida, to the same correspondent (Eliza Kingsley) are in *ibid.*, II, 597, 610–611.

The story of Jackson's conflict of wills with Governor Callava is well told by Bassett in his *Life*, pp. 301 ff., and at greater length by Marquis James, pp. 321

ff. Parton's account, which overemphasizes Callava's emotional version, has colored most subsequent narratives of the affair. The Vidal case was fought in the courts for years after Jackson's departure from Florida; and echoed in diplomatic circles even longer.

Jackson's suspicions that he had been exiled to Florida were expressed in undated notes in his hand in the *Jackson Papers*, as cited in Bassett's *Life*, p. 319.

Jackson's protest that he was not qualified to be president is reported in Parton, II, 354, and his support of Adams—and hostility toward Crawford— in a letter to James Gadsden, Dec. 6, 1821 (*Correspondence*, III, 140).

Buell, II, 157, quotes Rachel Jackson's complaints of the burgeoning presidential boom for her husband, citing her letter to Mary Donelson, "Feb. 1822."

Jackson wrote James Gadsden of his revealing conversation with George Campbell (*Correspondence*, III, 161).

Chancellor Kent's dazzling vision of the American future is cited by Douglas T. Miller in *The Birth of Modern America*, p. 21.

Chapter 16

The role of the Nashville Junto in Jackson's campaign and eventual election can hardly be overestimated. He probably could not have become President without the efforts of his shrewd, tough-minded amateur managers. But earlier biographers, who made much of Jackson's reluctance, have depicted him as an unwitting pawn of the Junto. It is clear from his correspondence that Jackson, after a period of indecision in 1821, fully intended to make the race and he gave every indication that he would neither give nor ask quarter.

John Overton had his political papers burned shortly before his death, and the loss of his 1824 correspondence with Jackson destroyed most evidence of his adroit direction of Jackson's campaign. Marquis James found in the Overton and Coffee Papers of the Tennessee Historical Society and elsewhere striking evidence of Overton's skill and resourcefulness as a political partisan, particularly in his masterful responses to slanders against Rachel Jackson in the campaign of 1827. James considered Overton the most able member of the Junto.

There has been disagreement as to whether Jackson responded to Grundy's letter. Bassett assumed that he did, but James maintains that Bassett mistakenly assumed that a letter to Dr. James Bronaugh was addressed to Grundy. In any case, Jackson's purported lack of interest in the prospect of becoming President was soon forgotten. The "reluctant" candidate began his insistence to numerous correspondents that though he had never sought public office, he was willing to place his fate in the hands of the people. Clear examples are his letters to Bronaugh (Aug. 1, 1822, S. G. Heiskell, *Andrew Jackson and Early Tennessee History*, III, 158; and to A. J. Donelson, Aug. 6, 1822, *Correspondence*, III, 174).

Eaton's role in Jackson's refusal of Monroe's proferred post of minister to Mexico was skillfully conducted, and revealed the senator as a resourceful political conspirator (Eaton–Jackson, Jan. 11, 1823, *Jackson Papers;* Monroe–Jackson, Jan. 30, 1823, Collection of Henry M. Flynt, New York City).

Edward Patchell's amusing letter of Aug. 7, 1824, to Jackson, documenting a crucial turn in Old Hickory's political fortunes, is in the *Jackson Papers,* and is reproduced in *Correspondence,* III, 263.

The unctuous letter to Jackson from John C. Calhoun, as Bassett noted, betrayed the South Carolinian's anxiety to win Jackson's goodwill, an effort that failed (Calhoun–Jackson, March 30, 1823, *Jackson Papers*).

The intriguing proposal of an Adams-Jackson ticket and Adams's estimate of its benefits to Jackson are found in Adams's *Memoirs,* VI, 333 and 633. The formation of this ticket would have reduced the excitement of the ensuing Jackson era, by eliminating the hue and cry over Henry Clay's "corrupt Bargain" with Adams.

The only extensive source for the Eaton scandal is Peggy Eaton's *Autobiography,* written in her old age, in 1873, and published in 1932. This uneven work, though refreshingly candid at times, leaves much unsaid. Peggy's life was more satisfactorily narrated by Queena Pollack in *Peggy Eaton, Democracy's Mistress,* in 1931.

Jackson's first defense of Peggy Eaton's virtue, to W. B. Lewis, Sept. 10, 1829, is in *Correspondence,* IV, 72.

Revealing comments on Jackson's political "image" when he became a serious candidate for the presidency were offered by Jackson himself to Coffee (June 18, 1824, *Correspondence,* III, 256); by Clay (*Works of Henry Clay,* 1857, IV, 368–369); by John Quincy Adams (*Memoirs,* VIII, 564); and by Martin Van Buren in his autobiography, J. C. Fitzpatrick, ed., American Historical Association *Report for the Year 1918,* II, p. 267.

Jefferson's comments about Jackson's fitness for the presidency, as reported by Webster, should be considered in light of Jefferson's letter to Jackson, Dec. 18, 1823: "I recall with pleasure the remembrance of our joint labors while in senate together in times of great trial and of hard battling. Battles indeed of words, not of blood, as those you have since fought so much for your own glory and that of your country. With the assurance that my attamts. [attachments] continue undiminished, accept that of my great respect and considn." (Bassett, p. 329, citing Jefferson Mss., Library of Congress).

George Ticknor Curtis in *Life of Daniel Webster* (1870), I, 222, offers an account of Webster's interview with Jefferson. One of Jefferson's grandsons later questioned the accuracy of Webster's quotation (Henry S. Randall, *Life of Thomas Jefferson,* [1858], III, 507).

Chapter 17

The text of Jesse Benton's attack against Jackson is found in his *Address to the People* (1824). This diatribe may have contributed to Jackson's growing popularity, and in any case failed to damage his cause. A leading politician of the time said despairingly, "General Jackson's popularity can stand anything!" (Parton, III, as cited by James, p. 401).

The Raleigh *Register* introduced Rachel Jackson's character as a campaign issue on Nov. 5, 1824, seven days before North Carolina voters went to the polls.

The frustration of those who attempted rational campaigning against Jackson was expressed by John Owen of North Carolina to Bartlett Yancey, July 21, 1824 (N.C. Department of Archives and History, *Misc. Papers*, series one, II, A. R. Newsome Thesis, p. 173). The same source (p. 165) reports the action of the pro-Jackson grand jury in Davidson County, North Carolina, in May 1824.

The Jacksons' journey to Washington in the large family carriage was criticized by hostile editors as unbecoming to a professed democrat (Parton, III, 51). Jackson explained that he took the heavy vehicle on the long, hard journey for the sake of Rachel's comfort (Jackson–Coffee, Oct. 24, 1823, *Correspondence*, III, 213).

The Alexandria *Herald*'s forecast of Jackson's "betrayal" in Washington was offered Dec. 1, 1824. As if in response, Jackson declared that he would spurn the presidency rather than stoop to intrigue (Jackson–Samuel Swartwout, Dec. 14, 1824, *Correspondence*, III, 268).

Rachel Jackson's concern over her acceptance by Washington society and her report of the busy rounds of social life were written to Eliza Kingsley, Dec. 23, 1824 (cited in Parton, III, 52).

The warning of fresh attacks on Rachel's reputation came from Charles P. Tritt (*Jackson Papers*, Jan. 9, 1825). Two earlier letters on the subject from Tritt have been lost. Jackson's forthright response was made Jan. 6, 1825, *ibid.*

Jackson's greeting by Clay in the Capitol was reported by Congressman R. K. Call in the *United States Telegraph*, Extra No. 10, May 10, 1828. Clay later declared he had no intention of traveling with Jackson (*Address*, p. 28).

The involved story of Clay's activities during the weeks of decision is well told in Marquis James, pp. 417 ff., with citation of numerous documents.

The charge of corruption against Clay in the *Columbian Observer* was published Jan. 28, 1825. Clay accused Jackson of complicity in or knowledge of the attack by Congressman Kremer.

Van Rensselaer's travail and final vote for Adams is told by Van Buren in his *Autobiography*, p. 152, the only account by a participant. Mrs. Margaret Bayard Smith observed the old man's distress after his interview with Clay and Webster. Another, and less persuasive, version of Van Rensselaer's decisive vote is offered by Nathan Sargent, in *Public Men and Events* (1875), p. 77.

Jackson branded Clay as "The Judas of the West" in a letter to W. B. Lewis, Feb. 14, 1825, *Correspondence*, III, 276. His conviction that Clay had accepted a bribe from Adams, expressed to George Wilson, was dated Feb. 20, 1825 (Tennessee Historical Society, Nashville).

402 · OLD HICKORY: A LIFE OF ANDREW JACKSON

Chapter 18

The rise of the Democratic party and the excesses of its first campaign are described and interpreted in a voluminous literature. Significant recent contributions, in the wake of Schlesinger's *The Age of Jackson,* are Edward Pessen's *Jacksonian America* and *Most Uncommon Jacksonians;* Glyndon Van Deusen's *The Jacksonian Era;* Douglas Miller's *The Birth of Modern America;* Leonard White's *The Jacksonians;* Robert Remini's *The Age of Jackson;* and Claude G. Bowers's *Making Democracy a Reality.*

The sketch of Martin Van Buren is drawn from the apt observations of Harriet Martineau in *A Retrospect of Western Travel;* Van Buren's *Autobiography;* and the *Dictionary of American Biography.* Van Buren's perfection of the spoils system, and his early allegiance to Jackson, are described in William G. Sumner's *Andrew Jackson,* pp. 100–101.

Major American labor organizations appeared almost simultaneously with the rise of the Jacksonian Democrats, demanding a ten-hour day, the end of imprisonment for debt, free public education, the elimination of monopolies, banking reform, and the prohibition of paper money. More than 200 active trade associations had been formed, with an estimated membership of 100,000 to 300,000. More than 150 strikes occurred between 1833 and 1837, most of them for higher wages.

Since he observed that political parties of workingmen generally ceased their independent existence at about the same time that the Democratic party began its anti-monopoly crusade, Schlesinger concluded that the workers had aligned with the Democrats and that the major thrust of Jacksonian democracy stemmed in large part from the working class.

However, subsequent scholarship has shown that there was not a major shift of labor groups to the Democratic party. In fact, as a recent labor historian writes: "What is of special interest was the tendency of labor leaders not only not to affiliate with the Democrats but, if anything, to attack that party with special vindictiveness, as though to counteract the belief inculcated by some Jacksonians that their party was peculiarly close to the laboring man"—(Douglas Miller, *The Birth of Modern America,* p. 110).

The alienation of northern Negroes by the Democrats is discussed by Edward Pessen in *Jacksonian America,* p. 215.

John Randolph's memorable attack on Henry Clay (made vivid by his allusion to Henry Fielding's characters Blifil and Black George of *Tom Jones*) is described in Charles H. Peck, *The Jacksonian Epoch* (1899), p. 107. The text is found in *Register of Debates,* 19th Congress, 1st Session, pp. 393, 395–399, and 401.

The Buchanan-Jackson meeting which set off such a furor was reported by Jackson in a clear and vigorous letter to Carter Beverly, June 5, 1827 (*Correspondence,* III, 355), and by Buchanan, in a somewhat contrived letter to his constituents, on Aug. 18, 1827 (John B. Moore, *Works of James Buchanan* [1908], I, 263). Marquis James, who discusses the affair at length, concluded that

Jackson told the truth, and that Buchanan's denial of his role as a Clay emissary was false.

Jackson clung to his belief in the "corrupt Bargain" between Clay and Adams for the rest of his life. But Carter Beverly wrote Clay in 1842, expressing regret for his role in spreading the accusation, since it remained unsubstantiated (*Niles' Register*, vol. 61, p. 403). Adams flatly denied the charge (Adams, XI, 431). Clay, who bore the odium of the charge to his grave, said in 1842 that he would have been wiser to have declined his appointment as Secretary of State.

As to Jackson's declaration that the Clay-Adams Bargain thwarted "the will of the people," later analysis of voting patterns revealed that Jackson won the votes of four states as a result of bargaining equally "corrupt." In New Jersey and Maryland, Crawford men supported Jackson in order to weaken Adams. In North Carolina, Adams men supported Jackson at the expense of Crawford; and in Louisiana, Adams and Jackson supporters combined to weaken Clay (*Annual Register*, I, 40).

Jackson's acceptance of the role of a crusader with the goal of turning opponents out of office was reported by Amos Kendall to Frank Blair on March 7, 1829 (*Blair-Lee Papers*, Princeton University Library, N.J.).

Clay's denunciation of Jackson's candidacy on the basis of his military career is cited by Daniel Mallory, *Life and Speeches of Henry Clay*, I, 555–557.

The origin of the expression "O.K.," sometimes attributed to Jackson, has also been linked to Van Buren, who was referred to in *The New Era*, April 11, 1840, as "O.K." ("Old Kinderhook," after his place of birth). (Reported in the *Saturday Review of Literature*, July 19, 1941.)

The popular appeal of Jackson's plebian qualities is assessed by John William Ward, *op. cit.*, pp. 80 ff. The observation that Jackson was opposed by the upper class is Parton's in III, 150. The comment of John Symes on Democrats as gentlemen is quoted by Pessen in *Jacksonian America*, p. 220.

A copy of Arnold's broadside accusing the Jacksons of adultery is in the Tennessee State Library, Nashville.

The furious letter to Henry Clay over which Jackson agonized for several days is cited by Marquis James, p. 467, as an undated draft in the collection of Andrew Jackson IV, Los Angeles. James concluded that since Clay failed to respond, the letter was probably never mailed.

Caleb Atwater's admonition to Jackson that he should ignore campaign attacks is in *Jackson Papers*, April 9, 1828, and that of Van Buren is in *Correspondence*, III, 384.

Jackson's anguish at reading published charges of his illegitimacy is described by Robert Remini in his *Andrew Jackson*, p. 13.

Duff Green's admission of his threats to attack Mrs. Adams in the *Telegraph* and Jackson's chivalrous reply are in the *Jackson Papers*, July 8 and Aug. 13, 1827.

Adams in his *Memoirs*, VII, 415–416, catalogues some of the ludicrous charges made against him during the campaign, including that of pandering at the Russian court. Sumner's *Jackson,* p. 115, cites the handbill in which Adams was pictured driving off a crippled soldier with a whip. Other examples of campaign literature in this vein are to be found in Van Deusen, *Jacksonian America,* p. 27; *The National Intelligencer,* Oct. 6, 1828; and Parton, III, 144.

The new waves of immigration during the period are described in Douglas Miller's *The Birth of Modern America,* p. 104.

Rachel Jackson's touching complaint of campaign attacks on her reputation appears in *Correspondence,* III, 416. Her exchange with Moses Dawson is cited in Parton, III, 153. The depressing effect of attacks by Adams partisans, by an anonymous observer, was reported in the Cincinnati *National Republican,* Jan. 23, 1829, under the name "L."

Eaton's attempt to persuade Rachel to accompany Jackson to Washington for his inaugural appears in *Correspondence,* III, 449.

Henry Wise, in *Seven Decades of the Union,* left his impressions of Rachel during these days, and cited her obvious apprehensions at the prospect of living in the White House (pp. 101, 113). Her homely hospitality to a visiting army officer is described in Parton, III, 162. Wise (p. 113) also reported Rachel's hysterical reaction when she discovered a particularly scurrilous campaign broadside in a newspaper office.

Rachel's death is described in Parton, III, 156 ff., and in Buell, II, 210 ff. Details of her condition were reported to the Winchester *Virginian* in January 1829 by Dr. Heiskell. Marquis James (p. 857) cites various documents to detail her passing. The funeral oration by the Reverend Mr. Hume is in a *Scrapbook of Jacksoniana* in the Tennessee State Library, Nashville.

Jackson's behavior at the funeral was reported in the Cincinnati *National Republican,* Jan. 23, 1829, and in the Louisville *Courier-Journal,* as cited by Ben Truman in *Field of Honor,* p. 283. The general's despairing letter to Coffee appears in *Correspondence,* IV, 2 (Jan. 17, 1829).

Chapter 19

Mrs. Trollope reported her glimpse of Jackson in *Domestic Manners of the Americans* (reprint, 1904), p. 125.

John Brown's letter and Jackson's reaction to it are in Bassett's *Life,* p. 408. Bassett commented, "Jackson was an average man; and his power to appreciate the views of the average man was one of his best traits."

Webster's report from Washington on the eve of Jackson's arrival is found in Daniel Webster, *Letters,* edited by C. H. Van Tyne, I, 142 (1902), and John Randolph's doomsday forecast is found in H. A. Garland's *Life of John Randolph of Roanoke,* II, 317–318.

Clay's departure is recorded in Glyndon Van Deusen's *Henry Clay,* p. 232, and Clay's farewell toast is in *Clay Papers,* XI, March 3, 1829 (Library of Congress).

Mrs. Smith's description of the city at the time is in her *Forty Years of Washington Society*, pp. 257 ff.

Jackson's refusal to call on Adams was reported by W. B. Lewis to Lewis Cass, about 1845 (undated letter in Bixby Collection, Huntington Library, San Marino, Calif.).

The fortunes of the Eatons at this time are described in Queena Pollack's *Peggy Eaton*, pp. 74 ff. The report of Timberlake's death, from the seaman Thomas Norman to Margaret Eaton, April 1829, is in the New York Historical Society. Eaton's letter to Jackson on his intentions to marry Peggy (Dec. 7, 1828) was cited by James as in the collection of Andrew Jackson IV of Los Angeles, as of 1932. Peggy, in her *Autobiography*, p. 80, gave her account of Jackson's response. Parton's version, cited here, differs in detail (III, 185).

Cambreleng's quip—an attempted quotation of Montaigne—is in the *Van Buren Papers*, Library of Congress, dated Jan. 1, 1829. Montaigne's remark was, "This is as they say, to betray the pannier, and then put it on your head" (Montaigne, *Essays* [Temple Classics], V, 109).

The contrast between Peggy and Rachel Jackson by Mrs. Smith is in her *Forty Years . . .* , p. 252.

The biographer's comment on Jackson's mercurial nature and its effect upon his political decisions was made by Bassett, *op. cit.*, p. 421.

The comment of James Hamilton upon the new cabinet is in the *Van Buren Papers* (Hamilton–Van Buren, Feb. 23, 1829). And Jackson's defense of his choice of Eaton is from Peggy's *Autobiography*, pp. 54–55.

The fullest account of Jackson's inaugural was left by Mrs. Smith (pp. 284 ff.). Francis Scott Key's comment is cited by Bassett, p. 422, and James Hamilton's reaction is in the *Van Buren Papers* (Hamilton–Van Buren, March 5, 1829).

Congressman Gilmer described his adventures at the reception in *Sketches of Some of the Settlers of Upper Georgia* (reprint, 1926), p. 244. Other details from Parton, III, 170; Bassett, p. 423; and Claude G. Bowers, *Party Battles of the Jackson Period* (1922), p. 47.

Louis McLane's tribute to Jackson's acuity was cited by Amos Kendall in his *Autobiography*, p. 634. Benton's observation is in his *Thirty Years' View*, I, 737; Paulding's is in W. I. Paulding, *Life of James K. Paulding*, pp. 287–288; Hawthorne's in *Writings of Nathaniel Hawthorne*, XXII, 158–160 (Manse ed.). Van Buren's account of his first visit to Jackson is in his *Autobiography*, pp. 229–232.

Arthur Schlesinger's estimate of Jackson as a national leader is from his *Age of Jackson*, p. 43.

Chapter 20

John McLean's interview with Jackson which led to his Supreme Court appointment was reported by Ben Perley Poore in *Perley's Reminiscences* (1866) I, 98. Ike Hill's pronouncement of a clean sweep in Washington is reported in Claude G. Bowers, *Making Democracy a Reality*, p. 97.

Marcy's ringing phrase, "to the victors belong the spoils," was uttered in defense of Van Buren's nomination during Senate debate (Parton, 111, 377–378).

The flight of Watkins is described by James Schouler in *History of the United States* (1913 ed.), III, 458. The default of Nourse, as recorded by David Campbell, June 3, 1829, is in the *Campbell Papers* (unpublished), cited by James as in the collection of Lemuel R. Campbell of Nashville, Tennessee.

Jackson's troubled relationship with Samuel Swartwout is revealed in Van Buren's *Autobiography*, pp. 262 ff. Jackson's harsh treatment of William Henry Harrison is cited by Claude G. Bowers, *op. cit.*, p. 98.

Jackson's exasperation after a few weeks of trying to cope with the horde of officeseekers, as expressed to Coffee, is in *Correspondence*, IV, 14 (March 22, 1829). For his impulsive generosity to the unfortunate woman who begged for help, see *ibid.*, 33.

Jackson's impatience with Silas Wright over the attempted removal of the elderly postmaster is related in John W. Forney's *Anecdotes of Public Men* (1873), p. 283; the story of the one-legged postmaster is in Buell, II, 213.

The appraisal of Jackson's approach to the spoils system is based on Leonard D. White's *The Jacksonians*, p. 5. The estimates of the numbers of officeholders removed by Jackson are from James, pp. 861–862, whose summary is based on Carl Russell Fish, *The Civil Service and Patronage* (1905), p. 51; and on "The Federal Civil Service under President Jackson" in the *Mississippi Valley Historical Review*, vol. XIII, pp. 529–530.

The description of Peggy Eaton's mode of flattery, and the prophecy of the troubles she would cause her husband, are by David Campbell of Virginia (May 24 and 27, June 3, 1829), Campbell papers.

Peggy Eaton's resolve to confront enemies directly is found in her *Autobiography*, p. 80, and in Queena Pollack, *op. cit.*, p. 86.

Jackson repeatedly protested that he had not gone to Washington to compose a cabinet acceptable to the city's society matrons. One such remark, similar to his retort to Calhoun, is in the *Jackson Papers*, April 26, 1829, addressed to an unknown correspondent.

Calhoun's disparagement of the Eaton affair is cited by Margaret Coit in her *Calhoun*, p. 548.

Parton, III, 186 ff., narrates the Reverend Ely's role in the Eaton affair, and cites Jackson's correspondence with him. Several documents are also found in *Correspondence*, IV, 35 ff.

W. B. Lewis's account of the cabinet meeting on the Eaton affair is in Parton, III, 202–205. Van Buren's version, written to James Hamilton, is in Hamilton's *Reminiscences*, p. 146.

Edward Pessen (*op. cit.*), p. 309, points out that Jackson's genius was in creating the impression he seriously believed that his enemies conspired against Peggy Eaton—a factor that transformed the sordid affair into a matter of principle.

Chapter 21

The Kitchen Cabinet was formed during Jackson's opening weeks in office, when the Senate adjourned for an eight-month recess without confirming the first batch of presidential appointments. Jackson's resentment to criticism of the group's influence was expressed to John Randolph (*Jackson Papers*, Nov. 11, 1831).

Criticism of Lewis as a dull-witted braggart came from the outspoken General W. G. Dunlap of Tennessee (*Jackson Papers*, Dunlap–Jackson, June 30, 1831). Claude G. Bowers, *op. cit.*, p. 102, cites Jackson's urgent recommendation of Lewis to James K. Polk.

Amos Kendall's role as the Svengali of the Jackson administration was appraised by Harriet Martineau in *Retrospect of Western Travel*, I, 155 (1838). Philip Hone's acid comment on Kendall is in Hone's *Diary* (Allen Nevins, ed.), p. 482. The description of the haggard Kendall riding on Pennsylvania Avenue was offered by Henry A. Wise on the House floor, Dec. 12, 1838 (*Congressional Globe*, 25th Congress, 1st Session, Appendix, p. 386).

Jackson's limited grasp of the complexities of national finance led him to rely on advisers for guidance. Felix Grundy submitted the most detailed proposal for a new bank, but this seems to have influenced Jackson less than an earlier scheme devised by John Randolph of Roanoke (*Jackson Papers*, Grundy–Jackson, May 22, 1829; Randolph–J. H. Burton, Dec. 12, 1829).

Jackson was also influenced by his friend John Catron, a Nashville lawyer who published newspaper attacks on Biddle's Bank (St. George L. Sioussat, "Tennessee Politics in the Jackson Period," *American Historical Review*, vol. XIV, p. 62).

An incomplete rough draft of Jackson's first annual message appears in *Correspondence*, IV, 97. The published version is in *Messages and Papers of the Presidents* (1899), II, 462.

Biddle's adroit political manipulations are described by Ralph C. H. Catterall in *The Second Bank of the United States* (1903), pp. 243–251. See also Reginald C. McGrane, *The Correspondence of Nicholas Biddle* (1919), pp. 63, 68, 70, 72. An illuminating modern study is Bray Hammond's *Banks and Politics* (1957).

The fate of Henry Lee is described by Margaret Sanborn in *R. E. Lee*, I, 71.

Surprisingly, in the triumph of democracy, 51 of the 76 departmental secretaries in the government in the Jacksonian era were college men—though there were only 3,400 college students among the 13 million Americans of that day. (Yale and the University of North Carolina were each represented by seven men, Princeton and William and Mary by four, Harvard and Dartmouth by three.)

Jackson's association with Colonel Anthony Butler had begun two years before Old Hickory's election. Butler's first letter to Jackson urging the annexation of Texas is in the *Jackson Papers*, Jan. 4, 1827. Jackson's instructions to

Van Buren and Poinsett on the opening of negotiations with Mexico are in *Correspondence*, IV, 57–61.

Robert Hayne had approached Jackson before his defeat of Adams, speaking for South Carolina's slaveholding free-traders: "Should you be elected, as there is every reason to believe, we shall look to you as a Pacificator" (Hayne–Jackson, *Jackson Papers*, Sept. 3, 1828). Though Jackson did not publicly commit himself for months thereafter, he had written James Hamilton, Jr., "There is nothing I shudder at more than the idea of a separate Union."

Jackson's reaction to the report by Lewis of Webster's triumph in debate is cited in Parton, III, 282. The exchange between Hayne and Webster at the White House is found in Charles W. March, *Reminiscences of Congress* (1850), p. 151.

Jackson's letter to Overton, offering Van Buren as his successor, is in *Correspondence*, IV, 108. Its significance is made clear through notes appended by Lewis.

Jackson's vow that he would not abandon John Eaton appears in a letter to Samuel Swartwout, *Correspondence*, IV, 77.

The remarkable memorandum read by Jackson to his cabinet is in *Correspondence*, IV, 123. For Jackson's accounts of the meeting, see *ibid.*, 163, 328. The published versions of Ingham, Branch, and Berrien, which differ from Jackson's, are cited in Parton, III, 303–309.

For the toll of the Eaton affair on Jackson's health, described by A. J. Donelson to John Coffee, Aug. 27, 1829, see *Andrew Jackson Donelson Papers* (Library of Congress).

Chapter 22

Though Thomas H. Benton recounted vivid details, it was Van Buren (*Autobiography*, pp. 413 ff.) who left the fullest account of the Jackson–Calhoun battle of toasts at the Jefferson Day banquet. The lengthy report in the *United States Telegraph*, April 17, 1830, is undependable because of its anti-Jackson bias.

Jackson's warning to South Carolinians through Congressman Potter is from Buell, II, 241 ff. For Benton's remark to Hayne that Jackson would carry out his threat to hang traitors, see *ibid.*, 245.

Bassett, who pointed out that Jackson's views of the Constitution were formed "through feeling rather than intellect," offers a concise summary of the controversy over internal improvements prior to Jackson's election (pp. 476 ff.). The account of Jackson's Maysville veto by James (pp. 525–527) leans heavily on the narrative of Van Buren, whose account is in his *Autobiography*, pp. 312–338. Bassett (pp. 374–396) offers other contemporary testimony.

Bassett (pp. 487–488) tells the story of Tecumseh Johnson's warning to Jackson that he should not veto the Maysville project bill.

Van Deusen in *The Jacksonian Era*, pp. 54 ff., comments on the partisan nature of the veto.

Jackson's discovery that Calhoun had secretly opposed him during the invasion of Florida, as narrated by W. B. Lewis, is in Parton, III, 322–325. The exchange of letters between Jackson and Calhoun is in *Correspondence*, IV, 136, 141, 151, and in the *Jackson Papers* (Calhoun–Jackson, May 29, 1830).

Crawford's venomous letter to the defeated Calhoun, Oct. 2, 1830, is in the *Jackson Papers.*

Peggy Eaton's plaint that the Donelsons made it impossible for her to visit the White House is in *Correspondence*, IV, 145 (June 9, 1830).

Edward Pessen, *op. cit.,* p. 322, charges Jackson with deceit—or self-deception—in his Indian policy.

Jackson's westward journey to confer with the Cherokee and Chickasaw chiefs is described in Seymour Dunbar, *A History of Travel in America* (1915), II, 484–587.

The visit of the Quaker delegation to Jackson is recounted in Buell, II, 401–403.

Commissioner Schoolcraft's recollection of Jackson's denunciation of white traders who victimized Indians is cited in Parton, III, 280.

Jackson's invitation to the Eatons, assuring them of a warm welcome at the Hermitage, is in the *Jackson Papers* (Aug. 3, 1830). The descriptions of Jackson's role as host, and his visit to Rachel's grave, were given by Peggy Eaton in her *Autobiography*, pp. 72–73.

The story of the birth of the *Globe* and the coming of Francis P. Blair, as related by W. B. Lewis, is in Parton, III, 336 ff. The sketch of Blair is drawn from a description by his partner, John C. Rives (unpublished thesis of Culver H. Smith, "The Washington Press of the Jackson Period," p. 252, Perkins Library, Duke University); and from William Ernest Smith, *The Francis Preston Blair Family in Politics* (1933) I, *passim.*

Jackson's denunciation of Duff Green was written to Lewis, June 26, 1830 (Mss. Collection, New York Public Library).

For Blair's estimate of Jackson's spirit of independence, see *Atlantic Monthly,* vol. LX, p. 187.

Chapter 23

Jackson's explanation of his inclusion of the challenge to Biddle in his first message to Congress was written to James Hamilton, Jr., Dec. 19, 1829 (Hamilton, *Reminiscences*, p. 151).

The expression of support for Jackson on behalf of "the open-mouthed million" is to be found in the *A. J. Donelson Papers* (Library of Congress, W. Catron–Donelson, Dec. 31, 1829).

John C. Calhoun's version of Jackson's attempt at reconciliation, and the final break, is to be found in J. Franklin Jameson (ed.), "Correspondence of John C. Calhoun," *Annual Report of the American Historical Association,* (1899), pp. 279, 283, and *passim.*

The fresh outbreak of the Peggy Eaton affair may be traced in Jackson's voluminous correspondence with Emily and A. J. Donelson and Mary Eastin in *Correspondence*, IV, 186 ff.

Jackson's defiant challenge to Samuel Bradford when he heard of the threatened resignation of 100 congressmen is in the *Jackson Papers* (Bradford–W. B. Lewis, Feb. 28, 1832).

The account of Van Buren's manipulation of Jackson and Eaton in the reorganization of the cabinet rests on Van Buren's narrative in his *Autobiography*, pp. 402–407.

Ingham's blustering note to John Eaton, which led to the climax of "the Eaton malaria," is cited in Parton, III, 365.

Dunlap's urgent plea that Jackson dismiss Lewis from his Kitchen Cabinet is in the *Jackson Papers* (June 30, 1831).

The appraisal of Kendall as the energy source of Jackson's administration is by Harriet Martineau, I, 257–258. Henry Wise's denunciation of Kendall appears in the *Congressional Globe*, 25th Congress, 3rd Session, Appendix, p. 386.

The description of the remodeled Hermitage is drawn from a report to Jackson by the contractor, D. Morrison, cited by Stanley F. Horn in *The Hermitage* (1938), p. 23.

Jackson's exchange of letters with Robert Hayne on the eve of the nullification crisis is in the *Jackson Papers* (Hayne–Jackson, Feb. 4; Jackson–Hayne, Feb. 6, 1831).

Calhoun's admission that the defense of slavery was at the bottom of nullification is found in a letter to Colonel Virgil Maxey of Maryland, Sept. 11, 1830, cited by Bassett (p. 547) as from "The Marcou Mss."

Jackson's firm reassurance to James Hamilton that he would save the Union (Nov. 12, 1831) is found in Hamilton's *Reminiscences*, p. 231.

Chapter 24

The sketch of Clay upon his return to the Senate is in Martineau, *op. cit.*, pp. 252–255. Clay's hope for better days was expressed to Francis Brooke, Dec. 9, 1831 (Clay's *Works*, IV, 321).

The Senate's rejection of Van Buren as minister to Great Britain, accomplished in executive session, is narrated in Parton, III, 375–380. Jackson's reaction to news of this defeat is reported in Henry Wikoff, *Reminiscences of an Idler* (1880), pp. 29–31.

Benton's prophecy of the effect of the incident may be found in his *Thirty Years' View*, I, 215, 219.

Jackson's exchange with John Randolph on the issues of nullification and the Bank charter is found in the *Jackson Papers* (Jackson–Randolph, Dec. 22, 1831; Randolph–Jackson, Jan. 3, 1832).

The removal of Jesse Benton's bullet from Jackson's arm was described by

John Campbell to David Campbell, March 8, 1832 *(Campbell Papers)*; and in Buell, II, 268.

Jackson's grim resolve to kill the Bank during the struggle was reported by Van Buren in his *Autobiography,* p. 625.

The account of the preparation of Jackson's veto of the Bank Charter Bill is based on Taney's narrative, as cited by Carl B. Swisher in his *Roger B. Taney* (1935), pp. 187–195. The message itself is found in Richardson, *op. cit.,* II, 576–591. Biddle's striking comment upon the veto is found in Calvin Colton (ed.), *The Private Correspondence of Henry Clay* (1856), p. 341. And Webster's final attack upon the message (July 11, 1832) appears in *Register of·Debates,* 22nd Congress, 1st Session, p. 1,240. Webster's indebtedness to the Bank and his status as a lobbyist are made clear in Swisher, *op. cit.,* p. 200, and in James T. Lynch, *An Epoch and a Man: Martin Van Buren and His Times* (1929), p. 357.

The Benton-Clay imbroglio on the Senate floor is reported in Parton, III, 414–415.

The effects of Biddle's loans to Webb and *The New York Courier and Enquirer* are reported by Ralph C. H. Catterall, *op. cit.,* pp. 258–264, and by Bassett, p. 625.

Chapter 25

Jackson's one-man propaganda campaign for hard money on his journey to Tennessee is described in Parton, III, 420, and his prediction that his veto would ruin the Bank is cited in Bowers, *op. cit.,* p. 251.

The Supreme Court's decision in the controversy between the state of Georgia and the Cherokees, as viewed by Jackson, was reported to Coffee April 7, 1832 *(Correspondence,* IV, 430), and his purported remark that John Marshall could enforce his edict is based on the memory of an unidentified Massachusetts congressman years afterward (Horace Greeley, *The American Conflict,* I, 106).

Jackson's comment that Calhoun was "prostrate" was made to Louis McLane, July 3, 1832 *(Jackson Papers).* His instructions to Secretary of War Lewis Cass to move troops and ships to South Carolina (Oct. 29, 1832) are in *Correspondence,* IV, 483. For Joel Poinsett's plea for arms for Charleston, Nov. 16, 1832, see *ibid.,* 488.

Hill's twenty-one reasons for the defeat of Henry Clay were reprinted in the Washington *Globe,* Sept. 25, 1832.

Channing's prescription for happiness among America's lower classes is cited in Elizabeth Peabody's *Reminiscences of the Rev. W. E. Channing,* (1880), p. 415.

Expressions of similar economic theories of the day appeared in the Boston *Courier* of June 28, 1834; in R. C. Waterston, *An Address on Pauperism . . .* (1844), p. 35; and in Edward Everett's *Address Delivered Before the Mercantile Library Association* (1838), p. 13.

Assumptions of Jackson's defeat in his bid for reelection were expressed by Fanny Kemble in *Records of a Girlhood* (1879), p. 549; and by Alexis de Tocqueville, as quoted in G. W. Pierson, *Tocqueville and Beaumont in America* (1938), p. 484.

The margin of Jackson's victory over Clay in terms of popular vote as given here is approximate. Chosen from a variety of reports, the totals cited are from Samuel R. Gammon, Jr., *The Presidential Campaign of 1832* (1922), pp. 153, 170.

The Boston *Courier*'s expression of the fervent wish for Jackson's early death was reprinted in the Washington *Globe*, Oct. 27, 1832.

Jackson's assurance to Sam Dale that he would stifle the threat of nullification is found in J. F. H. Claiborne, *The Life and Times of General Sam Dale* (1860), p. 178. The President's confidence that there would be no bloodshed in South Carolina is reported in Amos Kendall's *Autobiography*, p. 631; his promise of troops to Joel Poinsett (Dec. 9, 1832) is from *Correspondence*, IV, 498.

For the draft of the Nullification Proclamation as sent to Livingston by Jackson (Dec. 4, 1832), see *ibid.*, p. 495. The proclamation as issued is in Richardson, *op. cit.*, II, 640–656.

Governor Hayne's defiant attitude in the wake of Jackson's ultimatum, written to F. W. Pickens, is found in *The American Historical Review*, vol. VI, p. 755.

For the glimpse of the cowed Calhoun, trembling before Jackson's threats, see Poore, *op. cit.*, p. 138, and Benton, I, 143.

The spectacular speech by McDuffie in the House is from *Niles' Register*, Aug. 17, 1833. Calhoun's resistance to the Force Bill is graphically described by Coit, *op. cit.*, pp. 247 ff.

Jackson's comment that he would have hanged the leaders of nullification, given the opportunity, was reported by P. P. F. Degrand to Nicholas Biddle, July 4, 1833 (*Biddle Papers*, Library of Congress).

Jackson's prophetic vision of the coming Civil War was written to John Coffee on April 9, 1833, thirty-two years to the day before Appomattox (*Correspondence*, V, 56).

Chapter 26

Dr. Dunglison's treatment of Jackson with his plaster of powdered beetles is described by Percy G. Hamlin in *Virginia Cavalcade* (Summer 1972), pp. 14–21.

The glimpse of the aging Jackson in the White House is from Martineau, I, 111–113, 243–245.

Street paving and plumbing improvements in the capital are recorded in Constance M. Green's *Washington, Village and Capital* (1962), I, 125; and in W. B. Bryan's *A History of the National Capital* (1914), II, 237 ff.

Jackson's conversation with Blair about the soundness of Biddle's Bank is from Parton, III, 498, a report evidently based on Blair's recollection. James questions the accuracy of Blair's memory, since the soundness of the Bank was widely accepted at the time, and Jackson himself remained a depositor.

Biddle's loans to congressmen are revealed in J. G. Watmough's notes to

Biddle from March to May 1833 *(Biddle Papers)*. Jackson's persistent longing for retirement, when he had destroyed Biddle's "hydra of corruption," was expressed to the Reverend H. M. Cryer, April 7, 1833 *(American Historical Magazine*, vol. IV, p. 239).

Lee's warning to Jackson about Duane, Dec. 27, 1833, is in the *Jackson Papers*. Duane's interview with Jackson is reported in Parton, III, 513.

Lieutenant Randolph's attempted assault upon Jackson is detailed in an undated memorandum by Frank Blair *(Correspondence*, V, 102–104). Parton, III, 487, also tells the story.

The plight of Van Buren on horseback on Boston Common is reported in Josiah Quincy, *Figures of the Past* (1883), pp. 353 ff.

Jackson at Harvard is described in Andrew F. Davis, "A Tempest In a Teapot: Jackson's LLD" (*Massachusetts Historical Society Proceedings*, 2nd series, vol. XX [December 1906], pp. 490–493, 503; Josiah Quincy, *Figures of the Past* . . . [1883], pp. 361, 365; and Adams, VIII, 546).

Commodore Elliott's project involving the Jackson figurehead is described in Thurlow Weed, *Autobiography*, p. 482.

Nicholas Trist's glimpse of Jackson at the Rip Raps is recorded in Parton, III, 601, and the meetings with R. E. Lee and his family are drawn from Margaret Sanborn's *R. E. Lee*, I, 97.

Duane reported his final confrontation with Jackson in his *Narrative and Correspondence Concerning the Deposites* . . . (1838), pp. 102–103, and Jackson's farewell comment is found in *Correspondence*, V, 207. The denunciation of Jackson by Duane is from Parton, III, 601–602.

Biddle's resolve to crush the Kitchen Cabinet was confided to Robert Lenox, July 30, 1833 *(Biddle Papers)*; and his confidence that his Bank would survive was expressed to William Appleton, Jan. 27, 1834, and to J. G. Watmough, Feb. 8, 1834 *(Biddle Correspondence*, pp. 219, 221).

The visits of protesting delegations to the White House are described in Parton, III, 549 ff.; *Niles' Register*, March 1, 8, 15, and 22, 1834; Blair–George Bancroft, June 24, 1845 *(Correspondence*, V, 238n); and Buell, II, 328.

The amusing threat to Jackson from an anonymous critic in Cincinnati was reported in *Niles' Register*, Feb. 14, 1835.

As Jackson's twentieth-century critic Edward Pessen has noted, government deposits under Jackson flowed to politically loyal banks after Biddle's demise. Amos Kendall conceded that "those which are in hands politically friendly will be preferred," and a modern study reveals that 80 percent of presidents, cashiers, and directors of favored banks were Democrats. W. B. Smith, in *Economic Aspects of the Second Bank*, p. 263, maintains that Jackson's party never developed a sound banking system, and that as a result the United States lost its leadership in banking techniques.

Pessen, *op. cit.*, p. 229, quotes Azariah Flagg of New York to the effect that monopoly charters grew rapidly in the Jackson era.

Leonard D. White, *op. cit.*, p. 269 ff., recounts Amos Kendall's successes as Postmaster General.

The sumptuous dinner at the White House in 1834 was described by J. R.

Montgomery of Lancaster, Pennsylvania, to his daughter Letitia, Feb. 20, 1834 (cited by James as from the collection of Emil E. Hurja, New York City). The expenses of Jackson's larder are cited by Bassett, pp. 712–713, quoting undated items in the *Jackson Papers*.

Jackson's persistent problems with the hapless Andrew Jackson, Jr., in plantation management are recounted in James, pp. 666, 689, 710, and *passim*.

Chapter 27

The narrative of Jackson's negotiations of the French claims is drawn from the account of Bassett, pp. 663 ff., which is based on a study of records of the Secretary of State, *France*, vols. 24–27. The story of Jackson's protest at Donelson's alteration of his forceful message to Paris is told by Poore, *op. cit.*, pp. 112–113.

The chief source for the account of Lawrence's attempted assassination of Jackson is a letter from John Tyler to Robert Tyler, Jan. 31, 1835 (Huntington Library, San Marino, Calif., copy in author's collection). Harriet Martineau, who was present, added details of the incident, *op. cit.*, I, 161. Jackson's nonchalant dismissal of the attack is recorded in the *United States Telegraph*, Feb. 2, 1835, and in Van Buren, p. 353.

The comment on Jackson's vindictive nature by Niles was expressed to William C. Rives, June 14, 1835 (*Rives Papers*, Library of Congress).

Margaret Coit, *op. cit.*, pp. 308 ff., details Jackson's ambivalent policy toward delivery of Abolitionist pamphlets through the mails. Calhoun's comment that slavery was "a positive good" for both blacks and whites is found in Marquis James, p. 692, without citation.

Richard M. Johnson's career is sketched in Schlesinger, pp. 140–142.

The stout defense of Jackson's policy toward the French is cited in Parton, III, 577–578; and in Bowers, p. 155.

The last years of Biddle's life were blighted by his defeat by Jackson. After his resignation as president of the United States Bank of Pennsylvania, Biddle and four other former officers of the Bank were arrested on charges of conspiracy, but were acquitted, a victory that evidently inspired Biddle to further activity—a disastrous attempt to corner the cotton market.

At Biddle's death in 1844, at the age of fifty-eight, William Cullen Bryant bade him a bitter farewell: "He died at his country seat where he passed his last days in elegant retirement, which, if justice had been done, would have been spent in the penitentiary."

Philip Hone, who quoted Bryant in his *Diary*, II, 686–687, added, "How such a blackhearted misanthrope as Bryant should possess an imagination teeming with beautiful poetical images astonishes me; one would as soon expect to extract drops of honey from the fangs of a rattlesnake."

Chapter 28

Bassett, pp. 673 ff., offers a full account of Jackson's role in preliminary negotiations for the annexation of Texas. A hostile view of this phase of Jackson's diplomacy is presented by Richard R. Stenberg, in "Jackson, Anthony Butler, and Texas," *The Southwestern Social Science Quarterly,* vol. XIII (December 1932), pp. 264–286, and in "The Texas Schemes of Jackson and Houston, 1829–1836," *ibid.,* vol. XV (December 1934), pp. 229–250. Jackson's view that the Mississippi Valley was divinely destined for national control was written to Van Buren on Aug. 12, 1829 *(Van Buren Papers).*

Jackson's recall and denunciation of Butler is reported by Jesse S. Reeves, in *Diplomacy Under Tyler and Polk,* p. 69.

An able discussion of the specie circular and its effects is found in Van Deusen, *Jacksonian America,* pp. 105 ff. Anti-Jackson men, who felt that destruction of the Bank to expel paper money was "like killing the cat to keep mice away," have a modern ally in Edward Pessen, who concludes (pp. 330 ff.) that Jackson and his supporters played a double game in their attempted control of the currency.

Hugh White's fears of a potential dictatorship in America are recorded in his *Memoirs,* pp. 179–180.

Nicholas Biddle's prescription for Harrison's candidacy (Aug. 11, 1835) is found in *Biddle Correspondence,* p. 256.

Crockett's acidulous sketch of Van Buren's appearance is in his *Life of Martin Van Buren,* pp. 80–81.

The designation of Van Buren's administration as the third term of the Jacksonian revolution is Schlesinger's (p. 215).

Jackson's prediction that Houston would fight Santa Anna at San Jacinto was reported in the *New York Evening Post,* July 1853, citing the reminiscences of Nicholas P. Trist. Other details are from the Journal of Lieutenant Hitchcock, as cited in C. R. Wharton's *Texas Republic* (1922), p. 165.

Jackson's congratulations to Houston after San Jacinto are cited in Buell, II, 352.

The captive Santa Anna appeared in Washington, where he had several interviews with Jackson, and gave the President the impression that he was, in fact, a true friend of Texas. Bassett, pp. 682–683, comments on the only surviving document on this incident.

The expunging of the censure motion against Jackson is found in *Congressional Debates,* 24th Congress, 2nd Session, pp. 429 ff. and 440 ff.

Webster's final tribute to Jackson is cited in Buell, II, 297; Bryant's comment is in the *New York Evening Post,* Dec. 3, 1836; that of the German nobleman is in Francis J. Grund (ed.), *Aristocracy in America* (1839), II, 241–243; and that of Randolph was quoted by Abram Van Buren to Martin Van Buren June 3 (or 5), 1833 *(Van Buren Papers).*

Parton's estimate of Jackson's contradictory nature is found in I, vii.

The Chicago *Democrat's* styling of the era as the Age of Jackson is in the issue of Jan. 21, 1834—a concept adopted and impressively documented by Schlesinger. Douglas T. Miller, however (in *The Birth of Modern America*, pp. 170–171), challenges this concept, on the ground that Jackson, though a significant figure, did not dominate his age, "obstructed rather than furthered democratic causes," and had little to do with the most influential economic, social, and intellectual developments of his time.

Jackson's conversation with Blair and Allen is based on Buell's later interviews with the general's friends (Buell, II, 364–366).

Jackson's departure from Washington was described in *Harper's Magazine* (January 1855). His reception on the road near the Hermitage is recounted in Parton, III, 630.

Epilogue

The impoverished condition of Jackson at retirement was noted in an endorsement on a letter received from the Reverend A. D. Campbell, March 17, 1837 (*Jackson Papers*).

The urgent messages from the Hermitage to the White House concerning the financial panic were frequently delivered through Frank Blair, as on April 2, 18, 25, and June 5, 1837 (*Jackson Papers*). His claim that the public was aroused against banks was made to Kendall, June 23, 1837 (*Correspondence*, V, 489–490. A most insistent note of March 30, 1837, to Van Buren, is in *ibid.*, p. 467, and Van Buren's reply, of April 24, in *ibid.*, p. 477.

Kendall described his visit to the Hermitage to Van Buren, Nov. 20, 1838 (*Van Buren Papers*).

The wry remark by Jackson upon the ineffectiveness of committees is quoted in Horn, p. 189.

Jackson's theory that his political enemies brought on the financial ruin of Andrew Jackson, Jr., as expressed to Kendall on May 23, 1842, appeared in the Cincinnati *Commercial*, Feb. 5, 1879.

The refund of Judge Hall's fine is recounted from Jackson's point of view in *Correspondence*, VI, 143 ff., and is summarized in Bassett, p. 745.

Jackson's protest that he would starve before accepting the refund in the form of a gratuity was made to Frank Blair on June 4, 1842 (*Jackson Papers*).

Jackson's confession that he lacked the money for a trip to New Orleans, made to H. M. Cryer, Dec. 10, 1839, is in *Correspondence*, VI, 41.

The defection of Eaton and Jackson's angry reaction are related in Parton, III, 639–640, and in Bassett, p. 539.

Jackson's denunciation of Harrison as unfit for the presidency, to E. F. Purdy, March 16, 1841, was cited by James as from the collection of Arthur G. Mitten, Goodland, Indiana; Old Hickory's gratification at Harrison's death was expressed to Blair on April 19, 1841 (*Correspondence*, VI, 105).

President Tyler approached Jackson for aid on the Texas problem through Senator Robert J. Walker of Mississippi (Walker–Jackson, Jan. 10, 1844, *Corre-*

spondence, VI, 255). Jackson's subsequent notes to Houston were discovered by James in Houston, Texas, in the collection of the late Houston Williams, Sam Houston's grandson.

Jackson's pronouncement on Henry Clay's opposition to the annexation of Texas was made to Blair on May 7, 1844, and his dismay over Van Buren's stand, also to Blair, May 11, 1844, is revealed in *Correspondence,* VI, 286.

Polk's adroit use of Jackson's blessing is revealed in letters to Cave Johnson, May 13, 14, 1844 (Sioussat, *Polk Letters,* I, 239–240, 242). Jackson's admonition to Polk to attack Clay on the Texas issue, July 23, 1844, is in the *Polk Papers.*

Benton's explanation of his stand on Texas, May 28, 1844, is in the *Jackson Papers,* and Jackson's reaction, when he heard of Benton's reunion with John Quincy Adams over the issue, is reported in Bassett, p. 742.

For a detailed clinical analysis of Jackson's medical problems, see Francis T. Gardner, "The Gentleman from Tennessee," *Surgery, Gynecology and Obstetrics* . . . , vol. LXXXVIII (March 1949), pp. 404–411. This study concludes that Jackson's death was caused by amyloidosis, which resulted from chronic suppuration. Near the end of Jackson's life the flesh of his lower body had to be strapped to prevent its falling away. Dr. Gardner commented that "no structure ever endured under greater handicaps than the frame that supported the brain of the astonishing, the determined, the invincible gentleman from Tennessee." Dr. Bernard Wolff of Atlanta, a distinguished specialist, concurred in this sentiment after a review of the available evidence in 1976.

Jackson's lifelong battle against illness endeared him to Franklin D. Roosevelt, who also struggled with crippling disease. "The more I learn about old Andy Jackson," Roosevelt said, "the more I love him" (Elliott Roosevelt [ed.], *F.D.R. His Personal Letters, 1928–1945* [1950], I, 433).

Isaac Hill's account of Jackson's health in the final days of his life is found in *The Madisonian* (Washington, D.C.), March 29, 1845.

Davezac's birthday tribute to Old Hickory is in a scrapbook of unidentified newspaper clippings, Tennessee State Library, Nashville.

Jackson's protest over Buchanan's appointment as Secretary of State is found in Buell, II, 404; his urgent advice to Polk about the Oregon controversy, May 2, 1845, is in the *Polk Papers.*

Healy described his visit to the Hermitage in his *Reminiscences of a Portrait Painter* (1894), pp. 144, 149.

Jackson's reaction to his daguerrotype is by Horn, p. 202, citing family tradition.

Elliott's offer of the Roman sarcophagus to Jackson is recounted in Parton, III, 666–667.

The account of Jackson's death is drawn from Parton, III, 673 ff. Jackson's request that his family go to church is from the Diary of William Tyack, *Niles' Register,* June 21, 1845. Jackson's letter about the debts of Andrew Jackson, Jr., to J. B. Plauché was found by James in "an old newspaper clipping, apparently from a New Orleans newspaper"; the writing of the letter was described by Andrew Jackson, Jr., to Polk Oct. 10, 1845 *(Jackson Papers).* Other recollections of Jackson's last moments may be found in Andrew Jackson, Jr., to A. O. P. Nicholson, June 17, 1845 (*Jackson Papers*, New York Historical Society).

The belated arrival of Houston was related to James in 1927 by Nettie Houston Bringhurst of San Antonio, Texas, a daughter of Sam Houston.

The Profane Parrot at the funeral was described by a fifteen-year-old Cumberland University student, William Norment (Horn, *op. cit.*, 205).

Bibliography

As the first biography of Jackson in forty years, this work owes much to modern scholarship, whose landmark was Arthur Schlesinger, Jr.'s, *The Age of Jackson*. The later work of Douglas T. Miller, Edward Pessen, Robert Remini, C. G. Sellers, H. C. Syrett, C. R. Taylor, Glyndon G. Van Deusen, and John William Ward provided the basis for my interpretation of Jackson's political career. The studies of Samuel F. Bemis on John Quincy Adams, Van Deusen on Henry Clay, Charles Wiltse and Margaret Coit on John C. Calhoun, and Bray Hammond and C. R. Taylor on Jackson's Bank War are of special importance to an understanding of Jackson's presidency.

The primary source for any study of Jackson remains the Jackson Papers in the Library of Congress, whose 40,000 manuscripts are admirably represented in J. S. Bassett's *Correspondence of Andrew Jackson*. The Tennessee Historical Society of Nashville also houses an invaluable collection of the papers of Jackson and his contemporaries.

Charles Francis Adams, ed., *Memoirs of John Quincy Adams, Comprising Portions of His Diary* . . . (1876)

Susan Smart Alexander, *Reminiscences of Andrew Jackson, National Intelligencer*, Aug. 1 and 29, 1845

John Allison, *Dropped Stitches in Tennessee History* (1897)

James Douglas Anderson, *Making of the American Thoroughbred* (1916)

James L. Armstrong, *General Jackson's Juvenile Indiscretions* (1832)

Harriet Arnow, *Seedtime on the Cumberland* (1960)

Stanley Clisby Arthur, *The Story of the Battle of New Orleans* (1915)

Francis Baily, *Journal of a Tour in the Unsettled Parts of North America* (1854)

John Spencer Bassett, ed., *Correspondence of Andrew Jackson* (7 vols., 1926–33)
———, *Life of Andrew Jackson* (1911)
Samuel F. Bemis, *John Quincy Adams* (1949)
Jesse Benton, *An Address to the People of the United States on the Presidential Election* (1824)
Thomas Hart Benton, *Thirty Years' View* (1854)
Claude G. Bowers, *Making Democracy a Reality* (1954)
———, *Party Battles of the Jackson Period* (1922)
Wilhelmus Bogart Bryan, *A History of the National Capital* (1914)
Augustus C. Buell, *A History of Andrew Jackson* (2 vols., 1904)
Mary French Caldwell, *Andrew Jackson's Hermitage* (1933)
Samuel Carter, *Blaze of Glory* (1971)
Ralph C. H. Catterall, *The Second Bank of the United States* (1903)
Alfred A. Cave, *Jacksonian Democracy and the Historians* (1964)
W. N. Chambers, *Old Bullion Benton* (1970)
Michel Chevalier, *Manners & Politics in the U.S.* (1839)
Henry Clay, *Address of Henry Clay to the Public, Containing Certain Testimony in Refutation of the Charges Made by Gen. Andrew Jackson* (1827)
Margaret Coit, *John C. Calhoun* (1950)
Congressional Record, discussions about Jackson's birthplace, Feb. 23, 1922; June 18, 1926; May 24, 1928; and July 2, 1928
David Crockett, *Life of David Crockett* (reprint of 1865)
Matthew L. Davis, *Memoirs of Aaron Burr* (1837)
Jane Lucas de Grummond, *The Baratarians and the Battle of New Orleans* (1961)
Seymour Dunbar, *History of Travel in America* (vol. II, 1915)
John Henry Eaton, *Life of Andrew Jackson* (1824)
——— and John Reid, *Life of Andrew Jackson* (1817)
Margaret Eaton, *The Autobiography of Peggy Eaton* (1932)
T. D. Faulkner, reminiscence of Jackson's father, reprinted in the Fort Mill (S.C.) *Times*, Oct. 8, 1931
John W. Forney, *Anecdotes of Public Men* (1873)
H. R. Fraser, *Democracy in the Making* (1938)
Francis T. Gardner, "The Gentleman from Tennessee," *Surgery, Gynecology and Obstetrics . . .* , vol. LXXXVIII (March 1949)
Charles E. Gayerré, *History of Louisiana* (1866)
George Robert Gleig, . . . *Narrative of the Campaign of the British Army at Baltimore, Washington, etc. . . .* (1821)
Constance McLaughlin Green, *Washington, Village and Capital, 1800–1879* (2 vols., 1962)
J. C. Guild, *Old Times in Tennessee* (1878)
Bray Hammond, *Banks and Politics* (1957)
Charles Hammond, *A View of General Jackson's Domestic Relations* (1828)
John Haywood, *Civil and Political History of the State of Tennessee* (1823)
George P. A. Healy, *Reminiscences of a Portrait Painter* (1894)
S. G. Heiskell, *Andrew Jackson and Early Tennessee History* (1920–21)

Archibald Henderson, article about Jackson's birthplace, Raleigh (N.C.) *News and Observer*, Oct. 3, 1926; "Jackson's Loose Living Common Sin of the Period," *News and Observer*, Oct. 17, 1926

W. S. Hoffman, *Andrew Jackson and North Carolina Politics* (1958)

Stanley F. Horn, *The Hermitage, Home of Old Hickory* (1938)

Marquis James, *Andrew Jackson* (1938)

William James, *Military Occurrences of the Late War Between Great Britain and the United States* (1818)

Amos Kendall, *Life of Andrew Jackson* (1843)

Major A. Lacarrière Latour, *Historical Memoir of the War in West Fla. . . .* (1816)

Charles Edward Lester and Sam Houston, *Life of Sam Houston* (1855)

Louisiana Historical Quarterly, vol. VI, Grace King's translation of Bernard Marigny's pamphlet on the New Orleans campaign

Harriet Martineau, *A Retrospect of Western Travel* (1838)

———, *Society in America* (1837)

Bernard Mayo, *Henry Clay* (1937)

Douglas T. Miller, *The Birth of Modern America* (1970)

M. Myers, *The Jacksonian Persuasion* (1937)

Vincent Nolte, *Fifty Years in Two Hemispheres* (1854)

North Carolina Argus (Wadesboro), Sept. 23, 1858

Frederic Austin Ogg, *The Reign of Andrew Jackson* (1919)

W. G. Orr, Memoir of Weatherford's surrender, *Publication of Alabama Historical Society*, vol. II, p. 57.

John Overton, *A Vindication of the Measures of the President and His Commanding Generals in the Commencement and Termination of the Seminole War* (1819)

James Parton, *A Life of Andrew Jackson* (1859–60)

Edward Pessen, *Jacksonian America . . .* (1969)

Queena Pollack, *Peggy Eaton, Democracy's Mistress* (1931)

Ben Perley Poore, *Perley's Reminiscences . . .* (1866)

Milo Milton Quaife, *Diary of James K. Polk* (1910)

J. G. M. Ramsay, *Annals of Tennessee* (1853)

James B. Ranck, "Andrew Jackson and the Burr Conspiracy," *Tennessee Historical Society Magazine* (October 1930)

Robert Remini, *The Age of Jackson* (1972)

———, *Andrew Jackson* (1966)

———, *The Election of Andrew Jackson* (1963)

James D. Richardson, *. . . Messages and Papers of the Presidents . . .* (1909)

Mrs. Dunbar Rowland, *Andrew Jackson's Campaign Against the British or the Mississippi Territory in the War of 1812* (1926)

Mrs. Margaret Bayard Smith, *The First Forty Years of Washington's Society*, ed. Gaillard Hunt, (1906)

C. G. Sellers, *Andrew Jackson, a Profile* (1971)

Arthur M. Schlesinger, Jr., *The Age of Jackson* (1945)

Shooting at the President! The Remarkable Trial of Richard Lawrence . . . by a Washington Reporter, Washington, D.C. (1835)

William G. Sumner, *Andrew Jackson* (ed. of 1899)

H. C. Syrett, *Andrew Jackson: His Contribution to American Tradition* (1953)

Lieutenant-Colonel Banastre Tarleton, *Campaign of 1780–1781 in the Southern Provinces* (1787)

Major Howell Tatum, "Major Howell Tatum's Journal," *Smith College Studies in History,* vol. VII

C. R. Taylor, *Jackson Versus Biddle* (1959)

Frances M. Trollope, *Domestic Manners of the Americans* (reprint of 1904)

Major Ben Truman, *Field of Honor* (1884)

Frederick Jackson Turner, *The United States* (1830–50)

Martin Van Buren, *Autobiography of Martin Van Buren,* ed. John C. Fitzpatrick (1920)

Glyndon G. Van Deusen, *The Jacksonian Era* (1959)

———, *The Life of Henry Clay* (1937)

S. Putnam Waldo, *Memoirs of Andrew Jackson* (1819)

Alexander Walker, *Jackson and New Orleans . . .* (1856)

———, *The Life of Andrew Jackson* (1860)

John William Ward, *Andrew Jackson—Symbol for an Age* (1955)

Leonard White, *The Jacksonians* (1954)

Charles Wiltse, *John C. Calhoun* (1944–1951)

Henry A. Wise, *Seven Decades of the Union* (1872)

Index